Jewish Passages

THE S. MARK TAPER FOUNDATION

IMPRINT IN JEWISH STUDIES

BY THIS ENDOWMENT
THE S. MARK TAPER FOUNDATION SUPPORTS
THE APPRECIATION AND UNDERSTANDING
OF THE RICHNESS AND DIVERSITY OF
JEWISH LIFE AND CULTURE

Jewish Passages

Cycles of Jewish Life

HARVEY E. GOLDBERG

University of California Press

BERKELEY   LOS ANGELES   LONDON

The publisher gratefully acknowledges the generous contribution to this book provided by the Jewish Studies Endowment Fund of the University of California Press Associates, which is supported by a major gift from the S. Mark Taper Foundation.

University of California Press
Berkeley and Los Angeles, California

University of California Press, Ltd.
London, England

Library of Congress Cataloging-in-Publication Data

Goldberg, Harvey E.
    Jewish passages : cycles of Jewish life / Harvey E. Goldberg.
        p.   cm.
    Includes bibliographical references and index.
    ISBN 0-520-20693-2 (alk. paper).
        1. Judaism—Customs and practices.   2. Fasts and feasts—
Judaism.   3. Jewish way of life.   4. Life cycle, Human—Religious
aspects—Judaism.   I. Title.

BM700.G613   2003
296.4′4—dc21   2002151317

Manufactured in the United States of America
12   11   10   09   08   07   06   05   04   03
10   9   8   7   6   5   4   3   2   1

The paper used in this publication meets the minimum requirements of
ANSI/NISO Z39.48–1992 (R 1997) (Permanence of Paper). ⊗

*To our children
and our children's children*

Contents

Illustrations

Acknowledgments

This volume reflects the prodding, encouragement, criticism, and help of many individuals. The first push was given by Doug Abrams Arava, formerly of the University of California Press. Reed Malcolm of the University of California Press provided the constancy to complete the project. Peter Dreyer's editorial skill and knowledge improved the final version. Thanks are also due to anonymous readers who provided input along the way. Joëlle Bahloul and Marshall Leaffer warmly enriched my stay in Bloomington during the final stages of the project.

Friends and colleagues reacted to individual chapters or were generous with advice and support. I am grateful for the feedback, wisdom, and experience of Elisheva Baumgarten, Christina Burke, Sol Cohen, Steven M. Cohen, Tamar El-Or, Matt Futterman, Jack Kugelmass, Andy Sacks, Hagar Salamon, Susan Sered, and Chava Weissler. Etty Lassman lent invaluable aid in preparing the manuscript. Ariella Amar and Einat Ron of the Center for Jewish Art at the Hebrew University offered guidance in the selection of pictures.

The project moved forward with the help of several institutions. The Bellagio Study and Conference Center of the Rockefeller Foundation was the venue within which the structure of the book was conceived. Teaching in the Department of Sociology of Boğaziçi University, Istanbul, provided perspectives that have enriched the book. A fellowship at the Center for Advanced Jewish Studies of the University of Pennsylvania enabled me to deepen the historical exploration of several issues. A grant from the Memorial Foundation for Jewish Culture, for research in collaboration with Hagar Salamon, expanded my understanding of Israeli society. Support from the Harvey L. Silbert Center for Israeli Studies enabled me to sharpen the discussion of religion in Israel. A stay at Indiana University provided a helpful setting to put the manuscript in final form. I continue to be thankful for the congenial and stimulating atmosphere of my academic home—the Department of Sociology and Anthropology at the Hebrew University, and the Shaine Center for Research in the Social Sciences.

The book also grows out of the time—more than a biblical generation—spent with my wife, Judy Goldberg. The intertwining of our "life cycles" is echoed in the dedication.

Abbreviations

Some of these terms also appear in the glossary.

EJ	*Encyclopaedia Judaica* (New York and Jerusalem, 1971).
Midrash	Titles of books given in Hebrew. Most references according to standard numbering; a few according to page numbers in specific editions.
Mishna	References within tractates according to standard numbering.
Shulhan Arukh	References according to standard Hebrew subdivisions and numbers; see chapter 1.
Talmud	References within tractates according to standard subdivisions and pagination in Hebrew (Aramaic) editions.
TB	Babylonian Talmud
TJ	Jerusalem (Palestinian) Talmud
Yad ha-Ḥazaqah	Maimonides' halakhic work; references follow standard Hebrew subdivisions and numbers.
Zohar	Most references follow *The Wisdom of the Zohar*, 3 vols., trans. and ed. Isaiah Tishby and Fishel Lachower (New York: Oxford University Press, 1989), which provides references to standard texts and pagination.

1 Being Jewish

LIFE-CYCLE EVENTS AND JEWISH CULTURE

Life-cycle ceremonies are one of the axes around which Jewish life is organized. In marking the birth of children, celebrating bar mitzvah and bat mitzvah ceremonies, rejoicing at weddings, and mourning the dead, Jews feel emotions shared with humans everywhere and observe customs that parallel those found in other cultures. Jewish practice, however, is also shaped by an ancient textual tradition, expressed in the Bible and elaborated in the Talmud, which has continued through the Middle Ages up until the present. In addition, the life-cycle rituals of Jews reflect the experience of communities that have long resided in many lands of the Middle East, Europe, and, most recently, the Americas. Despite this diversity, and the many historical changes that have affected Jewish communities, Jews everywhere recognize similar markers in their lives, and each in his or her own way draws upon a shared pool of textual and cultural resources in celebrating and reshaping these milestone events. To celebrate a Jewish life-cycle ritual is to make a statement pointing to the Jews' collective future.

Today, only limited parts of world Jewry follow traditional rituals with the comprehensiveness and detail that characterized Jewish life in pre-emancipation settings. Many, however, while compartmentalizing the Jewish side of their lives, still adhere to some ceremonial practices derived from the Jewish past. Along with observing festivals such as Hanukkah, Passover, and Yom Kippur (the Day of Atonement), Jews expect their tradition and the various forms of identity they have chosen to receive expression in life-cycle events. Both the strictly observant who bind themselves to set obligations and communal regimes and Jews whose connection to their tradition comes to the fore only sporadically are involved in constructing identities and lifestyles that draw upon Jewish sources. At the same time, the reality of choice, which is part and parcel of the modern world, is an undeniable component of the cultural forms that they select. With the contemporary valorization of the individual, life-cycle rituals have become prominent in the ways Jews fashion and place themselves in ethnic, communal, and religious networks.

Explanations of and rules for life-cycle celebrations are found in many written works, but the nature of Jewish life today calls for a basic rethinking of the topic of Jewish life cycles in light of the current global emphasis on the individual and on private experience. Both in the United States and Israel, where together three-fourths of world Jewry now resides, there is increasing attention to the way individuals and families define the content and emphases of their own lives, without precisely fitting into prescribed patterns set by communities or by society.[1] This trend is encapsulated in the title of a book about American Jewry by Steven M. Cohen and Arnold Eisen, *The Jew Within.*[2] It is paralleled by developments in Israel where the experience of individuals has ceased to be dominated by the collective ideals of Zionism or by the wider society.[3] In both settings, however, families and individuals continue to value life-cycle events and often endow them with various Jewish symbols and meanings. Therefore, in addition to providing information about life-cycle rituals in the past and in recent times, another theme of our examination of life-cycle events will be to explore how "the individual" gradually surfaced as a culturally recognized sphere in structured Jewish life as opposed to being a muted or only implicit presence in earlier periods.

This new emphasis on the individual as a locus of Jewish expression should be placed in historical perspective. It is a development that was not obvious a century ago. At that time, there was still a large Jewish population in Europe. Some assimilation had been going on for several generations, along with religious reforms among some Jews and Orthodox reactions to them. The mass immigration of Jews from eastern Europe to North America, where there was hope for a better personal future, was under way. Zionism, which claimed that Jews would not be able to assimilate successfully as individuals in Europe, and that they therefore needed to reassert their national existence in their own country, had recently appeared on the scene. Tragically, this claim received historical reinforcement by the European ideologies that attributed a collective existence to Jews in terms of race. The Holocaust not only destroyed one-third of the Jewish people but also cut short the experiments of forging Jewish life in modern European settings. This left two major settings for Jewish existence: the United States, where Jews whose families had lived there for several generations were beginning to assert themselves with self-confidence as members of

American society, and the nascent state of Israel, which struggled for physical survival with a population made up mostly of immigrants, whether they were old-time Zionist pioneers, postwar refugees from Europe, or new arrivals from Middle Eastern countries. In each of these milieus, the question of how Jews might pattern their cultural and religious life could not be answered by simply referring to the ways of their forebears, but required a reappropriation of tradition, involvement in group efforts, and individual initiatives and commitments.

In the second half of the twentieth century, Jews in America built and attended synagogues, cultivated ethnic organizations, created new frameworks for Jewish education, and worked to support Israel. In that country, the major tasks at first took the form of political and economic challenges. Soon, however, issues stemming from Jewish history and religion—the meaning of the Holocaust, the justification of Zionist settlement in Palestine, and the place of Middle Eastern religious traditions in a society that had been mostly shaped by Jews from Europe—became central societal issues as well. Throughout all these developments, both in Israel and abroad, Jews continued to celebrate life's transitions, turning to the social networks in which they were engaged and calling upon various aspects of Jewish tradition even when these did not always seem to speak to the new life circumstances in which they were enmeshed. With time, however, both as a result of innovations by religious and cultural leaders, and on the basis of popular responses that merged intuitive feelings about Jewishness with current cultural assumptions, life-cycle events became active occasions for expressing and giving shape to contemporary ways of being Jewish. The theme of life cycles is thus also one angle from which it is possible to look at Jewish life in its diversity, and at the relation of that kaleidoscopic reality to the threads of the Jewish past.

My approach to the topic of life cycles is therefore not a catalogue of the customs that pertain to them. It is based on the assumption that in carrying out the rituals and celebrations associated with life-cycle events, people have linked themselves to the social and cultural settings in which they are enmeshed and reinforced their sense of connection to the Jewish past and its special sense of history. Whether or not individuals today give extensive forethought to rituals, preparation for and participation in them constitute gestures of collective identity, along with the enactment and reproduction of Jewish culture. In these settings, rituals and explanations of those rituals, which often are linked to Jewish texts, act in tandem. In today's reality, where involvement in Jewish life and tradition is largely voluntary, life-cycle rituals provide a window on the past and offer potential signposts for personal and communal identification in the future. My approach to the topic, which seeks both to look at life-cycle celebrations in the past and in the present and to appreciate the significance of these practices for individuals in their life settings, draws heavily on perspectives that grow out of the discipline of anthropology.

Anthropology complements the two main approaches to life-cycle celebrations that have been used in the past: a focus on normative texts and the tracing of historical development. Texts represent the authority of tradition, and older forms of historical documentation show how rituals and forms of celebration evolved and became standardized over the centuries. These approaches continue to be crucial to our understanding of life-cycle events, but they often lack what has been called an "experience-near" grasp of cultural forms as they have been meaningful to people in distinct and specific periods and places.[4] Such understanding is provided by an anthropological point of view and by its hallmark method of field research, or ethnography. These relate to the significance of canonical texts and to documents from earlier ages, while interpreting life-cycle rituals as the experiences of individuals who are bound up with ongoing familial and communal processes.

Several features of anthropology enhance our appreciation of life-cycle events. The first is the emphasis on diversity: taking into account a range of societies in different parts of the world, both past and present. With regard to Jewish life, this means attending to Jewish culture as expressed in the classic texts of antiquity, as well as to the historical societies of the Middle Ages, both in Christian and Muslim realms. With regard to more recent periods, historical study flows into ethnography and the depiction of Jewish communities in eastern Europe, the Middle East, and North Africa, as well as within smaller Jewish groups, such as those in India and Ethiopia.

One implication of the emphasis on diversity is that it leads to a questioning, and ultimately a greater understanding, of notions and life-ways that we take for granted or see as "given." This applies both to particular Jewish practices and to concepts from general culture that are applied to Jewish existence in a commonsense manner. One example is the very idea of "life cycles," which, as will be discussed, has not always been as pivotal in organizing Jewish life as it is among Jews today. Another related example, as already intimated, is the notion of "the individual," which, although now assumed to be a "natural" category, has a history that gave it its current cultural shape.

Whether in respect to societies with which we are familiar or to those distant in space or in time, an anthropological perspective entails several other emphases. One is an interest in "ordinary people." The study of Judaism has long been associated with expertise in scholarly writings. The past heroes of Jewish life have typically been rabbis, especially rabbis who wrote influential books. Even as Jewish social history, over the past century, began to explore these writings to see what they reveal regarding daily life, the points of view reflected in them were often those of a learned elite. The focus on the "average" members of Jewish communities, who were affected by many influences, including economic and social forces and the presence of Muslim and Christian neighbors, is an approach that helps illuminate Jewish culture as it was forged both by time-honored texts and by more proximate life experiences. Life-cycle ceremonies, in particular, reflect all these sources of influence.

Second, within the general category of "ordinary people," anthropology, like other disciplines, increasingly takes into account the actions, attitudes, and ideas of women. It is now well understood that neglect of female perspectives yielded a severely unbalanced view of history, culture, and society. This is undoubtedly the case for anyone wishing to look carefully at social and ritual processes connected with birth, marriage, and death. Steps towards the rectification of this imbalance are now under way in Jewish studies generally, and certainly within the anthropological study of Jewish communities and families. This reorientation also has relevance beyond the study of women per se.

Both the expanded view of "ordinary people" and a stronger focus on "women in society" return us to the theme of "the individual." Societies have always been made up of single human beings, but explicit attention to and valorization of the concept of the individual is a relatively modern phenomenon. One way of attempting to grasp notions of the individual in Jewish life is through a careful look at the milestone events that mark the lives of the members of a society. This entails an assessment both of individuals in traditional communities and of the changing nature of that relationship as societies passed through the sea changes that gave rise to the contemporary era. A combination of historical and anthropological perspectives in interpreting these developments provides a way of placing them on a broad canvas while simultaneously viewing them intimately.

THE ROOTS OF AN ANTHROPOLOGICAL
APPROACH TO JEWISH CULTURE

Before further elaborating on these and other aspects of the anthropological approach to life-cycle events, it might be remarked that in today's intellectual and interdisciplinary environment, it is not unusual to focus on the issues mentioned. It is only recently, however, that anthropological analyses of Jewish life have been carried out with some regularity and viewed with interest by other scholars of Judaica. There are various reasons for this, and considering them can provide a keener sense of what this approach can add both to the grasp of Jewish life in the past and to its present constitution. Anthropology was suspicious in its formative period of attaching too much weight to written sources, or to the interpretations offered by literati of the rituals and mores of their own traditions. One of the discipline's dogmas was that explanations offered by "natives" concerning their own practices are not helpful.[5] Anthropologists were then keen to substitute understandings growing out of their theoretical perspectives for those given by the members of a society they were studying. This approach, which privileged actual behavior over the oral or written interpretations of customary practice, flew in the face of Jewish scholarship, whether by rabbis or researchers, which heavily valued texts and saw social life as deriving from them. Today, however, the basic insight of social science that thought, speech, and writing often follow from behavior, rather than being the "reason why" people do things, has become widespread. At the same time, cultural researchers have come to view texts as formative components in social life.[6] Today, anthropologists often begin their analyses with close attention to the exegesis offered by members of the society with which they are concerned. Phrased differently, anthropology now takes the views that a group of people have of themselves and their traditions seriously.

This development reflects slow trends and changes over time within the discipline. Two images long accompanied the field and to some extent still persist. One is that of anthropology as the investigation of "primitive" or "exotic" societies. The other is of anthropology as concerned with the origin of human beings through the evidence of the fossil record. The second topic is closely linked to a third: the division of contemporary humans into what superficially appear to be distinct categories, popularly called "races." All these research directions created problems for the Jews, but, paradoxically, the last emphasis was partially adopted by some Jewish scholars as a way of regaining their own sense of worth and identity.

To evaluate the impact of the first image of anthropology, it should be remembered that for extensive periods of European history, Jews lived in close contact with Christians in Europe but were nonetheless perceived as outsiders. At times, Europeans viewed Jews as "Orientals," linked to their Middle Eastern origins.[7] When the New World was discovered at the end of the fifteenth century, a new collective fantasy arose, that the inhabitants of the Americas might be descended from Jews or from the Ten Lost Tribes. This now appears void of historical foundation, but the idea struck deep roots in European thought. Some societies on the other side of the Atlantic had food taboos, rules of menstrual avoidance, or unusual marriage patterns between relatives, practices that Christian Europeans associated with Jews and the Israelites of the Hebrew Bible. How deep this idea was may be seen in a book entitled *The Present State of the Jews (More Particularly Relating to Those in Barbary): Wherein Is Contained an Exact Account of Their Customs, Secular and Religious*, published in 1675.[8] The author, Lancelot Addison, was a minister assigned to the English garrison in Tangiers, where he met local Jews. A striking feature of the publication is its frontispiece, which depicts an "aborigine" (with some features that might be Amerindian and others that probably correspond to generic images of "natives" at that time) holding a banner bearing the title of the book (figure 1). No explanation is attached to the illustration, suggesting that the association between Jews and "barbarians" was familiar to the intended audience. When anthropology began to take shape as a discipline in the nineteenth century, it would have seemed normal to many Europeans to include within it the study of Jews, but this linkage was opposed by Jews themselves, who were then energetically asserting themselves as enlightened individuals fully deserving to be participants in the nation-states of contemporary Europe. In addition, they were interested in stressing the similarities between themselves and their neighbors rather than the differences. Jews thus resisted an anthropological gaze that might place them in the same category of "less-civilized" peoples. This resistance continued for many generations. For example, the philosopher Abraham Joshua Heschel, in considering the comparison of the prophets of Israel to members of tribal society who entered states of ecstasy, objected that this approach "reduced biblical prophecy . . . to a common anthropological denominator; the prophets were conveniently classified as a typical phenomenon of primitive or ancient society."[9]

An anthropological approach to ongoing Jewish life thus did not appear throughout most of the nineteenth century, but there were attempts to understand the Hebrew Bible in anthropological terms. William Robertson Smith, who is an important figure in the history of both biblical studies and anthropology, played a key role contributing to this effort.[10] Smith—a believing Christian—assessed biblical religion with the aid of anthropology, placing it on an evolutionary ladder that led to Christianity. More widely known, however, is James George Frazer, Smith's student at Cambridge, whose book *The Golden Bough* was based upon comparative anthropological data.[11] In the preface to his three-volume study *Folklore in the Old Testament*, Frazer wrote: "The annals of savagery and superstition unhappily compose a large part of human literature; but in what other vol-

Figure 1.   Frontispiece to Lancelot Addison's *The Present State of the Jews* (London, 1675). Courtesy Center
of Judaic Studies Library, University of Pennsylvania.

ume [than the Old Testament] shall we find side by side with that melan-
choly record, psalmists who poured forth their sweet and solemn
strains?"[12] Frazer's rhetorical question implies some sympathy for the literature of the Hebrew Bible, but it is also clear that such a formulation
might well offend people with a deep attachment to that text. A few Jewish
scholars were able to see past the ambivalent situation of applying folklore
to the study of Jews and grasp that it carried the potential of further exploring the Jewish past. Two rabbinic scholars, Louis Ginzberg and Jacob
Lauterbach, incorporated perspectives from that discipline into their research. The format of Ginzberg's multivolume *Legends of the Jews* may
have been inspired by Frazer's approach.[13] Lauterbach referred to folklore

in seeking to unravel the history of Jewish customs.[14] Their readiness to move in this direction may have stemmed from a distinction between folklore and anthropology later formulated by Raphael Patai in the following words: "[F]olklore is the study of the mental equipment of simple folk in civilized countries" and "excludes the customs and beliefs of backward countries and savages, these being the provinces of certain branches of anthropology."[15] With the prevalence of such conceptions, several more decades of developments within anthropology would pass before firm constructive links between it and Jewish studies began to be forged.

Part of the problem was that in addition to documenting different ways of life, anthropology was also identified with the study of race. At the beginning of the twentieth century, the field was sometimes synonymous with the term "race science." This too, must be seen in the context of the late eighteenth and the nineteenth centuries, and in reference to the study of language. It had recently been discovered that some languages in India were historically related to languages in Europe. This historical connection was not accepted by all immediately but became established over the course of several decades. During that time, there were still attempts to view India in the framework of a "Mosaic ethnology" based on the opening chapters of the Bible.[16] In that context, scholars assigning names to languages around the world sometimes drew upon the story in Genesis that saw all humankind as descended from the three sons of Noah—Shem, Ham, and Yefet. That gave rise to new nomenclature, such as the term "Semitic languages" (from the Hebrew name Shem), which included ancient Hebrew and Arabic. In the course of the nineteenth century, with the strengthening of racial ideas and the attempt to give them scientific validity, the category "Semite" took on more and more of a racial meaning (as did the term "Aryan," linked to ancient India) and was incorporated into the modern phenomena of racial anti-Semitism. At the intellectual level, anti-Semitism was expressed in theories and research on traits that were seen to be biologically inborn in Jews and persisting over their long history. Today, we understand how misleading those claims were, but at the turn of the twentieth century, they had gained the status of serious science.

After the horrors of World War II, so-called scientific racism became thoroughly discredited. Recent research, however, has shown that studying what was understood as race and trying to assess its role in history and behavior did not merely arise from conservative and ultranationalist politics. Some scholars with liberal orientations were also interested in the subject.[17] There was still an assumption that analyzing the physical characteristics of a group might be closely tied to its practices and "mentality," so that what are now called physical anthropology and cultural anthropology were seen as part of the same package. There were those who criticized this view, such as German Jewish anthropologist Franz Boas, who was a central figure in shaping academic anthropology in the United States.[18] The Viennese rabbi Max Grunwald, who is viewed as the founder of Jewish folkloristics, also wanted to develop a cultural approach to Judaism to combat negative images arising from the racial anthropological approach.[19] But race science remained respectable to many and stimulated a great deal of systematic research. At that time, many Jews, particularly physicians, participated in studying the Jews from a racial and anthropological point of view.

There were two reasons why the (physical) anthropological study of the Jews was a topic that attracted the attention of Jewish scientists. The first was that they wanted to combat the negative stereotypes of Jews linked to racial theories. As directly stated in the title of a book by the historian John Efron, they became the "defenders of the race."[20] They criticized studies with negative conclusions about Jews and demonstrated the positive qualities of what they understood as the Jewish race cum culture. One feature of this research tradition was that it paid increasing attention to history and ethnography. When these scholars began to look at Jewish populations in Central Asia, the Middle East, and North Africa, it became apparent how diverse Jews were in physical appearance. Understanding this required placing these groups within history. If one assumed that Jews had been a single "nation" in the ancient past, what explained their present diversity? The typical answer was that Jews had changed physically in response to environmental conditions. The study of "race" therefore had to be connected to the social settings within which Jewish groups found themselves. Thus Jewish "race science" had an important component of what is now called cultural anthropology, but it was still subordinated to the misleading assumptions of race theory.

A second reason that racial social research appeared relevant to some Jews was a "positive" one. It appeared to supply Jews with a "scientific" way of asserting their collective existence precisely at a time when many Jews were assimilating and adopting the languages, lifestyles, and values of the countries in which they had been granted citizenship. More and more Jews received schooling along the same lines as their fellow citizens, and many began to enjoy the rewards of higher education. They wanted to reap the benefits of modern life while asserting aspects of their ethnic identity in ways that were "rationally" based. Particularly when discussions of race flowed naturally into the consideration of historical and cultural questions, a "scientific" approach to ethnic roots was therefore appealing as a means of staking out a claim for continued Jewish existence in the contemporary world.

Today, of course, a racial approach to Judaism—or to any culture—has been discredited, but its disappearance has left a vacuum.[21] Are there ways in which it is still possible to discuss Jews all over the world as a belonging to a single "group," when they are often so different from one another as a result of participation in different national cultures? Does a common history in the distant past have any relevance to contemporary identities, particularly when people are free to pick and choose what aspects of history have meaning to them, or may try to ignore it altogether? Can one speak of "the Jews" in the absence of a centralized authority with the power to determine "what Judaism is," and when scholars writing about "Jewish tradition" now recognize that they are dealing with phenomena whose contents and boundaries are fluid?

I believe that an anthropological perspective on Jewish life, linked to the more established modes of Jewish self-representation through textual and historical study, can help provide an affirmative answer to these questions. Such a perspective began to coalesce in the second half of the twentieth century and slowly was able to overcome the resistance that Jews and Judaic scholars had to viewing Jewish life and texts through anthropological eyes. I shall attempt to show its attraction and potential by first referring to my own experience in bridging the two domains.

ANTHROPOLOGY AND JEWISH LIFE: A PERSONAL ADVENTURE

My entrance into the world of anthropology took place in the fall of 1959. The setting was my junior year at Columbia College, after having taken off a year from my studies to spend it in Israel. Previous to that, I had been exposed to the study of Hebrew and Jewish life in my home synagogue, in an Orthodox day school and high school, and—concurrent with my college courses—at the Jewish Theological Seminary of America. Although "the Seminary" was located only a few blocks from Columbia University, up until that point I had seen few connections between what I was learning in those two institutions. Beginning with my first course in anthropology, however, the twin experiences of having lived in Israel and of delving more deeply into anthropological literature became central to my grasp of Judaism.

Encounters with Jews from Middle Eastern backgrounds and the styles of Judaism they practiced were one crucial feature of my year in Israel. From my first weeks in the country, when I attended a synagogue of Jews from Morocco on the High Holidays, I was fascinated by the way that the pronunciation of Hebrew, the Sephardi liturgy, and the atmosphere in the synagogue were all very different from what I had known while growing up but, at the same time, understandable to me. This combination of strangeness and closeness, which I met with many times throughout the year, was especially intense during two months I spent in an agricultural village (*moshav*) that had become the new home of Jews originating in a mountainous region of Tripolitania in Libya. It was epitomized by an incident that I recollect as forming a permanent bond between myself and the people on the moshav, who became a link to Middle Eastern Jewry in general for me.

This took place during the synagogue prayers on a Sabbath morning, when, as a guest in the village, I was "called up" to recite the blessings over the Torah. While I knew the blessings by heart and had carried out such a *mitzvah* (religious deed) on numerous occasions in Ashkenazi synagogues, I was a bit nervous. This was because of a slight difference (of two words) in the Ashkenazi and Sephardi versions of the second blessing, and also because the decorum of going up to and coming down from the lectern where the Torah is read varies slightly in each community. Nevertheless, my performance of the mitzvah passed smoothly, and I was congratulated warmly upon resuming my place among the congregants. I remember reflecting at the time on the power of this ritual. I had come from a middle-class family in New York City, and they had come from an "obscure" area of North Africa. I had received a general education, learning broadly about the European/Christian world, and their formal education had been confined to a few years in a synagogue school. My version of Judaism had been filtered through several generations of savants, linking Jewish tradition and modern scholarship, and their upbringing knew nothing of this. But in the space of a few minutes, when I had ascended to the Torah, uttered two sentences, and then descended from the *bimah* (platform), our worlds intersected, with a sense of communion, both between us as people and with "the tradition" that we shared.[22] My overall experience on the moshav also left me with the as-yet-unformulated conviction that Jewish life is inherently constituted by intriguing and attractive diversity.

As the end of my year in Israel grew near, I had to think more seriously about the continuation of my studies. By then I had a definite notion that I was interested in the social sciences and began to read books that had been mentioned to me during the course of the year. I had been told that Jacob Katz's *Tradition and Crisis* was a "must," and I purchased a copy.[23] While much of the sophistication of the work was lost on me at the time, inasmuch as I was a novice in the realms of sociology and social history, I was struck by the topics presented at the opening of the book. The discussions of Jewish streets, houses, and language gave the various ideals and lofty images I had come to associate with traditional European Jewry (which was the background of my grandparents) a concrete aspect. The book showed me that Jewish history could be approached in a manner that saw Jews as real people, without denying the importance that the values of Jewish tradition assumed in their lives. In retrospect, I was on the way to translating the impression-laden year in Israel to a systematic path of intellectual and professional endeavor. This took the form of focusing my studies, upon returning to the United States, in the direction of anthropology.

My courses in anthropology suggested many parallels to my experiences in Israel and the approach to Jewish studies that had become meaningful to me over the years. Upon reading Bronislaw Malinowski's description of the Kula expedition off the coast of New Guinea, I was impressed by his sensitivity to the excitement of the young men who, for the first time, saw places that they had known about only through myths.[24] That excitement paralleled my own during the year in Israel when, upon traveling throughout the country, stories and metaphors from the Bible took on a full-blooded reality. At the intellectual level, I was intrigued by the stress on cultural relativism. Franz Boas had shown that American Indian languages had to be understood in terms of their own grammatical structures and could not be forced into the requirements of classic Greek and Latin. Continuing the threads of his work, Ruth Benedict made a strong case for the integration and integrity of each culture, even though it might have borrowed heavily from other societies with which it was in contact.[25] These notions were familiar to me from studies of the Bible. Umberto Cassuto had criticized scholars who were quick to emend the biblical text, arguing from assumptions growing out of the models of classical scholarship, and Yehezkel Kaufmann insisted that the specific segments of biblical literature had to be understood in the context of an overall monotheistic worldview that informed them.[26] These trends in biblical studies, it is true, emerged quite independently from anthropological concerns and were remote from the study of contemporary communities. The potential link between the two fields, however, was clear to me.[27] Although anthropology may historically have emerged as the study of "other," sometimes denigrated societies, it could also be placed in the service of self-examination, self-enlightenment, and at times self-criticism. Most basically, I perceived the discipline to be self-enabling. Prodded on by this hunch, I was confronted with the challenge of showing that the ethnographic method and anthropological insights could help illuminate the cultures of Jewish communities of our own times.

I soon discovered that I was not alone in envisioning such a project. Two books by anthropologists that came out in the 1950s demonstrated that the possibility was a real one. The devastating events of World War II provided the background for a study of eastern European Jewish life by Mark Zborowski and Elizabeth Herzog, published under the title *Life Is with People*. Based on interviews in the United States with individuals who had grown up in *shtetl* communities, it presented a portrait of Jewish small towns in Poland.[28] Whereas this book may be seen as a memorial to the past, another ethnographic study, Melford Spiro's *Children of the Kibbutz*, portrayed the new Jewish collective settlements (*kibbutzim*) that had emerged in Palestine early in the twentieth century.[29] I then learned that, precisely at the time when my interests were coming together, several researchers had set out to document the lives of Jews in Middle Eastern settings. Israel, the new home of many of these groups, was a natural center of such work, but life in other Middle Eastern countries, along with the experience of Middle Eastern Jewish immigrants elsewhere, also received attention.[30] Thus, Jewish immigrants to France from North Africa became the focus of anthropological fieldwork. The author of one study, Joëlle Bahloul, herself a Jew from Algeria who had experienced the colonial situation and then moved to France, later expressed her attraction to anthropology in terms I could readily appreciate. She explains how this perspective "aided my self-recognition with the savage in my culture," and how "I, the savage, reversed the roles; by casting an anthropological gaze upon my own group, I posed a challenge to that belittling glance [of others] by making it my own."[31] At the same time, various forms of Jewish religious and cultural activity in the United States among the descendants of immigrants from eastern Europe began to attract ethnographic attention as new generations of Jews sought to both interpret the past and participate in the ongoing formulation of their traditions.[32] A sustained anthropological engagement with Jewish life was beginning to take shape.[33]

The appropriation of anthropology by individuals interested and involved in Judaism was sustained by developments within the discipline itself. Historically, anthropology had been an enterprise of Europeans dealing with groups in "faraway places." Often the societies that ethnographers studied did not have their own written traditions, and anthropology remained the discipline of the "tribal" rather than the "scribal."[34] After World War II, this began to change. Anthropological research was increasingly carried out in "peasant societies," in which local village communities formed part of larger urban, regional, and international networks.[35] This had not only economic and political significance but cultural and religious ramifications as well. The way Buddhism, Christianity, Hinduism, or Islam was practiced among the nonliterate residents of villages and cities reflected both the hallowed teachings and texts of these traditions and various local influences.[36] Anthropologists were presented with the task of relating the skills they had developed in observing local communities to the insights gained from deciphering and interpreting historical texts and literatures. Paths were being opened for ways of connecting the legacy of ancient traditions to the immediacy of daily life, and there was no reason that Judaism should not have a place in this process.

This new potential was realized in several ways. Beginning in the 1950s, several leading British anthropologists known previously for their fieldwork in Africa and Asia published studies showing their interest in the Hebrew Bible.[37] This represented a return, with contemporary sensibilities, to the subject matter of Smith and Frazer. Somewhat later, Jewish historians began to incorporate anthropology as a source of insight with regard to textual materials from antiquity, the Middle Ages, and early modern periods.[38] For example, S. D. Goitein, whose work on documents from the Jewish community of Cairo has enriched the understanding of medieval Jewry generally, acknowledged the impact of his field research among contemporary Yemenite Jews and his friendship with Erich Brauer, who was the first Jewish ethnographer in Mandate Palestine, on his approach to earlier archival sources.[39] Along with anthropology, the parallel field of folklore has inspired a sensitive appreciation of European Jewry in recent centuries, a period that overlaps with the focus of the researchers mentioned above who delved into the historical backgrounds of Middle Eastern Jewish communities.[40] These developments now make it possible to inquire into the texture and sheen of Judaism and of Jewish lives as they are refracted by a discipline that views society from "close in," person-centered angles of analysis, while remaining connected to broad horizons of Jewish history and textual culture.

ANTHROPOLOGY AND JEWISH LIVES

How an anthropological perspective keeps us attuned to ancient texts, to the taken-for-granted assumptions of our own culture, and to the lessons of ethnography is illustrated by the notion of "life cycles" itself. To begin with, the idea of "life cycles" does not always emerge as a commonsense category or coherent theme in traditional Jewish culture.[41] For example, it does not appear as a guiding category in the sixteenth-century *Shulhan Arukh*, which continues to be a standard work and is often referred to as "the code of Jewish law." The *Shulhan Arukh*, like later commentaries based on it, is organized in terms of rubrics established by an earlier *halakhic* essay, the *Arba'ah Turim* ("Four Columns") of Rabbi Jacob ben

Asher, which codifies Jewish practice under four headings: (1) the daily religious routine (blessings, prayers, Sabbaths, and festivals, etc.), (2) ritual law (rules of *kashrut,* circumcision, mourning, etc.), (3) family laws (marriage, divorce, etc.), and (4) civil law (e.g., contracts). An inquirer into rituals linked to birth and circumcision would need to examine the second "book," called *Yoreh Deʿah,*[42] while for information about what we now call "bar mitzvah," marked by calling a young person to recite blessings while the Torah is read in the synagogue, he would have to look in the first book, *Oraḥ Ḥayyim* ("The Path of Life"). Information relevant to understanding weddings appears in the third volume, *Even Haʿezer.*[43] Rabbi Jacob Ben Asher, who was born in Germany and moved with his father to Spain in 1303, did not take the trajectory of an individual life as a major conceptual point of reference in his work, but organized the halakhic tradition according to other principles, within which men and women (mainly men) had to find their way.

This is not to say that Jewish textual tradition is blind to the life cycle, or does not recognize the dynamics of an unfolding life. The Babylonian Talmud notes that God dressed Adam and Eve in the opening chapters of the Pentateuch and buried Moses at its conclusion.[44] While the "first people" appear as adults, the text imputes to them some childlike qualities. In another passage from rabbinic literature, a midrash views the authorship of three biblical books, all attributed to King Solomon, through the prism of the stages of life. It claims that when Solomon was young, he composed the Song of Songs which is full of love poetry; in his middle years, he wrote Proverbs, reflecting his wisdom; and in his old age, he wrote Ecclesiastes, beginning with the statement: "Vanity of vanities, all is vanity." Who in fact wrote these books is not known, but this midrash clearly expresses the changing frames of mind of an individual in his adult years.[45]

More concretely, the mishnaic tractate *Avot* outlines the normative stages of the life of a Jewish male:

> At five years, the age is reached for the study of the Scripture, at ten for the study of the Mishna, at thirteen for the fulfillment of the commandments, at fifteen for the study of the Talmud, at eighteen for marriage, at twenty for seeking a livelihood, at thirty for entering into one's full strength, at forty for understanding, at fifty for counsel, at sixty a man attains old age, at seventy the hoary head, at eighty the gift of special strength, at ninety he bends beneath the weight of years, at a hundred he is as if he were already dead and had passed away from the world.

This passage was probably inserted in the Middle Ages, but its author clearly had a sense of progression of individual lives.[46]

Figure 2.   The "Four Sons" depicted in a Passover Haggadah printed in Amsterdam in 1712 as four stages of life. Courtesy Jewish National and University Library, Jerusalem.

   Given that notions of a life cycle were recognized at various points in Jewish history, they surely were structured differently at different times. A seventeenth-century illustration of a section of the Passover Haggadah called the "Four Sons," suggests that at this period a stronger sense of a life cycle may have been emerging (see figure 2). In traditional European communities, one remembered the date of death (*yahrtzeit*) of one's parents but did not normally celebrate birthdays. The precise date on which a male was born was important, however, in terms of counting the days towards his circumcision. This situation was common among Middle Eastern communities too. I recall an incident, from the 1960s, in an Israeli village settled by Jews from a rural area of Libya.[47] Entering one of the village houses, I found a bearded man (generally said to be in his seventies) sitting on the floor and gleefully peering into a tattered prayer book. He looked up at me and said with excitement: "I just discovered how old I am." The book had belonged to his father, and he had discovered that the latter had written in it that a son had been born to him on such and such a date. The man himself had been unaware of his own birth date. Generalizing from this situation, it appears that one had the obligation of knowing one's son's date of birth for religious reasons, but not necessarily one's own (or one's daughter's). The life cycle was perceived, but subordinated to collective purposes given shape by ancient texts.

This ethnographic vignette provides one illustration of the linkage between an appreciation of texts and the anthropological focus on social context. On the one hand, time-honored texts have played a central role in the lives of Jewish communities. On the other hand, it would be highly simplistic to assume that the actual way Jews behaved was a "printout," so to speak, of the contents of their sacred books. Rabbinical writings must thus be used cautiously as a source of social history, because it is often not clear when this literature expresses an ideal and when it reflects an existing state of affairs. It has been suggested, for example, that the Mishna Avot's "eighteen for marriage" was a rabbinical recommendation and not the average age at which men married in ancient Judea. This ideal, in a situation where average life expectancy was about fifty, was to enable men to live to see grandsons who would continue the study of Torah.[48] This suggestion recognizes the importance of textually based norms and simultaneously seeks to place them in their proper historical context. It should also be noted that the interpretation assumes that in ancient times, people took into account the interconnection of distinct stages of life.

Viewing life-cycle celebrations with an anthropological eye thus involves paying attention to both books and their social settings. On both these levels, one must be aware that what is now familiar in Jewish life may only partially reflect earlier periods or other places. For example, traditional Jews today think of the sixteenth-century *Shulhan Arukh* (with later glosses on it) as authoritatively defining ritual behavior in all spheres, but for several centuries a composition entitled *Maavar Yabboq*, published by a kabbalist from Modena, Italy, in 1626, provided standards of comportment for Ashkenazi Jews with regard to illness and death.[49] Placing this book and others like it in their social setting means paying attention to the burial societies that used them. Our consideration of burial societies in both Europe and North Africa will indicate the roles that these organizations played in the lives of communities well beyond the realm of death and burial. With regard to the diverse historical circumstances within which texts operate, it is obvious that an anthropological or ethnographic perspective is called for to capture the specific sense and social implications of rituals and celebrations as they were carried out in those settings.

One way of working towards the goal of understanding rituals as they were practiced in earlier periods is to try to imagine those settings as they might have been observed by an ethnographer on the spot. Thinking in these terms, one natural question regarding life-cycle customs is the possible influence of neighboring societies on practices we now call "Jewish." During the past millennium (and earlier), Jewish practice was exposed to outside influences both in the Muslim Middle East (in which Sephardi traditions became dominant) and in Christian Europe (where Ashkenazi practice evolved).[50] There was also at least one major Jewish schism, the Karaites, which was represented in both the Middle East and eastern Europe.[51] In addition, there were groups that were separated from the main centers of Jewish life for considerable periods of time, like those in India (affected by Hindu civilization) or the Beta Israel of Ethiopia (a Christian-dominated land surrounded by Muslim countries and also including non-monotheistic African traditions). In all these arenas, Jews came into contact with diverse practices and beliefs, and an examination of historical sources with the aid of ethnographic insights may help us grasp the dynamics and impact of such contact.

Many cultural traits of the surrounding societies, such as food habits and dress, became part of Jewish life. This process entailed many possible reactions. When new cultural features did not conflict with religious norms, they often were unnoticed by the historical record and silently slid into the range of practices internal to Jewish culture. If some tension were felt between Jewish tradition and new forms of behavior, the latter might be forbidden by religious leaders, or they might be reinterpreted and thus become acceptable within textually based culture. In addition, there were times in which Jewish practice and that of the majority directly clashed and competed, just as there were cases in which Jewish customs appeared as oppositional responses to the customs and beliefs of the wider society. Such situations emerged when majority religions that historically were derived from Judaism became rivals to it.

An example of the latter process may be seen in an unusual Jewish custom, reported from Tripoli, in Libya, on the occasion of the Muslim celebration of the Great Festival, which relates to Abraham's (or Ibrahim's) near-sacrifice of his son, who, according to the widespread Muslim claim, was the biblical Ishmael and not Isaac. The holiday is characterized by the slaughter of animals and their consumption in family gatherings, while multitudes of Muslims who have left their local communities simultaneously participate in the pilgrimage to Mecca. Observers in Tripoli towards the end of the nineteenth century reported that, in this context, some men in the Jewish quarter got up at night, or before dawn, to slaughter a sheep on the day of the Muslim festival. Their view of this practice was that the Jews, "jealous, so to speak, of the homage paid by Muslims to one of their greatest patriarchs" (Abraham), sacrificed early "in order to preempt for themselves the grace of the Lord."[52] The logic of this vernacular custom may be based on a standard Jewish-Muslim difference in another realm, that of circumcision; it seems to say: just as we circumcise earlier, at the age of eight days, so we may be able to preempt the blessing by sacrificing earlier in the day than the Muslims.[53] This popular polemic with Muslim practice is not recorded, to the best of my knowledge, in any rabbinical text. It appears to be embarrassing to any formal representative of Jewish tradition, but it illustrates the many strands of meaning, deriving from both official tradition and local influence, that may be enmeshed in what appear to be simple customary actions by ordinary Jews.

A popular bar mitzvah song from a neighboring North African country, Tunisia, supplies another illustration of religious impact from outside Jewish tradition, along with evidence of how Jewish communities both absorbed such influence and neutralized it.[54] The song, in the Arabic speech of Tunisian Jews, addresses various participants in the ritual—neighbors, members of the boy's family, and the celebrant himself—and ends with a stanza of appreciation: "There is no God but Allah, the festivities are at our place; all our former enemies have come and given us greetings." How do we grasp the reference to Allah in an eminently Jewish celebration?

Allah, in this context, can be translated as "God." The word appears regularly in the speech of North African Jews. More startling, however, is that the opening phrase of that stanza is, in fact, the Muslim profession of faith. Jews can easily agree to that brief statement, but cannot accept its second half (not incorporated into the song), which declares that Mohammad is the messenger of God. According to the researcher who recorded this song, who was himself born in Tunisia, the sentence was borrowed mechanically from Muslim chants, pronounced very differently in the speech of Jews, and treated as a refrain with little meaning. This shows how understanding Jewish celebrations at a local level involves exploring the concrete dynamics of interreligious contact, which may entail both the absorption of influence and, simultaneously, the disguising and denial of that process. My assumption is that such subtle interactive dynamics took place often in Jewish history, in both Europe and in the Middle East, although it is unusual to have close-up data that document the process.[55]

The above discussion is typical of classic anthropological concerns when ethnographic research was primarily concerned with the cultural diversity that distinguished different groups and with the outcome of contact among them. Anthropology today, however, along with other disciplines, is also attuned to the variety of "voices" within any society. In particular, historical researchers now seek ways of understanding the experiences of nonelite categories of people whose activities and points of view are less likely to have received direct expression in written sources. Ordinary members of families and communities in Jewish life were positioned differently than were rabbinic leaders and also were open to different kinds of cultural influence. It would be a mistake to approach this issue by simply dealing with separate topics, such as "learned" as opposed to "folk" religion. The previously cited examples show that various spheres of a society and its culture are intertwined. Unraveling the give-and-take between Judaism as it was lived by ordinary community members, on the one hand, and as it was expounded by representatives of rabbinical tradition, on the other, is an important goal of the anthropological study of Jewish rituals.

The greater openness to the category of "ordinary Jews" also pushes towards the inclusion of women in a broadened historical outlook. In the past, the involvement of women in life-cycle celebrations was often ignored, mentioned only briefly, or relegated to strictly defined roles. Scholars today realize that the lives of Jewish women constitute a subject of untapped potential. It is now a dynamic field of research, involving much debate, and having implications outside the academic realm. Anthropology has been mobilized in staking out different approaches to the topic.[56]

In the study of the Hebrew Bible from an anthropological perspective, the topic of women typically emerged in relation to family. In *Folklore in the Old Testament,* Sir James Frazer began his survey by discussing the family of "Father Jacob," including his marriage to two sisters.[57] He found that customs in "savage" societies (a term since rejected by anthropologists) could be compared to biblical family institutions such as the levirate—a man marrying the widow of his deceased brother. Placing the Bible in this comparative framework raises poignant questions about women in biblical society and religion.

Some see the Bible as expressing an unredeemable "patriarchy," in which women are dominated socially and devalued spiritually.[58] At times, this is viewed as a link between monotheism—the belief in one God—and the assignment of secondary status to women, for if there is only one deity, a choice has to be made as to whether "he" is male or female.[59] The world of the Bible is certainly dominated by men, but it is a document that took shape over many centuries, and scholars emphasize the diversity of sources and variety of points of view that are included in it. The Book of Ruth, for example, which portrays a close relationship between two women, can be read in contrast to the more "patriarchal" stories in Genesis.[60] It is also possible to understand some biblical material, such as the story of Judah and Tamar in Genesis, as taking a stance in opposition to popular beliefs, such as the misogynistic view that certain wives have a tendency to "kill" their husbands.[61] Critics who find no satisfactory place for women in biblical culture may dismiss such interpretations as "apologetic," but they are based on close readings of the original text and theoretically informed literary analyses. These readings show the special themes and internal dynamics of the biblical text, even while comparing biblical society to other societies.

In addition to narrative portions of the Bible, women also appear in biblical rules. Leviticus 15 outlines the restrictions of sexual intercourse during menstruation and the process of purification that follows. These rules have been interpreted as indicators of low religious and social status.[62] They are found, however, in a textual matrix that discusses impurity connected to flow from the sexual organs of men as well.[63] Classic writings thus engender various points of view, as may be seen in reference to ancient rabbinical texts, like the Mishna, as well.[64] In both instances of canonized literature, it should be stressed, we are presented with sets of rules. Anthropologists want to know whether these books reflect social reality, present a set of ideals, or are a complex weave of both. Whatever the answers, the textual scholar and the anthropologist can both agree that the first challenge is to understand how the texts imagine society and the place of women in it. Whether this leads to justification or condemnation, inspiration or dismissal, is a partially different matter.

With regard to the Middle Ages, we sometimes have a more concrete picture of how the lives of women were actually lived. S. D. Goitein utilized documents from the Cairo Geniza that are in Arabic, written in Hebrew script, to illuminate many aspects of daily life in the tenth through twelfth centuries.[65] For example, marriage contracts yield information on the content and value of women's wedding trousseaus. Goitein also showed how women entering a second marriage, after divorce or widowhood, had a fair amount of leeway in running their own lives.[66] It is also important to attend to religious realms that in the past were looked at only from the perspective of men.[67]

From later periods, there is more ample evidence of the religious lives of women. For example, in Europe, supplicatory prayers appeared in Yiddish to be recited by women on occasions such as lighting Sabbath candles, or at special times, such as pregnancy. Chava Weissler points out that these prayers were mostly composed by men, but in nineteenth-century eastern Europe, some supplications were written by women too.[68] With regard to North Africa, Joseph Chetrit has analyzed Judeo-Arabic poetry (poetry in the local dialects of the Jews) that was sung by women. Typically, it was linked to life-cycle settings: lullabies, weddings, and ritualized mourning. As such, it reflected universal human themes, but it also included Jewish concerns such as the longing for Zion.[69] Materials like these from recent centuries, whose social context is not fully clear, are occasionally illuminated by field data gathered in the past few generations.

The ethnography of contemporary communities teaches us that there is much Jewish belief and practice that is not recorded in, or derived from, written texts.[70] One may try to analyze "the attitude" towards women in books of *halakha* (rabbinic law), but women would relate to religious practices such as those concerning menstruation in a manner quite different from men.[71] Our perspective is further expanded by ethnographic studies that do not cite "women" as their subject but delve into realms, such as food preparation, in which women play a leading role.[72] Field experience also reveals that women are involved in aspects of religion from which we are accustomed to see them as excluded. A friend from Tripoli once remarked to me that women constantly had the synagogue on their minds. They "cared for" the synagogue, cleaning it during the week and making sure that spices, or oil for the lamps, were there on the Sabbath.[73] An expanded appreciation stemming from contemporary field studies sometimes allows scholars to read sources from earlier periods with greater sensitivity and to more fully grasp women's involvement in religion in preceding eras, just as it augments historical apperception generally.

Contemporary life is of value in itself, of course. One of the main factors reshaping the religiosity of women today is their entrance into the world of textual studies, a process that has also been illuminated by ethnographic research.[74] The expanded and more intensive study of Jewish texts not only has gone hand in hand with women assuming religious roles formerly limited to men but has also been mobilized to reinforce traditional "feminine roles" in today's society. Ultimately, a fuller view of women in Jewish life serves to enrich and revise our overall understanding of Jewish culture.[75]

Attention to women, and to various nonelite groups, leads to a consideration of another underappreciated category in Jewish life, "the individual." As already indicated, understanding individuals in relation to their cultural milieu presents a challenge both to anthropology and to Jewish studies. While stressing the imprint of cultural traditions upon those socialized within it, anthropology has also pointed to individual variation within cultures and has analyzed how actors manipulate and otherwise have an impact on the social and symbolic settings within which they are enmeshed. In addition to the concern with viewing human beings as active agents, anthropologists and historians now realize that the very notion of "the individual" is a cultural creation, and that different societies are predicated on varying concepts of "the person," "the self," and "the individual."[76] These questions grow in relevance as issues of individuality, individual rights, and personal meaning become ever more prominent in contemporary life.

The question of conceptualizing "the individual" has only occasionally been explicitly raised in discussions of Jewish history and culture. In exhorting Jews to follow the guidance of hoary texts and to emulate religious heroes of the past, spokesmen for Jewish tradition have built upon and encouraged the perception that figures from the past shared the same sense of "self" as they and their followers, or inhabited a life-world fully comparable to their own. In reality, however, all individual Jews today face a range of options far broader than those encountered by their cultural forebears in preemancipation Europe or in the traditional Middle East. Moreover, all contemporary Jews are endowed with a modern-day sense of being able to participate in current affairs and affect their surroundings, a basic perception and sentiment that was less widespread in past eras. This sense of individual empowerment is as true of Jews adhering to Orthodox forms of Judaism, who claim that they are faithfully following the dictates of law and tradition, as it is of Jews who follow other formulations of Jewish life that explicitly acknowledge that they have chosen to adapt Judaism to contemporary circumstances. The most basic exercise of choice by Jews deeply committed to tradition is, firstly, to live within frameworks defined by that tradition and, secondly, to select from a range of options that Orthodox approaches offer. All contemporary forms of Judaism, no matter how their ideologies view the past, are modern creations and partake of modern cultural assumptions about individuality. Both Orthodox and other contemporary Jews operate on the basis of senses of "the individual" that are distinct from the taken-for-granted notions of traditional Jewish society.

Expressions of "the individual" in traditional Jewish cultures are thus another theme that we shall examine in relation to life trajectories. Such expressions always existed, but they only rarely led individuals to separate themselves formally from the fabric of Jewish communal life, or even to imagine the possibility of such a separation. Enwrapped within and forming part of that fabric, the events of individual lives meshed with other cycles of Jewish life: the ritual calendar, the flow of communal activities, and the commitment to Torah study. If you were the youngest child, it was incumbent upon you to recite the "four questions" during the Passover seder. After getting married, in Sephardi tradition, an additional Torah scroll was taken out of the Ark and read in the synagogue on Sabbath in order to honor the newly wed groom. If you were a man whose wife had given birth to a girl, you were accorded a ritual honor in the synagogue on the following Sabbath and named your daughter on that occasion, while the community acknowledged a prayer recited for the recovery of her mother. Hymns composed for the festival of Shavuot likened Israel to a "bride" receiving the Torah from the "bridgeroom," God, while on the holiday of Simhat Torah, the person receiving the honor of blessing the Torah when the opening portion of Genesis was read was known as "the bridegroom of Genesis." During memorial rituals, portions of the Mishna were read aloud that were selected to form an acrostic of the name of the deceased. As in other societies studied by anthropologists during its classic phase, individual life milestones in traditional Jewish settings were deeply embedded in ongoing, intense, and taken-for-granted communal frameworks, and were expressed within meaningful webs of intermeshing practices, which continually reinforced them. Examining "the individual" in Judaism, therefore, inevitably entails taking into account different forms of Jewish "community."

The notion of community, of course, carries distinct implications in different historical contexts. Today, it cannot be separated from new forms of literacy and communication. Accounts of contemporary individual and social life must consider the impact of globalization providing people with an expanding range of information, images, and options for connecting to others. The anthropologist Arjun Appadurai has sought to grasp these trends by viewing local social action against the background of a series of "-scapes," such as "ethnoscapes" or "mediascapes."[77] For Jews, the creation of community typically places them within dynamic textscapes as well. These, while now often filtered through digital technology, define and express versions of Judaism and infuse social links to other Jews. For individuals, the new technology creates myriad opportunities for shaping tailor-made life celebrations embracing themselves and those close to them. In an era when some Jewish groups ideologically place themselves in strict opposition to others, they also find themselves facing the unprecedented possibility of mutual or overlapping communication.

Finally, Jewish communal life today cannot be fully understood except in relation to the broad national and political contexts within which it is constituted. The two countries within which the majority of Jews today are concentrated—the United States and Israel—provide very different frameworks for individuals pursuing personal and collective Jewish expression. The former offers a legally open arena for people of different religious orientations to shape varying styles of spiritual commitment and behavior, while the latter has established formal bureaucratic structures that entail limitations on many features of life-cycle events and other aspects of Jewish existence. Within both these societies, however, a kaleidoscope of Jewish practice may be observed, ranging from individuals seeking innovative religious forms to those adhering to strictly monitored communal norms.

The Israeli situation constitutes a highly dynamic and contested topic, impossible to summarize here, but deserving of discussion within a broad and global Jewish frame of reference. In both societies, as in other countries around the world where Jews live, daily decisions about how to live and celebrate Jewishly are made in reference to a venerated textual tradition and to assorted notions of a collective Jewish future.

The chapters that follow apply these anthropological perspectives to Jewish life-cycle ceremonies as they appear both in texts and in history and practice. Each chapter discusses a different life-cycle topic and draws upon these orientations in varying proportions. Each shows many aspects of ongoing lives and their celebration, but does not seek to provide exhaustive coverage. Rather, along with a presentation of some textual background to each subject, anthropological perspectives are employed to enrich the understanding of texts, and of previous historical study, by enlarging the field of explanations evoked by rituals and enhancing appreciation of the social and symbolic contexts relevant to them. For example, chapter 2, in exploring circumcision, offers an anthropological reading of the notion of "covenant" in the Hebrew Bible that brings together theological and everyday meanings of the ritual operation. Chapter 3, which focuses on rituals concerning the study of Torah, reviews a historical anthropological analysis that shows how this internal Jewish realm was affected by popular polemics with Christianity in the Middle Ages.[78] Chapter 4, on marriage, not only explores various aspects of women's lives in relation to it but illustrates the interweaving of elite rabbinical interpretations and popular social and sexual significations in the symbolic gesture of breaking a glass and demonstrates how their interlinking became persuasive and widely accepted.

An anthropological apperception also implies considering practices that have not conventionally been placed under the rubric of life cycles. Thus, chapter 5 discusses pilgrimage, because it is often a crucial act in the cultivation of individual religiosity for both men and women and now takes the form of identity-forming travel and tourism that are often linked to stages in a life trajectory. Modern travel brings about spatial contiguity among Jews of different backgrounds, adding a global dimension to hitherto isolated definitions of Jewish selves. Other aspects of "the individual" within Judaism appear in chapter 6, on death and mourning, where a consideration of *dibbuk* spirit-possession proves relevant to the emergence of inner psychological controls among Jews in the early modern period. Finally, chapter 7 deals with the topic of community, which both historically and in recent times has inevitably presented itself when individuals engaged those around them in marking life's transitions.

These are a few illustrations of some of the topics and issues that form part of our anthropological view of Jewish culture and lives. It is also appropriate to mention several other aspects of the anthropological perspective in order to guide the reader through the chapters that follow. First, anthropologists rarely attempt to understand rituals and ceremonies as things in themselves, but always try to place them in their human historical settings. The cycles of single lives are thus instructive avenues leading to other spheres of Jewish existence and expression. In general, life-cycle rituals are best grasped as highlighted moments within the flow of social and cultural processes. If at times the discussion moves away from a direct consideration of rituals and ceremonies, it is for the purpose of returning to them with greater precision and significance. A sense of context is crucial, particularly as we seek to incorporate materials from antiquity and the Middle Ages into an outlook that is relevant to contemporary society. For example, the development of modern hygiene, and the fact that Jews began to study in medical schools, proves relevant to practices concerning both circumcision and burial.

It may appear pretentious, on the part of a discipline or its practitioners, to claim to be able to bring together under one intellectual purview the distant past and its relevance to contemporary developments, textual treasures and their connection to ordinary behavior, and a grasp of broad social contexts coupled with their implications for personal experience. Anthropologists seek to take these various factors into account, however, precisely because ethnographic encounters have taught them that all these forces coalesce to give detailed shape to ongoing social life and patterns of customary behavior. The case for an anthropological excursion into Jewish life does not rest upon the desire to produce a reified and timeless summary of the content of Judaism, but upon the attempt to convey the dynamism in which a range of factors interact and create new forms that reflect the complex and conflicted present, while connected to the Jewish past. In tune with the insistence upon keeping myriad angles of vision in mind, I open the following chapters with short ethnographic vignettes from my own experience. Indeed, the variegated material that follows, from different periods, regions, and realms of life, is an attempt to share with the reader a glimpse of "being Jewish" that stems from this anthropologically informed respect for diversity, along with a sense of its fluid yet palpable interconnectedness. I shall be gratified if this point of view not only provides readers of any background with new information but also becomes incorporated into how contemporary Jews, following different paths, attend to and partially appreciate one another.

2 Beginnings

Birth, Circumcision, and Naming

The best-known ritual of early life in Judaism is the circumcision of baby boys. It is the only life-cycle ritual based directly on an explicit rule in the Bible. According to Genesis 17, it was the first commandment given to Abraham to be carried out by him and his descendants. Circumcision has been practiced by Jews for more than two millennia, and it has been a topic of debate over the centuries. These debates and discussions have engaged both Jews and Gentiles.

From the point of view of Western culture, no ritual has come to symbolize Jews and the special character of Judaism more than circumcision. One way that Christianity set itself off from the Jewish religion was by rejecting the requirement of circumcision and insisting that all peoples, not only Jews, could become part of the faith initiated by Abraham. Circumcision thus came to be associated with the "particularism" of Judaism, contrasted with the "universalism" of Christian teaching. Nineteenth-century students of religion saw in circumcision the vestiges of a "tribal religion," as they became aware that circumcision was practiced in many societies in Africa and in Oceania. This knowledge made biblical circumcision ripe for anthropological interpretations, which Jews had to take into account as well. The *Jewish Encyclopaedia*, published in New York in 1903, includes an ethnographic discussion of circumcision spanning three pages.

Debates over circumcision, which took different forms in different historical eras, did not bring Jews, as a collectivity, to abandon the practice. Benedict (Baruch) de Spinoza, familiar with the Marranos who kept their Judaism secretly in the Iberian peninsula, assessed the power of circumcision to maintain Jewish distinctiveness: "The significance is, as I think, so important, that I could persuade myself that it alone would preserve the nation forever."[1] Over the past decade or so, many Jews moving to Israel from the former Soviet Union who had not been circumcised there elected to undergo the operation as part of their reconnection to Jewish life. To understand how circumcision became a central and defining practice for Jews, it is useful to begin with a Jewish ethnographic perspective.

My first experience of a circumcision as an anthropological researcher took place in an Israeli immigrant village, a moshav inhabited by Jews from Libya, in 1964. About half a year earlier, my own firstborn son had been circumcised, in the United States, so I was well acquainted with the basic structure of the ceremony. I was eager to see in what ways heirs to the Sephardi tradition who had lived, as recently as fifteen years earlier, in a mountainous region south of Tripoli, had customs that were different from the ones with which I was familiar. Witnessing that circumcision, and following the events surrounding it, raised many questions, the complexity of which I only appreciated years later.[2]

As had been the case with my son, on the moshav, the ceremony, which is supposed to take place on the eighth day after birth, was delayed for medical reasons. This was not unusual, because under rabbinic law, the principle of preserving life takes precedence over the observance of other commandments. I was therefore surprised to learn that such delays had never taken place in the Libyan community abroad; circumcisions there had been carried out on the eighth day without exception. This was the first hint of a significant difference in the ways in which circumcision was part of their culture and of mine.

A second difference appeared after a date for the ceremony was finally set. At that time, I learned of a gathering to take place at the home of the family the night before the circumcision. This occasion was called *leilat az-zuhar*, the "night of the Zohar." On that night, a number of men came to the home and sat around and read from a chapbook that contained selections from the Zohar, the major work of Jewish mysticism. Later, they were served a meal. This was a completely new practice for me, but I subsequently discovered that it had formerly been widespread among some Ashkenazi Jews, as well as among Sephardi communities (see below, "Rabbinic Circumcision").

The following day, the circumcision took place. The *mohel* (circumciser) was a member of the community. In everyday life, he was a farmer like the other householders of the village. He had learned to be a mohel in Tripoli and continued to serve in this capacity in the Israeli village. The village was characterized by a high birthrate, so he was frequently called upon to perform circumcisions. That his craft had undergone certain changes was obvious from the fact that in preparation for the operation, he donned a white coat and opened a kit with modern surgical instruments, medications, and bandages. I had intended to ask him later about the transition from traditional to modern practice, and I was to learn, as will soon be explained, that it had not been an easy one.

The family into which the baby had been born was one with whom I had developed good relations, even though I had only been in the village a few months. Upon entering the house, I noticed a chair placed on top of a cabinet, with a prayer shawl draped across it. I was told that this was the chair of "Elijah the prophet," an element of the ceremony that had not been included in the circumcision of my son. Someone asked me if I wished to see the baby that was about to be circumcised. When I said yes, I was admitted into a back room in the small house, where I found the infant, his mother, and some other women. It was curtained off from the main area where men had gathered by a colorful hanging sheet, of the kind used by women in the village as an outer garment, draped around a woman like a sari. Aside from the infant and a few very young boys, I was the only male in this section of the house at the time.

The separation of males from females that was normal in village life was emphasized during the ceremony, and in the context, it was striking to observe the way in which the infant had been prepared for the occasion. The child was completely wrapped up in a way that gave no hint as to his gender, and his face was made up, particularly around the eyes, as if he were a girl. I immediately thought of the studies of initiation ceremonies in many societies that include genital operations like circumcision that are understood as making young boys—who are closely associated with women—into men. It was puzzling that this same type of symbolism appeared in the Tripolitanian community, where it was clear that the infant would be returned to the world of women after the ceremony.

Soon the infant was transferred from the women's room into the area of the male gathering. The ritual proceedings were basically similar to those I recognized from my own background. The mohel worked swiftly, the appropriate prayers and blessings were recited, and the infant was bandaged and handed back to the mother in the women's section. I also moved back into that section, taking advantage of the liberty that had been given to me as an outsider to move between the rigid gender categories of village life. A moment later, however, I was surprised by the appearance of a tall, bearded man, dressed in a black coat and large brimmed black hat that marked him as part of the Ashkenazi, Hasidic world, who unhesitatingly came behind the curtain.

The intruder assertively asked: "Where is the boy who was circumcised here a year ago?" The women pointed to one of the youngsters who was close by them. "Show me," the Hasid demanded. One of the women held the boy, while someone else pulled down his pants. The young boy was frightened, began to cry, and urinated in the man's face. The women immediately offered him a towel and showed him where he could wash himself, but he said "never mind," indicating that he was finished and impatient to leave. Moving into the men's area, he asked how he could get out of the village quickly. The men, speaking to him very respectfully, said that I, who had the only car in the village at the time, might be willing to give him a ride to the main road. While I found his manner offensive and would have preferred to stay with the celebrants, the deference shown to him by the villagers (who addressed him as *kevod ha-rav*, "honorable rabbi"), made it hard for me to refuse. This gave me the opportunity to ask where he had come from and what his intrusion was about.

In the car, he said that he was the chief inspector of all the circumcisers in Israel and had to check to see whether circumcisions were being carried out correctly. He had in fact missed the ceremony by a few minutes, but had taken the opportunity to examine last year's operation. I asked him how he knew that a circumcision was supposed to take place, particularly as it had been delayed past the first eight days. He gave a brief and puzzling answer to the effect that "he had his sources." He spoke condescendingly about immigrant *mohalim*, saying, "They come from abroad with their rusty razor blades." I am now quite sure that this was untrue—special knives for circumcisions were, in fact, fashioned by Jewish silversmiths in Tripoli—but it reflected the chief inspector's overall mind-set. One could not disqualify the immigrant mohalim, he explained, "people would continue to go to them anyway," and it was therefore necessary to "work with them slowly." Later, after returning to the village, it became apparent that the local mohel felt demeaned by the situation: not only by the surprise inspection but by the fact that he had not immediately been certified upon arrival in Israel. Several months after this incident, the long-awaited certificate of accreditation arrived in the mail.

This is the story of a single circumcision. Although it occurred forty years ago, it embodies elements of an extremely long history and raises questions concerning the similarity between Jewish circumcision and rituals in other societies, about gender symbolism and the role of women in the ceremony, and about the relationship between textual traditions and local customs. The final episode—the arrival of the inspector—places the issue of circumcision in the context of health supervision in modern nation-states. All these topics are explored in the sections that follow, beginning with a close consideration of circumcision in the Bible.

CIRCUMCISION: ANTHROPOLOGY
AND THE BIBLICAL TEXT

Circumcision in other societies often takes place within the framework of rituals that are often called "initiation ceremonies." The French ethnographer Arnold van Gennep, who coined the term *rites de passage*, drew attention to some basic characteristics of these celebrations for the male members of a society and showed that although they have also been called "puberty rituals," they are not connected to physiological puberty in the narrow sense, for they may take place within a range of ages from late childhood to early adulthood. Rather, they are associated with the transition from childhood to the beginnings of adult status in a society, a passage in which sexual maturation is only one element.[3]

Male initiation ceremonies are not known everywhere in the non-Western world but tend to be found in societies with certain characteristics. Prominent among these is the principle of patrilineal descent: children are assigned to the father's group and not to that of the mother. Often these societies are polygynous as well, enabling a man to have more than one wife if his economic and social situation allows. Both these features are found where the roles of men and women are clearly distinguished, and these societies inculcate a strong sense of male identity. According to some interpretations, initiation ceremonies in these societies are particularly dramatic and persuasive because in them, before initiation, young boys are found almost exclusively in the company of women.

An example of an elaborate initiation ceremony is found among the Thonga in South Africa.[4] Somewhere between the ages of ten and sixteen, boys are sent to a "circumcision school," which is held every four or five years. There, with their age-mates, they undergo severe hazing by adult males, which includes running the gauntlet between two rows of men, who beat them with clubs, strip off their clothes, and cut their hair. Next, the initiates meet men covered with lion manes, and each boy sits on a stone facing a "lion man." Someone then strikes each boy from behind, and when he turns his head his foreskin is seized and in two movements cut off by the "lion man." The boys are then secluded for three months and may be seen only by the initiated. It is especially taboo for women to approach them during their seclusion. If a woman should glance at the leaves covering the circumcised's wound, which form his only clothing, she must in theory be killed. Various aspects of the rites are "calculated to give the candidates the impression that they are new men."[5] Armed with this comparative background, we may explore whether features of patrilineal social structure, or of rituals like the one described, might be relevant to understanding biblical circumcision.

Circumcision, as it appears in the Bible, contains little detail paralleling the above account. Presented as a command (Gen. 17:1–14), it notes that Abram was ninety-nine when God appeared to him saying "I will make My covenant between Me and you, and will multiply you exceedingly." Along with this promise, God changed Abram's name to "Abraham,[6] for the father of a multitude of nations have I made you." God, having promised progeny to Abraham, then envisions an enduring relationship "between Me and you and your seed after you throughout their generations for an everlasting covenant." Moreover, Abraham and his seed will be given "the land of your sojournings, all the land of Canaan, for an everlasting possession; and I will be their God." God then announces Abraham's part in keeping the covenant: "between Me and you and your seed after you—every male among you shall be circumcised." Almost no details of circumcision are given, except that it shall be "in the flesh of your foreskin" and that every male "throughout your generations," who is eight days old shall be circumcised. This includes "the homeborn slave and the one brought from an outsider who is not your offspring." God's message ends with a warning: "And the uncircumcised male who is not circumcised in the flesh of his foreskin, that person shall be cut off from his people; he hath broken My covenant." The text of Genesis stresses the covenantal meaning of circumcision, including the promise of progeny (along with that of land), rather than the particulars of the operation and the ceremony. Since the nineteenth century, scholars have debated whether or not circumcision in societies with initiation rites has any relevance to understanding the commandment of circumcision outlined in Genesis.[7]

In addition to the covenantal ideology marking circumcision in Genesis 17, the very early age of eight days after birth also sets it off from typical patterns in other societies. Another difference is the definition of the ritual in terms of the individual and his date of birth, in contrast to group circumcision ceremonies. Still, comparing "tribal" initiation to biblical circumcision may be illuminating, in terms both of similarities and of differences.

The fact that customs of circumcision are so widespread among human societies implies that the institution is very ancient. It was known in Egypt and practiced by ancient Arabs (as suggested in the description of Abraham circumcising Ishmael when he first receives the commandment [Gen. 17:23]) and probably by other groups in the Land of Canaan. The Israelites did not invent circumcision, but came to practice it in a certain way and invest it with a purpose specific to their culture. In addition to having the theological meaning of a sign of the covenant, it appears as a mark of identity vis-à-vis Israel's long-standing enemies the Philistines, known in the Bible as "the uncircumcised ones," an epithet used by David before his famous confrontation with Goliath (1 Sam. 17:26). It also makes sense to inquire whether circumcision carried with it the additional associations of entrance into manhood, sexuality, and male fertility, found in other settings.

As indicated, analogies between other ceremonies and biblical circumcision are faced with an immediate question: the very young age at which the Bible requires males to be circumcised. Many argue that this difference negates the possibility that rituals in other societies have relevance for understanding the meaning assigned to circumcision in Genesis. Nevertheless, some scholars have argued that male fertility is precisely the point of God's covenant with Abraham.

One of these is Michael Fox, who has explored the meaning of the saying that circumcision is a "sign of the covenant."[8] He compares Genesis 17, which scholars assign to the strand of biblical literature that they call the Priestly Code, with other portions of the Priestly Code that feature a "sign" (*ot*).[9] From this perspective, circumcision creates a visible sign that will *"remind God to keep his promise of posterity."*[10] Fox thus incorporates an anthropological perspective on the meaning of circumcision in other societies and links it to a specific religious worldview within biblical culture.

This interpretation posits a connection between circumcision—a procedure on the penis—and the value of reproduction. It makes comparative sense when taking into consideration the patrilineal nature of Israelite society.[11] Fox does not offer an anthropological reason, however, as to why that connection should take the form of a *covenant*, a solemn agreement between two parties. Answering this question means examining other features of social life reflected in the Bible. The concept of *alliance*, which has proved helpful to anthropologists in analyzing links between kinship groups in other societies, is helpful here too.

The notion of alliance is relevant to societies based on patrilineal descent. Individual families typically formed part of a large patrilineal unit— the *beit av*, or "house of the father." At its fullest extent, a beit av would consist of a married couple, their sons and daughters-in-law, the latter's children, and any unmarried children. Daughters would usually leave the beit av upon marriage, taking up residence in the beit av of which their husbands were members.[12]

Batei avot were part of a still larger patrilineal unit—the *mishpaḥa*. In modern Hebrew, this refers to the individual family, but in the Bible mishpaḥa means a patrilineal clan. The Israelite tribes, each putatively descended from one of Jacob's twelve sons, consisted of a series of such *mish-*

paḥot. The beit av was the unit within which males grew up, acquired rights to land, and sought support in facing life's challenges. At the same time, there were tensions built into patrilineal family life.

The success of a beit av, an increase in its numbers and in the livestock it owned, created pressure on land. This was the basis of Abram's conflict with his brother's son, Lot, as portrayed in Genesis 13:5–9: "the land was not able to bear them, that they might dwell together; for their substance was great. . . . And there was a strife between the herdsmen of Abram's cattle and the herdsmen of Lot's cattle." This led to their separation from one another, with Lot founding his own beit av. Lot then elected to move to the "cities of the plain," Sodom and Gomorrah, near the Dead Sea, while Abram tented near Hebron.

The next chapter in Genesis tells of four kings from Mesopotamia making war on Sodom and Gomorrah and carrying off many captives, including Lot. When Abram hears this, he turns to his neighbors in Hebron and they set out successfully to rescue Lot. The neighbors are referred to as *baalei brit Abram*—Abram's allies or confederates. The term for alliance is *brit*, the same Hebrew term that refers to covenants that God establishes with humans.[13] The notion of "covenant," then, is a religious conception that has a basis in everyday social and political experiences.

In the Bible, relations of patrilineal kinship (the beit av) and those based on alliance (brit) complement and at times substitute for each other. When Jacob decides to leave Mesopotamia, taking his wives, Rachel and Leah, and two concubines with him, he in fact is separating from Laban's beit av and setting up his own. Consequently, to mitigate the tension between the two batei avot, which are now rivals, he makes a brit with Laban. Another example concerns the career of David. The book of 1 Samuel describes the drama of Saul cultivating young David, who came from another tribe, as part of his household, but eventually having to face the threat of David assuming the kingship instead of Saul's own son, Jonathan. The drama of the situation is enhanced by the close relationship between Jonathan and David. When it becomes clear that David is no longer safe in Saul's household, he feels forced to separate from Saul, explaining that he has obligations to his own mishpaḥa. At the same time, an enduring tie between David and Jonathan is set up in the form of a brit.[14] The language of that very human brit is almost identical to the language used in Genesis 17 when the brit of circumcision is established between God and Abraham's descendants. The idea of a "covenant" between God and Abraham's descendants is a religious notion grounded in everyday experiences and perceptions.

Not only is the notion of brit related to normal Israelite social life, but circumcision can be seen as an act that "naturally" symbolizes alliance (alongside its resonance with patrilineal descent and fertility).[15] The penis serves as a sign of social connection par excellence. This intuitive view is supplemented by associations in the biblical text. For example, circumcision's link to alliance, in the form of marriage, appears in the puzzling story of the circumcision of Moses' son by Moses' wife Zipporah (Exod. 4:24–26). In that context, Zipporah uses a term, "*ḥatan damim*—bridegroom of blood," that, while not fully understood, has clear implications of alliance.[16]

The foregoing discussion raises a question about the place of women, and the alliances they forge, in the world of biblical kinship. Over the course of the book of Genesis, in which God establishes several covenants with humans, the marriages of the patriarchs are a consistent concern.[17] A covenant with Abram is made prior to the one that announces circumcision, and it also entails the promise of progeny and of land. There is, however, a difference in the women who are prominent in the context of each brit. After the first covenant, Sarah, still barren, decides to give her Egyptian servant, Hagar, to Abram as a concubine (Genesis 16). Hagar then conceives and gives birth to Ishmael. After the covenant of circumcision (Genesis 17), three men visit Abraham and announce that Sarah will give birth the following year. As the story evolves, it becomes clear that Isaac, and not Ishmael, is Abraham's material and spiritual heir. The continuity of Abraham's special tradition, based on his relationship with God, is a function of who the mother of the heir is and, by implication, the influences to which he is exposed in the household.

This theme is repeated in later generations, in the story of Abraham's servant making a trip back to Mesopotamia to find the appropriate wife for Isaac, instead of the latter's marrying one of the "daughters of Canaan" (Genesis 24). Further on, Esau, the firstborn of Isaac and Rebecca, marries local Hittite women, a "source of bitterness" to his parents. Esau's local marriages and the decision to send Jacob to Rebecca's family in Mesopotamia are counterposed in the text (Gen. 27:46–28:2).[18] The overall setting of the lives of the "patriarchs" reflects a society in which males are the main actors in the public sphere, but women are significant figures as well, being important in both the realm of fertility and that of socialization.

After viewing the social institutions and thought habits within which the account of circumcision is placed, the narrative in Genesis 17 appears to be in a counterdialogue with meanings prevalent in other societies and probably also in ancient Israel. It does not abolish popular associations but seeks to reinterpret them. Instead of circumcision being an act of magical potency, or participation in cosmic forces of fecundity, it becomes a sign to "remind God" of his promise of progeny. Genesis deftly holds on to elements of a culture with which it is in disagreement while conveying its own view of those elements. It uses older forms to get across new messages.

The message is that human fertility is not the outcome of an automatic process but ultimately reflects the will of God. This is expressed in various biblical passages.[19] The first eleven chapters of Genesis contain genealogical lists of "begats" in which the act of procreation is designated by the Hebrew term *holid*, which is a male action (like the word "sired" in English). Women hardly figure in the picture. Against this backdrop, the stories of the progeny of the "patriarchs" that begin at the end of chapter 11 (v. 26) constitute a dramatic shift. Not only are the "matriarchs" central figures in these narratives, but "birth achieves the status of a miracle."[20] The story of the birth of Isaac hints at God's role in fertility by distancing it from "procreation-as-usual" in two ways. It stresses that Abraham and Sarah were *old*, with Sarah having passed menopause (Gen. 18:11). On the other hand, the commandment that circumcision takes place at a radically *young* age conveys the same message: fertility is ultimately in the hands of God. At the same time, the young age assigned to the ritual suggests another aspect of circumcision, that of socialization and education.

Initiation ceremonies in general (including those that feature circumcision) are sites of education into the tradition of a society. As in the Thonga example cited above, such education typically involves all-male groups. A central difference between circumcision at puberty (like that of Ishmael) and at eight days (like that of Isaac) is that the biblical requirement places the ritual squarely in the context of the family. Biblical circumcision does *not* remove a male from the world of his mother and other women, a feature made plain in the narrative that presents Isaac's circumcision as taking place *before* he is weaned (Gen. 21:1–8). At the same time, the act of circumcision may still carry with it associations of education, but education in a family setting.

The Bible itself implies a connection between circumcision and socialization. Among the laws of the Passover sacrifice, presented to the Children of Israel at the beginning of their history of liberation from Egypt, is the requirement that the sacrifice be eaten only by males who are circumcised (Exod. 12:43–50). This sacrifice, in contrast to others, is domestic in nature and is to be slaughtered and consumed in the context of the beit av (Exod. 12:3–4). In the future, according to the text, it will be the occasion for retelling the history of the "tribe" of the Jewish people (Exod. 12:26–27). This connection formed the basis of the Passover seder, in which a domestic reunion is the setting for both the obligation and the opportunity of hearing the history of the Exodus.[21] Because of the tight linkage between circumcision and participation in the paschal sacrifice, it is possible that circumcision, taking place in individual "houses," also set the stage for cultural instruction in which women play a role.[22] The story of Zipporah circumcising her son, in which Moses' name is not even mentioned, may also hint at the importance of women in cultivating tradition within the family circle.

CIRCUMCISION AFTER THE BIBLE: AN EMBLEM OF JEWISH IDENTITY

Anyone who has watched a skilled mohel at work knows that the operation of circumcision can be performed in a matter of seconds. The range of meanings that have been attached to the act in different historical settings, however, resounds with significance in varying and sometimes opposite directions. We have discussed the ritual's connection both to patrilineal descent and to alliances created through women: to continuity based on fertility as well as to continuity based upon education. In addition, the meaning of circumcision to Jews grew out of the contrast to other societies. Do these various interpretations of circumcision in ancient Israel have echoes in the way the ritual developed in postbiblical Jewish culture?

Some of the interpretations suggested in the previous section resonate with rabbinic sensibilities. The issues of both education and of alliance, expressed as marriage, appear in the formula recited at the end of a circumcision ceremony: "Even as he [the child] has entered into the covenant, so may he enter into the Torah, the nuptial canopy, and into good deeds."[23] Another salient expression of rabbinic culture, the "Grace after Meals," cites circumcision and the Torah contiguously: "We thank thee, O Lord our God . . . for the covenant You have sealed in our flesh, and for the Torah You have taught us." [24] Even more obvious is the way in which circumcision has continued to function as a marker distinguishing Jews from non-Jews in a variety of settings.

There is little direct evidence of the historical stages of the process, but circumcising young boys became standard in ancient Israel, and certainly among the exiles returning to the small state of Judea around 500 B.C.E. Perhaps the fact that the practice is mentioned only occasionally in biblical sources, and with few details as to how it actually took place, bespeaks the degree to which it became a taken-for-granted feature of Jewish life. The cultural power of an unquestioned assumption may be illustrated by reference to Islam. There is no mention of circumcision in the Quran, but the vast majority of Muslims would not dream of neglecting the practice. I assume that a similar situation held among Jews until about the third century B.C.E.

In 333 B.C.E., Alexander (the Great) of Macedonia conquered Judea as part of the wars that established his empire throughout the Near East. After his death, the region he ruled was split up among successors, one of which was the Seleucid dynasty at the eastern end of the Mediterranean. The state of Judea, including the rebuilt Temple, came under Seleucid rule and was exposed to Hellenic culture, which Alexander's conquests had brought to the region. This is the background of the Books of Maccabees, which describe the Maccabean revolt against the Syrian Greeks when Hellenism began to make heavy inroads into local religious life. They depict members of the Judean community as seeking an alliance with the nations around them and building "a gymnasium in Jerusalem according to the customs of the Gentiles. They made a foreskin, abandoning the Holy covenant; they attached themselves to the Gentiles and committed themselves to do evil" (1 Macc. 1:14–15). In Hellenic culture, participants in the athletic games appeared in the nude. The attempt to reconstitute a foreskin stemmed from the desire to be accepted into the culture of the ruling class that had established itself in Judea and throughout the region.

The foregoing account of the obliteration of circumcision describes self-motivated steps by some circles within local Jewry to become "like the Gentiles," but later on, according to 1 Maccabees (1:44–49), the ruler Antiochus Epiphanes actually forbade circumcision. His persecution went so far that mothers who circumcised their children were put to death, along with the babies and members of their families (1 Macc. 1:60–61). These and parallel actions stimulated the revolt of the Maccabees, which temporarily reestablished Judean independence and bolstered those committed to a Torah-based tradition. The broader culture of Hellenism could not be uprooted, however, and its influence among Jews increased, a process that continued after the Roman Empire established its hegemony in the region in 63 B.C.E. Both the values of Hellenic culture, which saw perfection in the human body and therefore abhorred any form of mutilation, and the ideas of Roman rule, which envisioned universal norms at work among Rome's subjects, had difficulty with Jewish insistence upon a bodily mark that was a permanent sign of their difference from other peoples.

The opposition to circumcision occasionally took the form of harsh persecution under the Romans as well—for example, in the second century C.E.[25] More profoundly, however, circumcision was challenged from within by a branch of Judaism, infused with Hellenistic ideals, that emerged under Roman rule and eventually achieved a dominant position within the empire. That was the challenge posed by Paul, who claimed that descent was no longer a critical feature in defining the community of believers—"it is men of faith who are the sons of Abraham."[26] Parallel to that, Paul downplayed the importance of circumcision and emphasized baptism as the ritual marking inclusion in the faith of Israel.

The challenges to circumcision, whether they stemmed from emulating the norms of "high society" or from ideological opposition, affected the way it was practiced within Judaism. It seems that in the period just discussed, the nature of the operation was different from what later became standard within rabbinic Judaism. According to the Mishna (*Shabbat* 19:2), edited at the end of the second century C.E., circumcision included three successive acts: the removal of the foreskin (*milah*), drawing down the prepuce (*periah*), and suctioning blood out of the incision (*meṣiṣah*—to be discussed later in the chapter). Periah, which entails removing the membrane that covers the glans, precludes the possibility of altering the penis to make it appear that the foreskin is still intact. If periah had always been part of circumcision, it would not have been possible for Jews in the time of the Maccabees or at later dates, as attested to by talmudic discussion of the issue, to "restore" their foreskins. Nissan Rubin has recently discussed this question, concluding that circumcision did not originally entail the act of periah.[27] Periah was probably included in the mishnaic code to combat attempts to obliterate the effects of circumcision. Most likely, it took some time for the mishnaic norm to take root.

Most developments concerning the practice cannot be dated precisely, but it is clear that from the time of the Mishna and Talmuds, circumcision had been universally instituted among Jews. Questions that arose concerned how it should be carried out under certain circumstances. For example, there was the question of whether circumcision, or the preparations for it, should be carried out on the Sabbath. The answer with regard to the actual operation was clearly affirmative. Other issues were more complex, and depended on how essential a specific preparation was. One involved children born without foreskins, or adult males who were not Jewish, but happened to be circumcised, and then converted to Judaism. In the latter case, the procedure of *haṭafat dam* was instituted, which involved letting some blood by pricking the area where the foreskin had been, so that circumcision that had taken place for reasons other than adherence to the Jewish religion retroactively took on the meaning of the commandment of the circumcision covenant. Crucial questions also arose when children died from bleeding after circumcisions. In some cases, if two sons of the same mother had died in this manner, a third son was not allowed to be circumcised.[28] This may point to an ancient grasp of the pattern of hereditary transmission of hemophilia.

Some practices accompanying circumcision are also very old. In the first century C.E., circumcision was already the occasion when the name of a male child was announced, as described in Luke 1:59. The Pharisees, the group out of which Paul grew, and against whom he later positioned himself, reacted against Paul by underlining certain themes within circumcision. Just as Paul played down descent and insisted that there was no difference between "Jew and Greek," or between "man and woman,"[29] so circumcision among the Pharisees, and their successors who shaped rabbinic culture, highlighted identity based on descent and the male side of circumcision.[30] As we shall see in the following sections, however, no matter how great the emphasis on maleness, the presence of women and female imagery remained part of the circumcision ritual.

RABBINIC CIRCUMCISION: THE PARADOX OF ELIJAH'S PRESENCE

The basic structure of the circumcision ceremony as we know it today is apparent from the Middle Ages onward. The structure is similar in the Sephardi and Ashkenazi regions, notwithstanding local variations between these traditions and within each of them. In Yiddish-speaking Ashkenaz, it became common to refer to the ceremony as *bris,* while among Sephardim, whether Judezmo or Arabic speakers, *mila* is a common designation. Each tradition linguistically selected a different aspect of the concept of *brit milah*—the covenant of circumcision. The precise texts recited during the ceremony also vary somewhat, but the basic format of blessings and readings interspersed with ritual acts is constant. Appendix 1 presents the structure of the ceremony on the basis of an Ashkenazi prayer book widely used in English-speaking countries in the mid twentieth century.

There may be various textual and customary embellishments on this basic service. Sephardim often introduce the ceremony by singing a hymn honoring Elijah the prophet. A father may recite the well-known *she-heḥeyanu* blessing, thanking God "who has kept us alive . . . for the present occasion." But rather than consider further examples of textual variations, I first discuss the way the prophet Elijah has become a figure associated with circumcisions throughout the Jewish world, illustrating how rabbinic texts can be linked to aspects of popular religion and social life.

The image of the prophet Elijah appears most prominently in the presence of a chair known as "Elijah's chair" (*kise eliyahu*) as part of the ritual. The basic notion is that the prophet is present at every circumcision. The claim is made palpable when a mohel places the child on Elijah's chair. Many Ashkenazi communities use two decorated chairs during a circumcision. The infant is placed for a moment on one of them (Elijah's chair), and then the person holding the child during the operation sits on the second. In some Sephardi communities, a special decorated seat built by a carpenter has the permanent function of being Elijah's chair. It is used when a circumcision takes place in the synagogue, or it may be passed around from house to house, according to where the circumcision is being celebrated. Among Aleppan Jews, any chair may be made into Elijah's chair by placing a special covering on it with the inscription *eliyahu ha-nabi* (Elijah the prophet).[31] Jews in Tunis had a special celebration honoring Elijah, which featured blind musicians and took place three days after the circumcision.[32]

Why is the figure of Elijah recruited to "attend" every circumcision? Elijah is described in 2 Kings 2:11 as having left this world in a chariot of fire, which ascended to heaven, and with this dramatic exit from normal history, he has become a ubiquitous figure in Jewish culture and lore.[33] He makes miraculous appearances, often in a form that hides his true identity (which is recognized only after the fact), helping individual people in difficult situations. According to the story in 1 Kings 17, Elijah revived a young child from death. He thus constitutes an appealing image of protection over young children at a time of potential danger. It is not difficult to see, in this context, how he would also be called upon to "watch over" male babies at the time of their circumcision.

The place that Elijah has achieved in circumcision ceremonies is expressed in a midrash known from the eighth century.[34] This midrash, however, calls upon another feature drawn from the biblical narrative, the portrayal of Elijah as a zealot for God's sake. Elijah describes himself as zealous on God's behalf in 1 Kings 19:10, and complains to the Lord of Hosts that the Children of Israel have followed other gods and "have abandoned Your covenant." The midrashic text connects Elijah to the figure of Pinhas in Numbers 25:1–15, who, full of zeal, executed an Israelite man and a Midianite woman while they were engaged in idolatry. After this act, Pinhas is awarded with the "everlasting covenant of the Priesthood [*kehuna*]." The midrash in fact suggests that Elijah *is* Pinhas. The midrash thus builds upon the textual links between references to zealotry, on the one hand, and to covenants, on the other. It states that God commanded Elijah to be present at every circumcision. Citing Malachi 3:23, the midrash calls Elijah the "messenger" or "the angel" of the covenant. It ends by explaining that at circumcision ceremonies, "the sages instituted (the custom) that people should prepare a seat of honor for the Messenger of the Covenant."[35]

The emphasis on the zealous side of Elijah's persona is somewhat puzzling with reference to circumcision. One of the features of zealotry is that it is blind to social relations, including kinship ties, in its enthusiasm to carry out a religious or political ideal. What, then, is a fanatic doing in the intimate atmosphere of a family celebration?

The midrash, and the custom that it justifies, may relate precisely to that paradox, and in fact build upon it. On the one hand, God appears to reward zealotry in the Bible, but, on the other hand, the midrash may be read as God reacting against the prophet's fervor. According to this view, He commands the prophet to be present at every circumcision in order to witness how the Children of Israel *do* steadfastly observe the practice that represents "the covenant," par excellence.

The presence of Elijah at circumcisions thus works in two directions. On the one hand, it adds an element of religious vigor to what might otherwise be seen as a routine occasion. Every family circumcising its sons joins the list of those who have been faithful to God's commandments over the generations. On the other hand, the custom "domesticates" the zealous prophet, presenting him as being concerned with each and every family. The two different sides of Elijah may in fact be linked, according to the anthropologist Victor Turner, who stressed how persuasive rituals often encapsulate symbolic associations of powerful import to personal lives, together with ideological meanings of central significance to a society.[36] The midrash builds upon the popular and personal attachment to Elijah as coming to the aid of the needy, and of male children in particular, and channels those sentiments into the expression of ancient Jewish values.

We return to the figure of Elijah later, but I would note here that two sides of a circumcision are wrapped up in a single symbolic figure: one focuses on the individual household and the other underlines the practice as representing Jewish tradition generally. This dual emphasis not only is a question of which elements in a textual tradition are highlighted, but leads to a more careful consideration of the specific contexts in which circumcision ceremonies are carried out.

HOME, SYNAGOGUE, AND THE ROLE OF WOMEN IN CIRCUMCISIONS

As already discussed, circumcision is a ritual that seems "naturally" appropriate to a domestic setting. Throughout most of Jewish history, births took place at home, and the most "logical" setting for a ritual involving a baby seven days later was the home. There was frequent variation in this regard however. From the time of the Geonim, who headed the Jewish religious academies in Iraq from the seventh to the eleventh centuries C.E., there is evidence of circumcision ceremonies taking place in synagogues. In the medieval Islamic world, Jewish circumcisions in the synagogue became an option, while in medieval Europe, they became the norm. For example, the Tosafist commentators on the Talmud, who lived in thirteenth-century France, mention that it was common to drink the wine of the Saturday night Havdalah ceremony or of the circumcision ceremony in the synagogue.[37] In the long historical view, circumcisions may be carried out in the home or in the synagogue (or, more recently, in a hospital or banquet hall), and the selection of a site could thus highlight different aspects of the ritual's social significance. As discussed in reference to Elijah's chair, different values relating to family on the one hand and wider loyalties on the other may be in tension with one another, not necessarily meshing seamlessly.

Rabbinic tradition views circumcision as a religious obligation of a father to his son.[38] Ideally, according to this conception, each father should physically circumcise his own child, but this is not now the general norm and has not been the practice for a long time. In the Talmud, various terms used to describe the mohel indicate that it was common to turn to a specialist to do the actual cutting. The formal blessings that accompany a circumcision, one to be recited by the mohel and the other by the father, are also mentioned in the Talmud. In a sense, bringing in an outside professional to perform what is basically a family-oriented ritual may be seen as setting aside the centrality of the father in favor of a formal representative of communal interests and practice. There is a custom in which, before the mohel takes charge of the proceedings, the father makes a pronouncement delegating the mohel to be his representative. This may be an attempt to symbolically redress the imbalance.

A close look at the traditions of reciting the formal blessings provides further evidence of the thin line trodden in balancing familial and communal perspectives. In rabbinic tradition, there is a lack of clarity as to the function of the father's blessing, which recognizes God as "having commanded us to enter the child into the covenant of Abraham." The typical pattern of reciting a blessing in conjunction with a mitzvah, or "commandment," is that the blessing is stated first and the ritual action then follows. This is not the case for the father's blessing, however, unless he happens to be the mohel as well. For that reason, various interpretations have been attached to the father's blessing. One is that it is a "statement of praise" with regard to the general commandment of circumcision, rather than a standard blessing that precedes the performance of a mitzvah. Whatever halakhic reasons may be offered, the textual and legal fuzziness may reflect the unresolved and perhaps unresolvable tension between the more familial and the more communal features of the rite.

When a mohel enters a home to conduct a circumcision, his presence stands for general Jewish norms, but there are also ways in which the family has an influence upon the communal realm, even if a circumcision takes place in the synagogue. Maimonides stated that it is preferable to carry out a circumcision as early on the eighth day as possible. In medieval Europe, when circumcisions regularly took place in the synagogue, it became common to carry them out just before the end of the morning prayer.[39] The format of the prayer, however, was partially a function of the family event. Rabbinic codes state that in a synagogue in which a circumcision is celebrated, the weekday prayer of penitence and supplication (*taḥanun*) is not recited, just as it is not cited on Sabbaths and festivals. The joy of the individual family thus partially defines the occasion for the whole community, even when the circumcision takes place outside the home.

Situated at a node between kinship links and communal structure, circumcisions provided a stage upon which social status could be enacted, enhanced, and contested.[40] An additional formal role emerged in the Middle Ages, that of the *baʿal brit* ("master of the circumcision") or, in the feminine, *baʿalat ha-brit*, who helped prepare the baby, brought it to the synagogue, and often held it during the operation. Later, the person holding the baby came to be known as the *sandek*, a term derived from a Greek word for a godparent in the rite of baptism. As in the Christian case, the relationship between the parents of the child and the "co-parents" was important. Another term emerging for this role was *kvatter*, derived from German, and the corresponding feminine *kvatterin*. The precise roles of the people so designated varied over time and from place to place.[41] In eastern Europe, *kvatterin* mainly meant the woman who brought the baby into the synagogue. The emergence and crystallization of roles within the jostling between home and synagogue was also tied to a struggle over the place of women in the ceremony.

The shifting place of women may be sensed in another site of textual lack of clarity: the halakhic conundrum concerning the blessing recited over the cup of wine as part of the ritual. There is no talmudic source for including wine in the ceremony, but the practice had become standard by the Middle Ages. While no proof is available, it is probable that rabbinic discussion and sanction followed in the wake of popular custom. If drinking and offering a blessing over wine is standard on other festive occasions, such as the Sabbath or at weddings, it is not surprising that it became part of circumcision celebrations as well. We may further speculate (in the absence of historical evidence) as to whether people began to drink wine, and then the rabbis insisted that the drinking be accompanied by a blessing, or whether the overall complex of blessing-plus-drinking was brought into the circumcision ritual based on models of other occasions, and the rabbis gave their approval to this innovation. In any event, drinking wine with a blessing has long been standard within the sequence of circumcision events.

The popular, as opposed to rabbinic, origin of the practice has left its mark in other ways: it is not clear who is supposed to drink the wine after the blessing is recited. As stated, it is normal for the pronouncement of a blessing to *precede* the ritual action to which it points. Not only that, it is prohibited to recite a blessing, including the mention of God's name, unless one in fact follows through with the apposite action. Reciting the blessing without the appropriate subsequent gesture would entail taking God's name in vain, or in rabbinic terminology, uttering a blessing for naught (*berakha le-vatala*). In Ashkenazi circumcision texts, it is often stated that the sandek drinks the wine and then passes it on to the mother, who, along with other women, is usually at some distance from the infant, mohel, and father. Some written guidelines mention only the sandek, and not the mother. There is no good reason that it is the sandek who drinks the wine. Why not the mohel, who recites the blessing, or the father, who in fact is the main celebrant fulfilling the commandment to circumcise his son? The answer stems from a situation in which the custom first arose in popular practice, and not through rabbinic deliberation, and then went through stages that are not in evidence today.

A textual analysis seeking to trace the evolution of the custom has been undertaken by the rabbinical scholar Daniel Sperber,[42] who focuses on the last paragraph in a ritual sequence of passages that bless the child after the circumcision has taken place. He shows that, historically, there were other passages that might be inserted into the ceremony at that point. One of them included a prayer for the health of the convalescing mother. The associated instructions from the earlier period suggest that the most common way of dealing with the wine over which a blessing had been recited was to "send it to the mother."[43] Not only that, but some of these earlier texts indicate that the mother might have had a more prominent presence at the ceremony than she had in later forms of the ritual.

At earlier times, it appears, a woman might serve as a sandek and hold the baby on her lap. The sources call such a woman by the term mentioned above, *ba'alat ha-brit*, "mistress of the circumcision." This woman often was the person who carried the baby from the mother to where the circumcision was taking place. It was not unusual for the mother to follow her in order to be near the proceedings. In these circumstances, it is not surprising that she, and/or the mother, were sometimes designated to drink the glass of wine after the blessing.

Figure 3. Circumcision portrait of a notable family in Baghdad, 1930s. Center: father holds the infant; the mohel (circumciser) is to their left. Women, not included in the portrait, are probably standing on the balcony above. Courtesy Babylonian Jewry Cultural Center Museum.

Later, there was a shift in prevailing norms in regard to those present at the ceremony. Sperber suggests that the shift had to do with the growing tendency to conduct the ceremony in the synagogue, a public space, dominated by males.[44] It was less appropriate for a woman to be a sandek in the synagogue than in a home. Rules were formulated that discouraged a woman from being a baʿalat ha-brit, and the mother from being present in the synagogue. The role of sandek became a male prerogative. These norms may have first emerged in the context of synagogue circumcisions, but once formulated, they eventually applied to those conducted in the home as well. The growing body of rabbinic law worked to restrict the place of women in the ceremony, and the consequences may still be seen today (see figure 3).[45]

THE EVE OF CIRCUMCISION CELEBRATIONS

Restriction of the place of women in celebrations related to circumcisions has been documented in another realm, celebrations on the eve of circumcision that took place in the home. Elliot Horowitz has discussed the trends affecting this form of celebration, which was common from the late Middle Ages until fairly recent times. Known variously as the *wachnacht* in Yiddish-speaking areas, the *noče de šemira* in some Judezmo-speaking communities (both meaning "night of watching"), or the *veglia* ("vigil") in Italy, it consisted of an all-night celebration preceding the circumcision on the following day.[46] The event assumed that before his circumcision, an infant was vulnerable and in need of protection from demonic forces (which was a factor in making the image of Elijah popular). The presence of many people, who stayed up all night, helped supply that protection. Horowitz's account draws upon observations of Jewish customs by Christians who recorded Jewish life after the Middle Ages. His perspective, that of a social historian, complements the above analysis by Sperber based upon a close reading of rabbinic literature.

These celebrations took place at home. Even though the home was a female domain, Horowitz shows how the custom underwent transformations over time in which the role of women was subdued. A central element in bringing this about was the introduction of communal readings from Jewish tradition into the ceremony. The analysis also places this trend within Jewish communities in the context of developments characterizing the wider society.

Horowitz cites a book published in 1603 by a Gentile Swiss scholar of Hebrew, Johannes Buxtorf, who depicts the eve of circumcision "as an all-night affair, involving, beside abundant food, such amusements as cards, dice, singing, and storytelling, all accompanied, especially among men, by rather heavy drinking, in which the circumciser must be warned against overindulging."[47] Drawing on a variety of other sources, he points to the practice of dancing in many of these gatherings and states that in some locales, such as Ancona in Italy, parallel celebrations and amusements took place among women and among men. Explanations for the celebration cited the protection of the newborn, implying the danger of harm from demons. Horowitz notes that the atmosphere in these nights of watchfulness, in which men and women took part with relatively little formal separation, "was typical of the popular religious culture of late medieval Europe, which saw no reason to sever the sacred from the profane."

An account of a celebration in Tripoli, Libya, dating from about a hundred years ago, helps shed light on the subsequent evolution of these celebrations. In Tripoli, the custom continued, even though it had been in decline in Europe since the early nineteenth century. Mordecaï Ha-Cohen, a native of Tripoli, provides a glimpse of the practice:

> As the shadows of evening lengthen, midwives and female relatives
> of the woman who has given birth gather [in her house] to grind

myrtle buds and other spices, for the community will recite the blessing "Who createst diverse kinds of spices" when the child is circumcised. While the grinding is going on, a group of old women, known
as the *zamzamat*, will ululate in joy and sing special holy songs [in
Arabic] for the occasion. At the same time, the old men, designated
for this purpose, gather and read portions from the Psalms (in former
days, it was customary for a boy to stand and pleasantly sing a certain hymn in Arabic, as is still done in the villages). Then the chair
of the Messenger of the Brit is hung on the wall in the room where
the mother is, and [it] is called here [in Tripoli] *kursi* (the chair of)
Eliyyahu. The father of the child distributes a glass of whiskey to
each of the old men and to the poor, sometimes giving them fruit
and money as well. He also gives boiled fava beans, and sometimes
money, to the synagogue school children who are present.

On the eve of the eighth day after the birth, the invited friends of
the father come to his house to hear the reading of a section of the
Zohar from the Torah portion *Lekh Lekha*.[48] Then they recite the
scholar's *kaddish*[49] and begin to sing hymns; the father of the boy
begins to distribute boiled eggs to everyone present. . . . The learned
men study all night in the home of the newborn, and the father of
the boy prepares a meal for them and distributes money according
to his means. . . . The baby is not put on the ground all night long;
he is held in the bosom of the mother or of other women.[50]

This event included the communal gathering of men and women, and of
singing and feasting, but compared to the earlier descriptions cited by
Horowitz, it is suffused with seriousness and interlaced with religious
readings and hymns. What explains this difference?

Horowitz relates the difference to the changes that took place in religious sensibilities in Europe that were connected to the Reformation and
the Counter-Reformation. In contrast to what was common in medieval
times, where amusement and frivolity were easily able to coexist with the
sacred, the mixture of those domains became problematic in the early
modern period, when religion became more one-sidedly austere. These
trends had their correspondences in Jewish culture. Horowitz quotes the
seventeenth-century Rabbi Aaron Berechia of Modena, who proposed reforming the festive atmosphere of the traditional celebrations before a circumcision, saying: "[H]ow beneficial it would be to recite [certain passages]
before the Chair of Elijah, together with the Psalms of David . . . as against
those who spend that night in merrymaking, men and women . . . young
and old."[51] This and parallel attempts to purify the traditional celebration
met with success. Eventually, ritual readings evolved from being an extra
feature added to the evening and came to define the content of the gather-

ing.[52] In communities near Tripoli, the evening goings-on described by Mordecaï Ha-Cohen came to be known in terms of the mystical text that dominated the occasion, "the night of the Zohar." Corresponding to this textual dominance, the activities of women were subdued and circumscribed.

CIRCUMCISION, BLOOD, AND PASSOVER: THE MANAGEMENT OF CUSTOMS

The previous three sections, all dealing with the Middle Ages, have pointed to tension and a shifting balance between contrasting social factors that enter into circumcision celebrations: home and community, women and men. This internal tension overlapped with another, rooted in antiquity, in which circumcision marked Judaism's contrast with its neighbors, especially Christianity. One feature of circumcision, blood, connects these internal and external factors. The threads of that connection lead to another theme from antiquity, the link between circumcision and Passover. How did Jews manage circumcision customs when those customs placed them, as a vulnerable minority, in opposition to their environment?

Lawrence Hoffman, a student of circumcision ritual, has emphasized the growing removal of women from any role within it during the European Middle Ages.[53] His explanation underlines a growing emphasis on the blood of circumcision as the ritual's central symbolic element. This implied a contrast, in his view, between the valued male blood of circumcision and the devalued menstrual blood of women. This contrast would represent a shift in symbolic emphasis from that of Leviticus 15, where menstrual flow is aligned with male semen.[54] In the Middle Ages, the male descent line highlighted by a father imposing upon his infant son the drawing of covenantal blood charged the blood of circumcision with salvific value. The Jewish claim that the blood of circumcision saves has to be understood in counterpoint to the Christian claim that faith, and not religious works, brings about salvation.

Circumcision clearly carries male overtones. Asserting the existence of that association, however, is not the same as explaining it, or as situating it fully upon a canvas with the other shades of meaning that it evokes. The cited trends within the Middle Ages notwithstanding, there are ancient textual aspects of circumcision that link it to women. The image of Zipporah severing a foreskin with a flint knife (Exod. 4:25), or of the mother in 1 Maccabees who insisted upon circumcising her son despite danger to her life, are indelible parts of circumcision tradition.[55] Some recent discussions of Judaism in antiquity and in the Middle Ages have also pointed to subtle feminine associations in the rite.[56] In addition, as has been noted, the domestic nature of the ritual tends to keep women in the picture in spite of attempts to limit their participation. Among Syrian Jews in recent times, the mother was not present in the room where circumcision took place, but she traditionally attended the accompanying meal, dressed in a long white gown.[57] Perhaps the historical thrust of rabbinical culture was less about excluding women than about asserting control over domestic affairs, wherein "women" represent the home and "men" are emblematic of communal authority. Beyond that, comparative studies of circumcision argue that feminine undercurrents are to be found precisely in rituals that try to obliterate the presence of women, but never fully succeed in doing so.[58]

Feminine echoes may also be discerned in a central and valued text of the circumcision ceremony that is connected to blood. Those familiar with circumcisions as they are conducted in Ashkenazi tradition recognize that one of the climaxes in the overall ceremony is the recital of a phrase from Ezekiel 16:6, "I said unto thee: 'In thy blood, live!' " (in Hebrew, "Va-omar lakh be-damayikh ḥayi"). Inserted into the paragraph that includes the naming of the child, the phrase is repeated just as it is in the book of Ezekiel. The mohel, in chanting it aloud, often emphasizes it, cuing the others present to repeat the words with him. Other factors, including both gestures and texts, further emphasize this phrase.

At this point, when the phrase with "blood" is chanted, the mohel dabs a few drops of wine, taken from the wine glass, into the baby's mouth. Alternatively, or complementarily, several drops of wine are placed into the infant's mouth at the end of the blessing when the sandek drinks from the cup. This act seems intended to soothe infants who suck the wine (today, typically from a piece of gauze). Wine is easily seen as symbolic of blood, but this is only a first level of explanation.[59] As has been pointed out by David Wachtel, there is a long, complex, and even paradoxical history to this verse from Ezekiel, both in terms of its content and with reference to its use on the occasion of circumcision.[60]

The verse, in its original context, constitutes a dramatic turning point. The previous passage (Ezek. 16:1–5) portrays a scene of total rejection. A baby is born, neglected, and cast out into a field. Normally, such a baby would die, but Ezekiel, in God's name, proclaims: "I passed by thee and I saw thee weltering in thy blood, and I said unto thee 'In thy blood, live,' and I said unto thee 'In thy blood, live!' " Blood, pointing to death, is mobilized in a reversal and becomes a sign of life. This is an apt trope for circumcision, in which blood is let at the outset of what, it is hoped, will prove to be a full Jewish life.

Equally striking, however, is that all the imagery associated with the baby in Ezekiel is feminine. The chapter is addressed to Jerusalem, which, as elsewhere in the Bible, is assigned a female character.[61] After being born to non-Israelite parents, the baby Jerusalem—representing the Jewish people—is abandoned until God comes along and rescues her. Not only does He save her life, He then possesses her sexually while she is still covered in impure vaginal blood (Ezek. 16:8–9). Ezekiel's vision presented a problem to rabbinic exegetes. One way of suppressing both the anthropomorphism of the prophetic poetry, and what appears to be God's violation of his own purity code, was to reinterpret the unusual Hebrew phrase "in your blood" (*be-damayikh*), which also can be translated as a plural: "in your bloods." The unexplained use of the plural is further complicated by the fact that the phrase is repeated. An ancient Aramaic *targum*, or "translation," of Ezekiel,[62] explicitly renders the repetition of "In your bloods, live!" as referring to the blood of circumcision and the blood of the Passover sacrifice.[63]

As pointed out by Wachtel, interpreting the verse in terms of established rituals in Jewish life opened the way for incorporating it into liturgy and ceremony. Its inclusion into circumcision practice eventually took place in Ashkenaz in the Middle Ages. The close link to circumcision gave it a male tinge, but female associations were never far from the surface. Feminine grammatical forms are salient in three of the four words of the phrase. In addition, as suggested, the obvious centrality of women in anything relating to an eight-day-old infant renders futile the attempts to attain total male hegemony over the whole ceremony. Perhaps the rabbinical shift of the verse's meaning to point to two domestic rituals stems from the implicit recognition of women's role in them.

The rabbinic interpretation of "two bloods" reflects another "reality factor" in Jewish culture, the similarities between circumcision and Passover. As already discussed, the links between the two rituals go back to the Bible, and both celebratory occasions, one focused on the individual male and the other forming part of the festival cycle, became part of Judaism's energetic debate with Christianity. They both crystallize competitive religious tension in reference to the Christian Eucharist, in which ingesting a wafer and wine are seen as partaking of the body and blood of the Christian savior.

There are different interpretations of the Christian Last Supper, but many see in it a Passover seder reworked to accommodate and underscore Christian theology and imagery. Jesus became a paschal lamb who had to be sacrificed on behalf of all mankind. As emphasized and detailed in a study by Gillian Feeley-Harnik, there is a deep symbolic challenge to Jewish culture in this claim: a holiday built upon the solidarity of the patriline and family is co-opted and utilized to make a claim of universality—obliterating the importance of kinship and descent in defining the true Israel.[64] Christianity challenged and attached completely new meanings to central elements of the Jewish Passover seder: unleavened bread, wine, the paschal lamb, and the importance of descent in transmitting a religious heritage. As emphasized in Hoffman's study, the rabbis were forced to react to these new claims. The saving blood of circumcision was tightly linked to descent through living males.[65] Later, aspects of the Passover ritual emerged in contrapuntal tension to Christian claims.[66]

The tensions between early rabbinic Judaism and Christianity that were embedded in the rituals of circumcision and Passover also appeared in later periods, conditioned by changing historical circumstances. As noted, the verse from Ezekiel became part of circumcision liturgy in medieval Ashkenaz. It is likely that this addition arose against the background of the rival meanings given to blood, and of charges leveled at Jews by Christians accusing the former of using Christian blood in their rites.[67] Various strategies might be employed to parry these claims. One was to abandon a practice that was only customary, if the custom had the potential of being misread by Christians. Thus, Avraham Grossman has documented the disappearance in Ashkenaz of the practice of hanging out a bloodied cloth on the door of a house in which a circumcision was taking place.[68] The essence of circumcision could not be abandoned, however, so here the emergent strategy was to invest it with reinvigorated meaning. Mobilizing the verse from Ezekiel, with its emphatic repetition, Jews asserted that the blood of circumcision, even when maligned by the competing and majority religion, was a source of communal and personal salvation. A fuller appreciation of these processes emerges when examining parallels between circumcision and the Passover seder.

Both circumcision and Passover are centered on the family, and there is a symbolic usage of wine in relation to texts that mention blood on both occasions. In the first setting, when the mohel reads the words: "In thy blood live," he dabs wine onto the tongue of the baby. During the Passover seder, when the list of the plagues that God visited upon the Egyptians, according to the account in Exodus, is read aloud, it is customary to spill a drop of wine at the mention of each plague. The first plague is that of "blood" and the last is the "slaying of the firstborn." Although the victims of the plagues, as recited in the text, were the ancient Egyptians, it does not take a great leap of imagination to surmise that participants at a seder who felt they were under spiritual or even physical attack easily identified the ancient Egyptians with contemporary rivals and foes.[69]

The theme of retribution against hostile Gentiles also appears in the seder ritual, after the Passover feast and the "Grace after Meals," in the recitation of several biblical passages. These vary from place to place but commonly begin with Psalms 79:6: "Pour out Your wrath upon the nations who knew You not, and upon the kingdoms who did not call Your name." This practice too arose in Ashkenaz in the Middle Ages and conveys an atmosphere of tension between Jews and their religious adversaries. There were further developments of this custom, linked to the prophet Elijah, who is perceived as attending each family during their seder, just as he is present at every circumcision. There is a widespread Ashkenazi practice of opening the door of a home just before reading "Pour out Your wrath" to "let in" Elijah. Sometimes the reading is prefaced with the welcome "Barukh ha-ba," which also opens circumcision ceremonies. Another popular custom is to prepare a special goblet of wine for Elijah, which he supposedly sips from when visiting the house.

The origins of these practices are not known, but some scholars attribute the custom of opening the door to the anti-Jewish accusations that were prominent at different times during the Middle Ages.[70] These libels insisted, for example, that it was a part of the Jewish Passover to use the blood of Christians in the baking of unleavened bread (*matzah*) for the seder. Such claims were often made in conjunction with the disappearance or murder of a Christian child or adult, leading to the accusation that Jews had murdered the person for use in their rituals. Against this background, it has been speculated that the opening of the door was symbolically addressed to the Gentiles to come and see the innocence of the Jewish seder. Others surmise that the gesture was a way of checking that no "informers" were nearby who might report to the authorities how Jews read the verses of vengeance.[71] The suggested close link of this practice to the Ashkenazi Middle Ages is reinforced by comparing it to customs in other settings. One Sephardi tradition is to keep the door of a house open from the beginning of the seder and close it only after reading "Pour out Your wrath," while among the Jews of Yemen, the whole tradition of a cup for Elijah was unknown.[72] Passover, with its use of unleavened bread and wine, shared with circumcision the challenge of both maintaining tradition and "managing" its interpretation in an inhospitable cultural environment.

The parallels between circumcision and Passover remind one of the verse in Ezekiel that was interpreted as referring to the blood of circumcision *and* to the blood of the Passover sacrifice and lead one to ask about its use in the Passover seder. Here, too, as analyzed by Wachtel, there is a complex history of religious management. The verse with the words "In your blood, live" does today appear in some versions of the Haggadah, the text that is read in the seder ritual, but its insertion there is relatively recent. The sixteenth-century kabbalist Hayyim Vital introduced it into the Haggadah, claiming that there existed an ancient tradition that it had been recited orally, but not written down.[73] If Vital's claim is correct that earlier generations did not commit the verse to writing, this caution may have reflected concern over Christian misreading and misuse of the text.

Wachtel argues that Vital introduced the potentially explosive verse into the Haggadah because, as a resident of the Ottoman Empire, he was not concerned with Christian reactions.[74] Indeed, he gave a kabbalistic meaning to the phrase "In your bloods live," which had sexual connotations. This interpretation hinted at God's sexual possession of Israel, imagery that harks back to the original prophecy in Ezekiel 16:8 in which God "spreads his garment" over Jerusalem and covers her nakedness. We thus see that, while buffeted by historic forces impinging upon circumcision and Passover celebrations, the biblical verse also retained its original resonance. The dual gendered connotations of circumcision were muted as the practice became enmeshed in a wider field of Jewish symbolism and encountered rival meanings, but they did not disappear completely and perhaps energized the ritual by adding to its emotive impact.

The polemics implied in customs were not always hidden from view, and Jews were not only on the defensive. Towards the end of the Middle Ages, criticism of Christian practice and belief began to be expressed openly within Christianity itself, and some opinions resonated with Jewish points of view. Daniel Lasker provides an example relevant to circumcision from the late Middle Ages, which compares the Christian Eucharist to the Jews' ritual use of a "chair of Elijah."[75] In the Eucharist, Catholics believe, the body and the blood of Jesus undergo "transubstantiation" into a wafer and wine. The ritual conveys the sense that Jesus is "present" every time a worshiper engages in the ritual act. Within Christianity, this belief was first challenged by heretics and later by Protestants. There also were Jews who questioned the ritual, asking: how is it possible for Jesus to be present at every time and place that the Eucharist is performed? Christians retorted by citing the "illogical" Jewish claim that Elijah is present at every circumcision. Lasker stresses that this was not a polemic of the religious elite: "Comparison of transubstantiation with Elijah's Chair was not a textbook discussion; it was the product of actual contact between Jews and Christians." The "official" meanings of rituals offered by learned teachers are often only a faint reverberation of ongoing popular processes of interpretation and reinterpretation that have taken place with regard to rituals over the generations.[76]

Jewish customs have "entered conversations" with Islam as well as with Christianity. The former religion shared the practice of circumcision with

Judaism. A basic difference between the two, however, is that Jews circumcise at the age of eight days, following the biblical rule, while Muslims may select any time during childhood, because circumcision is not mentioned in the Quran.[77] Against this background, we find an instance in which the custom of the Jews, who were in the minority, was closely scrutinized by the majority. A researcher among the Muslims of Tripoli, Libya, in the 1930s recorded: "The time of circumcision is variable. Some circumcise on the fortieth day, but this is rare, so as to be different from the Jews who circumcise on the seventh and fortieth day. Most of the [Muslim] residents of Tripoli circumcise from the second to the seventh year."[78] While based on a misperception as to the date of the Jewish practice, this statement shows that prestige could adhere to the practice of the Jews. In different ways, then, in both Christian and Muslim realms, circumcision for centuries marked the difference between Judaism and the religion of the majority.

SOME MODERN CHALLENGES

The place of religion in the life of Europeans became less dominant after the Middle Ages, and the polemical associations of circumcision diminished in salience. Recent centuries, however, have presented new challenges to the practice, along with much else in Jewish life that was shaped by rabbinical culture. Circumcision, by and large, has been retained in the face of those challenges, but not without debate, reinterpretation, and some changes in the way it is carried out. Aspects of the ritual came to signify differences among Jews, rather than between Jews and Gentiles. Jacob Katz has shown how controversies surrounding circumcision illuminate struggles and trends emerging with new forms of Jewish organization and religious outlook.[79]

There are many dimensions to the changes affecting European Jewish society at the end of the eighteenth century and the beginning of the nineteenth. One is the ideal, which came to be shared by Jews and non-Jews, that Jews participate in the national culture of a society, sharing its language, its basic education, and its moral and esthetic standards. A second dimension concerns the actual legal and social status of the Jews in modern nation-states: the assumption that they enjoy the same rights as any individual citizen, regardless of religious commitment. Today, these ideas are taken for granted and built into the organization of Western societies. These ideas, however, have a *history:* the ways that they grew and became institutionalized influenced how Jewish religion was practiced and came to be understood in our era.

With growing contact between Jews and Gentiles in western and central Europe, many Jews became concerned about the image of their religious practices in the eyes of non-Jews. They sometimes tried to "dress up" these practices to make them comprehensible and attractive to Christians. Thus, aspects of the synagogue service became more "decorous," even if there were no basic changes in the ritual and liturgy.[80] The attempt to give Judaism, and Jews, a new face often created a new vocabulary; in France, the country that first extended legal emancipation to Jews in hope of overcoming the age-old opprobrium sometimes attached to the word *Juif* (Jew), Jews were called *Israélites* or *Hébreux*.

In France, too, brit milah was often referred to as *circoncision* but came to be called *baptême,* or "baptism," as well. The selection of the term may indicate the Jews' desire to be part of French culture, more than the adoption of a religious perspective, but reflected the fact that the French were mainly Catholics and baptism was parallel to circumcision, inasmuch as it entailed a ritual at a young age. To the historical observer, however, the use of the term is full of irony, because of the Christian association of baptism displacing circumcision as an aspect of Christianity superseding Judaism.

The emerging modern states were not trying to convert their Jewish citizens. Rather, based on ideas that sought to limit the impact of religion on social and political life, they experimented with communal structures that enabled Jews to maintain their religious practices and beliefs. This could even reinforce traditional practices of Judaism. In Germany and the Austro-Hungarian Empire, early in the nineteenth century, religious communities had the duty of recording the birth of every child. Religious functionaries were charged with reporting each baptism or circumcision, as the case might be. One was born either a Christian or a Jew; no other category existed. Thus, the state became one of the factors supporting the circumcision of Jewish males.[81]

In nineteenth-century Europe, the possibility existed of Jews converting to Christianity, or having their children convert through baptism. This was a known phenomenon, although it became widespread only in certain locales and periods. What is less remembered today is the wish of certain Jews to remain within the fold of Judaism but to abolish circumcision. In the Austro-Hungarian Empire, this was both a Judaic and a legal anomaly. It challenged ancient Jewish rules and sensibilities, and made a claim for free exercise of religious conscience beyond that which had been envisioned by the current laws.

The claim that one could stay Jewish but ignore circumcision appeared as one aspect of religious reform within western European Jewry. The most prominent expression of the claim was in Frankfurt am Main in 1843, among a group called the "Friends of Reform," who put forth various arguments for it.[82] It was asserted that the ancient Hebrews had adopted the practice from the Egyptians, so that in present circumstances, when the wider society did not attach any importance to it, the ritual could be dropped. Another position, that paralleled ancient arguments within Christianity, stressed the spiritual nature of the Jewish contribution to civilization, which obviated the need for "physical" rites. These arguments were opposed by leaders of the emerging forms of Jewish Orthodoxy, as well as by advocates of religious reform who were not as radical in their demands for, and ideology of, change. Many grounds for maintaining the custom were offered: some were based on religious conceptions, others stressed ethnic loyalty, and still others cited health, claiming that circumcision helped prevent certain diseases.

Although most Jews continued to practice circumcision, new ideas of medicine and hygiene affected how they did so. As mentioned, the Mishna describes the ceremony as being composed of three separate actions, cutting the foreskin, periʾah, and meṣiṣah, or sucking blood from the wound. While circumcision with periʾah was maintained, reservations were expressed concerning meṣiṣah, and it was eventually dropped by many from the ceremony. This had to do both with modern sensibilities and with medicine.

To non-Jews, a mohel's sucking the wound he had made on the child's penis probably appeared bizarre.[83] Nineteenth-century Jews, concerned to make a good impression on their neighbors, often were uncomfortable with this aspect of the ritual. Moreover, it became questionable from a health point of view. Even before the germ theory of disease was established by Pasteur in 1861, it was assumed that diseases were contagious, and that illness could be prevented by avoiding contact between carriers and those who were well. Infant mortality was common, however, before the development of modern norms of hygiene and inoculations against childhood diseases. If a male baby died young, contact during circumcision was not singled out as a special cause.

In the nineteenth century, treatises that discussed circumcision from a combined Jewish and medical point of view began to appear. This reflected both the sensitivity of Jews to Gentile norms and the growing presence of Jews in medical schools. One study, published in 1831, cited a case in Kraków in which several babies had developed syphilis after having been circumcised by a mohel with that disease. This stimulated medical objection to a practice that had begun to make people uneasy for other reasons as well. Meṣiṣah might transmit disease from a mohel to an infant, or vice versa, and pressure mounted to abandon it.

As stated, debates surrounding circumcision were sensitive indicators of religious ideologies within Judaism. With regard to meṣiṣah, Orthodox Jews insisted it was integral to the ritual, being a "tradition given to Moses on Sinai," even though it is not explicit in the Torah. This position must be viewed as part of the struggle of Orthodoxy with religious reform. In addition to textually based arguments in favor of maintaining meṣiṣah, the practice now symbolized resistance to reform. To accede to reform arguments in this area was to accord legitimization to the reformers' approach to Judaism.

Those who advocated abolishing or changing the form of meṣiṣah, especially the moderate reformers associated with the "positive historical" approach to Judaism (the precursor of the Conservative movement in the United States), also had good arguments. While meṣiṣah appears in the Mishna as one of three main elements in the circumcision ritual, elsewhere it is clear that the motivation for the practice was to help heal the wound. Sucking blood from a wound was the accepted health practice of the day. Rabbinical authorities who felt loyalty to halakha but also acknowledged that Jewish practice had evolved in historical contexts claimed that with up-to-date medical understanding, meṣiṣah no longer made any sense. It should be abandoned or carried out in a different way. Thus, a cotton swab soaked in appropriate chemicals also served to draw out blood from the wound and this could be used instead of the traditional meṣiṣah.[84]

Parallel to the arguments of rabbis were popular sentiments that also went in different directions. As Jewish participation in general society expanded in scope, a basic perception of the custom as contrary to modern life spread. At the same time, in large circles of Jewish society, a positive attitude to the practice persisted. Basing themselves on interviews with Polish Jews born in the early part of the twentieth century, Mark Zborowski and Elizabeth Herzog write: "In the old tradition, the greatest honor of all [in a circumcision] is that of *metsutsa* [sic], performed by a venerable pious man who sucks the first drop of blood."[85] Nevertheless, changing attitudes to meṣiṣah began to appear among Jews in eastern Europe as well.

Along with attitudinal changes came technological innovations. Devices were developed (one in Poland and another in England) whereby suction could be applied without direct contact between the mouth of the mohel and the baby. Steps to improve circumcision did not begin in the nineteenth century. Before then, progress in metallurgy enabled the making of new types of knives, and shields were invented to protect the penis when the foreskin was removed.

The medical side of circumcision has always been entailed in broader cultural issues, both among Jewish groups and within the wider society.

The idea arose that circumcision was a positive health measure, according to modern science. Although this notion clearly fits in with modern Jewish apologetics, it may also echo ancient views of circumcision as having apotropaic qualities. In the United States, the medical view was reinforced by practice among Christians. Around the turn of the twentieth century, it became widespread in America to circumcise babies while in hospital.[86] For years, many American Jews had their babies circumcised in this manner without attaching religious significance to the operation. Among Reform Jews, a trend to reinvest the act with meaning became evident after World War II, while Israeli Jews widely assume that an experienced mohel (with medical supervision as part of his training) will be more efficient in carrying out the operation than a doctor.[87] The relation between religious currents and other societal trends never reaches final equilibrium.

In recent years, the medical benefits that were attributed to circumcision have been called into question. Studies have been said to show, for example, "that circumcised males have a lower incidence of urinary tract infections, and that circumcision offers almost complete protection against penile carcinoma," but medical science cannot be unequivocally mobilized on behalf of circumcision, because a report of the American Academy of Pediatrics also "states that proper hygiene of the uncircumcised penis would equally prevent carcinoma."[88] Moreover, there have been different attitudes as to what, in principle, is the relation between religion and science. The *Jewish Encyclopedia*, published in New York in 1903, cites medical opinions concerning the operation, but the idea that the basic rationale for Jewish circumcisions stems from health reasons is presented as a historical curiosity. Even more skeptical is the anthropologist Mary Douglas's view apropos of the dietary laws of Leviticus: "Even if some of Moses's dietary rules were hygienically beneficial it is a pity to treat him as an enlightened public health official rather than as a spiritual leader."[89] Still, many contemporary Jews would surely question circumcision if there were a clear indication that it caused harm.

The most recent questions about circumcision relate to areas difficult to measure. There is now a challenge to the ritual because of its putative emphasis on maleness and social power,[90] although, as we have seen, it can be interpreted on a variety of levels. There is also growing concern with bodily mutilation, cruelty, and the pain felt by the infant or its psychological effects. Even those assenting to circumcision ask why it cannot be done with the administration of anesthesia. Both the critics of traditional circumcision and those who defend it speak in terms of Jewish values, the former citing, for example, the prohibition against cruelty to animals (ṣa'ar ba'alei ḥayyim).[91] Some defenders state that the experience of some degree of pain is not always bad. One author mentions stress on the father as a factor to be considered.[92] Expanding these outlooks somewhat, there emerges an attitude that parents are not always able to keep children from pain but can exercise influence on how to interpret it.

Today, it is universally expected that circumcision will be performed taking into account current health standards and medical refinements, but the meanings attached to the ritual are as diverse as might be expected given its long history. Both non-Jews and Jews associate it with Judaism, but it is less exclusively Jewish in some settings than in others, being more common among Gentiles in the United States than in Europe. Agnieszka Holland's 1991 film *Europa, Europa* employs circumcision as a mark of Jewishness as the premise of a drama of individual survival during World War II. Jews in Muslim lands, numbering close to one million at mid twentieth century, lived in an environment in which circumcision was taken for granted and never questioned. In some cases, such as in Egypt, medical issues concerning circumcision arose, but there were also instances in which the first impact of modern medicine upon the procedure took place when traditional Middle Eastern communities migrated to Israel. The incident in the Tripolitanian moshav, cited above, is an example of the latter.

Migration to Israel has provided the context for other episodes in the story of circumcision. I have already mentioned that many uncircumcised adult males arriving from the former Soviet Union elected to be circumcised in Israel. Another concerns Jews from Ethiopia who call themselves the Beta Israel (House of Israel). There are debates about the origins of the Jews there, but a salient fact of their history is that they lived in proximity to Ethiopian Christians. This branch of Christianity retained aspects of ritual life based on what it calls "Old Testament" texts. To the present day, for example, it is not unusual to find rural Ethiopian Christians circumcising their sons. Although the Beta Israel and Ethiopian Christians have emphasized the many differences between them, the parallels in the culture and religion of the two groups, in which the rules of the Hebrew Bible play a prominent part, are striking.[93]

Basing their religious lives directly upon the Bible, the Beta Israel seem to have bypassed rabbinic law. This perception was one of the factors that initially kept them from being categorized as Jews with regard to Israel's "Law of Return," under which a Jew anywhere in the world has the right to immigrate to Israel and instantly receive citizenship. So long as religious authorities in Israel were unsure of the Jewishness of Beta Israel, they hesitated to apply the Law of Return to them. A change in this situation took place in 1972, when the then Sephardi chief rabbi of Israel, Ovadia Yosef, declared the Beta Israel to be Jews. Basing himself on an opinion by a sixteenth-century authority in Egypt, Rabbi David Ben Zimra, he explained that they were descended from the biblical tribe of Dan, and had been separated from the centers of Jewish life, but now were in a position to reconnect to Judaism by following the dictates of rabbinic law. That decision provided an opening for many Ethiopian Jews, and some 22,000 of them arrived in Israel in two mass migrations in 1984 and 1991, leaving very few Beta Israel on Ethiopian soil.

Although they became full citizens of the State of Israel, immigration based on the Law of Return did not automatically resolve the religious anomalies attributed to them. Rabbi Yosef's decision notwithstanding, many rabbis would not treat them as full Jews unless they met all the requirements of conversion.[94] These included ritual immersion in a ritual bath (*miqveh*) or an otherwise appropriate body of water, and circumcision. The latter was a problematic demand, because the males of the Beta Israel had all been circumcised as babies, in accordance with the rule in Genesis and Leviticus. Those rabbis who demanded circumcision expected them to follow the ancient procedure of haṭafat dam (see above, "Circumcision after the Bible"), which was applied when a male who was already circumcised converted to Judaism.

Many Ethiopian Jews found this demand, and the demand for ritual immersion, insulting. They argued that they had scrupulously followed laws of purity and separated themselves from non-Jews over many generations. They were not about to demean themselves by accepting rabbinic claims that they were lesser Jews. This stance meant that most members of the rabbinic establishment were not prepared to marry Ethiopian Jews. This was a crucial decision, for Israeli law empowers rabbis to decide who may be legally registered as married under the rules of the Ministry of the Interior. The dilemma was mitigated somewhat by a small number of rabbis who took a more accommodating stance in recognizing the marriages of Beta Israel among themselves and with others.[95]

The fact that Ethiopian Jews were only partially accepted by the religious establishment may also be illustrated by an incident involving circumcision. In one case, a baby boy was born to an Ethiopian family living in an immigrant absorption center.[96] In such situations, decisions often were taken by workers in the center, rather than by the families themselves. In this case, an administrator took the initiative of calling a mohel to come on the eighth day after birth. The mohel found that day inconvenient and decided instead on another date. No medical reason was given for the postponement. Among the Beta Israel in the past, exceptions were not made with regard to the timing of circumcision. More to the point, such a postponement is unacceptable according to rabbinic law, unless the health of the child is entailed. The attitude of the mohel only can be explained by assuming that he did not fully relate to the Ethiopian immigrants as Jews.

Another contentious custom preserved by some of the Beta Israel is the practice of "female circumcision,"[97] sometimes also called female genital mutilation (FGM), or, more neutrally, "female genital operations," which involves "cutting away parts of the external female genitalia or other injury to the female genitals."[98] It is mostly customary in regions of Africa and some parts of the Middle East and was also known in ancient times. Although not usually associated with Judaism, it was and is practiced by some Ethiopian Jews. The Roman writer Strabo, describing female excision among Egyptians, linked it to male circumcision and attributed both to the Jews.[99] A medieval Iraqi source, on the other hand, sees the absence of female excision to be a Jewish characteristic.[100] A modern link between Jewish practice and African excision customs was made by Jomo Kenyatta, who eventually became president of Kenya, who averred that Europeans would have to learn to accept the latter practices, just as they did circumcision among the Jews.[101] Recently, it has become identified with Islam in the eyes of many and attracts attention in the West.[102] For example, a recent court dispute pitted Islamic groups seeking to maintain the practice against Egyptian health officials trying to ban it.[103] Some feminist opinion is unsure how to relate critically to a practice often defended by women because of its importance in their culture. In this case, as in that of male circumcision, medical opinion and cultural perspectives within the wider society are likely to intertwine and jostle against one another for a long time to come.

RECOGNIZING GENDER: BIRTH, THE FIRSTBORN, AND NAMING

The centrality of circumcision within Jewish tradition has meant that other aspects of infancy have at times been overlooked. Not only are girls excluded from discussion, but a focus on circumcision sometimes overshadows the consideration of birth itself.[104] Other topics that also deserve more attention include the redemption of firstborn males and the naming of infants. Whereas boys typically receive names at circumcision, recent sensibilities and trends affecting early childhood rituals are involved in the naming of baby girls.

While scattered material on customs relating to birth is available, ethnographies of Jewish life often are sparse, if not silent, with regard to the process and events surrounding it.[105] At times, ritual awareness of birth appears in unexpected places. In parts of central Europe, local custom assigned the honor of opening the doors of the holy ark at the time of Torah reading to a man whose wife was reaching term. Similar customs existed in the Ottoman Empire.[106] Referring again to central Europe, pregnant women there might bite off the tip of the *etrog* (citron) at the end of the Sukkot festival and pray for easy childbirth.[107] In a village in Tripolitania, in instances of difficult labor, a ritual ram's horn (*shofar*), used on the High Holy Days, might be sounded to assist the newborn's passage.[108] Aside from scattered information on customs like these, the sparseness of discussion concerning birth has now partially been rectified. Chava Weissler has explored the religious world of Ashkenazi women, expressed in prayers in Yiddish, providing a window on their views of menstruation and child-bearing.[109] Other research has shed light on birth celebrations among women in Saná, Yemen.

Ethnographic reconstruction among Yemenites, carried out in Israel, reveals an elaborate custom of ceremoniously visiting a woman at home, where she gave birth.[110] This pattern continued over four to six weeks, taking place irrespective of the sex of the baby. During this period a woman was pampered, receiving massages and additional nourishment. She did not prepare refreshments for her guests; visiting women brought their own coffee. They sat in a special room for this purpose, chatting, relaxing, and smoking a narghile. At the same time, there was a formal side to these visits, focusing on the postparturient mother.

The new mother sat in a corner of the room, facing her guests, enclosed in a triangular wooden box, which was partially covered, the cover serving as a table, upon which she rested her arms. Dressed in a festive blue or black cotton dress embroidered with silver and red threads, along with an unadorned black velvet or brocade hood, a young mother was expected to sit with composure in a fixed position. The room was furnished with rugs, mattresses, and cushions, and there were characteristic decorations on the corner box and walls (figure 4).

In addition to the triangular corner box, triangles prominently decorated both the mother's dress and the walls. Triangles often represent female sexuality, closely linked to fecundity. The latter theme also appeared in hanging ostrich eggs, as ostriches lay many eggs at a time. Ester Muchawsky-Schnapper's reading of the symbolism in the room highlights this theme and sees the box as hiding the lower part of the mother's body, simultaneously signaling both modesty and fertility. Other complex messages are coded into the dress, which is the same garment that is taken to the grave, and in the triangular shape that is associated locally with tombstones. The Jews of Saná, like many other societies, saw common features in the womb and the tomb.[111]

Figure 4.   Museum display depicting a festive setting
for a Yemenite woman after childbirth. Courtesy Israel
Museum, Jerusalem. Photo David Harris.

The room's decorations and the customs attached to the process dramatized the value of fertility and the place of women in it. This occurred in a
society that, at the same time, maintained sharp gender boundaries and
limited women to domestic realms.[112] Muchawsky-Schnapper notes that
the custom was observed in its most elaborate form when a woman gave
birth for the first time, thus proving her reproductive ability.[113] The ambivalence associated with the special place of women in reproduction also
appears in another ritual, usually thought of as the arena of men, that of
pidyon ha-ben, or "redeeming the firstborn male."

Redeeming the firstborn male is based on a biblical injunction (Exod.
13:12–13).[114] It is to take place after the firstborn reaches his thirtieth day,
and entails "redeeming" the child from a *kohen,* or priest, by paying five
shekels. In discussing this practice, Nissan Rubin points to a general notion,
in the Bible, of the sanctity of "firstlings" which applies to produce, to flocks,
and to humans.[115] A firstborn son, a *bekhor,* is holy by virtue of birth, and
must be redeemed to be removed from the category of the holy. The payment to the priest constitutes an exchange; prosaic funds are devoted to
priestly purposes and the child is released from the class of the sacred.

The rule applies only to firstborn sons, not daughters, although women are central to the definition of the practice. The Bible distinguishes between the firstborn son of a male, which entails privileges of inheritance, and the firstborn son of a female: the first to "escape" her womb. According to some, the term for a man's firstborn son—bekhor—is better understood legally as meaning the "preferred son," the father having the option of designating the son of his choice.[116] The firstborn of a woman, however, stems from a biological fact and confers a status of sanctity, thereby requiring an act of redemption. This definitional feature is the basis of mothers' having some role in the ceremony as it later developed, even while the obligation to redeem falls solely upon the father.

To speak of "the ceremony" of redemption is not simple. The biblical rule does not take ritual form, in contrast, for example, to the ceremony outlined for bringing first fruits to the priest (Deuteronomy 26). It is surmised that fathers living near the sanctuary in ancient times brought sons there for an exchange-redemption, while those living at a distance simply gave the appropriate sum of money to priests when bringing other Temple gifts. When the Temple no longer stood, redemption funds were given to local priests. The Mishna, however, gives no indication of a fixed redemption rite.

It is only in literature after that period, from both the Palestinian and Babylonian Talmuds, that we learn of a celebration and recitation of blessings. Subsequently, in both Palestine under Byzantine rule and Babylonia under Muslim rule, there seem, moreover, to have been significant variations in the role of the father vis-à-vis the kohen and the inclusion of the mother in the ceremony.

In one instance, the father recited both the blessing "Who has sanctified . . . and commanded us on the redemption of sons," and the she-heḥeyanu ("Who has kept us in life . . . ") blessing, while in another instance, the priest uttered the latter blessing. In one Babylonian tradition, the father recited the two blessings as above, the kohen added three blessings including one on wine and on fragrant herbs, and the mother announced, "This is my firstborn, with which the Holy One, Blessed-be-He, opened the doors of my womb." Following that, the mother recited a formal blessing, praising God for "sanctifying Israel through the firstborn and their redemption." According to Rubin, this is the only instance in ancient rabbinic literature in which a woman was expected to pronounce a set blessing in a public ceremony, but this Babylonian tradition did not become standard practice in successive generations.[117] The overall field of textual variations did, however, find expression in various pidyon ha-ben ceremonies known today.

A custom in North Africa has the father and the kohen engage in mock bargaining over the price, and eventually "agreeing upon" an amount (set in the Bible at five shekels), in order for the father to "get his son back."[118] This might be related to an exchange of letters preserved in the Talmud in which a Rabbi Ashi and a kohen differed over the amount to be paid.[119] In some communities, parallel to the Babylonian custom mentioned, a woman is asked to declare that the boy in the ceremony is the first child to exit her womb. She could not make this statement if she had previously miscarried or had given birth to her son by Caesarean section. Another practice in several locales is that the mother dresses specially for the occasion, for example in her wedding garb.[120] Today, a mother might assume a formerly "male" role, such as giving a Torah lesson as part of the ceremony (figure 5). In some communities, the ceremony of pidyon is carried out quickly and simply, while in others it is enacted in an elaborate manner. The importance of the firstborn is also reflected in a Sephardi custom of assigning the Hebrew name Bekhor to a boy, either as a first or supplementary name.[121]

The assigning of names is a realm that reflects many aspects of social and religious life.[122] As stated, it has long been standard to give boys a name at circumcision, but customs with regard to girls have been more varied. In a number of communities, the naming of girls takes place at home. In Tunis, this occurs on the seventh day after birth.[123] Among Iraqi Jews living in Calcutta, naming girls often took place on the sixth day after birth, preceded by a festive gathering—the *sitti* ("the sixth")—the night before.[124] In both cases, the occasion was not known for its content, but by a term reflecting its conventional timing.

Among Sephardi Jews, there developed an occasion for naming a girl that was called *zeved ha-bat* ("gift of a daughter").[125] The word for gift, *zeved*, appears in Genesis 30:20 in connection with the naming of Leah's last male child, Zevulun. The following verse mentions the birth of her daughter, Dinah. Some think that this custom was a Jewish revision of a naming practice adopted from Spanish neighbors that involved the invocation of fairies.[126] There was also a naming custom in various parts of Ashkenaz called *holekreish* (there are many spellings), which many historians link to German beliefs in a Frau Holle who threatened newborn infants. It took place in homes, on a Sabbath. The baby was lifted up and given a name, while the adult who raised the baby (sometimes, a cantor) was surrounded by children. They called out "holekreish," which other scholars see as deriving from French: *haut la crèche*, "up with the cradle." The nature of the practice varied. In some locales, it was the way girls were named. In others, the ceremony was conducted for both girls and boys,

Figure 5.   Redemption of the firstborn in a Jerusalem synagogue with mother presenting a Torah lesson and father holding baby. Courtesy Amir Busheri.

while the latter were given their Yiddish names (having received a Hebrew name at circumcision).[127]

In Ashkenazi Jewish communities, it became standard to announce the name of a baby girl in the synagogue. This often took place on the first Sabbath after the birth, or sometimes on the first occasion that the Torah was read, such as a Monday or Thursday. The father of the baby girl was given the ritual honor of reciting blessings over the reading of the Torah in the course of the morning prayer service. His completion of the blessings marked the opportunity for a prayer, called *mi she-berakh* ("He who has blessed . . . "), asking for the health of the mother and the well-being of the daughter, and also for proclaiming the baby's name. A recent development is connected with the presence of the mother in the synagogue (she need not be there). In that case, she might, from the woman's section of the synagogue, recite the blessing for having emerged alive from a dangerous situation: "Blessed are you, O Lord, our God, king of the world, who acts beneficently towards the undeserving, and who has dealt kindly with me." Special refreshments were sometimes served at the termination of the service. Today, many variations on this pattern are common in both Ashkenazi and Sephardi synagogues (figure 6). The public recognition given to newborn girls was relatively muted in comparison to that at a circumcision.[128]

Figure 6.   Baby-girl naming ceremony in a Jerusalem synagogue. Photo Harvey E. Goldberg.

In the past two generations, religious rules that distinguish between women and men have come under scrutiny. In America, many parents began to experiment with ceremonies, seen as paralleling the brit milah, that introduced baby girls to the Jewish community and announced their names. The practice rapidly became common; one set of parents stimulated others to follow suit, and information was disseminated in publications. Parallel to this, religious leaders put forward suggestions as to appropriate ways of naming newborn girls. Soon, much literature on the subject was available, providing an overview of the emerging trends and accompanying ideas.[129]

The term applied to the girl-naming ceremony varies. One name is *simḥat bat* (the joyous occasion of a daughter), while less frequently *zeved ha-bat*, from the Sephardi tradition, is used. Others have selected to stress the parallel between boys and girls and call the occasion *brit banot* (the covenanting of daughters). The suggested timing also varies. Some authors of new ceremonies stress their lack of satisfaction with the traditional naming in the synagogue, because it is not always possible or comfortable for a postparturient mother to be present. Any convenient day might be chosen, while a publication of the Jewish Women's Resource Center lists various possibilities providing a reason for each:[130]

1. At eight days, paralleling a brit milah.

2. At fourteen days, with the termination of ritual impurity associated with the birth of a girl (in contrast to seven days for a boy), according to Leviticus 12:5.

3. At thirty days, because rabbinic law perceives a child as viable after that period (there is no formal mourning for children who die before the age of thirty days).[131]

4. On a Sabbath, because the Bible presents the Sabbath as a covenant between God and Israel.

5. On Rosh Hodesh, the New Moon festival, which traditionally has been associated with women.[132]

Each of the above suggestions links the birth ceremony with other aspects of Jewish ritual life.

Most commonly, these ceremonies take place at home, while sometimes the synagogue is selected. Very often, parents take the initiative, particularly if they are knowledgeable about Jewish culture. They create texts for the occasion based on established liturgy and precedent, but also containing innovations and adaptations for the specific family and child. A rabbi may be invited, sometimes to "officiate," but often simply as a friend. Frequently, portions of the prepared ceremonial readings are assigned to different participants, with grandparents playing a salient role. A new development is the introduction of "Miriam's cup," which may be a feminist echo of "Elijah's cup" (in the Passover seder) and of the imagined presence of Elijah at circumcisions.[133] In some instances, following the model of a circumcision, a birth ceremony is placed in conjunction with the morning service. One mother indicates that she led the service (did the "davening") prior to the naming celebration. Universally, the celebration includes refreshments or a meal. A meal attached to the fulfillment of a commandment is known as a seʿudat mitzvah (a meal celebrating a mitzvah).

Several themes appear in these ceremonies. One stresses the miracle of birth and of creation. Another highlights the child as a gift, stimulating a deep sense of appreciation. Often the notion of a covenant with God is underlined, joined to the idea of becoming part of the Jewish people. Aside from obvious hints of circumcision ritual, symbols are borrowed from other ceremonies such as weddings or lighting candles on the Sabbath. Another comparison is between a young child and young tree. This draws on a custom cited in the Talmud, in which a tree was planted at the birth of a child and branches of that tree were later used in the person's wedding canopy.[134] The tree-child metaphor has also been elaborated in birthday celebrations inspired by the Zionist renewal.[135]

Certain texts appear with frequency. One, taken from a midrash, pre-sents God, at Sinai, asking the Israelites for guarantors so that He will be sure that they will guard the Torah He is about to give them.[136] Several suggestions are made by the Israelites and rejected by God. Finally, the offer is made: "Our children are our guarantors." The midrash continues: "The Holy One, Blessed be He, said: They are certainly good guarantors. For their sake I will give the Torah to you." Other standard texts are the blessing over wine and the "she-heheyanu" blessing. Sometimes blessings are taken from the "seven blessings" of the wedding ceremony, such as the one ending with the phrase: "creator of humanity" (appendix 4). That phrase translates the Hebrew "*yoser ha-adam,*" which also could be ren-dered in English as "Creator of Man," "Mankind," or "Humankind." *Adam* is the word appearing in Genesis that is sometimes translated as the name Adam, and sometimes as a generic name for "man." While the orig-inal Hebrew text is retained in the ceremony, the translation is sensitive to possible gender bias.

A leader of Orthodoxy in England presents different rabbinical views on applying the blessing "He who is good and the source of good" to the birth of a girl.[137] Non-Orthodox approaches introduce new Hebrew texts, based on older standard versions. The same ceremony that utilizes "yoser ha-adam" also includes: "Blessed are you, O Lord, our God, king of the world, who brings the joy of children to parents." The Hebrew is modeled on another of the standard blessings in the wedding ceremony, which speaks of the "joy of the groom and bride."[138]

Some new blessings show great readiness to experiment with ancient forms. An example, which innovates in several ways, is: "Blessed are you, O Lord, our God, king of the world, who has made us holy through His commandments and has commanded us to enter our daughter in the chain of the generations of Israel and to renew the Covenant." It is not part of rabbinic tradition to include two topics (the chain of generations *and* the covenant) in a single blessing. Also, not since ancient times have rabbis felt that they could compose a blessing with the words "who has made us holy through His commandments and has commanded us," when no explicit commandment of that nature appears in the text of the Torah. Parents with secular worldviews also seek to link themselves and their offspring to Jew-ish culture. In place of the "she-heheyanu," the Ann Arbor Jewish Cultural Society offers: "We rejoice in our heritage which has given us the in-domitable spirit that has preserved our people and sustained us and brought us forward to celebrate this joyous occasion."[139]

In addition to using older Hebrew blessings in new contexts, revising blessings, and composing new liturgical forms, recent ceremonies incorporate personal prayers and poetry written for the occasion, or poetic passages selected from general literature. In addition to solemn tones, rhymed poems directed at the family add levity to some of these occasions. Needless to say, in North America, the ceremonies as a whole are bilingual events, including both Hebrew and English elements. Hebrew plays a salient textual and symbolic role with regard to the giving of a name.

Many ceremonies borrow from other life milestone occasions in elaborating upon the letters of the child's Hebrew name. In the Book of Psalms, some chapters are composed on the basis of an acrostic; Psalm 119 is built of sets of eight verses, each beginning with a letter of the alphabet. In one naming ceremony, verses are selected from that psalm so that the first letters of the selected passages spell the baby's name. This parallels the practice on memorial occasions of reading portions of the Mishna that begin with the letters of a deceased person's name.[140] Another "letter-play" device in Jewish tradition is *gematria*. Because each letter of the Hebrew alphabet has a numerical value, any Hebrew word can have a quantitative value attached to it. Figuring out the gematria of words can thus lead to unsuspected "equivalences" of meaning. Some ceremonies explain what the significance of a given name is in terms of recent family history but also succeed in discovering unsuspected resonances by creative gematria manipulations. This interpretive device is often used at weddings, enabling a rabbi to discover hidden meanings in the names of the bride and groom. Such customs, at both birth and marriage, weave threads of significance that connect the individual to the fabric of Jewish culture.

There is a deep linkage between the contemporary wealth of publication, the ease of communication, and the widespread appearance of rituals concerning daughters. Formal Jewish tradition as expressed in written materials minimally recognized the birth of girls, but anthropological intuition suggests that there must have been many local customs that gave expression to these events. Because such customs were not linked to textual production and preservation, we are left with large areas of silence as to how the birth of daughters was marked in the Jewish past. If local practice was referred to, here and there, by rabbis commenting on the peculiarities of specific communities, it was not thereby incorporated into the pool of broadly shared norms of halakha and custom. Today, this silence has been permanently broken, partially because writing about Jewish practice is not only confined to a rabbinic elite. Birth rituals for girls are thus one indication of a general shift in, and diversification of, patterns of authority in religious life and mechanisms of transmission of Jewish culture.

RECENT DEVELOPMENTS

The emergence and acceptance of new naming customs reflect a meeting of Jewish tradition and halakha with contemporary social and cultural trends. They partially stem from the fact that the birth of girls is ignored, downplayed, and sometimes devalued in classic Jewish sources.[141] An initial question that presents itself is what sense to make of this bias. Whatever explanation is adopted by a set of parents will be reflected in the way they inject Jewish tradition into the lives of their children (if at all). The examples of new ceremonies cited above show commitment to Jewish tradition and continuity, while, at the same time, their innovating approach stems from a critique of aspects of that tradition.[142] The materials from which these examples were taken vary in a number of significant ways.

I have focused on ceremonies for girls, but the ideology behind the ceremonies may lead to an insistence on changes with regard to brit milah as well. While the actual procedure of circumcision is usually not changed, the accompanying texts may be modified, or added to, so as not to privilege boys over girls. There also may be changes in personnel; the Reform movement now trains both men and women to be circumcisers.[143]

The rituals for girls and boys may be homogenized in other ways. An example is the use of a *tallit* (prayer shawl) in both, an object that traditionally has been associated with males.[144] The suggestion also has been made to achieve gender equivalence by adding a gesture that impinges on the body of baby girls. One idea put forth was to pierce the hymen of the baby, an act that would yield blood as in a circumcision, and would be in tune with contemporary casualness about premarital virginity. This idea has not met with acceptance.[145] Another suggestion is washing a baby girl's feet, a gesture that has been incorporated into practice to some extent. It bases itself on the episode in Genesis 18:1–16, when Abraham and Sarah are visited by three "angels" who announce that Sarah will give birth to Isaac. There, Abraham welcomes the visitors by telling them to wash their feet, and Sarah takes part in the welcome by preparing cakes. Just as the visitors were greeted warmly into Abraham's encampment, so the infant newcomer is welcomed.

The sense that greater recognition ought to be accorded to girls is found in many Jewish groups today, but its expression varies according to religious ideology. Those adhering to Orthodox ideologies and ways of life would not change circumcision ritual or the forms of the blessings but can easily embellish the limited ceremonial acknowledgment of the birth of girls that characterized traditional communities. Both they and non-

Orthodox ideologues try to anchor new forms by reference to traditional sources. This is not always easy to achieve while maintaining intellectual consistency. Frequent reference is made to the zeved ha-bat precedent in Sephardi tradition, but an examination of the text of that liturgy reveals that it asks for the newborn girl to be blessed with male children, with no mention of daughters.[146] Innovators are thus faced with the question of how to present their new practices. Do they insist that they are only perpetuating the values and customs of the past, or do they forthrightly claim for themselves the authority to change Jewish tradition or to add to it what did not exist before?

In seeking perspective on new ritual forms, it is useful to look at them comparatively. One level is to compare contemporary rituals to those of the past. Alternatively, rituals among Conservative and Reform Jews, or among groups deriving from them, may be compared to those among groups with Orthodox ideologies. Finally, developments in one country may be compared with those in another. From many points of view, ritual life among Israeli Jews is very different from that common among American Jews, but in several aspects they share characteristics of modern industrial societies.

Beginning with the last comparison, many Israeli Jews see themselves as totally secular. Still, certain Jewish practices are widely maintained, even though their explicit religious content is not of much concern to the participants. Often, religious specialists participate in ceremonies in a most perfunctory manner. Early in 1996, a newscast on the radio carried the following "human interest" story. A family in the Tel Aviv area had engaged a mohel to perform a circumcision that was to take place in a rented hall. A mohel showed up a little early, quickly performed the circumcision, was paid, and began to leave.[147] Just then, a second mohel appeared, causing great commotion. It turned out that he was the one who had in fact been invited. Aside from a telephone call, however, there had been no contact between him and the family, and the first mohel had taken advantage of the circumciser's anonymity. As it happened, the child's father was a policeman, and the imposter quickly found himself under arrest.

Secular Israelis typically keep their distance from religious officialdom. One outcome of this stance is that many Israelis do not envision the possibility of forms of religious expression that are at variance with the established Orthodox patterns. Nevertheless, social changes that have led to religious innovation are felt everywhere, and the expectation of a ceremony for the birth of a girl also has emerged among secular Israelis. Everyday Hebrew has assigned a term to these events: *britah* (adding the feminine ending, *ah*, to the word *brit*). This makes no sense from the perspective of language "purity," but some linguists who recognize that language is a social process as well as a cognitive one have welcomed the neologism, which is now part of normal Israeli speech. There is no established ritual or textual content to these gatherings. Even without explicit "ritual," they have clear functions of "announcing newcomers" to the family, activating kin and friendship ties, and being an occasion for presents that form part of a larger scheme of gift exchange. They also indicate that the notion that one only marks the birth of boys is no longer acceptable.

Various broad social trends form the background to the emergence of these sensibilities, and the search for new customs is found among Jews everywhere. Middle-class life and extensive geographic mobility both separate the individual family from an immediate kin context and highlight the mutuality of spouses within it. One of the first descriptions of a celebration for a daughter to be widely published was provided by a family that decided to have a birth at home, and emphasized the husband assisting the mother as much as he could.[148] While in many ways "modernity" has challenged and changed preindustrial family forms and traditional observances embedded in them, its products have also been utilized to reconstruct and reshape traditions. Grandparents can easily travel thousands of miles to be present at a celebration for a grandchild, and word processors enable the quick and esthetic presentation of new composite texts that parents feel appropriate to the ritual for their child. Food processors similarly enable young couples to prepare spreads that would have demanded hours more of work on the part of their grandmothers.

Changes in basic cultural perceptions with regard to gender impinge upon everyone, including those who are opposed to and resist those changes. Developments among American Jews with regard to women in ritual are affected by trends in the wider society, even though they may not exactly mirror those trends. Indeed, reactions to issues concerning conception, birth, and the care of infants are far from unidirectional in America. Faye Ginsburg has documented different worldviews associated with the debate over abortion in America in a midwestern city, and Janet Dolgin has pointed to the internal contradictions in American court decisions as to what the "natural" roles of fathers and mothers are.[149] Even though American Jewry, which is largely urban, middle-class, and educated, is not as internally diverse as American society as a whole, it is not surprising to find various trends within it. These trends are sociological as well as ideological.

Larger numbers of intermarriages and one-parent families and a higher incidence of adoption make a birth or naming ceremony more optional than it was in the past. Decisions have to be made about many matters, including how one deals with non-Jews who are close friends or relatives present at the ceremony. A text tailor-made for the occasion not only expresses the worldview and commitments of the parents but provides a simple way of explaining rituals to those unfamiliar with them, whether Jewish or non-Jewish. These ceremonial occasions become public statements about the way a couple intends to live its life and to educate its children. While in the past a circumcision, or the naming of a girl in the synagogue, welcomed the newborn into an extant community, contemporary celebrations are frequently part of a process of *creating* communities.

This creation of community around an ancient ritual goes hand in hand with the rereading and reappropriation of texts. The brief account in Genesis is often revisited, with contemporary points of view, such as the one offered above from the perspective of anthropology. Parents who choose and shape the ceremonies surrounding the birth of male or female infants join generations of Jews who both followed and forged these rituals through loyalty to a tradition that, whether in an obvious manner or not, was always responding to a wider social and cultural environment. In Genesis, circumcision is referred to as the "sign of the covenant," and the biblical word for sign—*ot*—became the Hebrew word for "letter." Consciousness of literacy and textuality were thus ceremonially imprinted on the lives of individual Jews from their earliest days.

3 Rituals of Education

A favorite item displayed in Jewish museums is an object called a *wimpel*.[1] It is a long thin piece of cloth, with decorations, made for binding Torah scrolls. A wimpel is not a short sash, to be tied in a knot or fastened with a clip, but a lengthy linen strip wound around the scroll many times. The first known Torah wimpels date from the sixteenth century in western Ashkenaz, some of which are still in active synagogue use in places like Strasbourg, France. What is notable about the wimpel, however, is not its geographic range but how it is made.

A wimpel was prepared from a piece of linen first used to wrap a male child during his circumcision. Once this event was over, mothers devoted special treatment to the cloth employed in the ceremony. It was cut into four strips, which were sewn together into a single band. This band was then embroidered or painted in watercolors. It often included the names of the child and of his father and the date of birth. Other textual material appropriate to the wimpel was the blessing encountered in circumcisions praying for "Torah, the bridal canopy, and good deeds." These themes were given visual expression in pictures of the Torah scroll and *ḥuppah* (bridal canopy). On a special occasion, such as the boy's bar mitzvah, the decorated strip was presented to the community to be used to bind a Torah scroll in the synagogue.[2]

I first became aware of the custom of the wimpel in the Museum of the Diaspora in Tel Aviv. A diorama of a family scene from central Europe provided the background to the custom. Instead of stressing the Yiddish word *wimpel,* the exhibit explained the decorative cloth using the Hebrew *ḥitul.* In contemporary Hebrew, this term also refers to diapers. The topic of Torah was thus linked to the earliest physical experiences of a baby boy. In discussing circumcision in chapter 2, I suggested that, in addition to permanently marking the male body, this ritual is also an element in the edu-

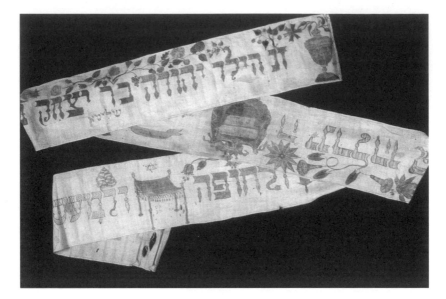

Figure 7.   Decorated Torah binder (wimpel) from nineteenth-century Germany. Courtesy Collection Mishkan Le'Omanut, Museum of Art, Ein Harod, Israel. Item Sc. 7652, yod-73.

cational process. The museum exhibit made me aware of how Jewish culture builds up intimate connections to the value of Torah through various life stages, so that an individual's progression in relation to "Torah" also becomes the object of ritual marking and celebration (see figure 7).

MEANINGS OF TORAH

When the word "Torah" is used today, it carries multiple associations, each hinting at its long history. In the Bible itself, it has several meanings. At times, it refers to a specific set of rules, such as those pertaining to *kohanim* in sacrificial rituals. In other contexts, prophets use the term to describe messages they have received from God. In some settings, it is associated with written documents and in others with oral instruction. The more generalized sense of the term, referring to a whole set of teachings and instructions, is characteristic of Deuteronomy, the last book of the Ḥumash, or "five books [of Moses]" (the equivalent of the Greek-derived "Pentateuch").

Over time, the tendency for Torah to take on an all-inclusive meaning grew stronger. For example, the revelation on Mt. Sinai most explicitly entailed the Ten Commandments,[3] but later traditions offered different understandings of what was transmitted on that occasion. Some sought to limit the imagination as to what portion of the divine message was audibly heard by the people of Israel, while others claimed that even the content of rabbinic rulings, a millennium later, was revealed to Moses at the time.[4] The notion of an "oral Torah" complementing the "written Torah," and integrally related to the latter, provided the basis of the broad notion we use today.[5] Thus "the Torah" can refer to the physical Torah scroll (sefer torah), which must be hand-written on parchment and is normally prepared by a trained scribe, or to the same contents in the form of a book, the Ḥumash. The widespread image of traditional Judaism was that "the Torah" was revealed to Moses and the Jewish people at Sinai. "Torah," however, sometimes implies the other, and later, sections of the Bible—the Prophets (Nevi'im) and the Holy Writings (Ketuvim)—along with the works of rabbinic culture: the Mishna, Talmud, and the discussions and codifications of talmudic literature produced from ancient times to the present. To begin the study of Torah by learning the Hebrew alphabet and acquiring the ability to read verses of the Bible is to take the first steps into a vast cultural universe.

RECEIVING THE TORAH AND ACCESS TO IT

The Bible tells the story of God revealing himself to the Children of Israel at Mt. Sinai. An outstanding feature of the revelation was that it was a public event, taking place before the whole people. The precise account is complex, however, with various players having differential access to the main "action." According to Exodus, God revealed the Ten Commandments to Moses at Sinai. God's teachings were directed to the Children of Israel as a whole, but the awe of facing God was an experience from which the people retreated (Exod. 20:18–21). This raised the question of who was religiously rigorous and sturdy enough to survive the encounter and could thereby represent the people before God. An implication of that question is: What category of people would enjoy the privilege of being close to the source of "Torah," the written record of God's revelation?

The answers to these questions have been a matter of differing views over the generations. One issue concerns the relative places of men and women. The issue of gender at Sinai was read into the narrative by later generations. Citing the verse "And Moses went unto God, and the Lord called unto him out of the mountain, saying: 'Thus shall you say to the House of Jacob, and tell the Children of Israel' " (Exod. 19:3), the rabbis comment that "the House of Jacob" refers to the women and "the Children of Israel" to the men. This midrash thus underlines that the revelation was directed towards all—that is, both genders. At the same time, the biblical text later intimates that separation and the avoidance of sexual activity was appropriate to the situation (Exod. 19:15). Moses tells the people: "Be ready for three days; come not near a woman." Other commentators point out, however, that Moses created this prohibition on his own; he is not repeating an explicit command to him by God. Thus, from ancient times, the issue arose as to the place of gender division and sexuality in gaining access to God's written revelation.[6]

Another line of division concerns the priests (kohanim). The narrative in Exodus first expects that these will be with Moses when he faces God. This puzzled medieval commentators, because the assignment of a special ritual role to the children of Aaron has not yet been made in the text. They therefore interpret the term *kohanim* to mean the firstborn of each family.[7] In the end, Moses alone experiences the full revelation, the written record of which is two stone tablets with divine qualities.[8] They become the kernel of the written Torah, which, in principle, is directed to all the members of God's people.

The norm that everyone should study Torah emerged only gradually. The idea is embedded in the prelude to the revelation, however, when the whole people are enjoined to be a "kingdom of priests" (Exod. 19:6). This phrasing reflects the social reality of the ancient world in which literacy and the knowledge of sacred texts were confined to the priesthood.[9] It also corresponds to actual developments in the biblical period, when the priests had a special role in guarding the divine teachings. They, and the Levites, were in charge of cultic matters and responsible for transmitting the contents of Torah to others. The notion that all Jews, regardless of their lineage, should be educated in the Torah was only realized over the course of many centuries.

The ideal is stressed in Deuteronomy, chapter 5 of which recapitulates the Ten Commandments, given to the Israelites in the first months of their journey from Egypt (Exod. 20:1–17), and stresses that Moses' later teachings, almost forty years after the revelation, carry the same religious authority. Moses' words at that time were addressed to the generation born in the desert that did not directly experience revelation at Sinai. This created the challenges of educating them and of their educating their own children in the future, the topic of chapter 6 of Deuteronomy.

In a paragraph that has become known as the Shma' Yisrael, based on the first words of Deuteronomy 6:4–9, the Israelite is commanded to "love the Lord your God with all your heart, with all your soul, and with all your might." He is then directed to teach "these things (or words)" to his children, speaking of them "when you are in your house, and when you walk by the way, when you lie down and when you rise up"—that is, at all times and places. A person should also "tie them [the words] as a sign upon your hands, and they shall be for frontlets between your eyes." A physical connection should, in other words, be made between God's words and a person's body.

The verse in Deuteronomy does not specify the form of the "sign upon your hands and . . . [the] frontlets between your eyes," but rabbinic culture took this phrase as the basis for the use of *tefillin*, a pair of square black leather phylacteries containing portions of the Torah that are traditionally worn by males on the arm and the forehead during morning prayer. The form of tefillin we know today is quite ancient. Remnants of tefillin from about two thousand years ago have been found in the Qumran caves near the Dead Sea. Some medieval rabbinic discussions compare the region on the forehead where the head-tefillin[10] are placed to the corresponding region on the forehead of a high priest described in the Bible, where he was to wear a gold headband inscribed with the words "Holy to the Lord" (Exod. 28:36–37).[11] Thus Deuteronomy, and later trends in Second Temple times, expanded the intimate bodily nexus between person and text from the restricted circle of the priesthood to the arena of all male Jews.

Each of the two leather boxes contains the four sections of the Ḥumash that include rules interpreted as requiring tefillin (see appendix 3). Two sections are taken from Exodus and two from Deuteronomy. In the first two sections, from Exodus, there is also the mention of Passover and of the redemption of the firstborn.[12] Tefillin thus contain references to sacrificial worship (the Passover) and the potential priesthood (the firstborn), while simultaneously stressing the messages of Torah as the lot of every Jew. Echoes of the sacrificial roles of priests also reverberate in the rule that the leather of tefillin must be from a ritually pure (kosher) animal.

Tefillin thus appear to straddle the opposing thrusts of Torah tradition, which place it in the hands of specialists, on the one hand, and encourage wide participation, on the other. When the Temple stood, there were certain biblical passages recited daily by the priests, and these included the Ten Commandments and the paragraphs of the Shma' Yisrael. The Shma' consists of three sections, the first two of which are the same as the second set of verses from Deuteronomy that are found in tefillin. As indicated, the first of those two sections follows upon the Ten Commandments in the Deuteronomic text. The ancient tefillin from Qumran contain both the Ten Commandments and the four standard passages in tefillin as they are known today.[13] The Shma', in addition to its placement within tefillin, was incorporated into the daily prayer, and its third section is from Numbers 15:37–41 (see appendix 3 for a comparison of the different groupings of texts). The latter passage requires Israelites to wear fringes on the corners of their garments in order to remember God's commandments. Scholars have made comparisons between these fringes (*tzitzit*), to be worn by every man, and the garments worn by kohanim. The whole complex of tzitzit—fringes on the contemporary prayer shawl (tallit), tefillin, and accompanying prayers—creates a ritual bundle that links the individual, his body, his clothes, and the Torah.[14] This rabbinic complex grows out of parts of the Bible that may be read as an incipient program of individuals becoming their own priests.

The process first appearing in Deuteronomy became prominent in Second Temple times and later when religious leadership shifted to the hands of learned rabbis, instead of kohanim. Still, the priesthood remained a valued part of Jewish culture. Priests blessed the congregation in the synagogue with the formula from Numbers and continued to redeem firstborn sons (pidyon ha-ben).[15] They also observed other biblical laws, such as refraining from entering cemeteries, except when burying a first-degree relative.[16] Other practices became widespread, such as first turning to a kohen to lead the grace after meals, or designating a kohen to be the first person called to recite the blessings over the Torah when it is read in the synagogue. Reading the Torah in public, of course, was one way of making it available to everyone, but this institution did not completely erase cultic features connected to the sacred book.

Traces of the priesthood were found in Torah education as well. According to a midrash, a young boy beginning to learn to read the Torah should start with the third book of the Ḥumash, not with Genesis.[17] That book, Leviticus, details the routine of the priests in the sanctuary, and a midrash explains: "Let pure ones [young children] come and deal with matters of purity." The historical background to this custom is the connection linking the priesthood, literacy, and the laws of the Torah.[18] In the early Middle Ages, there seems to have developed a different opinion about the importance of Genesis in childhood education, because of the theological principles embedded in it, but this view did not prevail.[19] Even when the norm became taken for granted that all boys should have a basic Torah education, the historical tie between the priesthood and schooling still echoed in practice. Moroccan scholars likened the distribution of books to the offering of a sacrifice.[20] It was also a common organizational device in North Africa for a community to utilize taxes on the kosher slaughter of meat for supporting basic Torah education. A modern reverberation of that link may be seen in the practice of placing collection boxes for Torah institutions in butcher shops and kosher restaurants.[21]

The tie between the priesthood and the study of Torah may have had other consequences as well. Consider the following passage from the Jerusalem

Talmud: "In a city inhabited only by priests, and the priests raise their hands [that is, recite the blessing from Numbers], whom do they bless? Their brothers in the North, their brothers in the South, their brothers in the East, and their brothers in the West. And who replies: Amen [to the blessing]? The women and children."[22] If one category of people imparts a blessing, this required the presence of other categories to receive it, or to answer "Amen." The Talmud presents the relationship of priests to non-priests as paralleling that of men to women and adults to children. Applying this logic to the realm of Torah, it implies that men are the "officiants" and women the "recipients." With this pattern taking hold in antiquity, the democratization of Torah remained only partial.

The gendering of Torah, and of expressions of Torah like tefillin and the tallit, appeared in many spheres. Sometimes the world of Torah was imbued with meanings of male sexuality. In a nineteenth-century letter from Tripoli describing the education of boys, the depiction of a successful student uses a term meaning "demonstrating male potency."[23] A dream interpreter in Baghdad, at the same period, was approached by a man who reported that he had been dreaming that he had donned his head-tefillin on his arm and his arm-tefillin on his head. The rabbi-interpreter concluded that he had been having anal intercourse with his wife and told him to desist from the practice. The man acknowledged the rabbi's insight.[24] In North Africa, youngsters normally began to wear a tallit during prayer after their bar mitzvah, parallel to donning tefillin. It is a widespread custom in Ashkenaz, in contrast, that a tallit is worn only from the time of marriage. In some Sephardi settings, weddings do not take place under a canopy (ḥuppah), but the tallit worn by the groom is spread over the head of the bride. This is often explained by reference to the story of Ruth, in which Boaz "spread his wing" over her (Ruth 3:9), an image that may intimate sexuality.[25] These symbolic mechanisms may have strengthened the identification of men with Torah culture, but Jewish society paid the price of limiting the world of Torah to one gender.

ENTERING THE WORLD OF TORAH

We do not have in-depth knowledge of basic education in the biblical and rabbinical periods.[26] Nevertheless, Jews in the medieval period sought to make sense of their institutions in terms of their earlier sacred sources. One model that may have been before their eyes was that of biblical Samuel (1 Sam. 1), the conditions surrounding whose birth led his mother,

Hannah, to dedicate him to God. She brought young Samuel to the sanctuary in Shiloh that housed the tablets of the Sinai covenant to be trained by Eli, the priest. Samuel had been born to Hannah after years of barrenness, and in this, her story resembles that of the matriarch Sarah in giving birth to Isaac. Rabbinical tradition linked the two biblical episodes by providing that both be read on Rosh Hashanah, the New Year, or "the day the world was conceived."[27] As discussed in chapter 2 above, Abraham held a large feast when Isaac was weaned. I have argued that, contrary to some interpretations, this was not to be viewed as the celebratory feast—*seudat mitzvah*[28]—of Isaac's circumcision. A hint of the meaning of the feast may be found in the story of Samuel. The account mentions four times that his transfer to Shiloh took place only after Hannah weaned him.[29] Weaning, which took place when a boy was about two years old or even older, was a significant marker of a boy's step out of the circle of the family, represented by his mother, into a male framework of training and education.[30] The passage to schooling was an event marked by gender.

Arnold van Gennep, who formulated the concept of "rites of passage," argues that transition rituals relate mainly to social changes in an individual's situation, not to bodily changes.[31] Throughout the generations of Jewish history, the movement into the world of literacy and Torah was a major life-crossing. It was not unconnected, however, to biological realities. It was dependent on a boy's having attained some basic cognitive abilities and on his being toilet-trained, as well as entailing a move out of the home and away from the constant connection to his mother.[32]

Ivan Marcus has provided a detailed analysis of the ceremonies that introduced little boys to the study of Torah in medieval Ashkenaz.[33] His research not only helps us understand one ritual of childhood but provides a broad cultural perspective on Jewish life in the twelfth century. The sources he uses are both from the Rhineland, where the Yiddish language was formed, and from France, where Rashi founded his school and where the Tosaphist talmudic dialecticians resided.[34] In one case, an extant manuscript includes illuminations, which add a visual dimension to understanding the practices involved. While each source differs from the others in some details, taken together they contain a number of central elements: (1) carrying the child from his home to the synagogue; (2) the teacher's exposing the child to Hebrew letters, which he in some form ingests; (3) engaging in incantations intended to ward off forgetfulness; and (4) walking to the river from the synagogue. One basic difference between the French and German sources is that in France, the ceremony took place whenever a child reached the appropriate age, while in the Rhineland, it was prescribed for the festival of Shavuot (Pentecost).

Many elements of the ceremony recall older textual traditions in the Talmud or the Midrash. At the same time, the way that ritual acts and textual elements were combined in Ashkenaz reflects the immediate setting of Jewish life in medieval Europe. Marcus's analysis not only highlights the intricate web of internal references to other Jewish practices and texts but also shows how the ceremony has to be understood in relation to the Christian environment.[35]

An example of internal Jewish references is the link between the entering-school ceremony and the celebration of Shavuot. This ties a transition in the life of a specific child and his family to the broader community and to the wider Jewish world as well. The calendar transition from Passover to Shavuot corresponds to the period between the Israelites' leaving Egypt and their arrival at Mt. Sinai to receive the Torah. The child's beginning to learn the alphabet from his teacher is thus made parallel to Moses' initial transmission of the Torah to the Children of Israel.[36]

The linkage between Passover and Shavuot in the ceremony may fit into a pattern found in the Bible itself. Chapter 2 discussed the connection between circumcision and the festival of Passover, which, in biblical terms, opens the ritual year.[37] Just as circumcision carries with it notions of instruction in the family, and Passover—an occasion of family teaching—leads inevitably to Shavuot, so circumcision leads inexorably to the next stage of learning, entrance into school. Both circumcision and the festival of Shavuot are determined by counting a set number of days from a preceding event. The first occurs on the eighth day (7 + 1) after birth, and the second on the fiftieth day (7 × 7 + 1) after Passover.

Yet another feature of the ceremony builds upon biblical images. The account of the revelation at Sinai features both the people hearing God's voice and the creation of a written testimony on stone tablets of that revelation (Deut. 4:12–13). The Bible and later Jewish tradition stress that both the oral and the written are central channels of transmission. With regard to the poem at the end of Deuteronomy, Moses, facing his death, is commanded to "write ye this song for you, and teach it to the children of Israel; put it in their mouths" (Deut. 31:19). In a vision of Ezekiel, the two channels are merged; the prophet is commanded to eat a scroll on which is inscribed a divine message (Ezek. 3:1–3).[38] Ezekiel, in a passage that later resonated in the medieval ceremony analyzed by Marcus, finds the words to be "sweet as honey."

In medieval Ashkenaz, the child brought to the school for the first time was wrapped in a prayer shawl and sat on the lap of the teacher. In some cases, he licked a tablet on which Hebrew letters were written; in others, he ate honey cakes made in the shape of the letters (and in some instances, he did both). Ancient associations were brought together in these acts, relating to biblical verses that mention wheat, honey, and so forth. At the same time, the ceremony related to the challenges emanating from the Christian environment.

For example, two of the illuminated figures depicting the ceremony in the *Leipzig Maḥzor* are Jewish reworkings of the Madonna-and-child theme found throughout Christian art.[39] This comparison can be understood on the background of many textual illusions. In Numbers 11:12, Moses' care for the children of Israel is likened to a nursing figure carrying a young child in its breast. A midrash interprets the verse from the Song of Songs 4:5: "Your breasts are like two fawns" to mean Moses and Aaron transmitting the Torah. The teacher on whose lap the child sits is thereby imbued with motherly qualities and teaches Torah in the form of baby foods: milk and honey. The young male child imbibing Torah is pitted against the infant Jesus suckling at Mary's breast.[40]

The Christian Eucharist, already discussed with reference to Passover and circumcision, is another referent of the Jewish school ritual. In twelfth-century Latin Christendom, the idea that the Eucharist embodied Jesus as a child, and not only when he died as an adult, became increasingly prominent. The Eucharist thereby came to stand for a child sacrifice. Among the Jews, several lines of interpretation linked the study of young boys in school to the act of sacrifice.[41] Thus the Jewish ritual, in addition to the internal and external meanings already considered, also constituted an answer to the claim that it was the sacrifice of Jesus that saved the world. The pure young child studying Torah atoned for the community; reenactment of the ceremony carried the message that it was the study of Torah that saved, not faith in Jesus.

Returning to internal matters, the desire that a young boy master literacy and learn the Torah was accompanied by anxiety that he might forget what he had learned. This was an ancient concern with regard to the knowledge of adults, and there was a tradition of incantations to combat this danger. The rabbis were worried about Potaḥ, the prince of forgetfulness, and took steps to protect against him, including parts of the *havdalah* ritual at the end of the Sabbath. Just as demons threatened a child about to be circumcised, so entering school entailed dangers. The child ritual borrowed from adult traditions in other realms; thus, incantations to banish Potaḥ were written on an egg in the synagogue, or recited at the river bank.

A walk to the river with the teacher was the closing phase of the ceremony. In contrast to the move from home to synagogue, when he was carried, the child assumed a more grown-up status by going to the river on his own two feet. Reaching the river carried several meanings; one of them was the completion of the trek starting in "Egypt" that took the child through "Sinai" in the synagogue school. The walk to the river corresponded to the rest of the journey through the desert, bringing the Israelites to the banks of the Jordan River. The ceremony effected a passage for the individual and simultaneously provided an opportunity for the community to celebrate its historical sacred passages.

OTHER TORAH EDUCATION CEREMONIES

The Ashkenazi ceremonies of entrance into Torah study declined in the late Middle Ages. A new celebration, which came to be known as bar mitzvah, grew in prominence at that time. Yet, remnants of the child celebration persisted, both over time and through diffusion in space. Aspects of it are known both within the expanded Ashkenazi sphere and outside of it.

The feature of separation from the mother in order to further an ideal appears in Mark Zborowski's portrait of eastern European shtetl life at the beginning of the twentieth century: "The child cries, . . . but wrapped in the father's prayer shawl the boy is carried out of babyhood, out of the home circle. . . . And though the mother may weep, she would never oppose the commandment to teach Torah to a 'big boy who is already three years old.' "[42] The world the child enters, while sweetened with honey in his first encounter with it, is not an easy one. According to the poet Chaim Nachman Bialik, the hardest of substances cannot match up in toughness to a "A Jewish Child Engaged in Torah."[43] Parallel features have been described among Jews from Kurdistan in Jerusalem in the 1930s and 1940s: "When a boy comes to school for the first time, the teacher writes out for him the whole alphabet on a sheet of paper. He then smears honey on the letters, and tells the child to lick it." Then the following is said: "Oh Lord, just as honey is sweet, so may the Torah be sweet in the mouth of this boy." The same description also makes clear, however, through another saying, that entering school will not be easy; studying will not be "a picnic."[44]

We do not know if the practice of physically linking honey to the Torah diffused from Ashkenaz to Kurdistan, or whether they both reflect older Jewish customs and ideas. As ceremonies evolve and "travel," they sometimes lose elements and add new ones. At times, the addition of new elements may be stimulated by analogy with other ritual occasions. David Cohen describes a rite in Tunis in which very young boys were honored in a festive meal on the Thursday before they heard the reading of the Ten Commandments in Sabbath services for the first time.[45] He finds some parallels between this celebration and those in Ashkenaz on the eve of circumcision.[46]

A possible connection between circumcision and "entering Torah" ceremonies may be seen in some contemporary ritual developments among *haredi* (ultra-Orthodox) Jews in Israel, who customarily begin boys' education at the age of three. This entails up-to-date forms of the custom depicted for medieval Ashkenaz. Close to the same time, however, sometimes at a boy's third birthday, he goes through another ceremony in which his hair is cut for the first time. The cutting of hair as a component of beginning Torah study in the world of "men" was known in eastern Europe, but did not take place in an elaborate ritual context.[47] Today, there is a growing trend towards giving the first haircut on the festival of Lag ba-'Omer, thirty-three days after Passover, in Meron in the Galilee, where it forms part of the pilgrimage to the tomb of Rabbi Shim'on Bar Yohai (discussed in chapter 5), but it can take place near home as well on the same date. The haircutting ceremony is commonly known in Israel as *ḥalaqa*. The word is Arabic, and historically may have been adopted by Ashkenazi Jews in Palestine from local North African Jews with whom they were in contact.

Linguistic matters aside, the practice was also known in the Maghreb, where frequently a boy would be given his first haircut at the age of three near the tomb of a local sainted rabbi (*tzaddik*). The custom of cutting hair on this occasion may have been taken from North African bar mitzvah celebrations, where it often is a standard part of the ceremony (in Algeria, a visit to the "Turkish bath" was part of pre–bar mitzvah preparation as well).[48] At another level, one may see haircutting as paralleling circumcision.[49] Whether it correlates with entrance into the world of Torah or the creation of a symbolic relationship with a sainted rabbi, the cutting of hair, like circumcision, marks a critical passage in the Jewish development of the youngster.

Among Ashkenazi Jews, giving a boy his first haircut at the age of three may have been a custom that traveled from Palestine to eastern Europe, where it acquired a Yiddish name, *upsheren*. Most recently, the practice has taken root among some traditionalizing middle-class American Jews. What meaning the ceremony, which often had connotations of sexual differentiation, takes on in groups that champion gender equality is a matter worth exploring.

Along with symbolic links, there were concrete connections between the child's world of Torah education and other aspects of communal life. The children in synagogue schools in North Africa were taught to sing as well as to read and chant from sacred texts. They learned melodies for Hebrew liturgical poetry, composed in the Middle Ages, known as *piyyutim* (from the

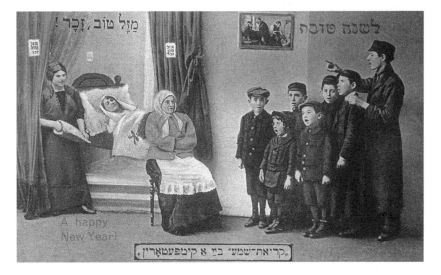

Figure 8.   Synagogue schoolchildren recite Shmaʿ Yisrael for the mother of a newborn boy. Polish postcard reproduced in New York in the early twentieth century. Courtesy Joseph Hoffman Jewish Postcard Collection, Folklore Research Center, Hebrew University, Jerusalem.

Greek *poiētēs*, which is also the root of the English word "poet"). In their musical version, these poems and hymns were known as *pizmonim*. On the basis of this training, children were summoned to life-cycle ceremonies to sing the appropriate hymns. The description of schoolchildren on the eve of circumcision celebrations in Tripoli, mentioned in chapter 2 above, is one example of this practice. In Tunis, the group was known as *ulad el-bayyut*, or "children of the piyyut."[50] This sort of arrangement took place in eastern Europe too (see figure 8), and schoolchildren both there and in North Africa would be called upon to play a role in funeral processions as well.[51] From the point of view of the young children, these occasions provided a break in the school routine, while their involvement was a vivid enactment of the cycle of life and the way Torah education was threaded through it.[52]

BAR MITZVAH

Some aspects of the medieval school rite, like licking honey off a slate with Hebrew letters, continued until the present era, while other features of it, such as the incantations against Potaḥ, disappeared. The invention of printing in the fifteenth century reduced the importance of memory in transmitting religious culture. More generally, developments beginning in the high Middle Ages and expanding thereafter, such as growth in urban life and in trade, engendered a sense of choice and the importance of consent in different spheres of life. Marcus argues that this led to parallel changes in the religious life of Jews and Christians. In the Christian world, there appeared opposition to placing children in monasteries at a very young age. Among European Jews, the notion began to be institutionalized that boys reach religious maturity, bearing responsibility for their own actions, only at the age of thirteen. This was the context for the development of the bar mitzvah ceremony.

The age of thirteen, with regard to boys, is mentioned in various forms of rabbinic literature as being an age of transition. At that age, for example, a boy is required to fast on the Day of Atonement.[53] In a midrashic passage, it is suggested that a person is punished for the sins of his children up until the age of thirteen.[54] Other notions of the age of maturity existed as well. Numbers counted males as adults in the census from the age of twenty upwards. In the Middle Ages, Maimonides, while recognizing the ages of thirteen for boys and twelve for girls for religious purposes, such as fasting on the Day of Atonement,[55] says that at thirteen, a boy is not old enough to understand and be a witness to transactions involving real estate.[56]

In the late Middle Ages, the various sources, some of which did not originally constitute halakhic rules, were consolidated into established norms. At this period in Europe, a debate arose over the age at which a male is both permitted and obligated to put on tefillin. A boy's thirteenth birthday came to mark a fixed boundary between childhood and religious majority. From the late fourteenth century on, there is evidence of a "bar mitzvah" ceremony. These developments were connected with the growing recognition of the special qualities we now take for granted as inherent to the special stage of life we call childhood, which meant that a child was no longer seen simply as a "miniature adult."[57] These trends in Europe may be contrasted with the situation elsewhere. In Yemen, "It was the aim of parents and children alike that the boy should become a man and that he should leave the state of ignorance as soon as possible."[58] This implies the absence of a concept like "adolescent," and in fact, in Yemen, no bar mitzvah ceremony evolved. The bar mitzvah did spread to North Africa, but often, until recently, was celebrated whenever a boy was capable of reading the prayers and blessings correctly.[59]

In the late sixteenth and early seventeenth centuries, the personal and communal elements we now associate with bar mitzvah coalesced into a pattern. This is seen most clearly in Italy.[60] The year before a boy's thirteenth birthday was devoted to special instruction. Not only was he expected to master the appropriate synagogue skills, but his teachers exhorted him as to the new moral and religious expectations he would face. The obligation to observe all the commandments was made public in his putting on tefillin. The question arose of whether it was appropriate to have a seúdat mitzvah, which celebrates the performance of a prescribed commandment, on these occasions.[61] This question continued to be considered in Morocco up through the twentieth century, but except for in Yemen, bar mitzvah celebrations everywhere became milestones in the lives of Jewish males and their families.[62] Bat mitzvah celebration was not to appear until the nineteenth century.

The term *bar mitzvah* means, "son of the commandments" (*bar* is the Aramaic word for son), or "falling into the category of being obligated by the commandments." Central among the commandments is the requirement to study Torah, and, as in the school-entering ritual, which it came to overshadow, the bar mitzvah ceremony highlights the link between the individual and the Torah. Typically a boy is called upon to recite the blessings over the reading of the Torah, or, in addition, to read from the Torah himself. Marking a bar mitzvah on a Sabbath frequently involves reading a section from the prophetic books of the Bible—the *haftara*—as well. Sometimes the boy presents a Torah lesson—a *derasha*. It is common for preachers to emphasize that a youngster should see the occasion as initiating further involvement in Torah, and not only as a sign of past achievements, while many teenagers today (and perhaps in the past?) feel that they are at last escaping from the burden of compulsory religious education.

The "bar mitzvah" concept, of course, took on various meanings in accordance with local situations and practices. In parts of North Africa, bar mitzvah implied that a boy would begin to work, as expressed in songs sung on that occasion. It might also be the occasion when males smoked their first cigarette. In the style of Orthodoxy represented by Habad Hasidim, it is often the time at which a young man begins to wear a black hat, characteristic of his group.[63]

The term *bar mitzvah* became common in Ashkenaz for the rituals and celebrations marking religious majority, while in many Sephardi communities, the term *tefillin* is prominent in designating those events. The lesson taught by the celebrant may be called *derashat tefillin*. In some Sephardi communities, the overall celebration has two phases. One is putting on the tefillin for the first time, which typically takes place on a Monday or a Thursday when the Torah is read in the synagogue; one does not don tefillin on Shabbat. After a youngster puts on a prayer shawl (with the appropriate blessing), he recites the blessing "Blessed are You . . . Who has commanded us to put on tefillin" and then tightens the "arm-tefillin" on his left arm (left-handed people do it on their right arm). Next, male members of the family may take turns at wrapping the strap around the boy's forearm, until the requisite seven wraps have been made. In everyday worship, the wrapping is done by the individual himself, followed by his putting on the head-tefillin. On the day of the initiatory donning of tefillin, which, in different regions may be called "wearing tefillin" or "the time of tefillin,"[64] the youngster will be called to recite blessings over the reading of the Torah for the first time (see figure 9).

The second phase of the overall Sephardi celebration is on Shabbat. Then, as mentioned, the boy may be called to read from the Torah, or from the Prophets, with the proper cantillation. The former task, in any community, is more challenging, because the Hebrew in a Torah scroll has no vowels and no written indication of the musical notes for each word. The prophetic texts are usually read from a printed book, in which vowel markings are inserted above and below the consonantal letters, as is musical notation (*te'amim*), demanding less memorization. The extent of the young boy's performance of these tasks (he might lead part of the prayer service as well) indicates the degree to which he has progressed in his education. At the end of the service, he is often encouraged to continue learning Torah and to follow the commandments to which he is now obligated.

The above features became widespread in the Jewish world, but variations continued to exist. The Jews of Shiraz, in Iran, refer to the occasion of putting on tefillin for the first time as *ben mitzvah* (also "son of the commandments," but in Hebrew rather than Aramaic), and are flexible about the age when this begins. The event was not marked by a celebration or party.[65]

The Jews of Cochin in southern India, who were far away from the major centers of Jewish life but had some contacts with the Sephardi world, structured the relation between these elements in a different manner.[66] A boy read his first haftara at the age of five or six. This probably reflects Hindu influence, because the number five represents the completion of a cycle in Hindu thought. It also fits in with a possibility provided in Sephardi tradition whereby a religious minor may read from the haftara in the synagogue, after the corresponding blessings over the Torah have been read by someone who has reached majority. At the age of thirteen, a boy in Cochin was called upon to read from the Torah scroll for the first time, as elsewhere in the Jewish world. This ceremony was not called bar mitzvah, but *bar minyan*. This meant that he would now be counted in a *minyan*, the quorum of ten adult males required to conduct public prayer. Both of

Figure 9. Postcard of a teacher showing a boy how to
put on tefillin before his bar mitzvah. Early-twentieth-
century New York. Courtesy Joseph Hoffman Jewish
Postcard Collection, Folklore Research Center, Hebrew
University, Jerusalem.

these occasions were times for celebration among the Jews of Cochin, but
the first celebration was much more elaborate than the second.[67]

THE TORAH AS A PERSON

Various customs we have considered, whether in relation to early education, participation in the life-cycle events of others, or the attainment of religious majority, weave the theme of Torah into the life courses of individuals. This process was intertwined with rituals that sometimes focused on

the Torah scroll itself. It is essentially the presence of a Torah scroll that turns a room or building into a synagogue. For ritual purposes, it is necessary to read from such a hand-written scroll, and in order to function smoothly, a synagogue needs several of them. Great care is exercised in the use and guarding of the scrolls. The symbolic and emotional investment of Jews in the sefer Torah has sometimes been so intense that often the Torah itself was envisioned as a person.

A Torah scroll, consisting of parchment rolled around two wooden poles (often called an 'eṣ ḥayyim—a tree of life), is always covered when it is not being read. In Ashkenaz and parts of the Sephardi world, a cloth coverlet (frequently made of velvet) is used, with two holes in the top, through which a protruding 'eṣ ḥayyim can be inserted. The "dressed" sefer Torah can be further embellished with silver ornaments. In some areas of the Sephardi realm, and particularly in Middle Eastern communities, a Torah scroll is typically referred to as "the *sefer*"—*the* book par excellence, and it is common for scroll and poles to be fitted into a round or octagonal wooden case, which opens in one direction, like a door. This case, too, can be further enhanced with kerchiefs draped upon it along with ornamentation reminiscent of a crown or of finials—*rimonim*—placed over the wooden poles (see figure 10).[68] Adding dress and ornaments to a sefer contributes to a perception of the Torah scroll as a person. Mystical literature from the Middle Ages compares the Torah to a "coquettish and seductive damsel," hidden in a palace, who only slowly reveals herself to a suitor on the outside.[69]

These mystical musings are not remote from human experience. A woman from Tripoli, in describing her early years when she did not leave her home until she was married, likened herself to a closeted sefer. Among my own childhood memories of synagogue life is an occasion upon which a scroll lay on the lectern after the Torah reading was finished, and there was a delay in moving on to the next stage of the service. A man born in eastern Europe motioned to me to stand next to the scroll, saying that where he had grown up, the Torah was never left alone. In Yemen, the mantle covering a Torah case was called a *guftan*, the term for standard male dress.[70] I have heard both young children and adults compare the dressed sefer Torah to a human persona. Some suggested male figures; others mentioned female figures, such as a bride or a queen.[71] While in traditional synagogue ritual, it is men who deal with taking the scroll from the "holy ark,"[72] the kerchiefs or coverings adorning the sefer are often contributed by, or embroidered by, women.[73]

There are many metaphorical expressions associating Torah, and the teaching of Torah, not only with individual human beings, but with the biological continuity both of the family and of the Jewish people. In both

Figure 10.   The "holy ark" in an Israeli synagogue,
with an open Sephardi Torah scroll flanked by
wrapped Ashkenazi scrolls. Photo Harvey E. Goldberg.

North Africa and eastern Europe, a childless couple, if they could mobilize
the means, might purchase a Torah scroll and make it available for the synagogue's use, hoping that it would bring them the blessing of offspring.[74]
In any event, the scroll, adorned with an inscription of their names, would
provide physical continuity, representing their lives after they had died. In
the medieval school ceremony described above, a child was wrapped in a
prayer shawl when carried to the synagogue, just as a Torah scroll is
wrapped when being carried from one place to another.[75] The same association appears in the custom of dancing with young children in one's arms, or
on one's shoulders, during the festival of Simhat Torah. That holiday celebrates the annual cycle of completing the reading of the Torah and begin-

ning it anew, and it is a widespread custom to dance in the synagogue while grasping the Torah scroll. Torah and children seem to be interchangeable in this setting. Symbolism along the same lines also appears in reworked forms. A common feature of bar and bat mitzvah ceremonies in Reform and some Conservative synagogues today is the "handing down" of the Torah. Just before or just after it is read, a Torah scroll is placed in the arms of the grandparents of the young person, who hand it to the celebrant's parents, who then hand it to the celebrant at the center of the occasion.

The parallels in ritual between the festival of Shavuʿot, when the Torah was given on Sinai, and the experience of young children entering school were discussed earlier. Another metaphor, elaborated in kabbala, and prominent in Sephardi tradition, treats Shavuʿot as a wedding. God is a bridegroom who, by giving the Torah, establishes a lasting relationship with his "bride," the people of Israel. In various versions of Sephardi liturgy, a piyyut is read on Shavuʿot, designated as the *ketubba*, or marriage contract, between God and Israel. The male-dominated setting of synagogue ritual thus absorbs imagery representing the receivers of the Torah as female. The versatility of symbolism also allows the Torah scroll "to mourn." In a synagogue in Istanbul, when the sefer is taken from the *heikhal* on the fast of Tishʿah be-Av, which commemorates the destruction of the Temple, it is placed on a chair and read, rather than being put on its normal raised table. Like the other members of the congregation, who sit on the floor on that sad day, the scroll "lowers itself" in an act of mourning. This vein of symbolism perhaps may be traced to ancient sources, for the Talmud compares a person breathing his last breath to a sefer Torah going up in flames (BT *Moʿed Qaṭan* 25a).

Beyond specific gender associations, a sefer Torah is often the ritual focus of the concerns of individual Jews. In the synagogue, when the sefer is taken from the *aron kodesh*, it is paraded through the congregation, giving worshipers a chance for personal contact with it. In traditional synagogue life, the proximate worshipers were male; women were in a separate section of the synagogue, which, in Europe, was sometimes a gallery above the main floor. In many North African synagogues, particularly in the smaller communities, there was no special space for women, but some of them would appear when the Torah was taken out of the heikhal, as described by Mordecaï Ha-Cohen: "Even though the women do not know how to pray, on Sabbaths and holidays a number of them stand at the entrance to the synagogue to look at the letters of the sefer Torah. When it is taken out [of the heikhal], they raise their palms upwards to pray for their well-being and that of their families. On the festivals, the women cry out [ululate] joyously in honor of the sefer Torah: ru-ru-ru-ru-ru."[76]

The desire of Jewish women to be close to the Torah is widespread. The gesture of women raising their palms towards the Torah is part of many traditions, for example in the Sephardi community in Turkey. It is also a common custom to pull back the curtain of a *meḥitza*, the synagogue divider separating men from women, during the reading of the Torah. This is not only for greater ease in hearing its contents, but a matter of physical contiguity. In some innovative Orthodox communities today, a sefer Torah, when taken from the aron kodesh, is paraded through the men's section and then passed on to a woman to carry through the women's section before it is brought to the lectern from which it is read. In synagogues where men and women are not separated, everyone has a chance to kiss the Torah in procession, either directly or with the touch of the hand, a prayer book, or a prayer shawl.

Beyond these various gestures of contact, it is universal practice that when the Torah is out of its cabinet, and among the congregation, prayers are said for individuals and their families, as in the case of the mi she-berakh ("He who has blessed . . . ") prayer recited after childbirth for the health of the mother and child. It is also standard to bless a person who has recovered from an illness or escaped danger. The individual in question is called to the Torah to recite the blessings when it is read, and then to recite the *ha-gomel* ("Who acts beneficently . . . ") blessing. However, an individual prayer can be said for any person, whether in need or because he or she is celebrating a happy life event. The recitation of a mi she-berakh in this setting connects the highly personal concerns of individuals to an existing community, and does so in the physical presence of the all-embracing symbol of God's relationship to the Jewish people—the Torah. While not normally expressed, there probably always have been sentiments that the concrete closeness of the Torah contributes to the efficacy of the blessing.

In the grammar of human cultures, it is common that a person or an object possessing the power to bless also has the power to curse. In Renaissance Italy, when the sefer was out of the ark, women took the opportunity to utter maledictions against their enemies. Opposition to this practice by community leaders has preserved it in the historical record.[77] This "logic" is not only the lot of women, or those with little exposure to formal Torah training. The same thought occurred to a young man in the twentieth century who was on his way to being a learned Talmud scholar.[78]

The notion suggesting that the physical presence of the Torah creates a "channel" through which the prayers of individuals reach On High has a hoary precedent. It is made explicit in a passage of the Zohar that it recommends be recited when taking the Torah from the heikhal.[79] The recommendation eventually led to inclusion of this passage in the liturgy.[80] The first wish of the prayer is: "May Thy good will ever abide with Thy people Israel," and then it asks: "May it be Thy will to prolong our life in happiness." A few lines later, the prayer stresses the unmediated connection between the worshiper and God: "I am the servant of the Holy One, blessed be He, before whom and before whose glorious Torah I bow at all times."[81] This form of obeisance is contrasted with another: "Not in man do I put my trust, nor do I rely on any angel, but only in the God of heaven who is the God of truth." Some scholars understand the word "angel," a translation of the Aramaic *bar elohim,* but which may also be rendered "son of God,"[82] to be a polemical allusion opposing the belief in Jesus. But in addition to matters of belief, the Zohar, a product of late thirteenth-century Spain, may also be distancing itself from the adoration of saints' images as "intermediaries" between the individual and the Almighty. Instead, the sefer, as an embodiment of Divine power, takes on anthropomorphic qualities and becomes the focus of intimate prayers. Its presence is available to both women and men, and to the barely educated along with the learned. In this manner, a tangible expression of "accessibility to all" is woven into the otherwise religiously stratified synagogue service.[83]

TORAH AND WOMEN

The section from the Zohar just cited also provides an entry into the topic of Torah and women. Its last sentence, as it appears in Ashkenazi prayer books, beseeches: "May it be Thy will to open my heart to Thy Torah" and concludes by asking God to "fulfill the wishes of my heart and of the heart of all thy people." Many Sephardi prayer books include a request in parentheses between the two parts of the sentence asking that "You give me sons who shall carry out Your will."[84] That parenthetical statement is found in the original Zohar passage, which explicitly uses the expression "male children" (*bnin dikhrin*).

The preference for males is linked to ancient attitudes that exclude women from the sphere of Torah. This exclusion has been extensive, but never total.[85] The Mishna, in the tractate Soṭah (3:4), states two views, one (of Ben Azzai) that a man must teach his daughter Torah, and another (of Rabbi Eliʿezer) that "he who teaches his daughter Torah teaches her lasciviousness." Modern critics of traditional attitudes often quote the latter passage, along with a statement from the Jerusalem Talmud in relation to the Mishna: "better burn the words of Torah than give them to a woman."[86] The discussion in the Mishna refers to a woman who, suspected by her husband of adultery (a *soṭah*), must submit to an ordeal of drinking "bitter waters."[87] The one-sidedness of the biblical rule notwithstanding (men suspected of adultery are not submitted to an ordeal), there are attempts to "rescue" these statements, showing that they are not as misogynist as they appear to be. Regarding the Mishna, Blu Greenberg explains that it refers to the possible merit a sotah may have that would warrant postponing punishment. She adds: "Very few rabbinic statements have been taken so far afield from their context."[88] Daniel Boyarin discusses the positive opinion of Ben Azzai and analyzes the differential treatment of the latter's view in the Jerusalem and Babylonian Talmuds.[89] Even recognizing contextual factors, and testimony to the contrary, we are left with the conclusion that the assumption throughout most of Jewish history has been that the world of Torah is basically one of males.[90]

The exclusion of women from the study of Torah did not mean they were detached from the values surrounding it. Women were eager to have their menfolk engage in study, and the success of their husbands, brothers, sons, or sons-in-law in this realm redounded to their communal standing. From the medieval material in the Cairo Geniza, S. D. Goitein records: "A married woman, together with her mother, once bought for her brother the highly estimated (and highly paid for) honor of reciting the book of Esther during the service."[91] In medieval Ashkenaz, women sewed together the parchment leaves of a Torah scroll.[92] We have already noted women's roles in connection with circumcision. In many different Jewish communities, mothers or grandmothers embroidered the cloth bags or cases in which a youngster carried his prayer shawl after attaining the age of bar mitzvah. It was also the task of kinswomen, in preparing a boy for a bar mitzvah in North African communities, to dress him in the clothes that would mark him as a man as he set off for the synagogue on the day he was to read the Torah.[93] Men in those societies recognized the import of women sharing the value of Torah. Those who came from rural areas of North Africa, many of whom were away from home for long periods of time as peddlers and craftsmen, recall the significance of mothers in developing correct attitudes towards synagogue education among their sons.

Pushing boys to the study of Torah could even begin in the cradle. "Teira is der besta skheira" ("Torah is the best merchandise") ran a Yiddish saying in eastern Europe, intimating that it was better to grow up as a scholar than a merchant. Somewhat ironically, this phrase appeared in lullabies in that region about a century ago, often when a father had sailed to America to set himself up economically before bringing over his wife and young children. Mothers in eastern Europe sometimes conveyed more than attitudes. "As soon as the baby starts to talk," write the ethnographers of traditional Polish Jewry, "his mother teaches him religious blessings and sometimes a few simple Hebrew words."[94] In that setting, a mother might have known the Hebrew blessings only orally, or she herself might have had some education in reading Hebrew-Yiddish script.

Women may not have learned to read and write Hebrew, but the languages they spoke were suffused with Torah-based culture. The common reference to Yiddish as *mamma loshen*—mother tongue—suggests a simplified contrast: Hebrew and Torah being associated with men, and the local language with women. Yiddish, however, became a vehicle through which women became familiar with Jewish tradition. The invention of printing encouraged the publication of works in various genres, including materials that might not in an earlier period have been considered "serious" enough to put in permanent written form in Hebrew. One such publication was the Yiddish book *Tzena U-re'ena*, by Jacob Ashkenazi in Kraków in 1620, first aimed at men with little Torah education. It consisted of homilies and midrashim organized on the basis of the weekly Torah readings and quickly became popular reading among women. This shows that many women could read Yiddish, reflecting education received at home. Others listened to the content of the book at times like Shabbat afternoons, even when they could not read themselves.

Another genre of literature, books of *tkhines*, supplicatory prayers in Yiddish, to be recited by women on various occasions, appeared at this time. Chava Weissler has used these books to understand the religious life of Ashkenazi women.[95] Some prayers are related either to the home, to be said on occasions like family meals, or to reproduction, such as a prayer for children or specifically for a son. Others were appropriate to the religious activities of women, such as seeking the intercession of relatives buried in the cemetery. Still other prayers concerned the synagogue and were keyed to liturgical moments, such as taking the Torah from the ark or the sounding of the shofar on the coming of the New Year. For the most part, these books were composed by men. At times, however, they may be read as challenges to the standard place of women, as in the prayer that likens a woman lighting Sabbath candles to the biblical high priest.[96] The daring implied in that image may be contrasted with another candle-lighting supplication, from a set of tkhines translated into English, which requests: "And this household should be a God-pleasing one, the consecration of real womanly virtue of peace and harmless innocence in order that it may serve the man as reposing shelter, as refuge where he snugly reposes after his toilsome daywork."[97]

Another challenge appears in the image of women in Paradise studying Torah, which they were normally barred from doing during their lives on earth.[98] Tkhines dating from eastern Europe in the eighteenth and nineteenth centuries were sometimes written by women themselves. As a class, these later supplicatory prayers show greater interest in communal affairs and are less concerned with the special ritual life of women.[99] This may be linked to a growing frustration on the part of women as to their inability to participate actively in the life of Torah, even though we have few direct expressions of that frustration.[100]

Other vernacular Jewish languages, in oral as well as written forms, have been conduits of contact between women and formal religion. In the course of the eighteenth century rabbis created literature in Judeo-Spanish directed to a non-learned audience that eventually included women.[101] Another example is from the realm of oral literature: a series of twenty-two proverbs in Judeo-Spanish, transmitted from one woman to another within a Jerusalem Sephardi family, in which the link between the popular and learned, or literate, realms exists on two levels.[102] Most basically, a form of oral literature is organized according to written norms: the order of the Hebrew alphabet. Second, the contents of the proverbs recall the oldest alphabet-based collection of proverbs in the biblical book of Proverbs (Mishlei), in the chapter that praises a "woman of valor."[103] This is not an esoteric reference, because, after the sixteenth century, the custom developed of reciting in the home from that chapter at the beginning of the Sabbath Eve meal.[104] The existence of separate religious spheres of men and women often entails a linkage between them.

Parallels to the situations described for Yiddish-speaking and Judezmo-speaking areas also existed in Arabic-speaking regions. In Tunisia, where the religious life of women had been a matter of oral tradition, the introduction of Hebrew printing presses led to the flourishing of Judeo-Arabic literature (Arabic written with Hebrew letters) in the nineteenth century.[105] As a result of publication, many aspects of rabbinic tradition became familiar to Jewish women throughout North Africa. Knowledge of tradition reached them, not from reading religious classics in Hebrew, but from hearing Judeo-Arabic literature read aloud on various social occasions.[106]

Our discussion has assumed that women rarely were bearers of Judaism's literary tradition, but, as already noted, there were exceptions to the rule. Tradition celebrates women such as Beruriah, the wife of the second-century sage Rabbi Meir, and the daughter of the medieval scholar Rashi, but the historicity of these claims is far from clear.[107] Documents from the Cairo Geniza present a case in which Maimonides was asked to consider whether a woman might be permitted to teach boys Torah in a school.[108] Another example, which calls for more research on the topic, is a Hebrew poem from medieval Spain by the wife of Dunash ibn Labrat.[109] The ability to assess the participation of women in a written culture is often limited, but women's access to Torah has been a possibility within Jewish culture.[110] In early modern Italy, women were sometimes Bible teachers to young boys, and some girls also acquired basic education in Hebrew, but usually in the form of private instruction in the homes of their families or in those of female instructors.[111]

Before modern times, regular education for girls was an isolated phenomenon. The well-to-do would bring in tutors to teach their sons, and sometimes their daughters, but providing a basic education as the right of every family and child is a recent phenomenon. Looking back at the society emerging from the documents in the Cairo Geniza, Goitein concluded: "The educational gap between male and female was the ultimate source and manifestation of the repression of womanhood in civilized societies."[112] It was only in the nineteenth century that the ancient inequality in which men were expected to be educated, while women were only occasionally tutored, was fundamentally undermined.

JEWISH WOMEN AND MODERN EDUCATION

One feature of modern societies is the ideal of universal elementary education, for girls as well as boys and for all social classes. Its appearance affected Jewish communities in different ways, some of them paradoxical and contradictory. In the course of the nineteenth century, Jews were incorporated as citizens in various western and central European states and thereby entitled and expected to receive a basic education along with all children of the country. This expectation extended to girls as well as to boys. One implication of the new trend was that the study of the Hebrew alphabet, language, and traditional texts became an aspect of private education, provided by families or by schools attended voluntarily in the framework of synagogue life. It still was common for boys to learn to pray and to be trained to recite the blessings and read the haftara at the age of bar mitzvah, but there was often tension between the "modern" studies in state schools, or in Jewish schools organized by the community with state supervision, and religious education, which preserved traits of earlier forms of pedagogy. This new situation also did little, at first, to challenge the existing assumption that Torah education for girls could be ignored. Attitudes like these persisted in North Africa as well, where the Paris-based Alliance Israélite Universelle provided European-style education for many youngsters beginning in the 1860s.[113] One of the "battles" fought by Alliance teachers was against parents who took girls out of school when they approached puberty and were eligible for engagement and marriage.

One major expression of the fragmentation of the Jewish world during the nineteenth century was the existence of competing educational ideals and institutions. In some cases, there was outright resistance to modern education by Orthodox religious leaders. In some eastern European locales, this produced the paradox that girls received a modern education, while boys, being religiously more highly valued, were "protected" from it. This "Orthodoxy" was basically a European phenomenon, but disjunctions were found everywhere. In Tripoli, daughters of middle-class families were enrolled in Italian schools from the end of the nineteenth century on, and efforts were made to teach them productive crafts, but no thought was given to schooling them in Judaism. The first time that women in that city studied the Hebrew language was in the 1930s, in the context of a fledgling organization called Ben Yehudah, inspired by ideals of Zionism and the revival of Hebrew.[114]

Eventually, it became clear, even within the Orthodox world, that some degree of exposure to and control over modern education was imperative. There thus emerged modern forms of Orthodox education, including some Torah education for girls. An innovator in this field was Rabbi Samson Raphael Hirsch in Germany (1808–88), whose approach to education tried to combine Jewish and general culture, touting a phrase from the Mishna that advocates the linking of Torah and *derekh eretz,* "the way of the land."[115] By the first part of the twentieth century, leaders of Orthodoxy in eastern Europe could not avoid dealing with the issue of girls' schooling. One source of concern was that the lack of education for women restricted the pool of potential brides for the emerging class of male yeshiva students.[116]

The most vigorous response to the general issue was led by Sarah Schenirer, who, alluding to the midrash cited above with regard to Mt. Sinai, established the network of Beis Yaåkov (House of Jacob) schools at the end of World War I.[117] Her efforts received ideological legitimation from an outstanding haredi leader, the "Hafetz Haim" who boldly stated: "Now, because of our many sins, the tradition of the fathers has been greatly weakened. . . . It is surely a great mitzvah to teach [girls] the Ḥumash and also the Prophets and the Holy Writings and the Ethics of the Rabbis."[118] Although this statement represented a dramatic innovation in eastern European Orthodox views, it also differentiates between the education appropriate to women and men.

The door to the study of Torah was opened for women, but they were not expected or allowed to study Talmud, the pinnacle of Torah study. Blu Greenberg depicts the following situation among Orthodox Jews in New York City in the 1950s: "Beginning with elementary school, the girls studied Israeli folk dancing while the boys studied Talmud. In the yeshiva high school, the girls' branch had no course of study in Talmud; the boys' branch had three hours a day. In Israel, in the Jewish studies seminar, all of the classes were coeducational except Talmud."[119] The issues of what aspects of Torah should be accessible to women, and in what manner the content of Torah is studied, are alive in many Orthodox groups today. For example, there is a debate as to whether women students should be exposed to the entire text or merely selected portions of it.[120] In some contemporary groups, the limitations defining appropriate study for women are continually being tested. If they study Talmud at all, women still typically do so in the context of separate education, but various new forms of study have emerged. In some circles, frameworks for women studying Torah have served to introduce new strains of discourse into Orthodox life. These may integrate insights from literature, psychology, or feminist theory into Torah texts.

NEW RITUALS OF EDUCATION: CONFIRMATION AND BAT MITZVAH

In the Jewish world generally, the challenges of modern education brought about changes both in religious training and in the accompanying rituals of boys and girls. Where emancipation was under way, it began to be felt that traditional bar mitzvah training, focused on the Hebrew text, was becoming mechanical, with little meaning for the participants. This led to the creation in Germany of the confirmation ceremony, originally a kind of complement to the bar mitzvah, celebrated by individual families for their sons, either at home or at school. Aspects of confirmation were directly copied from Christian models. A boy was presented with questions concerning Jewish faith and behavior, and he demonstrated his ability to answer before adult witnesses. This took place in the vernacular language, German, and indicated that a youngster was moving into Jewish adulthood on the basis of understanding and consciousness. Confirmation was first instituted in 1803. One early confirmand, in 1807, was Leopold Zunz, who later was a founder of the Wissenschaft des Judenthums movement, which created the modern historical study of Judaism.[121]

As a new form based on intentional innovation, confirmation ceremonies evolved rapidly in the first half of the nineteenth century and spread both to other parts of western Europe and to the United States. Classes were organized to prepare youngsters for confirmation, which included girls as well as boys. The ceremonies were shifted to the synagogue, so that whole classes were confirmed at the same time. Later, the festival of Shavuòt was selected as the appropriate time for confirmation, drawing upon the ancient understanding of Shavuòt as the time of the "giving of the Torah." Another old custom, the origins of which are obscure, involved decorating synagogues with greenery on Shavuòt.[122] This popular practice was retained, and it became common to adorn confirmation ceremonies with esthetic floral arrangements.

In many ways, confirmation ritual closely paralleled the nineteenth-century process of reforming synagogue ritual, making it more "decorous" and modeling it upon contemporary Christian sensibilities regarding behavior in a house of worship. The introduction of choral singing was one aspect of these changes and became common in confirmations. Christian influence on this new ritual was obvious and consciously understood, but with time, confirmation developed its own dynamics and absorbed some aspects of time-honored synagogue life. It thus was adopted by some traditional rabbis, who recognized the needs it addressed, so long as it did not include practices in direct contravention of accepted ritual rules. In the United States, in the twentieth century, confirmation was espoused by many Conservative synagogues. Both they and Reform congregations tended to raise the age of confirmation to fifteen or sixteen, clearly separating it from bar mitzvah and making it parallel to a later phase in the development of young people, in which they became more fully aware of the range of life choices confronting them.

Some changes were not explicitly ideological but evolved gradually as the assumption that girls and boys should have the same education came to be taken for granted. In America, social mobility and the move to the suburbs after World War II led to the creation of "afternoon" and Sunday schools connected to synagogues and Jewish centers.[123] At this period, the number of Conservative congregations expanded significantly. The education provided in their schools stemmed from traditional conceptions of learning to read Hebrew (they were typically called "Hebrew schools"), gaining familiarity with parts of the prayer book, and the ability to recite blessings when called to the reading of the Torah. Boys and girls took part in these classes side by side, and both gained an introduction to synagogue skills in "junior congregations" within this educational constellation.

One goal of this education was a successful bar mitzvah ceremony at the age of thirteen, in which a "bar mitzvah boy" was called to the Torah on a Sabbath and also recited the haftara, for which he was specifically trained for close to a year prior to the event. Many congregations also had bat mitzvah celebrations for girls. These shared some features of bar mitzvahs, but also were distinct from them. It was common for a bat mitzvah ceremony to take place on a Friday night. Girls recited the blessings over the Sabbath candles and recited the haftara portion of the week. That reading, however, was not part of a full Torah reading as on Saturday mornings when boys were "bar mitzvah-ed."[124]

We do not have a social history of the notion and forms of bat mitzvah celebration. Articles in encyclopedias cite celebrations in France and Italy early in the nineteenth century and innovations associated with reform in Germany later in the century.[125] In eastern Europe, a synagogue celebration involving a young girl in Lemberg in 1902 led to demonstrations and debates in the press.[126] In nineteenth-century Baghdad, Rabbi Yosef Hayyim recommended that when a girl reached the age of *mitzvot* (when she should keep the commandments), the occasion be marked in her home by donning a new set of clothes, justifying her recitation of the she-heheyanu blessing. The context of his innovation is not known. Rabbi Hayyim might have been addressing traditional sectors of Baghdad Jewry or, as he himself was from a wealthy family, he might have been stimulated by European influences on Baghdadi merchants with extensive international experience.[127] A contemporary of his in Alexandria, Rabbi Eliahu Hazzan, is mentioned as having organized a bat mitzvah celebration in a synagogue early in the twentieth century, although no further information is provided.[128] Later in the century, bat mitzvah rituals took place in Italy, although the description available from one small town does not make clear details of the event.[129] The celebration took place on Shavuot, which may have been reserved for (all) girls reaching twelve in a given year, rather than taking place at the time of an individual birthday, which was standard for a boy's bar mitzvah.[130] Within American Judaism, the bat mitzvah celebrated in the early 1920s by Judith, the daughter of Rabbi Mordecai Kaplan, is often cited as a precedent. When bat mitzvah became standard in the United States at mid twentieth century, it developed in a setting in which the Jewish education of boys and girls was basically the same.

An aspect of that educational effort was summer camps. Informal educational frameworks were part of Hirsch's program in the nineteenth century, and camps became common in Jewish life in twentieth-century America.[131] A recent museum exhibition suggests the centrality of that experience.[132] While camps were often set up under the auspices of organizations with defined orientations and ideologies, the concentration of young people, consisting of both campers and their counselors, separated from the immediate supervision of elders, provided a field for experimentation with new ideas and practices. In a Ramah camp, associated with the Conservative movement, there was at least one instance in the 1950s in which a girl read the haftara as part of a Torah service while a boy recited the blessings. This took place in the presence of an eminent talmudic scholar.[133] The *havura* movement in the late 1960s through the mid 1970s, which stressed the equality of men and women in ritual roles, gave expression to educational and social trends that, for a considerable time, had been gathering momentum off center stage.[134]

Eventually, the idea of a bat mitzvah moved into Orthodox circles, taking several forms. Among many Orthodox Jews, it has been common for a while for a young woman who has reached the age of twelve to have a bat mitzvah celebration at home, not as part of synagogue service. During the event, she demonstrates her abilities by giving a *dvar torah* (talk based on Torah learning). Most recently, some Orthodox Jews committed to ideals of equality have begun to organize prayer quorums (*minyanim*) made up only of women, which include a Torah service during which the bat mitzvah celebrant reads from the Torah or recites the blessings while it is read by another woman. In some avant-garde settings, these all-women services take place in a synagogue while men are present sitting on the other side of the divider that separates the genders in the prayer hall. The notion of bat mitzvah has entered some segments of the haredi world as well. Many Beis Yaakov schools have a special breakfast, to which mothers are invited, for a class in which the students have reached the age of mitzvot.[135]

ADULT STUDY AND RITUALS

Jewish tradition conceives the commandment to study Torah as incumbent upon adults throughout life. Brief selections from the Bible and rabbinical literature have been included at the beginning of the daily liturgy to encourage the keeping of this commandment, even if at the level of perfunctory reading. Another way this has been expressed is in the set of books known as Ḥoq le-Yisrael, a collation of texts from the Bible, rabbinic literature, and the Zohar, organized in accordance with the weekly Torah reading.[136] The book was used not only in Europe but in North Africa, where a section was read each morning after prayers. A different setting of adult study was found in voluntary groups that got together to read from a given sacred book, which also constituted mutual aid societies to cover burial costs and to ensure proper ritual treatment when any member of the group died. This social function of study was critical before the emergence of systems of national insurance. Transformations of this institution emerged in the twentieth century, for example among retired people in Miami Beach who got together both to study and as investment groups.

Study and a concern for the future, both in "this world" and "the next world," appears in other forms. When a group of ten studying adults finishes a session, it is proper to recite the "scholars' kaddish." This "kaddish" differs slightly from the better-known "mourners' kaddish." Included in it is a prayer for "Israel [the Jewish people] . . . the rabbis . . . their disciples . . . the disciples of their disciples . . . and all who engage in the study of Torah in this place and in any other place." The repetition of words and the drawn-out formula in this version of the kaddish contribute to the sense of extended continuity in time, as well as in space. The kaddish, in fact, contains no reference to those who have died. It was first associated with the conclusion of Torah study and only later became linked to mourning and memorialization.[137]

Jewish communities have generated a variety of adult groups that set aside time to meet the religious requirement of continued study. Samuel Heilman has provided ethnographic portraits of some contemporary study groups, both in the eastern United States and in Jerusalem.[138] He calls these groups *khevruse*, a Yiddish-based term deriving from the same stem as the Hebrew word *ḥaver*, which carries connotations of general sociality.[139] These groups meet once a week to study Talmud. Heilman analyzes processes within the groups in addition to the acquisition of talmudic knowledge. These include not only cultural performances that express and teach social and religious norms, but the enjoyment of fellowship and play. The use of language is especially interesting in these groups, for much talmudic literature is in Aramaic rendered in Hebrew characters. The shift back and forth between talmudic Aramaic and the vernacular of the participants, whether it be American English or contemporary spoken Hebrew, is evidence of the interpenetration of worlds, using the Talmud to comment on today's realities and thereby continually reinvesting the ancient text with new meanings.[140] As much as these are sessions of intellectual mastery, they are also ritual dramas that influence the social and religious lives of the participants.

In addition to the ritual processes inherent in the weekly sessions, life in khevruses is periodically marked by a special celebration known as a *siyyum*. A siyyum is called for when a scribe finishes the long and exacting task of writing a sefer Torah, and also when a person, or a group, finishes studying a tractate of the Talmud. While the word *siyyum* means "to bring to an end," one feature of these celebrations is that they often include a formalized beginning of the study of a new tractate, or other book of Torah literature. As explained to the anthropologist Barbara Myerhoff in Venice, California, in the 1970s: "Your study doesn't ever finish, it goes around again in a circle, as long as you are living."[141] A siyyum has the same structure as the festival of Simhat Torah, which takes place on the last day of Sukkot. On Simhat Torah, the last section of the Humash (Deut. 33–34) is read, but the Torah service also includes opening up a second sefer and reading from the beginning of Genesis. Simhat Torah means "Joy in the Torah," and the Yiddish term *simkhe* (derived from the Hebrew word for joy) refers to a festive family occasion such as a bar mitzvah or wedding. The term *simkhe* is applied to one of the siyyums recorded by Heilman, showing the interweaving of the cycle of study with the flow of individual lives.[142]

If even a single individual finishes studying a talmudic tractate, it is a matter for general rejoicing. This is seen in a celebration that takes place the morning before Passover begins, that is, the morning preceding the Passover *seder.* Jewish tradition prescribes that firstborn males fast on that day, commemorating the fact that "they" were spared while the firstborns of the Egyptians were smitten by God. There is a way out of the requirement to fast, however. One may avoid this burden by partaking of a seudat mitzvah. Once having done so, one need not continue one's fast. A siyyum is an occasion for a seudat mitzvah.[143] It therefore became customary in many synagogues for one individual, the rabbi or another learned person, to finish studying a tractate of the Talmud on the morning of the fifteenth day of Nisan. This is done upon concluding the morning prayers, attended by many men who are firstborns. One individual's study cycle thus touches upon a collection of firstborn males and, indirectly, on the families to which each of them belongs.

The khevruses studied by Heilman all represent different forms of Orthodoxy. In each, "learning" was a male activity. In one case, a decision to meet in a synagogue, rather than rotate among different homes, seems to have provided a "refuge from daily domestic struggle."[144] Women were incorporated into these groups when they reached the time for a siyyum; it was taken for granted that they shared in the joy of the occasion, and also that they would prepare refreshments. These are matters that now are in continual flux. A few years ago, I was invited to a study group in an East Coast American city in which the tone was set by Orthodox participants, but there were also members of the group with Conservative orientations. Women participated actively in the study session, but during the break for Saturday afternoon prayer, gender separation was the norm. There are also those who oppose new trends. In the politically organized haredi world of Israel, the opposition to including women in Torah-related activities along with men is still strong. This includes the attempt to prevent woman reporters from covering a mass rally celebrating the siyyum of a multi-year cycle of Torah study.[145]

Changing patterns of study bear implications for the nature of religious authority, and the link between the acquisition of knowledge and the exercise of authority is not simple.[146] The more people know, the more they may exercise individual judgment in the realm of religion, as in other realms of life. From another perspective, Jewish culture has emphasized *Torah li-shmah*, the study of Torah for its own sake, without any reward or application. This orientation can dilute the connection between learning and binding religious obligations.[147] Thus one response of Torah scholars in modern times has been to separate themselves from the realm of halakhic decision-making and the establishment of new norms.[148] It also has been a trend of the postemancipation era, in which Jews are free to fashion their own style of religious life, that rabbis in congregations function more as teachers and providers of sermons, than as deciders in matters of religious law.[149]

One expression of the changing relationships among study, religious authority, and the role of rabbi has been the ordination of women in Reform and Conservative Judaism. This trend, which has now become established, reflects ideas that were raised and debated throughout the twentieth century.[150] Recently, the case of the ordination of Regina Jonas, in Germany in 1935, has come to light.[151] The institution in which she studied was not prepared to take the innovative step at the time, but an individual rabbi and instructor in the school was prepared to pass on to her the authority of a rabbi. Her certificate of *semikha* (ordination) was later signed by Leo Baeck, a leading figure in Reform Judaism, in 1942. While Orthodox streams in Judaism have not found ways to ordain women, the growing access to Torah knowledge among women in contemporary Orthodox circles also challenges accepted forms of rabbinic authority.

Along with changing notions and practice of what constitutes rabbinic leadership, the regular study of Jewish sources by laypeople figures in many forms of religious expression today. Riv-Ellen Prell depicts classes organized by a West Coast group that prayed together.[152] The group was one expression of the havura movement, which first emerged in the late 1960s.[153] The word *havura* is linguistically parallel to *khevruse*; both suggest the fellowship aspect of prayer and study. Study was also central to some members of a gay and lesbian synagogue in New York City.[154] The widespread availability of Judaica in English, including translations of classics, as well as the contributions of recent authors, feeds into the whole range of modern-day commitments to Jewish tradition.

The manner in which traditional texts are studied and related to is sometimes an indicator of personal identity in adulthood. Stuart Schoenfeld discusses the case of a 24-year-old woman in North America who had not had a bat mitzvah at the age of twelve, and who remembered saying at the time, "Thank God I was born a woman" and rejoicing that she did not have to "go through the agony of learning for the bar mitzvah."[155] In college, however, friends who were non-Jewish and who were interested in spiritual matters questioned her about her religious identity. "I couldn't answer their questions, and that really bothered me because I was known by many of my Jewish and non-Jewish friends as being very strongly Jewish." This woman, Miriam, joined a "Jewish spiritual development group." One of their activities was to role-play biblical characters. This led her to decide to celebrate a bat mitzvah. Through friends, she learned to chant the haftara for the weekly Torah reading and prepared to deliver a talk on the occasion. The weekly reading happened to feature her biblical namesake— who was Moses' sister. While drawing on older patterns, Miriam put these elements into a special configuration appropriate to her situation. Schoenfeld sees this as typical of modern forms of religiosity that celebrate individuality and the uniqueness of the personality. At the same time, this uniqueness appears in a recognizable configuration. In addition to ancient Jewish writings, modern texts such as *The Jewish Catalogue* and journals such as *Shma*, *Moment*, and *Lilith* contribute to such patterning.[156] Within all these recent developments, maintaining a Jewish identity combines the ancient nexus of ritual and study.

The theme of study has received some attention in Israel in recent years among those worried about the sharp distinction between religious and nonreligious Jews.[157] Among both those who see themselves as "religious" and those who declare themselves to be "secular," some view the issue as critical for the society as a whole. In addition, a growing number of secular Israelis are concerned about the gap opening up between them and the textual sources of their historic culture. The topic is discussed in terms of the monopoly on Jewish tradition enjoyed by "the religious" in Israel. Opposition to a monopoly is also echoed by the small numbers identified with the Reform and Conservative movements, known respectively as "Progressive" and "Traditional" Judaism in the Israeli context. These concerns have led to some small-scale, but at times highly intense, efforts to resuscitate familiarity with classic texts among nonreligious Israelis, even as there are disagreements as to how to understand them and as to their implications for behavior in today's world.

These efforts appear in various formulations and have taken on different organizational forms. Some educators speak of having all Israelis gain acquaintance with the basic "Hebrew bookshelf." The notion is that everyone should be familiar with the classic sources (and Hebrew, in its modern version, is their mother tongue), which would then be available to individuals as a cultural resource as they make decisions shaping their styles of life. Others have stressed that religious and nonreligious Jews should experience studying together in an atmosphere of openness, seeking to understand one another's approaches to texts without trying to "convert" those holding opposite positions. This is the format of one study program in Jerusalem, which seeks to create a "new language" for talking about Jewish tradition that goes beyond the simplified "religious versus nonreligious" dichotomy. Another initiative by a private foundation has sought to create "learning communities" among secular Jerusalemites, and turned to all interested people in an open advertisement, appealing to families with young children. The response to this call shows that the issue is of some concern to nonreligious Israelis. The program stresses groups forming their own approach to study and participation, while making various kinds of resources available to members to aid them in this purpose.

These ideas and programs are a few examples of efforts to encourage positive engagement with Judaic culture and Jewish tradition within sectors of Israeli society perceived as alienated from religion. Recently, groups undertaking such endeavors have sought ways to cooperate with one another. A new magazine, *Eres Aheret* (An Alternative Land), with the subtitle "On Israeliness and Judaism," also reflects this aspiration.[158] There also are attempts to link American Jewry to Israeli Jewry through the study of texts. A program calling itself Bavli-Yerushalmi (Babylonia-Jerusalem), recalling the designations of the two editions of the Talmud, has organized study groups in both New York and Jerusalem and made it possible for them to meet with one another.[159] Electronic communication helps in this effort, and, in general, the computer age has added new dimensions to the study of texts that are put to use by Jews of many different religious orientations.[160]

Whether new social and ritual forms will emerge from attempts to reconnect to ancient sources from secular points of view is still an open question. There is, however, continued dynamism in this realm. A group of college teachers linked to the kibbutz movement, once the symbol of antireligious Zionism, has recently published a user-friendly edition of the Passover Haggadah that includes the standard rabbinic text along with modern interpretations and alternative readings from which secularly oriented Jews may select.[161] At about the same time, the book section of the *Ha'aretz* newspaper featured on its first page a review of a prayer book published in the United States that was compiled on the basis of a feminist ideology.[162] To what extent such initiatives echo interests and activities among Israeli Jews is hard to determine, but it is clear that the social and symbolic potential of textual study and interpretation, and their relevance to unfolding lives, have yet to be exhausted. One indication of a wider sense of search in this direction is an initiative by the program, mentioned above, seeking to forge a "new language" to approach the Jewish classics, which offers short, intensive "courses" directed at couples soon to be married. These meetings, aimed at creating a sense of familiarity with both texts and other people, encourage active engagement in relating to "the sources," and have succeeded in attracting participants from different backgrounds.

4 Marriage

On several occasions I have been asked to be a witness at a wedding, to sign my name on a wedding contract, or *ketubba*. One memorable instance was in the United States in the late 1970s. A colleague was getting married, and after the wedding, she and her husband were planning to spend a year in Israel. The officiating rabbi was a well-known figure in American Jewish life. Otherwise, upon arrival, I knew almost no one among the guests. Soon, however, I heard my name called; I was being summoned to play a role in the ceremony.

The rabbi, knowledgeable about life in Israel, was concerned that the marriage be recognized there if a question ever arose among the Israeli rabbinic authorities. The couple had some thoughts about living in Israel and, as a Conservative rabbi, he envisioned the possibility that his credentials or the version of the ketubba he used might be questioned.[1] Israeli law did not give the rabbinate the power to challenge the personal status of Jews married abroad, but the rabbi wanted the contract to be as free of objections as possible. He therefore sought two male witnesses who could sign in Hebrew and be identifiable to Israeli authorities. Apparently, I was the only one present aside from himself fitting this description, and I was called to a small room to be the second witness on the document.

After affixing my signature to the ketubba, the rabbi asked me to stand next to him under the *ḥuppah* (wedding canopy) so as to be an eyewitness to the part of the ceremony in which the bride accepts a ring from the groom and he declares her to be consecrated to him "according to the law of Moses and Israel." According to the Mishna, the transfer of something of monetary value is one of the ways in which a man "acquires" a woman. In order to witness this transaction, I found myself walking down the aisle with the rabbi, with my thoughts turning to the ceremony about to unfold.

A traditional wedding contains various features, in addition to the "acquisition" of the bride by the groom, which reflect a society in which a woman's position was weaker than a man's. This hardly fit the two people in question, both of whom were educated professionals. In fact, the year they were about to spend together in Israel constituted a step forward in her career, rather than his. At the same time, other aspects of the ceremony struck me as uncannily contemporary. The last of the seven wedding blessings praises God for creating "joy and gladness, bridegroom and bride, mirth and exultation, pleasure and delight, love, brotherhood, peace and fellowship." I realized that wedding rituals are very complex and even contradictory constructions, bringing together not only a man and a woman but other differences and opposites as well. They merge ancient practices and attitudes with present social concerns, attachments to tradition with hopes for a future, and ideal visions of human relationships with a recognition of the problems arising in everyday marital life. A consideration of wedding rituals entails all these subjects and more.

It has been remarked that marriage is "the most elaborate ceremony in Judaism,"[2] but the salience and intricacy of weddings are features of all traditional societies. The Jewishness of a wedding celebration intermingles with many panhuman features. Marriages permanently change the personal situation of individuals, set the social stage for biological reproduction, constitute occasions for the movement of wealth, and also call upon the representatives of religious authority. While often relying upon the legitimacy offered by ancient traditions, people expect marriage rituals to speak to current notions and sensibilities. These various facets of Jewish weddings, and how ancient rites, customs, and texts have been interpreted to make sense in new situations, are the subject of this chapter.

MARRIAGE, WOMEN, AND MENSTRUATION: IDEALS AND REALITY

Marriages create a special social bond both for women and for men, but often weddings are viewed as *the* celebration in the lives of women. As discussed earlier, giving birth itself was only minimally marked in traditional Jewish societies, and not in a way that linked it to the learned culture.[3] Similarly, the fact that girls were only occasionally provided with a Torah education, and then only as a result of the initiative of individual families, meant that there was no communal recognition of their advancement through life's early phases. From this perspective, marriage was a woman's first and central ceremonial appearance in a publicly valued status. Detailed accounts of marriage celebrations figure prominently in the life stories of Jewish women from Mediterranean countries.[4]

The centrality of women in marriage also stems, of course, from their indispensable part in procreation. The fourth of the seven blessings recited at a wedding (see below) praises God for making man in God's image, and for building out of him a mechanism for perpetuating himself ("hitqin lo mimenu binyan 'adei 'ad"). This refers to sexual reproduction in the human species. The use of the term "build," which appears in the creation account in Genesis 2:22, is one aspect of that reference.[5]

Given the fact that procreation depends on women and has been a major value in rabbinic culture, it is puzzling that Jewish tradition pays almost no attention to the onset of menarche.[6] A contemporary effort to compose a prayer appropriate to the occasion cites no precedents, and minimal attention is paid to the topic in the ethnography of Jewish communities.[7] A portrait of the Polish shtetl states that when a girl reports the appearance of blood to her mother, "she will be roundly slapped on both cheeks." It will later "be explained that this is in order to make her rosy and beautiful."[8] Esther Schely-Newman reports that in some Tunisian communities, there was a ritual use of oil when a girl first noticed vaginal blood: it was smeared on her face, or she was made to look at her face in a bowl of oil. In both instances, positive comments were attached to the gesture: "so things will always be smooth," or that the girl "will always be shiny and good-looking as she was at that time." In Yemen, according to Alana Suskin, a mother took melted butter and poured it on the hands of a newly menstruant daughter. The explanation was that "blessing will flow from her hands."[9] None of the gestures or statements cited connects to traditional texts or to formal normative practice.[10] In all cases, other parts of the girl's body become the focus, perhaps directing attention away from the perplexing genitalia and providing reassurance at what might appear as a troublesome juncture. Ambivalence over menstruation on the occasion of menarche also appears within the world of men. A remedy for epilepsy that entails ingesting the blood of a first-time menstruant has made its way into the writings of rabbis.[11]

Menstruation, of course, has not been "unnoticed" in Jewish tradition.[12] A tractate of the Mishna, Niddah, is devoted to the subject, focusing on identifying the situations that constitute menstrual flow and specifying the rules leading to purification and the resumption of sexual contact between a man and his wife. The topic of niddah has been open to differing interpretations. Some recent views contrast the devalued blood of menstruation, which may symbolically invoke death, with the valued blood of circumcision, which in rabbinic writings brings salvation and life.[13] It should also be noted, however, that menstrual impurity is not a permanent state; it always comes to an end. This leads to a restoration of purity and the ability to procreate, which should figure into an overall understanding of the topic as well. Moshe Idel, for example, discusses a rabbinic idea in which sexual relations between a couple in purity have a positive impact on the Divine Presence.[14] In general, one rabbinic tendency is to highlight the implications of niddah for the *relations between* a man and wife, rather than to link it to woman's "essence" or general status in society. A variety of messages, which sometimes compete with one another, may be drawn out of time-honored texts.

In many cultures there are symbolic associations linking women and the moon. The perceived likeness between lunar cycles and women is evident in the term *menses*. This association was elaborated later in Jewish history in the special attachment of women to New Moon observance, which became a minor festival for them.[15] A symbolic connection between women and the moon may be hinted at in the Bible. In the creation story, the sun is called "the great luminary" and the moon "the small luminary" (Gen. 1:16), probably to avoid the standard names of these heavenly bodies, which pointed to the polytheistic mythologies of surrounding cultures. Nevertheless, former mythological symbols of gods and goddesses may resurface in mundane guise in biblical literature and be utilized for the Bible's purposes.

In Genesis 1:16–18, the two heavenly luminaries are given "dominion over" the day and the night respectively. The word "dominion" here is a translation of the Hebrew stem *mashol*. That stem reappears twice in subsequent narratives in the beginning of Genesis, and a third time in the story of Joseph. After woman disobeys God by leading Adam to eat from the forbidden tree, both are punished; part of her punishment is that "your desire will be towards your Man, and he will have *dominion* over you" (Gen. 3:16). Almost identical wording appears soon thereafter in the story of Cain and Abel. There, in a phrase that grabbed the imagination of John Steinbeck in *East of Eden*, Cain is told that he may have *dominion* over sin (Gen. 4:7). Despite this warning, he murders his brother.

Later in Genesis (37:8), the stem *mashol* appears in Joseph's dreams that suggest that he will have dominion over the members of his family.[16] In the second dream, his mother and father are explicitly compared to the moon and the sun. The dissimilarity between the sun and moon is thus linked to several themes: human beings' rule over one another, disobedience to God, the shedding of blood, and the difference between men and women. The texts struggle to project a vision of an ideal humanity while recognizing the reality of how the world seems to operate under "normal" conditions. Later generations envisioned the messianic era as entailing the expansion of the moon so that it is equal in brightness to the sun (Isa. 30:26).[17]

In considering laws related to menstruation, or any other topic seen as indicative of the status of women, it is possible to focus on ideal formulations of rabbinic culture or on actual historical trends, to the extent that they are known. To anthropologists seeking to understand a religion and its ideals in concrete contexts, both are important. In the absence of direct historical or ethnographic evidence, comparative examples are often cited. With regard to menstruation, Nissan Rubin states that understanding the religious rules of antiquity should take into account the biological and demographic realities of the era, as suggested by studies in parts of the world where patterns of family life in peasant societies have been observed. On the basis of this comparison, it is possible that because of long periods of nursing, which suppresses menstruation, and because of the tendency to become pregnant again soon after a child is weaned and lactation ceases, women in talmudic times did not experience menstrual bleeding as frequently as we might imagine.[18] If this is correct, the rabbis' interest in the topic might relate to the symbolic features of the elaborate laws of niddah, as much as to their concrete regulatory functions in daily life.

In the Mishna and Talmud, one finds strict demands for the separation of "a *niddah*," along with opinions that restrain those demands.[19] An example is the expectation that women be confined to a special room or hut during periods of menstrual impurity. This practice was not incorporated into rabbinic norms, but the physical separation of menstruants from normal domestic routines is found in groups on the margins of Jewish life. For example, Ethiopian Jewish women moved to a menstrual hut, where they were provided with food and visited by female friends. Their migration to Israel entailed a major reorientation with regard to this institution. Among the Samaritans in Nablus, a menstruant refrains from preparing food or engaging in other domestic work, including touching her own children. Her tasks are taken over by her mother-in-law or sisters-in-law. This is only possible because of the extended-family structure characteristic of the group. At the same time, the menstruant-avoidance rule makes it indispensable to Samaritan life for related nuclear families to reside in the same household.[20] Jews in Kurdistan in the middle of the nineteenth century also provided a hut for menstruants, but no further information is available about this.[21]

Other local practices developed in connection with niddah. Mordecaï Ha-Cohen reports, with regard to the Jews of the Nefusa mountains in

Libya, that the men "are very careful to keep their distance from a woman during her menstrual period. A man may not even step on the straw mat that she has walked on, nor may he look upon her face."[22] It is not clear whether this reflects a very strict separation of men and women in other realms, because the same author notes that the women of the region opposed rabbis in the city of Tripoli who wanted to impose greater seclusion on them generally.[23] This may be a case of differing perspectives on the part of men and women with regard to menstruation.[24]

Ha-Cohen entertains the possibility that the Nefusa customs derive from Karaite influence, as Karaites are known to have stricter rules of menstrual avoidance than rabbinic Jews. He then rejects his own hypothesis, but the comparison with Karaite rules is illuminating.[25] Karaite women do not enter a synagogue while menstruating.[26] This custom arose among Jews in some regions in the Middle Ages, but many rabbinic authorities did not accept it and ruled that women may touch a Torah scroll while in a state of niddah.[27] On the other hand, menstruating women in a Tunisian community separated themselves from the preparation of *matzot* before Passover, while within the popular North African practice of visiting the graves of a sainted rabbi, the norm was that menstruating women could not enter the tomb of a tzaddik.[28] In Baghdad, there was a custom of women wearing special garments during their menstrual periods.[29]

This scattered information on actual practice shows that the theoretical understanding of rabbinic literature must be placed side by side with specific historical developments. It has been said that the Mishna "demoted" women in relation to the Bible, because the former focuses on the impurity of niddah as a subject in itself, while the Bible treats the impurity of flow from sexual organs of both men and women within the same textual framework. In other ways, however, the Mishna may be seen as elevating the place of women in comparison to the Bible. Judith Hauptman notes that the mishnaic texts seem to address an audience that includes women, while much of biblical literature speaks to men *about* women.[30] She also points out that "the Mishna invented the halakhic category of *bogeret*, a mature woman (over twelve years) who has the power to agree to or refuse entering a marriage, while no such category exists in the Bible."[31] The ketubba, or marriage contract, that guarantees rights for women is also a postbiblical institution.[32] The extent to which these powers and rights were actually exercised in specific communities is a matter that only can be determined by research. In considering Jewish weddings and marriage celebrations here, I shall first outline the formal structure of the ceremony and then elaborate upon variations in the ways in which marriages were arranged, planned, and took place.

THE MARRIAGE CEREMONY

Jewish marriage, as stated, has been based on the notion that it is men who acquire rights with regard to a woman, while a woman agrees to his acquisition of those rights. Wedding ceremonies, as now structured, consist of two phases, which in antiquity were separated in time. The first phase is called *kiddushin* or *erusin*, and the second is called *nesuin*. *Nesuin* is normally translated as "marriage," while the term *erusin* is used in modern Hebrew for "engagement." *Kiddushin* and *erusin* in the context of formal marriage procedures, however, do not mean "engagement" in the contemporary sense, but refer to the part of the ceremony that establishes a ritual and legal relationship setting a woman aside exclusively for a man who performs the act of kiddushin. The term *kiddushin* resembles the Hebrew word *kadosh*, "holy," and the Talmud interprets it as implying that a woman has been "set aside" or devoted to a single sacred purpose; after that no other man may have sexual access to her.[33]

Once the ceremony of kiddushin takes place, a permanent relationship is established between a man and a woman. If there is a decision not to continue with the marriage, it entails writing a *get*, a formal bill of divorce according to rabbinic law.[34] In antiquity, some time passed (typically a year) between kiddushin and full marriage, after which a woman began to live with her husband permanently. This created a complex and somewhat contradictory state for couples during the period between kiddushin and full marriage. In eleventh-century France, it became the practice to have a single ceremony, beginning with kiddushin, followed immediately by nesuin. This practice was widely adopted in Europe and later became common in other parts of the Jewish world.[35] In several Middle Eastern communities, the separation of the phases continued until much more recent times.[36]

The word *kiddushin* comes from a tractate in the Mishna with that name. The opening chapter in that tractate, however, does not use the word *kiddushin*, but mentions three modes of how a man's rights with regard to his wife are established.[37] These are through money; through a written document; or through sexual congress. According to the Mishna, an appropriate act in any of these modes, initiated by a man and agreed to by a woman, can bring about acquisition. As the wedding ceremony developed in postmishnaic times, aspects of all three acts were included in it, so instead of being alternate modes of creating a relationship, they were included in a total sequence of marriage ceremonies and thereby reinforced one another.

The feature of transferring money is typically expressed in the ring the groom gives the bride (see appendix 4 for the basic structure of the ceremony). The use of a ring is a posttalmudic development, and the Jews of Yemen preserved the practice of utilizing a coin in the ceremony.[38] Aleppan Jews, in Syria, used both a coin and a ring.[39] The ring has to have a minimal ascertainable monetary value, and two witnesses must be on hand to testify that the man put the ring on the finger of the bride. They also should pay attention to the fact that when the woman received it, she knew its value and accepted it for the purpose of kiddushin. When the ring is given to the bride, the groom recites: "Behold, you are consecrated [*mequddeshet*] to me with this ring according to the law of Moses and Israel." It is common practice that a wedding ring be plain, without any gems. There may have been magical reasons for this in antiquity, but rabbinic tradition reinterpreted the practice as making clear the value of the ring, so that the monetary issue not be clouded by "extraneous" jewels.[40]

Two blessings introduce the kiddushin phase of the ceremony.[41] The first is the blessing over wine. The second relates to the institution of kiddushin and praises God "who has sanctified us by his commandments, and has commanded us concerning forbidden unions, and has forbidden to us those who are betrothed [to other men], and has permitted to us those who are married by the rite of the nuptial canopy [ḥuppah] and kiddushin." The blessing is read by the rabbi, but its language represents the point of view of the man in relation to the woman whom he is "marrying" while she is "being married." Similarly, in the subsequent act of giving the ring and reciting: "Behold, you are consecrated . . . ," the man is the initiator of the marriage link. There have existed other rabbinic versions of "Behold, you are consecrated . . . " in which women also pronounce a statement of relationship. These, however, do not alter the basic ritual/legal logic of kiddushin. There does appear a degree of mutuality in some of the customs of drinking wine after the first two blessings are recited. Both the bride and groom drink: sometimes the rabbi gives the cup to the groom and then to the bride, and sometimes the groom hands wine directly to the bride after he drinks. Other permutations, including drinking of the wine by the parents of the couple, are known as well. An unusual custom found among both the Georgian Jews of the Caucasus and the Cochin Jews of India involves placing the ring of kiddushin in the cup of wine to be drunk.[42]

Often, with the conclusion of the betrothal phase of the ceremony, the wedding contract, or ketubba, is read. The basic purpose of the ketubba is to record the economic obligations of a man to a woman if the marriage relationship terminates. It is a socially sanctioned contract between the parties, and its precise contents have varied over time and place. For example, it specifies the dowry brought into the marriage by a woman, and during much of Middle Eastern Jewish history, it included a list of personal and household items and the value of each. The ketubba is not the same as the written document that can bring about kiddushin according to the Mishna, but it does include a paragraph corresponding to the statement of the man acquiring the woman. The ketubba is signed by two witnesses, who should also witness the actual giving of the ring and the following parts of the marriage ceremony.

Some aspects of the ketubba reflect changing historical circumstances, but other features are relatively invariant. For example, marriage contracts are still written in Aramaic, the language spoken by Jews at the time of the Mishna and the Talmuds. A historical variation is provided by Sephardi *ketubbot*, which may stipulate that if a woman has no children, a man may take a second wife, albeit only with her permission.[43] It is not required that the whole ketubba, written in an ancient language and containing much legal terminology, be read as part of the ceremony. Very often part of it is read, and/or its contents are summarized and explained by the rabbi.

One variable, and potentially attractive side, of the ketubba is the way it is decorated. Because they are essentially secular contracts, ketubbot can be written plainly, or can even be produced in a standard printed form, upon which the details of a given wedding are filled in. At various periods, however, traditions of elaborate ketubba illumination developed. Historical illuminated ketubbot are favorite items in museums and books of Jewish art.[44] In recent times in North America, the practice of having an individually designed and highly decorative marriage contract has become widespread. Typically, such ketubbot are prominently displayed in the homes of young couples as an expression of their joint and mutual commitment to marriage. This is very different from the traditional disposition of these documents, in which a ketubba might be hidden away in the home of the woman's father to be retrieved if life's fortunes brought her to make the economic claims guaranteed in them. Rabbinic literature typically talks of the sum mentioned in the document as "her ketubba," because it gives rights to a woman and places obligations upon a man.

After the ketubba is read or summarized, the next phase of the ceremony is nesuin, entrance into the full status of marriage. In antiquity, the hallmark of this stage was the movement of a woman from her parent's home into the home of her husband. Standing under the wedding canopy has come to symbolize that act, the image of a canopy perhaps deriving from a tent into which a bride entered in ancient times. The canopy as we know it today, however, has not always been in use. In some places, in both Europe and the Middle East, it was customary for the groom's prayer shawl to be spread over the bride as she stood next to him.[45] Frequently, the statement of Ruth to Boas, that he should "spread his wing" over her (Ruth

3:9), has been invoked with reference to this custom, as has a parallel phrase from Ezekiel 16:8 in which God affords protection to abandoned Jerusalem.

Entering the ḥuppah also is seen as standing for the third form of wife-acquisition mentioned in the Mishna—sexual congress. The act of being together under one roof is taken as a sign of full conjugal life. Another gesture expressing that association developed in Ashkenazi tradition—the custom of *yiḥud*. Yiḥud means being together alone "as one," and the practice evolved of the bride and groom going into a room by themselves immediately upon the conclusion of the ceremony under the ḥuppah. Witnesses are stationed to see that the couple in fact entered a room and stayed there for a few minutes. According to strict moral and religious norms, only a married couple are allowed to be alone in such a manner, and the fact that they do remain by themselves in a closed room becomes evidence of the "consummation" of a marriage. In most instances these days, the couple simply relax for a few minutes or, if they have followed the tradition of fasting all day until the time of the ceremony, they take the opportunity to have a bite to eat. In Israel today, where Ashkenazim and Sephardim live side by side and about one-fourth of all marriages that take place are between men and women from those two backgrounds, it is common for yiḥud to be part of many ceremonies.

The nesuin phase of wedding ceremonies also has its own blessings. These are now known as "the seven blessings." In the Talmud, they are known as the "blessings of the grooms" (*birkot ḥatanim*). Some claim that they are a list of blessings appropriate to the occasion of a wedding, and that the Talmud did not envision all of them having to be said on the occasion of every wedding. At the same time, it is possible to see a certain logic in their sequence. One way of highlighting their overall structure is the following ordering (see appendix 4):

1. The blessing over wine
2. Three blessings citing God's creating humanity and humanity's power of procreation
3. A blessing over the ingathering of Jews from the Diaspora to Jerusalem
4. Two blessings citing the joy of the bride and groom.

The blessings move from the most inclusive category of humanity through the mentioning of Jewish peoplehood and conclude with a focus on the single couple. Another movement may be discernible if the Hebrew *ha-adam* in the third and fourth blessings is translated as "mankind" rather than "humanity." This would involve the presentation of blessings with male resonance (*man*kind), followed by one with female echoes (Jerusalem is pictured as a woman), and concluding with a stress on the couple.

Both the fifth and the last blessings refer to the return to Zion and Jerusalem. This theme is also associated with the well-known feature of Jewish weddings of breaking a glass. In many Sephardi communities, it was standard to break a glass between the kiddushin and the nesuin part of the ceremony, while among Ashkenazim it took place as the very last act under the ḥuppah. Breaking a glass is a custom; it in no way affects the legal and religious transition from being single to being married. How it became central in the Jewish imagination will be discussed below, after considering other features of marriage in which rabbinic rules and interpretations intermix with both diverse social conditions and popular practices and understandings.

HOARY TEXTS AND LOCAL PRACTICES

Marriage has always been highly valued in Jewish culture. This continues to be the case in contemporary Israel, which has one of the highest marriage rates found in a Western-oriented industrial society. The centrality of marriage goes back to the stories in Genesis 24, which spells out in detail how Abraham's servant found a wife for Isaac, and the tribulations of Jacob stemming from his love for Rachel (Gen. 29:17–21). A legal discussion of kiddushin asserts that one can take it for granted that a man will prefer to be married rather than live alone.[46] The value of marriage is also expressed in the legend of a Roman matron who challenged the religious belief of Rabbi Yose ben Halafta, asking him how God spends his time now that he has finished creating the world. Yose's answer, that God spends his time in deciding on matrimonial matches is greeted with mockery by the matron, who claims that she is capable of doing the same thing, and more quickly. She proceeds to line up 1,000 male and female slaves and pairs them off, assigning them to marry one another. The next day, the matron finds all these couples engaged in physical fights and consequently acknowledges the truth of the Torah and Rabbi Yose's wisdom.[47]

Genesis 24 also forms part of wedding-linked liturgy in many Sephardi communities. Among them, it is customary for a groom to be called to the Torah in the synagogue on the Sabbath after his wedding. A special reading takes place in his honor, from the narrative of Abraham's servant finding Rebecca and bringing her back to Isaac. In some versions of the custom, an additional sefer Torah is taken from the ark, and the reading is done directly from the scroll.[48] No parallel convention of reading exists today in Ashkenaz, but there it is customary on the Sabbath before a wedding to "call up" (*uf-ruf* in Yiddish) a groom-to-be to the reading of the Torah, honoring him with the recitation of the blessings. In both instances, the community salutes the act of marriage and the formation of a new family in its midst.

The heavy value placed on marriage has its "down side," to adopt a contemporary phrase and point of view, in that pressure to marry begins at a young age. In earlier periods, this might take the form of childhood betrothal and marriage, particularly for females. A rabbinic elaboration of the biblical story of Isaac and Rebecca pictures her as being three years old, while Isaac was aged forty according to the Bible itself.[49] This interpretation does not easily harmonize with another rabbinic gloss, which, citing the fact that Rebecca's parents asked for her opinion (Gen. 24:57–58), recommends that women should be married off only with their consent.[50] As mentioned above, the Mishna created the category of "mature woman," in reference to someone who had passed the age of twelve, but did not absolutely prohibit fathers from marrying off their daughters before that age. The Mishna also indicates, and the Talmud acknowledges, that ideally a father should not arrange kiddushin for his daughter while she still is a young girl,[51] but practice did not always follow these norms. The Tosaphists, medieval commentators on the Talmud, in discussing this passage, wonder why in their own communities, they ignore the norm and take it upon themselves to represent their daughters and accept kiddushin for them when they are still minors. Their answer is that "every day the Exile lies more heavily upon us, and if a man is able to provide a dowry for his daughter at this moment [he should do so], lest he not be able to later and find that she remains unmarried forever."[52]

Aside from the strictly legal side of things, the younger a woman, the more likely that her choice will be influenced by her family. Even though the Mishna claims that a mature woman must assent to kiddushin, it is striking that Jewish tradition did not formulate a conventional verbal response on the part of a bride, such as "I do."[53] Proof of her acceptance is determined by witnesses observing her actions when she is given the monetary token of kiddushin (a ring). Historically, the circumstances affecting the degree of choice exercised by women were quite diverse. Examples from the Middle Ages are found in documents from the Cairo Geniza, which indicate that a woman was often married off by her parents at an early age and had little freedom and leverage in the home of her husband. She would be treated as a child who had to be educated, and in fact she was frequently much younger than her husband. The Geniza also reveals many cases of divorce, and divorced women did not necessarily "return to the father's house," as Genesis has it.[54] They were fairly independent in negotiating another marriage and in conducting their own affairs. Still, in this new situation, they did not have all the legal rights that men had and often had to be represented in official contexts by their brothers.

The main object of the socialization of girls was their future roles as wife and mother. This persisted even when women began to be exposed to formal education, so relatively early marriage was not unusual even in the not-so-distant past. A trend towards later marriage developed in recent centuries among Jews in Ashkenaz, while the pattern of early marriages, arranged by the parents, may have been preserved among the economic elite able to support their children and actualize the ideal of maintaining a son-in-law who was a Torah scholar.[55] Early marriages continued to be common in the Middle East. A member of the Baghdadi community in Calcutta supplies an account from the nineteenth century: "My mother was about eleven and going to school. One day, she was being brought home from school when she passed the home of a relative, who called her in. A sweet was put in her mouth and she was told she was engaged. My father was fourteen then. He was seventeen when they married and my mother was thirteen and a half. They had no voice in it really."[56] In Baghdad itself, towards the end of the nineteenth century, the Jewish leadership felt the need to issue an ordinance prohibiting the marriage of children under thirteen.[57] At the same period of time, in North Africa, teachers in the Alliance Israélite Universelle educational network complained that young girl students were being taken out of school by their parents to be married.[58] In many instances, both girls and boys were married off with little choice, but there also were instances of young women being married to men far older than them.

The early age of marriage is intertwined with other issues of both an attitudinal and a material nature. There are a number of statements in rabbinic literature indicating the preference for boys over girls.[59] Some probably reflect the exclusive access of males to Torah as discussed in chapter 3.[60] Others may stem from the economic reality in which daughters entail dowry payments, while sons will be a source of income.[61] The latter situation repeated itself in many Jewish communities over the centuries. Within the circle of Baghdadi Jews in the late nineteenth century, a local observer wrote in a Judeo-Arabic newspaper: "Woe to the father of girls. Our sages have written that at the hour a daughter is born the sun is darkened and even the angels shed a tear. Perhaps they said that in relation to the daughters of Baghdad in our day."[62] He criticizes the institution of early marriage, pointing out that as a girl gets older, the amount of dowry the parents have to pay rises as well. The burden of marrying off daughters was well known in eastern Europe too; it forms a basic element in the portrayal of the family of Tevya the Milkman in the writings of Sholem Aleichem (see below). This did not mean girls were seen in negative terms only. Folksongs from Tripoli about the birth of boys and girls that reflect the point of view of mothers tell of the joys and difficulties of each.[63] It is also important to distinguish between the social and cultural biases operating against girls and matters of interpersonal sentiment. A former member of the Baghdadi community in Calcutta who moved to England recollected: "My father wanted his eldest child to be a son. He was disappointed when I was born. He wrote me a letter when I left India saying how I had made up for his disappointment a thousandfold."[64]

The traditional norms pressing for early marriage, and the exercise of the will of the parents over that of their children, in particular the will of young girls, does not mean that the inclinations and choices of young people were totally ignored. Before an engagement was announced in a traditional community, a great deal of information was discreetly exchanged as part of behind-the-scenes maneuvering. A marriage decision involved the social standing and economic interests of the parents, but the likes and dislikes of the children might also be taken into consideration. Young men in Yemen would seek opportunities to catch glimpses of young women in everyday settings, such as when they drew water at a well or when they were working to prepare for Shabbat, for on those occasions they were dressed in ordinary work clothes. On other public occasions, young women dressed in elaborate garb and clearly were "on show."[65] In Jewish communities generally, the cycle of religious festivals provided the opportunity to "see and be seen," either at home, near the synagogue, or in more relaxed settings, such as pilgrimages to tombs of saintly figures.[66]

The flow of wedding festivities, in particular, were major occasions to observe young women, not only by young men, but by their mothers. Jews in Syria held a women's party in the *hammam*, or Turkish bath house, which was rented for the occasion by the family of the bride.[67] At this gathering, she might be inspected by the mother of the groom and immersed herself before the marriage to be purified according to the rules of niddah. In all Middle Eastern communities, there were festivities in which a bride-to-be was decorated with henna, and these also allowed the viewing of unmarried young women who were part of the bride's entourage. Henna evenings could be utilized cautiously by young men as well, even though during most of the celebration, people were confined to same-sex groups. In henna parties in Libyan villages, there was a phase when young men entered the circle of women surrounding a bride singly to place coins on her henna-covered feet. On this occasion, a man seeking a wife might quietly mention the name of one of the village's young women. This resulted in a series of tactful inquiries to see if the person named and her family were interested. If they were not, the subject was dropped without anyone losing face.[68]

In more urban settings, the delicacy of exploring, hinting at, and sometimes retreating from a possible marriage gave rise to the role of "matchmaker" in both Europe and the Middle East. Yitzhak Avishur provides some details from Baghdad. After preparatory work, the parents of a young man would visit the home of a prospective bride together with the matchmaker who had suggested the agreement. The parents of the woman prepared their house carefully and also made sure that no other unmarried daughters were around on the occasion. It was customary, after the guests were seated, for the prospective girl to come into the room and offer the guests a certain kind of candy. If they were not favorably impressed upon first appearance, the guests would refuse the candy and leave soon thereafter. If they were interested, they would stay and examine the potential daughter-in-law in every way they could. Women guests would use their hands as well as their eyes. They would try to see if her breasts were really developed or whether their appearance was the result of padding. They did not want a woman who was cross-eyed and watched her walk to make sure she did not limp. They were also wary about someone with too much makeup. Physical beauty was esteemed and the ability to bear children was, of course, a concern, but families also wanted evidence that a girl had been educated in the ways of modesty.[69]

In Tripoli, as described by Mordecaï Ha-Cohen, it was possible for a groom and his relatives to see a bride in her parents' home before serious negotiations were finalized. The meeting was called a *tijliyah*, or "revealing," which is comprehensible in terms of the woman from Tripoli mentioned in chapter 3 who likened her situation before marriage to a Torah closeted in the synagogue ark. Ha-Cohen also cites revulsion at the custom because of the disgrace experienced by the girl and her family if she were rejected, and explains that it was abandoned.[70]

Many Jewish communities in modern times were dramatically altered by migration, which led to the discarding of older forms of courtship and the rapid adopting of new ones. When large numbers of people from the same background migrated at the same period, modes of courtship underwent modification more gradually. An example of how new factors influenced the choice of a mate, while the changes were contained within traditional forms, is found among the Jews of Georgia in the Caucasus mountains. In that region there are traditions, among both Christians and Jews, of various forms of bride-capture and kidnapping. In a few instances, this involved actual abduction and rape, while in other instances, a woman would be captured and held and pressure put on her parents to assent to a marriage. Once she was in that position, it was not simple for her parents to take her back and pretend that she was in the same pristine unmarried state as before, so they often assented to the marriage. Maya Meltzer-Geva gathered information on cases of bride kidnapping among Georgian Jews who moved to Israel beginning in the late 1960s.[71]

In recent times, such "kidnappings" were often prearranged by a young man and woman. They might take place among a couple who were mutually attracted when the parents did not approve of the young man. Alternately, they could be a way out of a planned marriage imposed by parents on their daughter. After these ritualized kidnappings, the parents in most instances eventually agreed to a marriage. The contemporary utilization of this form undoubtedly reflects the growing desire of young people to marry partners of their own choosing, but the "ritual" also upholds traditional norms. It reinforces the premise that a woman cannot assert her will against that of her parents. It is only acceptable that she enter a marriage in opposition to their wishes when that step appears to arise from external conditions over which she and the family have no control.

DOWRY: NEGOTIATION AND CEREMONIES

Viewed sociologically, the high investment that families have in the marriage of their children is the obverse of the limitations placed on young people in determining their own marriage partners. This investment is constituted by both material wealth and social reputation. There is little in the way of direct data on the subject in historical Jewish societies, but it is likely that precisely the most well-to-do families, who might also be the most "educated," had the greatest interest in controlling the marriage choices of their offspring. By contrast, those of limited means had less leverage in imposing choices on their children. In any event, a marriage involved the exchange of money and of gifts between two families. In some Middle Eastern locales, it was expected that a major gift or "bride-price" be given to the father of the bride, while in other settings, both in the Middle East and Europe, the dowry brought by a woman to a marriage was the major economic investment. Both practices must be seen as part of a series of exchanges launching a new family into economic existence. There is almost no systematic study of the institution of bride-price in Jewish communities, but Abraham Marcus notes that in eighteenth-century Aleppo, bachelors were exempted from communal taxes to allow them to accumulate the funds necessary to attract a bride.[72] More attention has been paid to the mechanics of dowry.

Dowry is an ancient and widespread custom in Jewish life, but the actual amounts and goods included reflected current economic realities.[73] The amount given by the parents of a woman in her dowry was frequently written into the marriage contract, sometimes on the basis of assessments made by community notables. Both monetary transfers and goods brought by a woman to a marriage went into the sum promised to a woman in her ketubba. In the course of married life, the husband has control of those funds but also knows that he will have to return the money if he divorces his wife. Similarly, his heirs have to pay the amount in the ketubba if he predeceases her. In mid-twentieth-century Istanbul, a dowry might include buying and furnishing an apartment for a new couple and even purchasing a small factory to be run by the husband. A young man who showed an aptitude for business was in a position to attract a larger dowry than a person who had only proved himself in school.[74]

As noted, recent centuries have witnessed extensive migration and considerable social mobility among Jews as they became citizens of nation-states and participated in the economic and social life of the countries in which they resided. Rapid changes also entailed the possibility of downward mobility or simply social "stagnation." Often, men set the pace in new work settings and business ventures, while women either did not enter the labor force or stayed within a restricted range of "feminine occupations." This meant that their social status, and that of their parents, was closely linked with the kinds of marriages they made. A male could bring his potential earning power to a marriage, while a woman would be expected to bring actual capital. Daughters with limited or no dowries might be maneuvered into marriages that lowered them and their families on the social ladder; conversely, one of the strategies available to upwardly mobile males was to attract a woman with a generous dowry.

Families in which daughters outnumbered sons were clearly disadvantaged. One family sizing up another for a possible match would assess their potential partners' capabilities: the female/male ratio among the younger generation was also a factor taken into account. Attitudes reflecting this situation were found throughout the Jewish world where ancient norms intermingled with new economic realities and expectations. A development that fundamentally modified dowry transactions was the advanced education of women and their movement into expanded occupational and professional markets. The "dowry" made available to a woman was the education she received in endowing herself with professional credentials. This provided a wider range of options in the "marriage market," a process that has been evident among North African Jews who migrated to France beginning in the 1950s.[75]

Permanence of marriage and the stability of the economic arrangements entailed have always been major concerns. It took time to negotiate and reach understandings in such arrangements, to say nothing of the time needed for a young woman or man to become accustomed to the idea of being committed to a life together with someone whom she or he knew only very partially. The medieval practice of combining kiddushin—"betrothal"—with nesuin, cited above, left a vacuum in terms of an appropriate preparatory period before a marriage takes place. It is not surprising, therefore, that other kinds of ceremonies arose that sealed the social and economic agreements between two families. These ceremonies committed them to marry, in the combined "kiddushin and erusin" ceremony, at a later date. In Europe, the agreements reached in such a situation were called *tenaim*, or "conditions." A term with a similar meaning, *shart*, was common in parts of the Judeo-Arabic world.[76] *Tenaim* was also the name given to the celebration that finalized the prenuptial agreement.

The signing of tenaim in Europe could be an occasion almost as serious as a wedding. The major difference is that tenaim, from a legal point of view, did not contain the element of kiddushin, or ritual consecration. If the agreement established by tenaim was broken, there was no requirement of a rabbinic divorce. Dissolving a tenaim contract, however, could be exceedingly difficult and painful. These agreements normally stipulated heavy fines to be paid by the party calling off the engagement. Rejected families lost face in the community, and a broken engagement was especially damaging to the subsequent marriage prospects of a young woman.

The weightiness of a tenaim agreement was matched by the exuberance of the festivities that accompanied its signing. These celebrations rivaled weddings in their intensity. The custom of breaking a glass at weddings stimulated the adoption of a similar practice at tenaim celebrations, in which a plate was smashed as part of the ceremony. These plates were often decorated, and as is common in Jewish art, Hebrew words were part of the decoration. Some plates carried the word *qnas*, or "fine." The plate-smashing ceremony was interpreted as reminding the parties that they would face a heavy fine were they to go back on the agreement they had just made. The eighteenth-century leader of Lithuanian Jewry, Rabbi Elijah ben Solomon Zalman, the famous Gaon of Vilnius, required that tenaim plates be ceramic.[77] He claimed that just as a ceramic plate cannot be repaired, so the families should be warned not to renege on their commitments.

MODESTY AND VIRGINITY

The social worth of families stemmed from their economic position, but also from other values, such as mastery of Torah study. A statement in the Talmud exhorts a man to sell all that he has in order to marry the daughter of a *talmid ḥakham,* a scholar of Torah, or to marry off his own daughter to a talmid ḥakham.[78] This ideal could only be realized by some members of a community, but, as noted, it sometimes played a significant role in the self-image of Jews. Women themselves were not measured by this scale of achievement, but were judged in terms of values attached to their roles as wives, housekeepers, and mothers. "[P]ropriety and a good education are part of the family capital of which the young woman is the bearer," Abraham Udovitch and Lucette Valensi note of the Jews of Jerba. "These qualities are manifested by her modesty, her quiet demeanor, her knowledge of all household skills, and her docility."[79] This description, with little modification, could apply to traditional Jewish communities in Europe as well.

If this cluster of features had to be summed up in one word, it would be "modesty." The value of modesty, in its various dimensions, was highlighted in the course of weddings. A young woman and man might get to know each other somewhat during their "engagement," or might have been acquainted during childhood, but many communities assumed that they would not have contact in the period immediately before their wedding. This highlighted the "purity" with which they approached the marriage and showed their capacity for self-restraint and their acceptance of prevailing mores. During henna nights and other prenuptial festivities in Middle Eastern communities, a bride was expected to sit very still and show no emotion while singing, drumming, and dancing went on about her.

The norm of modesty also is expressed in the practice of *bedekn,* known from eastern Europe and practiced in many contemporary weddings. Just before they approach the ḥuppah, the groom comes to the room where the bride has been sitting with her family and friends and lowers her veil so that her face is covered (see figure 11). He then rejoins his own "party." The bride thus comes to the wedding canopy separate from the groom, radiating modesty, accompanied by female relatives and friends (see figure 12). It is common to connect this practice with Genesis 24:65, in which Rebecca, upon encountering Isaac for the first time, covers herself with a veil, or for onlookers to quote the words "Our sister, may you bring forth tens of thousands" from earlier in Genesis (v. 60). Some also link the Yiddish word *bedekn,* and the practice, with the Hebrew *bodeq,* "to examine," and recall Genesis 29:25, in which Jacob does not know that he has married his beloved's sister until after the marriage has been consummated. Here, as

Figure 11.   Bedekn: the groom places the veil over the bride before approaching the ḥuppah. Courtesy Yisrael-Kloss.

elsewhere, there is an interplay of rabbinic textual glosses and popular social values.[80]

There was also a norm of modesty with reference to grooms. On the Saturday night that initiated wedding festivities in Yemen, a groom was dressed in a special manner by a *mori,* or rabbi. This took place in a festive atmosphere, accompanied by hymns (*piyyutim*), in the home of the groom along with his friends. Moris usually limited their participation in these events, leaving soon after the formal dressing. So long as the mori was present, the groom and other guests acted with restraint and propriety. Once he left, the atmosphere became lighter and freer.[81] The major burden of modesty, in Yemen as elsewhere in the Jewish world, fell, however, upon the young woman. Ultimately, the notion of "modesty" referred to her sexual status and behavior.

It was expected that a woman married for the first time would be a virgin. The value of virginity was encoded in both formal rabbinic law and popular practice. The Mishna sets the minimum value that a man must stipulate in his wife's ketubba. It is double in the case of a virgin (200 zuz) in comparison to a widow (100 zuz; in both cases the sum can be much higher).[82] If it should happen in a case of widowhood or divorce that the actual ketubba is not preserved, a dispute may arise as to what the status of a woman was when she was married. This would make a big difference in the

Figure 12.   Bride accompanied to the ḥuppah by her family and friends in a
Jerusalem wedding. Courtesy Gili Cohen-Magen.

amount a man or his heirs would have to pay. In such cases, the court accepted testimony from witnesses as to the nature of the celebration at the
time of marriage. There were customs that differentiated the festivities in
connection with the marriage of a virgin from those of a woman who had
been married previously. One convention was that a virgin would appear
publicly with her hair uncovered. Another, according to one opinion, is the
distribution of parched corn.[83] The talmudic discussion of the mishnaic
principles adds the passing of a certain kind of wine before the bride as indicating her status as a virgin. It also mentions that customs in Babylonia
differed from those in Judea.[84] We find here a recognition, by rabbinic law,
of the power of local custom.

Another aspect of female virginity, and its public display, was the need to
prove it. This could not take place before a wedding, but was built into the
widespread custom of showing a sheet, stained with the blood of the bride,
after the first sexual union on the night of a wedding. One of the oldest examples of this practice is alluded to in Deuteronomy 22:17. It continued to be
common in many Middle Eastern communities, among both Jews and non-
Jews, up to the present, even though it is by no means a fully adequate test.[85]
There was even an attempt among Jews in the Middle Ages to institutionalize a blessing appropriate to the occasion, but authorities such as Saʿadiah
Gaon and Maimonides disapproved of it.[86] The custom was also known to

Figure 13.   A miqveh, without water, in a synagogue complex in Marrakesh.
Photo Harvey E. Goldberg.

Ashkenazi rabbis in Italy at the time of the Renaissance.[87] Deuteronomy
speaks of a legal claim, showing the proof before the (male) elders in the city
gate, if a husband declares that his wife was not a virgin when they married,
while the ethnographic record reflects popular expectations and usually depicts the event taking place among older women, in particular the female relatives of the couple. Mothers of the groom wanted to make sure that the
sheet demonstrated the virginity of the girl, but their family was also "on
trial," because the virility of the young groom was also being tested. Relatives of the bride were there to be vindicated and enjoy public recognition
that their daughter had received a proper, modest education.

There was a basic cultural tension in this aspect of the celebration, in addition to the uncertainty felt by those waiting until the test was passed successfully. Matters of sexual intimacy were usually treated discreetly in Jewish life, but at the time of weddings, they were on public display. This
inherent contradiction was partially handled by the fact that the direct public was made up of women, while the values they represented concerned all
the members of the community. This balancing of opposing elements also
appears in the ritual immersion of a woman before her wedding.

Earlier I mentioned the practice of women having a party at a Turkish
bath before their marriage. The use of a ḥammam paralleled what was
known in Europe as going to a miqveh. The term *miqveh* is derived from

the Hebrew phrase *miqveh mayyim,* a gathering of water,[88] and rabbinic tradition defined the minimum amount of a natural collection of water within which a woman was to totally immerse (see figure 13).[89] The fanfare of prenuptial "miqveh parties" may be contrasted to the conventional modesty and discretion that pervades "going to the miqveh" during routine married life, before a couple resumes sexual relations after a woman's period.[90]

HENNA AND TRANSITIONS

Some aspects of a wedding, like the formal rabbinic kiddushin, or the popular showing of a sheet after consummation among Middle Eastern Jews, constitute dramatic crossings of a threshold. Other parts of a wedding consist of many individual acts drawn out over the long festive period both before and after the formal religious ceremony. It is common to talk of the "seven days of feasting" based on the biblical reference to Samson's wedding (Judg. 14:12, 17), but the cycle of celebrations before the wedding night could be shorter or longer.[91] In Middle Eastern communities, some of these celebrations involved applying henna to the bride, and it was common that one (or more) of the nights before the wedding was known as "the night of henna."

The henna plant (*Lawsonia inermis*) is mentioned in the Bible, in the Song of Songs (1:13–14):

> My lover is like a bundle of myrrh
> He dwells between my breasts
> My lover is like a bundle of henna
> In the orchards of Ein Gedi

It continues to have connotations that are saliently associated with weddings, and implicitly with sexuality, among Middle Eastern Jews. In Algeria, the night of henna was also called the "night of opening." It was the occasion upon which a bride-to-be was verbally initiated into the "realities of marriage."[92]

The actual way henna was incorporated into prenuptial ceremonies varied greatly. In Tunisia, more than one night was identified with henna.[93] While the central use of henna was its application to the fingernails, toenails, and hair of a bride, in Saná (Yemen) and Tunisia, it was also ceremonially applied to grooms. The opposition of Yemenite rabbis who claimed that this violated the rule of not dressing a woman like a man (Deut. 22:5) did not succeed in squelching the practice.[94]

In the villages of Libya, on one henna night, a decorated bride sat outside on a low stool, her face and hair completely covered, but with her henna-covered hands and feet exposed. As already mentioned, young men would approach her, walking through a crowd of women gathered about her, and place coins on her toes and then leave them in a basket. One loquacious informant of mine said that young men might press the coins on her toes with great pressure, explaining that the act gave them vicarious erotic pleasure.[95] Many other more "conventional" explanations are assigned to the use of henna, which symbolically condenses various aspects of a marriage. Even the act of grinding up the leaves and preparing the mixture had ritual import.[96] The application of henna is seen, for example, as purifying the bride before the wedding. Another common reason, relating to the placing of henna on grooms as well as on brides, is that it wards off evil spirits, or opposes the evil eye operating within a community. This reason is given often, but yields only a superficial level of understanding. The very diversity of interpretations shows the need for other levels of understanding.

There are several characteristics of the henna plant and dye that make it appropriate for marriage ritual. While the plant itself is green, after being ground and mixed, it turns a darker color, sometimes described as red-brown and sometimes as yellow-brown. The change from green, the color of freshness and fertility, to red, the color of deflowered virginity, is particularly apropos, but even without focusing on the specific colors, the far-reaching transformation itself is a central feature from a sociological point of view. In addition, henna dye, when applied to the nails, hair, or the palms of the hand, is relatively lasting. It cannot be washed away immediately, but fades slowly over a period of weeks or more. It thus corresponds to a desired but not universally attained end-state of marriage ceremonies—that of permanence.

A general social science view of the use of henna does not mean that the explanations of warding off demons or the evil eye are devoid of sociological merit. As a major transition, a wedding entails charting unknown territory for the couple and for their families, a situation entailing anxiety. The belief in demons or the evil eye gives a concrete focus to anxieties and provides socially recognized ways of combating them. Such beliefs and actions may also mask other sources of ill feeling. As summarized by Eric Wolf with respect to weddings in peasant societies: "When one man succeeds in marrying a woman and receiving her dowry, a new household is formed; but the unsuccessful suitors will hang their head in despondency, or react with envy and shame." He adds that two families concluding a successful alliance may be the targets of gossip and ill will emanating from those "upon whom fortune has not smiled." The general sense of gaiety at weddings may thus drown out, but not eliminate, tensions that inevitably arise in the course of daily life. As in other communal celebrations, "participation does not end the hostilities between households, but rather affirms the existence of that larger social and moral order within which the hostilities are both contained and constrained."[97]

TENSIONS IN MARRIAGES: DIVORCE AND POLYGYNY

A marriage is an alliance between two households, but even in the most traditional of settings, it is based on daily cooperation and accommodation between individuals. The expectation that the man is "in charge" and the woman obedient, once common in many communities, was often contradicted by reality and depended on the individual spouses involved. In his study of marriage customs in Morocco, Issachar Ben-Ami describes practices he calls "rites of supremacy."[98] These may take the form of each member of the couple "putting his/her foot down" on top of the other's foot, or a contest over cutting fish. These playful rites, which have parallels in eastern Europe, are not necessarily declared to be tests of future domestic strength, but are embedded in other practices and gestures. Throughout North Africa, there were postnuptial customs involving fish, expressions of hoped-for fertility.

The wishes and blessings for harmonious life notwithstanding, some marriages end in divorce. Rabbinic tradition has discouraged divorce, and has encouraged couples to make every effort at reconciliation. It recognizes, however, that there are circumstances in which marriages should be dissolved. Even if rabbinic tradition wished to prohibit divorce, because of the value placed on marriage and procreation, it would be next to impossible, because divorce is explicitly recognized in the Bible. Deuteronomy 24:1 mentions a document called *sefer keritut*, a "bill of divorcement."[99] Thus divorce entailed creating a formal written document from early times. It is noteworthy that there is no biblical mention of a written document in the case of marriage, parallel to the rabbinic ketubba. In fact, the rabbis partially justify the possibility of marrying a woman through a written document by enunciating the general principle that one can learn laws concerning marriage from the laws of divorce, because the two subjects are juxtaposed in the passage of Deuteronomy just cited.[100]

There is also symmetry between divorce and marriage in rabbinic law in that they are both actions taken by a man, which a woman acquiesces in (or refuses).[101] Some suggest that the term "repudiation," of a woman by a man, would be a more accurate description of the formal aspect of Jewish divorce. The necessity of having a woman agree to accept a bill of divorce was instituted by authorities in medieval Ashkenaz, and is attributed to Gershom ben Yehudah of tenth- to eleventh-century Mainz.[102] Another development was the ability of a woman to pressure her husband, through the court, to issue her a *get*, or bill of divorce.[103] From a strictly legal point of view, however, the initiative lay solely with the man.

A get is a short document, addressed to a woman by her husband, that simply releases her from her commitment to him and makes her "permissible to any man." There are strict rules as to how it should be written. In contrast to a ketubba, it cannot be a standard form in which the names and date are filled in, but must be written expressly for the divorce in question. It is often explained that the detailed requirements concerning the preparation of a get are intended to create a "cooling-off" period, during which a man has time to rethink his decision. After a get is written, it must be handed to or delivered to a woman, and it must be clear that she has received and accepted it.[104]

There have been different views as to what constitutes a good reason for a man to repudiate his wife. The last Mishna in the tractate Giṭin (9:10; *giṭin* is the plural of *get*), offers several opinions. The followers of the sage Shammai say that divorce is justified if a woman is promiscuous, while the followers of Hillel claim that even her spoiling his cooked meals is grounds for divorce. The talmudic discussion that follows this Mishna concludes with the statement that even the sacrificial altar (in the Temple) sheds tears when a man divorces his first wife.[105] Historically, a common reason for seeking a divorce has been barrenness. The norm developed that if a woman did not give birth after ten years of marriage, her husband was justified in divorcing her. The sixteenth-century Polish sage Moshe Isserles states that the practice of divorcing a woman after ten years of childlessness had fallen into disuse.[106] Another option in those circumstances, which continued to exist in Sephardi tradition, was to take a second wife, as will be discussed shortly.

The decision to divorce and the writing of a get became matters of great gravity in rabbinic culture. Not only does divorce challenge the value of marriage, but, as noted, it calls for legal caution and precision. If there are mistakes in a get, or a lack of clarity, it may be claimed that a woman is not formally divorced. If she then enters into a relationship with another man, she is committing adultery. This was considered less of a legal problem with regard to the husband, because the Torah did not prohibit him from having more than one wife. Rabbinic concern, moreover, was not only about a woman's "morality" but about the status of any children she might bear in a second marriage.

Children born as the result of an adulterous relationship would be designated *mamzerim* (singular *mamzer*, Deut. 23:3), a word translated into English as "bastards." This is a misleading translation, however, because the question of a mamzer does not entail inheritance rights, nor is it only a matter of social opprobrium. Rather, it concerns the basic status of the individual within the Jewish community. A mamzer is any individual born as a result of sexual intercourse forbidden in the Torah, such as with one's sister or daughter or another man's wife.[107] A mamzer may only marry someone of the same status (although a convert, who can marry any Jew, may also marry a mamzer). The rabbinic stress on the correctness of a get, then, was linked to the desire to avoid creating or expanding a class of outcastes within Jewish society who were forbidden to marry other Jews.

Overall, it is very easy to marry according to Jewish tradition, but getting divorced is a slow and painstaking legal process. If a man past bar mitzvah age gives an unmarried woman a ring in front of two witnesses, recites the phrase of "kiddushin" (above), and she accepts the ring, there is good rabbinic opinion that a marriage has been effected according to halakha, even though this is not the recommended way of marrying today. If a man were to try to give his wife a get in such an informal and unsupervised manner, there would be myriad ways of challenging the validity of the procedure, and the working assumption of traditional rabbis would be that she was still married until a get had been given under their watchful eye. In modern times, now that Jews are able, or required, to marry and divorce according to civil law, the lack of coordination between civil divorce and Jewish divorce has created the problem of the *aguna*.

Aguna is a term from rabbinic tradition referring to a woman who is "tied down," or caught in a marriage that is no longer active, but who, at the same time, is not free to remarry.[108] The classic situation creating the status of aguna was a husband who left home in uncertain circumstances, such as going to war, or even going on a long journey for purposes of business, and then did not return. If there was no firm proof of his death, or he did not send a get to his wife through a legally empowered messenger, there was no way of terminating the marriage at her initiative. Rabbinic tradition sought ways of handling this problem. One was to relax the rules about witnesses who would be accepted to testify that the man had in fact died. Another was to have a husband who went off on a long or dangerous journey prepare a conditional get for his wife, which would become actual if he did not return after a defined amount of time. This was common among medieval traders, and the obligation that a man prepare conditional bills of divorce was even stipulated in betrothal contracts.[109]

In modern times, aside from the anonymous deaths of the Holocaust, the question of an aguna appears in two common versions. One is in Diaspora countries, where a couple may be divorced under civil law but not necessarily under Jewish law. If the couple is not concerned with rabbinic tradition, then the question does not become a personal problem. If the woman does want a get, however, or a man whom she later wants to marry is concerned that she have one, her former husband has a way of "tying her down" by refusing to issue it.

The second form of modern aguna arises in Israel, where marriage and divorce can only take place under religious law (Jewish, Muslim, or Christian, as the case may be), and the supervision of these matters among Jews is under the control of the Orthodox rabbinate. The established rabbinate has followed the principle that a woman can be released from her marriage only through a get issued by her husband, even when it is clear to them that the marriage no longer has any substance, and that it may even be harmful to her to continue in the relationship. There have been cases of men incarcerated in order to persuade them to provide a get but who preferred to remain in jail rather than release their wives. This has created a category of women in Israel who "have been refused a get," and who come under the rubric of aguna. The rabbinate has been slow and hesitant in finding halakhic solutions to this problem, which now is a major concern of organizations dealing with women's rights.

One halakhically possible solution is annulment of the original marriage by a rabbinic court. Historically, rabbis have been reluctant to take upon themselves the power of annulment, but recourse to it in recent history has been documented by Zvi Zohar, who studied the rabbinic response to a problem that arose among the Jews of Egypt in the nineteenth century.[110] After the construction of the Suez Canal (1869), Egypt began to attract migrants from Europe, including Jews from eastern Europe. Many of the latter were young men who came to Egypt looking for economic opportunities. They came in contact with local Jewish families, which included old Egyptian families and others who had migrated to Egypt from elsewhere in the Middle East. In some instances, European men began to court the daughters of these families. The young men could be relatively "free" in their behavior, while the young women both came from more traditional backgrounds and were more directly exposed to the scrutiny of their families and community. When couples reached a stage of growing sexual intimacy, men sometimes persuaded women to take the step of full sexual intercourse by saying they would marry them privately, and later let the parents know when the man had established himself economically. As indicated, this could be done by the man simply reciting the kiddushin in front of friends, and the woman accepting something of monetary value. This became a common occurrence, but in some cases, the men later left Egypt without a trace before publicly acknowledging the fact of their marriage. The abandoned women, telling their sad story, explained that they had agreed to sexual contact because of the ceremony of kiddushin. In facing this new situation, which was more extensive than a few individual cases, rabbis in Egypt took the daring step of annulling the private marriages. Zohar stresses the willingness of these rabbis to respond to a new social problem in a manner that enlarged the options in halakha, rather than to hold on to safer, conservative opinions. He claims that this willingness stemmed from the fact that there were no organized religious movements in Egypt that challenged traditional rabbinic authority, so that the rabbis there could allow themselves to cultivate the possibilities of change within halakha. This suggests that the stances of contemporary Orthodox rabbis to issues like that of aguna may overlook opportunities for halakhic solutions for reasons that are not inherently halakhic.

This issue of the aguna easily becomes a prism through which contemporary religious and political divides in Judaism are refracted. In the United States, the issue was addressed by the Jewish Theological Seminary of America, representing Conservative Judaism, in the 1950s. Based on the formulation of a leading Talmud scholar, Saul Lieberman, a version of the ketubba was put forth including a clause in which a husband agreed in advance that should problems arise in the marriage concerning religious matters, he empowered scholars at the seminary to summon him before a rabbinic court (*beit din*) and to impose monetary compensation from him. The assumption was that the threat of a big fine would deter men from refusing to supply a get just out of stubbornness.[111] The idea of the new ketubba was vociferously opposed by most leaders of Orthodoxy. In an intimate setting, I heard a leading Orthodox rabbi explain that there was nothing wrong with the "Lieberman clause" from the point of view of halakha, but that the new policy would bring Conservative rabbis to deal with the writing of bills of divorce, rather than rely on Orthodox rabbis to deal with this legally intricate matter as they had done in the past.

This explanation indicates that religious debates between religious streams in Judaism today are not always over religious content per se, but also, and sometimes mainly, over who is empowered to make decisions with regard to that content. Some Orthodox rabbis did express halakhic objections to the "Lieberman clause." They are mentioned by a well-known "modern Orthodox" spokeswoman on feminist matters, who also warns that rabbinical positions on issues should not be ruled out "just because Conservative or Reform or Reconstructionist Judaism got there first."[112] In 1996, a modern Orthodox rabbi, Emanuel Rackman, who has had a prominent career in both the United States and Israel, founded a beit din in New York to deal with the problem of *agunot* (plural). This court has since released many agunot based on the rabbinic principle of annulment. The majority of rabbis in the Orthodox world have not recognized these decisions, however, and are not prepared to preside over the marriages of these women to new husbands. It seems that matters of maintaining solidarity and authority get inextricably mixed into deliberations concerning individual families and lives.

In Israel, Conservative or Reform rabbis are not recognized to deal officially with matters of marriage or divorce. They have no standing in the eyes of the Ministry of the Interior, by which changes of personal status are registered and given legal validity. There, the issue of an aguna by virtue of a husband's refusal to provide a get pits individual women against established Orthodoxy. Some of the groups concerned with the problem view it in its most general terms because the same halakhic issues exist in various countries even though the context of national civil law differs. The International Coalition for Agunah Rights, for example, claims that rabbinic courts could make greater use of annulment to overcome the monopoly that men have with regard to the power of divorce.[113] Others encourage halakhic moves similar to the principle used by Lieberman: the inclusion of an agreement within the ketubba on steps to be taken in the event of a divorce.[114] In some aspects of family law, rabbinic authority in Israel has responded to pressure and agreed to the appearance before a beit din of professional female advocates in cases of divorce.[115] Whether the entrenched rabbinate will eventually permit developments that relieve the basic imbalance of divorce rights entailed in traditional Jewish marriage is a matter of speculation.

The other side of the advantage given to men by rabbinic law in relation to a get is that they can initiate divorce. As mentioned, lack of children was considered a legitimate motive in this regard. An alternate way of meeting the problem of barrenness was to take a second wife. The Bible recognizes polygyny; it appears in the lives of the patriarchs (Jacob marrying Leah and Rachel), in Deuteronomy 21:15, and in the political alliance marriages of David and Solomon. It sometimes assumes the form of concubinage, and no less a figure than Abraham provides the precedent for taking a concubine (actually offered to him by Sarah) in order to have children (Gen. 16:1–3). At the same time, domestic life as portrayed in later biblical literature, like the Book of Proverbs, seems to take monogamy as both the normal and ideal situation. This is the case in classic rabbinic culture as well, although the sages of the Mishna and Talmud never banned polygyny and were content to follow what had become accepted, rather than forbid what is explicitly permitted in the Torah.

Polygyny, however, did not completely disappear from Jewish life. It continued in some areas and was restricted or outlawed in others. From about the eleventh century on, it was banned among Ashkenazi Jews. This ban is commonly attributed to Rabbi Gershom of Mainz, mentioned above, but probably emerged even before his time. It is likely that the norms of the Christian surroundings, which viewed marriage as a concession to human weakness, influenced Jews to institutionalize the limitation of married life to one woman.

Classic Sepharad was at first heavily exposed to Islam, which permitted polygyny, and later to Christianity as well. In that setting, polygyny was not forbidden but was discouraged by means of the marriage contract. In addition to the standard stipulations of a ketubba, other provisions might be included at the agreement of the parties. A condition, for example, might be that a man could not take a second wife unless his wife agreed to it, or that if he did take a second wife, he automatically had to pay his first wife the sum of "her ketubba." Alternately, a ketubba might state that if a woman did not bear children after ten years, a man could take a second wife with the first's permission. Examples of such ketubbot or the laws on which they are based were found, among other places, in the Cairo Geniza, and in a collection of the ordinances of Sephardi rabbis after they had lived in Morocco for several generations.[116]

Polygyny continued to be an option among Jews in parts of the Islamic world. Mordecaï Ha-Cohen writes of Tripoli at the turn of the nineteenth century that Jewish men would come there from Italy in order to marry a second wife, something they could not do in Italy itself.[117] Typically, rabbis in Tripoli only agreed if the first wife had borne no children. Among poor families in nineteenth-century Baghdad, young women who had no dowry to offer sometimes migrated to India, where they married local Jewish men in the Bombay Bene Israel or the Cochin communities. These men were so pleased to have Baghdadi wives that they even agreed to marry a second penniless bride, often a relative of the first.[118] There also were cases of polygynous marriages in the twentieth century in North Africa and in Yemen.[119] In Aden, the practice was explained as a way of ensuring the birth of a son who would recite the *kaddish* prayer after the death of his father.[120]

There were undoubtedly regular tensions built into polygynous families. In Jerba, where polygyny was forbidden by the Tunisian state in 1958, "people preserve the memory of a rabbi at the beginning of this [twentieth] century, whose four wives exhausted themselves in domestic battles."[121] With regard to the Jews of Yemen, we have information from S. D. Goitein at the time of the mass immigration to Israel.[122] Goitein found two women living together in a village outside of Jerusalem in 1950, who were then widows but had been co-wives of the same man in the past. The second woman had come into the household after the first one had borne no children. The new wife gave birth to several children, and they still continued to be good friends. The latter gave the following account: "We two women were like two doves. The man was one week with her and the next week with me. I did embroidery and she the household work. I produced the children, and she reared them."[123] A more rounded perspective is provided by Laurence Loeb's discussion of polygyny among the Habbani Jews of southern Yemen, which notes that "co-wives, who could often be in vigorous competition for affection, attention, and influence, often were socially affable companions in the absence of their husbands." Loeb also indicates that males "were quite aware of the disadvantages of polygyny: conflict between co-wives for a husband's attention and over inheritance, interfamily hostility, expense, and . . . sexual responsibility."[124] He summarizes that "in retrospect, Habbani women [in Israel today] . . . comment negatively on their naiveté, especially in their consent to polygyny and early marriage."[125]

PRESERVING, REVIVING, AND INTERPRETING CUSTOMS

Institutional arrangements like polygyny are mainly a matter of historical interest, but other aspects of traditional marriages and wedding celebrations have been maintained, reshaped, and even revitalized in new circumstances. In many marriages in Israel, brides now wear white dresses, as has long been de rigueur in Europe. It is quite common, however, if the couple or even one of the partners has a Middle Eastern background, to have a minor henna ceremony a few days before the wedding, during which the woman dresses in the traditional wedding garb of her parents' (or husband's parents') country of origin (see figure 14). Sometimes this is done to satisfy the expectations of the older generation, but in other instances, the bride-to-be wishes to express family and ethnic continuity. It also is not unusual for a woman of Ashkenazi background to want to taste the prac-

Figure 14. A bride prepared for a henna ceremony among Habbani Jews from southern Yemen in Israel. Courtesy Carmela Avdar.

tices and traditions that have meaning to the family of her future husband. The practice is so common that many catering companies advertise their services for "henna parties" along with a list of events like brit milah and bar mitzvah. Contemporary henna celebrations are by no means close replicas of the ones conducted in the countries from whence immigrants to Israel came. I have seen a home video of a henna celebration by two Libyan families in Italy in a fancy Rome hotel, with elegantly dressed guests.

Another example of restored continuity, in relation to the European world, is the custom of bedekn (see above), which is part of the wedding ceremonies of many observant couples in Israel today. It has also undergone something of a renaissance in North America among people choosing to shape a traditional Jewish life for themselves. There, it is sometimes tied to another practice revived in these circles, the *tish*. The Yiddish word *tish* means "table," and the institution was adopted from eastern European Hasidic traditions, where many kinds of celebrations take place on the occasion of a meal around a table.[126] Typically, the leader of the Hasidic group, the *rebbi*, is the main figure at a tish, but in weddings, the groom holds center stage.

After the bedekn, the groom and the bride separate, each with his or her same-gender companions. The groom, and these days sometimes the bride, sets out to deliver a brief Torah lesson to those present. Ostensibly, this shows how cherished the value of Torah study is, being attached to every occasion. In fact, however, no sooner has the groom begun to speak than he is interrupted by his guests' bursting into song, cued by a word from him that calls to mind a familiar melody. The groom's "lesson" is thus jokingly frustrated, and an atmosphere of gaiety prevails. There was also a tradition of interrupting the groom's Torah lesson at the festive meal (*se'udat mitzvah*) after a wedding.[127] In the case of a prenuptial tish, when the joking and partying ends, the next stage is the actual approach to the ḥuppah.

One possible view is to regard this interrupted lesson simply as a form of wedding fun arising within communities to whom the study of Torah is a central value. At another level, the pretense of giving a lesson and having it stopped corresponds to, and even goes beyond, the rule in the Mishna that on his wedding night, a groom is exempted from reciting the Shma' Yisrael prayer.[128] The Mishna seems to assume that a young man getting married will not concentrate on the meaning of the Shma' and its religious message and therefore releases him from that obligation. With this rule in the background, the custom, as it were, presents a groom so committed to the study of the Torah that his friends have to remind him that there should be other things on his mind just then. This interpretation is offered as one of many intricate ways in which rabbinic tradition and popular culture interact on the stage of wedding celebrations. Another practice in which it is possible to view the complexities of that interaction over the long haul of Jewish history is the custom of breaking a glass.

BREAKING THE GLASS

"Up to the present day, the breaking of a glass has remained one of the most characteristic features of Jewish weddings," the noted anthropologist Edward Westermarck observes in his ambitiously titled *History of Human Marriage.* He notes that the custom may take several forms: the bridegroom may break a glass with his foot or it may be broken by the rabbi.

"Various fanciful explanations have been suggested for this ceremony," he adds, "but its true meaning, as I understand it, has to my knowledge never been recognized."[129]

One can still claim, over a century later, that the breaking of a glass is a characteristic feature of Jewish weddings, but today's anthropologists resist the notion that we can know the "true meaning" of this or any other custom. Rather, they claim, customs have various meanings for different members of a society, or for the same members of that society on different occasions. The best an analyst can do is to specify the diverse situations in which a custom comes into play and record them in detail, along with the reactions to and comments upon the custom. Customs do not have set, stable meanings that are good for all times and places.

With this skeptical approach, contemporary anthropology also questions what once was a basic dogma of the discipline: the belief that explanations offered by "natives" concerning their own customs are not very illuminating. Interpretations growing out of a scientific perspective were preferable to those given by members of the society involved. Today, however, it is a commonplace that anthropologists, or any so-called "objective" observers, themselves offer a variety of interpretations, none of which can be authoritatively established as the true one.

It is not easy to distinguish between "insider" and "outsider" explanations in the case of Jewish culture, with its ever-expanding storehouse of understandings, enshrined in texts produced over the generations. This corpus of interpretations contains many sophisticated insights. Often, rabbinic commentary on laws and practices yields "native" interpretations that parallel ideas found in social scientific discussion.

An appreciation of these issues emerges when examining the custom of breaking a glass at weddings. Several explanations that seem "fanciful" (Westermarck's term) when taken alone, make sense in the context of a set of interlocking interpretations. Glass-breaking, which is seen as part of Jewish "folk culture," provides a richly complex case of the meeting of textual and popular culture in Jewish life over the centuries.

It is common knowledge, often repeated at weddings, that the breaking of a glass is interpreted as a sign of mourning for Jerusalem and the destroyed Temple of antiquity. At the moment of their highest joy, a new couple must remember the plight of their people. This explanation is relatively "recent," however, in terms of the development of Jewish law and lore. It has no explicit basis in the Bible or the Mishna. Many later rabbinic authorities linked the practice of breaking a glass to a passage in the Babylonian Talmud (see below), edited in the fifth or sixth century C.E. This connection is indirect, however, as will be explained. The interpretation of the custom in terms of mourning for the Temple is known only from the fourteenth century in Ashkenaz. It is also only from the late Middle Ages that breaking a glass appears as a *prescribed* part of the marriage ceremony. It is therefore a puzzle why this custom, and its now quasi-official explanation, became firmly implanted in Jewish practice and awareness despite the "recency" of the Temple-mourning interpretation.

One facet of the success of the glass-breaking custom and its explanation is their inclusion in standard rabbinic codes compiled in the sixteenth century and after. These are all based on the *Shulhan Arukh*, a legal compendium by the Sephardi scholar Yosef Caro, to which the Polish sage Moshe Isserles added extensive glosses, based on Ashkenazi tradition, and included the "Temple-memorializing," or *zekher la-ḥurban*, explanation. The two works were printed together around 1570, and many times thereafter, and this may be one factor accounting for the widespread diffusion of the practice within the Jewish world.

This explanation of the custom's vitality can only be partial. Modern Jews have ignored and abandoned many traditional customs, the existence of proof texts notwithstanding. Why should they privilege the breaking of the glass and its zekher la-ḥurban justification? Other perspectives are called for to supplement and make sense of the persistence of this feature of Jewish weddings.

It must be noted that it is not only anthropologists who raise questions forcing us to look twice at the conventional meaning attached to ceremonial glass-breaking. In his description of the customs of the Jews of his native Tripoli, Rabbi Mordecaï Ha-Cohen of Libya implicitly challenged the "remembrance of the destroyed Temple" thesis, with reference, not to the glass broken as part of the wedding ceremony, but to two other vessel-breaking events.

In Tripoli, when a procession accompanied a bride to the home of the groom, the latter climbed to the top of his house and threw down a clay jug in front of her, forcing her to walk through the shattered pieces before entering the house. Upon entering her new abode, the bride took a raw egg that she had been carrying, and threw it at the opposite wall. Both these acts were viewed by Tripoli's Jews as "remembering the Temple." Ha-Cohen wonders, however, why, if the point is to recall a sad event, the smashing of the jug is accompanied by the high-pitched joyous ululation of female onlookers? He further observes, in describing life in a mountainous region south of Tripoli, that Muslim Berber brides also smashed eggs against the walls of their new homes. He ponders: "What connection exists between the Muslim Berbers and the destroyed Holy Temple?" Ha-Cohen's questions make it clear that there was something at work in these local customs beyond their time-sanctioned Judaic explanations, and the same is true of related practices in other Jewish communities as well. For answers to these questions, one seeks to supplement the historical study of ancient Jewish texts with insights based on actual practice.

As stated, breaking a glass as part of the wedding ceremony proper is not mentioned in early rabbinic literature, but when the practice became established, later authorities linked it to a talmudic precedent. The Babylonian Talmud describes two spontaneous events of glass-breaking that took place during wedding festivities. In the first: "Mar, son of Ravina, made the wedding feast for his son. When he noticed that the rabbis were merry, he brought a precious cup worth 400 zuz, and broke it before them. They immediately became sad."[130]

The second story is an almost exact parallel of the first. Both stories appear, not in relation to the topic of weddings, but in a discussion of the appropriate attitude to be maintained during prayer, which cites a phrase from Psalms 2:11, "rejoice with trembling," indicating complex and contradictory emotions.

In a 1925 article "The Ceremony of Breaking a Glass at Weddings," Jacob Lauterbach cites this talmudic reference and then follows the custom of breaking a glass at weddings through posttalmudic literature. He concludes that it reflected beliefs concerning demons. The purpose of the act, he claims, was to distract, or drive away, harmful demons from the joy of a new couple. He also sees the belief in demons and concomitant actions as implicated in the events reported in the Talmud.[131]

Posttalmudic rabbis, in Lauterbach's view, were aware of what he called the "superstitious" bases of these actions and would have preferred to eliminate them. They could not eradicate the glass-breaking custom, however, because of its popularity. The rabbis' strategy, he surmises, was to let the practice continue without commenting upon the dubious beliefs it implied. That is why no allusion to it appears in the centuries after the talmudic period. The custom is mentioned only in twelfth- and thirteenth-century Ashkenaz, when breaking a glass first appears as part of the wedding ceremony. In the fourteenth century, as noted, the practice is first interpreted as a gesture of mourning over the Temple. The subsequent persistence of the custom, Lauterbach asserts, stems from linking an ancient practice, which was questionable from the point of view of pure monotheistic belief, to the rabbinic explanation. He further argues that the acceptable interpretation of the glass-breaking custom did not immediately displace older demonic understandings, but that these persisted for several centuries.

Lauterbach's reconstruction seems plausible, given the sources available. The talmudic stories he cites do not mention demons per se, but they approvingly describe incidents in which a limit is placed on mirth during wedding celebrations. His explanation of why the rabbis *did not comment* on the glass-breaking custom from the late talmudic period until the twelfth century—a span of almost 700 years—remains in the realm of speculation.

From a contemporary point of view, these demonological interpretations are limited. Notions concerning demons were certainly widespread in Jewish communities, but anthropology does not now see ritual action as growing only out of the logic of belief systems. The belief in demons itself requires explanation. It reflects social processes, in particular the transitions and stresses of individual and communal life.[132] In addition, the explanations of rituals often do not help us understand their "origins"; they are better viewed as attempts to make sense of already existing practices. Lauterbach's exposition, by trying to elucidate the "logic" that links ritual acts to what he sees as no-longer-tenable beliefs, ignores the grounding of ritual in universal aspects of social life.

Ruth Gladstein-Kestenberg supplements Lauterbach's analysis by discussing the sexual symbolism of the glass-breaking, the meaning that was obvious to Westermarck.[133] She anchors her thesis in comparative study but also provides a talmudic prototype. Earlier, we noted that the Talmud contains information on the customary celebration of weddings. One practice was the passing of a vessel of wine in front of a bride. The Talmud further specifies that the shape of the receptacle depended upon whether she was a virgin or not.[134] A slender container was used in the case of a virgin, and a wider-mouthed vessel in the case of a widow. This dramatizes a direct link between virginity and a vessel used at a wedding.

According to Gladstein-Kestenberg, the talmudic sources underlined by Lauterbach and the ones that she cites were brought together in the wedding ceremonies performed by Rabbi Jacob ben Moshe of Moellin in fifteenth-century Germany. Rabbi Jacob used two different kinds of vessels to recite the blessing over wine. He utilized a narrow glass appropriate to a virgin and a wider ceramic cup for a widow. In the former case, a bridegroom would drink from the first cup of wine, then turn towards the north and smash it against the wall of the synagogue. One talmudic text was seen as the source for ceremoniously breaking a glass, while the other pointed to the shape of the vessel to be used. By linking the practice to old rabbinic sources, Rabbi Jacob not only underscored the validity of glass-breaking, but also seemingly acknowledged the sexual overtones of the rite.

Gladstein-Kestenberg also surmises that this practice was in fact older than the date of its first documentation. In some instances, at least, its sexual connotations must have been recognized. The same distinction appears in an account of Jewish weddings in seventeenth-century Morocco by the English clergyman Lancelot Addison, who writes: "If the bride be a virgin, they give her wine in a narrow cup; if a widow, in a wide one, for excellent reason no doubt." It is likely that Addison did not observe this directly among Jews in Morocco but copied these details from a description based on Jewish life in central Europe (Rabbi Jacob's milieu).[135] In any event, it was not difficult for him to "read" the sexual reference. Jacob of Moellin emphasized ties to the talmudic text, but he was also responding to meanings associated with the ceremony in popular sentiment.

Both the talmudic passage cited and Addison's comment suggest that a metaphoric connection between femininity and a vessel was by no means opaque. Contrary to Westermarck, an appreciation of the juxtaposition of glass-breaking with the conjugal act has never been obscure. In weddings I have observed, the ability to break a glass decisively was often associated with the "strength" of the groom in the form of jokes by onlookers concerning his "virility." Contemporary rabbis also have commented on this type of jesting; typically, they disapprove of it.[136]

The association of wedding glass-breaking and the end of virginity also appears in other guises in Jewish tradition. In late medieval central Europe, a wedding wine glass was thrown forcefully against a synagogue wall, leaving a red spot.[137] The stain on the wall may visually hint at another aspect of weddings mentioned above, proving the virginity of a bride by showing a blood-stained sheet.[138] Concerns over the successful initiation of sexual intercourse on the part of a newly established couple, an issue present at any wedding, received partial expression in the glass-breaking ceremony. Depending on time, place, and participants, an explicit grasp of the sexual resonance of the gesture was not very far beneath the surface.[139]

Gladstein-Kestenberg wonders why the sexual connotations of the symbolism are not made explicit in traditional sources. She cites Westermarck, who surmises: "That this intention has been more or less disguised, is not to be wondered at, considering the nature of the subject." Another reason that this level of explanation fails to appear in rabbinic writings may, however, be because it concerns a panhuman facet of marriage, rather than an issue with specific Jewish content. Rabbinic silence as to the sexual side of the practice may have repressed the awareness that Jewish life stemmed from the same human forces that affect everyone, as much as it reflected unease over issues of sexuality. Thus, the twelfth- to thirteenth-century sources that first mentioned glass-breaking, and linked it to the

Talmud, may have sought to actively "judaize," or give a Jewish cast to, a custom that had clear non-Jewish parallels.

Attention to explanations given for customs in neighboring cultures broadens the range of interpretations applicable to Jewish customs as well. We recall Ha-Cohen's observation that egg-breaking among Libyan Jewish villagers was also found among the local Muslims.[140] In one Muslim community, the act took place when a bride entered the room in which she would soon be deflowered; there is also the suggestion that it represents the desire for fertility. Similar attributions are made by Westermarck in referring to customs in many parts of the Muslim world and in Mediterranean lands generally.[141]

The Libyan Muslim data yield other understandings as well. For example, there is the interpretation that the act points to the loosening of social ties between the bride and her original family. Muslim villagers in a second Libyan community, on the other hand, state that the practice brings harmony to the new house.[142] These two explications of the same act may be seen as different aspects of a single process; it is only by neglecting, or permanently altering, the old ties that a new family can be successfully formed and sustained. Comparison with other cultures thus shows that our custom reflects the making and breaking of social ties, in addition to its patent sexual associations.

The symbolic understandings offered thus far bring together distinct ideas, which in some instances may be seen as opposites of one another. The rupturing of the hymen that constitutes the *termination* of virginity is associated with the *beginning* of procreation and the building of a new social unit. The *breaking* of an object points to the *creation* of a new social bond. In both instances, opposite types of processes are closely linked. Let us explore the latter association further by examining what happens when a vessel is smashed. First, the breaking of a glass entails a dramatic change of state. A second feature of the process is the move from wholeness to destruction. A third is the *irreversibility* of the change involved. This is the feature that seems most closely to match the aspired-for developments in the realm of marriage.

Judaism, as discussed, places high value on stable and peaceful family ties, but also recognizes the possibility of divorce. The rabbinic marriage ceremony and ketubba can encourage a successful and permanent union, but cannot totally guarantee that outcome. The unpredictable course of a marriage thus calls forth popular expressions of its durability. Breaking a glass seems to say: "Just as a broken vessel cannot be reconstituted, it is to be hoped that what has been done at this ceremony will not be undone." Standing the well-known injunction from the Episcopal Book of Common

Prayer sometimes heard at non-Jewish weddings on its head, the breaking of a glass challenges the onlookers of a ceremony: "Let no man join together what has here been rent asunder!" Its social-symbolic *use*, however, is precisely the opposite: to hold intact that which is inherently fragile.

This idea is also hinted at by Westermarck when he cites the explanation given in Boeotia, Greece, for the custom of burning the axle of a wagon that carried a bride to the house of a groom, thus culminating the wedding procedures. Once the marriage has taken place, there is no return. Westermarck does not apply this reasoning to his egg- and glass-breaking examples, but it applies there as well. The logic is that of the most widespread riddle in the English language: Humpty Dumpty. Once the egg—Humpty Dumpty—is broken, "all the king's horses and all the king's men" cannot reverse the process. Humpty Dumpty highlights the paradox that the *breaking* of an object stands for irreversibility and *permanence*.

Making a connection between Humpty Dumpty and wedding ceremonies is not arbitrary, because the children's verse is in fact a riddle (the answer is "an egg"), and there is an ancient connection between riddles and weddings. Samson presents a riddle to the Philistines to be solved by them on the occasion of his wedding (Judg. 14:12). In Italy and Holland in the seventeenth and eighteenth centuries, learned riddles were composed as an aspect of wedding festivities.[143] Galit Hasan-Rokem, in reference to this practice and to riddles generally, stresses the quality of irreversibility as inherent in riddles as a literary form.[144]

The logic of these symbolic associations, including that of irreversibility, was not lost on rabbinic commentators. After the custom of breaking a glass and the explanation tying it to the destroyed Temple were incorporated into rabbinic codes in the sixteenth century, rabbinic discussion of the practice and others related to it grew. One development stressed the distinction between the two cups of wine drunk in the wedding ceremony, one in the kiddushin phase and the other as part of the nesuin. Most rabbis insisted that only the former cup be broken, because to break the latter—in the marriage phase—would be an omen that the newly established marriage bond might not survive. Above, I cited the insistence of the Gaon of Vilnius that couples smash a ceramic dish, which cannot be repaired, as part of their prenuptial agreement (tenaim). Even when the explanation with reference to the destroyed Temple was well established, rabbis continued to elaborate their understanding of the glass-breaking and related customs.

Thus far we have viewed the breaking of the glass at Jewish weddings in terms of popular beliefs and various social scientific explanations. These may be sufficient to account for the wide diffusion of the custom and its persistence in Jewish life. From this standpoint, the connection between the glass-breaking and its well-known rabbinic explanation appears arbitrary. The explanation seems to supply a Jewish veneer to universal social and symbolic processes. Building upon this analysis, however, I would also argue that the destroyed Temple explanation is not totally arbitrary. It involves an intricate latching-on of a powerful theme in Jewish culture to the abiding human concerns of individuals and families. This linkage takes place because internal Jewish symbolism and the panhuman symbolic elements we have considered share similar structures of opposing and paradoxical meanings.

In a book introducing the study of symbolism, the anthropologist Edmund Leach illustrated the principle that symbols within a culture must be understood in relation to one another by pointing to the logic of colors worn by brides and widows in European society. White stands for the entrance into marriage, and contrasts with black, which represents the exit from the married state upon the death of the husband.[145] Examining Jewish tradition from this perspective leads to the observation that, more saliently than oppositions, one finds many parallels between the cultural markers of marriage and of mourning.

There are many examples of this parallel. The mishnaic rule that a groom on his wedding night is not obligated to recite the Shma' Yisrael was cited above. The next chapter of the Mishna states that a person whose deceased relative has not been buried is also released from that obligation.[146] In the Talmud, a discussion of the blessings recited at a wedding flows into a consideration of the blessings appropriate in the presence of mourners.[147] In a different realm, there exists the custom, in diverse Jewish communities, of preparing an undergarment for a bride that is worn first at her wedding but ultimately is used as a shroud. The connection between marriage and funerals also was elaborated in Jewish mysticism.[148] In some mystical traditions, the death of a righteous person was marked annually by a festive celebration called a *hillula*, because the return of his soul to its origin was perceived of as a kind of wedding.[149]

Returning to the practice of glass-smashing, symbols of breaking or severance are central both in Jewish weddings and in funerary ritual. Breaking a glass is standard in weddings, and tearing a garment is a required component of Jewish mourning. With regard to marriage, the prescribed nature of the act developed in the medieval period, but the act of rending a garment at the time of death has roots in biblical culture.[150] In the case of mourning, the symbolic link between tearing a garment and the irreversible rupture of ties is apparent, and we have argued that this is a central signification of glass-breaking with reference to marriage. The now "semi-official" interpretation that links the joy of marriage to sadness over the destruction of the Temple raises the question as to whether a woeful setting, such as a funeral, can be designated as having some positive features.

I personally experienced this question more than a decade ago at the time of the death of my father. A rabbi friend[151] explained to me and my family that the obligatory rending of our garments at the funeral signified the *end of sorrow*. This interpretation, pointing to an eventual return of gladness, did a somersault with the most obvious significance of the gesture, which resonates with the permanent breaking of a social bond. It is also obvious that my friend's consoling interpretation was more appropriate to the immediate human situation than were my own dubious anthropological ponderings. Religious thought in many societies is sensitive to unexpected reversals in human lives. In Jewish tradition, this is exemplified, and epitomized, in the close linkage between sorrow over the destruction of the Temple and the hope of rebuilding it.

The remembrance of the sorrow of Jerusalem by breaking a glass at weddings is a "recent" development in Jewish history, but it easily meshes with more ancient notions and texts. Bringing the topic of Jerusalem into the wedding celebration is not new. As already mentioned, two of the seven blessings from the Talmud that are recited at weddings express the hope that Jerusalem will be rebuilt. The wish of one of the blessings that speedily there will be heard "in the cities of Judah and the squares of Jerusalem, the sound of joy and the sound of happiness, the voices of bridegrooms and the voices of brides" is taken from Jeremiah 33:10–11, where it is to be understood as a *reversal* of the similarly phrased prophecy recorded earlier in Jeremiah 7:34, where it is warned that "the voices of bridegrooms and the voices of brides" will no longer be heard in Jerusalem. The fourteenth-century document that first invokes the destroyed Temple as an interpretation of the custom, and does so in the context of a discussion of the rules of the fast day commemorating that event, the laws of Tishah be-Av, did not make this connection de novo, but built upon a long tradition of cultural associations.

In fact, glass-breaking as Temple remembrance appears to have supplanted another custom recalling the Temple's destruction. Rabbi Jacob ben Asher of fourteenth-century Toledo, whose father moved from Ashkenaz to Spain, records that in the latter region, ashes were rubbed on the forehead of the groom, on the place where head-tefillin are placed, as a sign of Temple mourning.[152] The verse cited as explaining that custom, taken from Isaiah 61:3, addresses the mourners of Zion and speaks of replacing their ashes with glory. The phrase constitutes a play on words, in which *pe'er* (glory) takes the place of *'epher* (ashes).[153] The logic of a text-based reversal inserted into a wedding context thus existed prior to the emergence of the structured glass-breaking ceremony. Another medieval source suggests that the practice of applying ashes to the groom's forehead was relinquished on principle, because many grooms did not regularly don tefillin.[154] I suspect that it fell into relative disuse (it continued in Yemen as part of the ceremony of placing a prayer shawl on the groom)[155] because the glass-breaking custom, carrying with it the energy of popular roots, more powerfully encapsulated the multileveled message of reversal.

In Jewish tradition, remembrance of the destroyed Temple is typically intertwined with the hope of its rebuilding. This is expressed, for example, in the idea that the day of the destruction of the Temple, marked by the fast of Tish'ah be-Av, is also the day on which the Messiah, who is to rebuild the Temple, was born.[156] The same idea is found in a talmudic story about the sage Rabbi Akiba, who laughed upon seeing foxes run through the ruins of the Temple, while his colleagues cried. Akiba explained that now that he had seen the prophecies of destruction fulfilled, he could be certain that the predictions of redemption would be realized.[157] The paired elements of destruction and reconstruction have become so closely tied together in Jewish tradition that the one, pointing to the other, can also stand for its opposite. Given these associations in Jewish lore, the application of the destroyed Temple explanation to glass-breaking appears, not as an arbitrary choice assigning a meaning to a custom based on "superstition," but as a "natural" and persuasive development.

The seemingly effortless step that links a rabbinic interpretation to general symbolic processes connected with the breaking of vessels reflects the parallel logical structure found in both sets of associations. Universal glass-smashing symbolism, which startlingly proclaims that shattering can point to permanence, absorbs another bundle of symbols in which opposites are intertwined that is particularly and intensely Jewish. In addition, the paradoxical dimension of the ritual may function as an interpretive engine pushing towards further elaboration of ritual action and thought.

It is precisely the human conundrum that destroying and creating can be tightly interlocked, and even symbolize each other, that is ostensibly "resolved" by re-presenting familiar cultural content that shows that this connection appears again and again in a valued sphere of Jewish life. In this manner, a widespread symbolic association found in many societies becomes a vehicle for more culturally specific symbols.

The successful linking of culturally specific and universal symbolism has an impact upon individuals and ties them to the collectivity and its traditions, as seen in Jewish mourning ceremonies. Mourning ritual expresses the irreversible breaking of social ties, but the individual mourner is also reminded, in conventionalized fashion, of the mourning for Jerusalem. Upon exiting a cemetery after burial, or upon concluding a visit to a house of bereavement, visitors take leave of mourners with phrases such as: "May the All-Present console you among the other mourners of Zion and Jerusalem." Taken at face value, this is not a felicitous formula, for the memory of destroyed Jerusalem could just as easily compound the mourner's anguish![158] Characteristically however, the memory of Jerusalem's desolation is utilized to constitute a gesture of *consolation*. This can only be understood on the assumption that the destruction of Jerusalem assures its eventual restoration. Just as remembering the destroyed Temple intrudes into the mirth of a wedding, so recalling Jerusalem's sadness points to the eventual return of joyfulness to a mourning family. The symbolic processes seeking to connect the person to the group are parallel to what is stated explicitly in the Passover Haggadah, in which each individual is required to view himself as if he had left Egypt. Breaking the glass at weddings utilizes widespread folk symbolism to create a deep sense of identification between the newly formed family and the saga of the Jewish people.

In addition to the contexts of weddings and funerals, glass-breaking and its interpretation also held their grasp because similar cultural associations were reiterated in other realms of Jewish life. One salient realm is that of the Friday night service and liturgy, in which some of the oppositional symbolism we have discussed may be found. The Friday night hymn "Lekhah Dodi," which treats the Sabbath as a bride, is also a product of the sixteenth century, like the widely printed *Shulhan Arukh*, which includes the glass-breaking interpretation.[159] That hymn richly draws upon imagery from the latter part of the Book of Isaiah, which celebrates the radical reversal in the status of the exiled Israelites in ancient Babylon and heralds the return of the Jews to Jerusalem. In one verse, for example, an image of Zion as a bride is addressed:

> Those that trampled you shall be trampled
> All those that despoiled you shall be routed
> Your God shall rejoice in you
> As a groom is joyful over his bride[160]

Moreover, in Jewish life, this set of textual associations may be woven into ritual situations connected to mourning.

Jewish law forbids mourning on the Sabbath. Even those who have lost a close relative are to refrain from sitting at home and observing the laws of mourning on the Sabbath that falls in the first week after death. Rather, mourners are expected to join in public worship; coming to the synagogue on Friday night constitutes one of the first acts of reintegration into normal communal life. It became customary, in Ashkenazi tradition, for their entrance into the synagogue to be coordinated with the end of the singing of the "Lekhah Dodi" hymn. When that hymn is concluded, according to widespread Ashkenazi practice (there is variation among Sephardim in this matter), worshipers turn to the entrance of the synagogue and mildly bow, as if greeting someone, while the concluding words of the hymn, "Come, O bride; come, O bride," are recited. At this point, the entering mourners are greeted with the phrase cited above: "May the All-Present console you amidst the other mourners of Zion and Jerusalem." The meeting of the sadness of mourning, and the joy of the image of the Sabbath as a bride, both linked to the memory of Jerusalem, have thus been inserted into the weekly liturgical cycle, sinking into the consciousness of many Jews. When similar associations arise in wedding ceremonies, far from appearing as an arbitrary interpretation pasted on to the glass-breaking custom, these meanings are sensed as appropriate, as if they have been inherent in the situation from time immemorial.

The long and intricate story of the glass-breaking continues today. We now find the custom in popular films serving as a sign of Jewish weddings, thereby adding new "textual" dimensions to Jewish practice. The presence of non-Jews at contemporary Jewish weddings also encourages interpretations that are not specifically Jewish. At a wedding in the United States that I attended several years ago, the officiating rabbi, while not ignoring other explanations, claimed that the gesture reminds us of the fragility of life and its vicissitudes. This interpretation appears in a seventeenth-century work by Leon de Modena (in Italy), the first book written in a European vernacular by a Jew aiming to explain Judaism to Christians.[161] At the same wedding, the young couple themselves distributed a decorative brochure, prepared on a word processor, explaining various "laws and customs of the Jewish marriage ceremony." Included was "the breaking of the glass." It pointed out that the destruction of six million Jews is now included among the sobering thoughts that one must keep in mind, even at the hour of "greatest happiness." A variety of appreciations of the custom, stemming from both ancient wisdom and current sensibilities, still reinvigorate one another as modern technology abets the linkage of panhuman concerns that emerge in weddings to rabbinic texts and traditions.

Marriage thus appears as one of the most stable institutions of Jewish tradition, while, at the same time, the practices and understandings composing it have responded to the material reality and cultural sensibilities of different regions and periods. The interplay of rabbinic law and popular custom is evident from ancient times through the Middle Ages up to the present. Always a scene of opposites, between the genders, between aspirations and anxiety, or between joy and sorrow, weddings continue to merge the desires of individuals, the institutions of family and community, and religious traditions in their official and vernacular forms. They also constitute a sort of midpoint along the path of personal lives, where the family of childhood is left behind and new routes of travel must be charted and navigated. Marriage turns this journey into a joint effort, but does not obliterate the process of self-definition or the realm of private visions.

5 Pilgrimage and Creating Identities

In the summer of 1994, I spent five weeks with American Jewish teenagers on a trip to Israel. Most were members of youth groups affiliated with Reform synagogues. Travel to Israel was a high point in their Jewish education. They had been in the country for less than two weeks when one girl came up to me as I was jotting down notes and asked whether I had learned anything that day.

"Yes," I answered simply, and asked her the same question.

"I learned a lot," she said. "I just wrote five pages in my journal."

"About what?" I asked.

"About myself. Now I feel that I have two homes: one in America, and one here. Before that, Israel was just out there. Now it's part of me."

"How does that happen so fast?" I queried, and at first she did not reply. Following with another question, I inquired: "Was there a specific moment or event that made you feel the change?"

She answered immediately, "The Wall." "What did you expect would happen at the Wall?" I continued. "I thought it would be cool," she explained, "writing down a note and putting it in. But when I got there, I broke down into tears. It was emotional."[1]

The Western Wall, or "the Kotel," as it is often called, using the Hebrew word for wall, remains from the time of King Herod at the beginning of the Christian era. It was a retaining wall against the hill on which the Temple stood. The Temple, at that time, was a focus of pilgrimage for Jews both in the surrounding province of Judea and from the Diaspora. Even after they were destroyed, the Temple and Jerusalem held a central place in the religious imagination of Jews. Throughout the ages, Jews returned to Jerusalem, if only for a visit. From the sixteenth century on, we know of the practice of Jews gathering near the Kotel to pray. In the nineteenth century, "the Western Wall" became a salient visual image in the ideology of Jewish nationalism. The connection of Jews to the Wall is thus shaped by cultural currents that have a powerful popular base. Simultaneously, consciousness of the Wall sets the stage for deep personal experiences that may take place at different stages of life.

As in the case of the American teenager, such experiences reach their peak when actually visiting the Wall as a "pilgrim," a "tourist," or a combination of the two. A visit to Jerusalem is not a standard life-cycle event for all Jews, but travel for the sake of exploring or reinforcing one's identity is now becoming widespread. In addition to the Kotel, Jews have identified other sites of collective memory and instituted regular travel to them. With the advance of mechanized transportation and the attainment of financial ease, visits to places of religious and cultural significance are now a common way for Jews of diverse ages and stages in life to express their prayers and commitments or delve into the meaning of their heritage. Beyond rites of birth, entrance to school, or bar/bat mitzvah, through which youngsters may be processed while exercising little choice, these individualized rituals of passage are consciously chosen and have multiple meanings for their participants.

The pilgrimage sites developed by Jews are diverse in locale as well as in cultural content. One traditional site in the city of Tlemcen in North Africa was once regularly visited by Jews from Algeria and neighboring Morocco. This was a pilgrimage briefly described in 1913 by the French ethnographer Arnold van Gennep, who found Jewish women "in costume" and men in "European fashion" at the tomb of fourteenth-century Spanish Rabbi Ephraim Ankawa, known locally as the "Rabb" (rabbi). They usually came there to make a vow linked to a prayer for healing, success in matchmaking, a prosperous business, or—especially—male offspring.[2]

In recent decades, American and Israeli Jews have created many other centers for meaningful travel. A shared example is the death camp in Auschwitz, Poland, a locus of vicarious identification with the victims of mass murder that asserts the importance of future Jewish existence.[3] Pilgrimage sites thus reflect historical events and shared cultural sensibilities, while also providing the context for the coalescence of a personal path in relation to life's flow.

PILGRIMAGE IN THE BIBLE AND SECOND TEMPLE TIMES

Pilgrimage has been part of Jewish life since biblical times. The Pentateuch does not directly name Jerusalem as the site of the Holy Temple, but does require pilgrimage to the place that "God will choose" (Deut. 14:23; 16:2, 6). Visits are obligatory three times during the year: on the festivals of Passover in the spring; Shavuòt, which comes seven weeks after Passover; and Sukkot, at the end of the summer. The requirement is for the Israelite male "to be seen by the Lord," that is, to travel to the sanctuary with a gift or sacrificial offering.[4]

The pilgrimage festivals correspond to phases of the agricultural cycle but also recall historical stages in the sojourn from Egypt to the Land of Canaan. Passover commemorates the Exodus (e.g., Deut. 16:1), Shavuòt came to represent the revelation on Sinai,[5] and Sukkot reminds the Israelites of God's providential care during the vulnerable period of forty years in the desert (Lev. 23:43). Associating these festivals with visits to a central sanctuary gives the opportunity of personally presenting an offering of gratitude for the harvest, while highlighting shared national memories.

This scheme may have been a prescribed ideal, rather than a reflection of actual pilgrimage practice. Its ideal nature is suggested by the verse encouraging pilgrims to leave their homesteads and come to the central sanctuary by assuring them that "no one will covet your land" during the period of the visit (Exod. 34:24). Another indication that the scheme is normative, and not necessarily in tune with actual custom, is that the commandment of "being seen" by the Lord is directed to males only.[6] In most traditional societies, pilgrimages were very important in the religious lives of women.

I first became aware of the importance of pilgrimages to women during my work in the Tripolitanian moshav in Israel in 1964.[7] At the time, I was the only person in the village with a private car, and people would often ask me for a ride to the main road. On one occasion, I was stopped by a family including members of three generations: a grandmother, mother, and daughter, accompanied by a related male. When the grandmother got into the back of the car, she tried to sit on the floor, being unfamiliar with that mode of travel. It was the first time she had ridden out of the village since arriving there early in the 1950s. Clearly, this was an important occasion.

The family asked to be let off at the main north-south road. I asked them where they were headed, and they said "Haifa." After I pressed them further, they explained that they were going to visit Elijah's cave just south of Haifa. Haifa, a port city, is located at the tip of the Carmel range, an area prominently associated with Elijah's activities in 1 Kings 18.[8] I saw that my passengers were reluctant to answer questions, but knew that the youngest of the three women, the daughter, was well past the age at which women normally were married. I surmised that the visit to Elijah's cave was to pray for his intercession in making a match. I also sensed, as was made explicit to van Gennep in Tlemcen, that on such occasions, it is best not to make one's prayer public.[9] Within a year, the young woman was married to a Tripolitanian living in a neighboring town. I assume that there was later a return visit to Elijah to fulfill the original vow.

A story of this nature (without an anthropologist present) occurs in the Bible with regard to the birth of the prophet Samuel.[10] It is told (1 Sam. 1) that Elkanah and his two wives regularly made pilgrimages to Shiloh, where the Ark of the Covenant was located before the establishment of the monarchy and David's selection of Jerusalem as a capital. One wife, Hannah, had no children, and was taunted by her rival, Penina, who was blessed with offspring. One year, Hannah boldly came to the entrance of the sanctuary and prayed for a male child. Her behavior, in which "only her lips moved," must have been somewhat unusual, because Eli, the priest at the sanctuary, first thought she was drunk (1 Sam. 1:13). When realizing the purity of her purpose, he, too, prayed that God grant her request. Hannah became pregnant and gave birth to Samuel. Eventually, she returned to Shiloh to repay her vow and dedicated Samuel to a life in the sanctuary.

This story is well known because it is read in the synagogue as part of the haftara on the first day of Rosh Hashanah. It parallels the account of the miraculous birth of Isaac to Sarah (Genesis 21), which is part of the reading from the Torah on the same day. The major actor in the story is Hannah, and the Talmud cites her behavior as the norm in daily prayer when it became established in later generations.[11] The prominence of women on such occasions is underlined by the mention of daughters partaking of the pilgrimage feast, and, subsequently, by the criticism of the sons of Eli for taking sexual advantage of women seeking closeness to the sanctuary (1 Sam. 2:22–25). Given the background of this story, which seems to reflect real aspects of ancient pilgrimage culture, the biblical laws that confine the festival pilgrimages to men may not correspond to actual practice.

In many pilgrimage settings, behavior is often more open and relaxed than in daily life. Men and women may mix more freely, or individuals of lower status and lesser wealth may rub shoulders with more affluent members of society from whom they usually would be quite separate. This is a phenomenon discussed by Victor Turner in terms of what he calls "communitas," a term that he first elaborated in discussing rites of passage. During the transitional phase of these rites, individuals going through the ritual together are symbolically separated from their previous identities, a process that highlights the basic human features they have in common. Rather than relating to one another by the status markers that assign them their social places in everyday life, initiates often experience communitas—"a generic human bond without which there could be no society." Turner links his notion of communitas to that of the "I and the Thou" of the philosopher Martin Buber.[12] Communitas is a transitory experience, but one that reenergizes social life when people return to more structured situations. It also appears to be one aspect of pilgrimages.[13]

This is exemplified in pilgrimages to Jerusalem in the late Second Temple period (the first century C.E.), discussed in a study by Jackie Feldman.[14] Some rabbinic laws relating to pilgrimage behavior fit the notion of communitas, in that they emphasize the sameness and equality of the pilgrims in comparison to their differentiated positions in everyday social life. For example, one law forbids people living in Jerusalem to rent their homes to pilgrims; instead, they have to make them hospitably available to them, as if they all were owners of the property.[15]

Another set of special pilgrimage rules concerns the distinction between the "ordinary people" (*am ha-ʾareṣ*) and those who took upon themselves special religious restrictions regarding food. One such category of people, known as *haverim* ("friends," or "comrades"), were strict about only eating food from which they were sure the tithes had been separated (Deut. 14:22–29). Normally, they would not eat food provided by an *am ha-ʾareṣ*, for fear that such an ordinary person might not have given the tithe from his produce, or might have ignored certain purity rules.[16] In the pilgrimage situation, however, some of these restrictions were suspended. The law stated that an *am ha-ʾareṣ* should be trusted in matters of observance as if he were a member of the special category, creating a sense of oneness in contrast to the daily consciousness of social and religious distinctions. The Palestinian Talmud expresses this by stating that Jerusalem was a city that gave all Israelites the status of haverim, with the double entendre that all Jews were "fellows" or "friends."[17]

POPULAR PILGRIMAGES: THE TOMB OF SAMUEL AND MERON

After the destruction of the Temple, it was no longer possible to conceive of pilgrimages in terms of the biblical legislation requiring an Israelite to "be seen before God." Nevertheless, as has been shown by Elchanan Reiner, pilgrimage was a significant form of religious behavior in the Middle Ages. Pilgrims no longer connected their acts to the laws of the Bible or the Mishna, but regularly visited the Land of Israel and various sites within it.[18]

Pilgrims reached the Land of Israel from the two realms within which the Jewish Diaspora was spread: Christendom and the domain of Islam. In lands within the latter realm, the practice of Jews visiting holy sites may have been stimulated by the centrality of pilgrimage in the Muslim religion. Islam, in fact, contained two pilgrimage traditions: one focused on Mecca and based on the Quran, and the other to the graves of sainted individuals.[19] The latter may have provided the background for the appearance of Jewish shrines outside of the Land of Israel, like the tomb of the prophet Ezekiel in southern Iraq, near ancient Babylonia.[20] Visits to this and other shrines, like the synagogue outside of Cairo that came to be known as "the synagogue of Moses our Teacher,"[21] were part of the accepted culture of Jewish communities in the Middle East.

The culture of visits to the Land of Israel, or of taking up of residence there, which originated in Latin Christendom, had a strong ideological character. It involved individuals who, though few in number, were part of a religious intellectual elite. Examples are the twelfth-century philosopher and poet Yehudah Ha-Levi, who left Toledo in Spain towards the end of his life, and Yehiel, head of a yeshiva in Paris in the thirteenth century, who set out for the Land of Israel but died on the way.[22] These visits and permanent moves dramatized the importance of the physical Land of Israel and Jerusalem in the worldview of Jews in the medieval era who were compelled to face the topic by the Christian Crusades, which began at the end of the eleventh century. Recalling our discussion of breaking the glass at weddings, it may be that awareness of rivalry over the Holy Land was one of the factors that reinforced the interpretation of the practice in terms of remembering the Temple.[23]

The popular Middle Eastern pilgrimages, which were often local in character, were less ideological. Visitors to the holy sites engaged in rituals and prayed. They hoped for the mundane blessings of health and family, or rain and prosperity, as do pilgrims everywhere. Reiner demonstrates how, beginning in the thirteenth century, popular traditions began to intermingle with text-based religion. One expression of this trend was the appearance of written pilgrimage guides describing sanctified sites in the Land of Israel identified as the graves of biblical figures or rabbis known from talmudic literature. The guidebooks located these sites geographically and sometimes spelled out the prayers to be recited and the rituals to be carried out at them. They circulated among Jews in Europe, so that popular local shrines of Middle Eastern Jews became known in a systematized fashion far beyond the realm of the Mamluk Empire ruling over Palestine and neighboring lands at that period. The region with the greatest concentration of sainted graves was the Galilee, in the north of the country. Gatherings of Jews there had less chance of stimulating interreligious tensions than might large-scale pilgrimages to Jerusalem, which was a physical and spiritual center in the Holy Land for the two other monotheistic religions as well.

Nevertheless, Jewish pilgrimage sites also developed near Jerusalem. Best known was a shrine on a hill northwest of Jerusalem that was called Ramah by the Jews and Nebi Samwil by the Muslims. The Arabic name, which means Prophet Samuel, and by which the site is still known today, is based on the belief that the site was the burial place of the biblical Samuel. This identification crystallized at the time of the Crusades, even though it is clear that the medieval site was in a different region than the Ramah associated with Samuel in the Bible (1 Sam. 1:19).[24] In any event, the pilgrimage that developed there among Jews was nourished by a tradition, documented from the ninth century, that Samuel had died on the twenty-eighth of the Hebrew month of Iyyar, in late spring. It is not known how this date was selected, as there are no hints as to the date of Samuel's death in the Bible, but the following speculative explanation is in tune with the mixture of textual sources and popular traditions that gave Samuel's grave, and other shrines, their Jewish aura.

The Bible injects symmetry into the geography of Samuel's life. It tells the saga of Samuel from conception and birth until his death and juxtaposes these in the narrative when it tells us that Samuel was buried in Ramah, the city of his birth (1 Sam. 25:1, 28:3). Shifting from geography and space to the sphere of time, it is notable that the Talmud claims that righteous people die on the same date on which they were born, because their religious merit earns them the fullness of years. The claim that Samuel died on the twenty-eighth of Iyyar may therefore imply that this was also the date of his birth.[25] Our speculation thus returns to the question of the significance of that particular date.

The Hebrew month of Iyyar precedes that of Sivan. Eight days after the twenty-eighth of Iyyar is the sixth of Sivan, the date of the Festival of Shavuòt. If Samuel was circumcised on the eighth day after his birth, the claim that he was born on the twenty-eighth of Iyyar assigns his circumcision, or "entrance into the covenant," to the holiday celebrating the revelation on Sinai.[26] The pilgrimage tradition linking Samuel's birth to the festival that celebrates the giving of the Torah thus resonates with the biblical story in which Samuel's birth leads to his consecration to serve the priests in the sanctuary at Shiloh. Whether this conjecture as to the origin of the date is correct or not, the associations it evokes received expression in an event concerning pilgrimages to Samuel's tomb at the end of the Middle Ages.

Rabbi David ben Zimra, a noted Sephardi rabbi living in Cairo in the sixteenth century, received an inquiry concerning the custom of giving a young boy his first haircut at the shrine of Samuel.[27] The father of the boy had made a vow that he would cut the boy's hair when visiting Samuel's tomb. Shortly after he made this vow, however, a powerful Muslim sheikh took control of the site and put an end to the Jewish pilgrimage there. The father wanted to know whether he still was obligated to fulfill his vow. Rabbi ben Zimra attached importance to the question, because it was common practice on such occasions to weigh the shorn hair and then contribute funds to the shrine proportionate to its weight.[28] The money might go to buying oil or wax used to light lamps in honor of the saint, or to kindle a large bonfire as part of the celebration. Some money also went to charity, and vows of this nature were not to be taken lightly.

This custom, too, resonates with the story of Samuel, who was brought to the shrine of Shiloh (which in fact was in the region north of the site identified with Ramah) after he was weaned (1 Sam. 1:22–24). Jewish parents in the Middle Ages could not consecrate their sons to sanctuaries, but they could make an "offering" in the form of oil, which was symbolically linked to the child by equating the weight of the cut hair with the amount spent for the oil. Cutting hair, as already remarked, may be seen as an act parallel to circumcision, both involving severance and separation.[29] Just as it has been argued that circumcision set the stage for aspects of education,[30] so the first haircut at the shrine of the prophet Samuel implied the child's separation from the bosom of the family and meant that a male child could begin his Torah education. As already discussed with regard to ḥaredi youngsters, this symbolic nexus receives expression today (see figure 15).[31]

It is possible to track other aspects of the celebration at Samuel's tomb from the early modern period to the present by following another trail that combines popular with textually grounded religiosity. As stated, Muslims put an end to the pilgrimage at Ramah, but they did not quench the attachment to the popular practices at the large gatherings there: the dramatic bonfire, vows with regard to the health of children, hair-cutting, and other matters of personal import.[32] According to Abraham Yaʻari, the spiritual energies that had been focused on Ramah near Jerusalem were soon transferred to a burial site in Meron in the Galilee.[33] Meron had been a pilgrimage site since the Middle Ages as well. It too combined vernacular and elite-literate religious components in a complex manner.

Inside a certain cave at Meron, near the city of Safed, a pool of fresh water periodically replenished itself without flowing from any visible source.[34] Claims were made that sometimes the caves were dry, but that water appeared precisely at the time that pilgrims visited. This claim turned the natural phenomenon into a miraculous sign, making the site a particularly appropriate place for people to pray and express personal re-

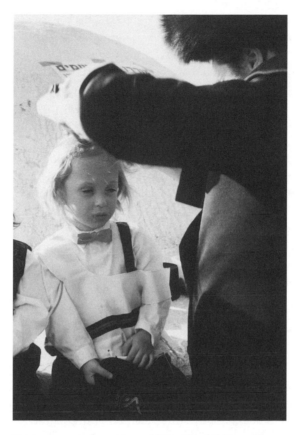

Figure 15. A three-year-old Hasidic child brought to the Tomb of Rabbi Shim'on Bar Yohai at Meron for his first haircut. Courtesy Tami Levi.

quests. The site was "judaized" and identified with the graves of the prominent mishnaic sages Hillel and Shammai.[35] Other traditions mentioned the cave as the burial place of Rabbi Shim'on Bar Yohai, a mishnaic scholar who had to hide from the Romans in the mountains of the Galilee along with his son Rabbi El'azar in order to continue the study of the Torah.[36] Documents from the Middle Ages, however, emphasize Hillel and Shammai, relegating the putative graves of R. Shim'on and R. El'azar to a secondary place.

In the late medieval period, however, another learned influence, Sephardi rabbis who had fled from the Inquisition and the forced conversions in Spain, entered the arena of the Galilee. Many of them settled in Safed.[37] Among various branches of Jewish learning, they delved into mysticism and the study of the Zohar. In this setting, the claim that the shrine

at Meron was the burial place of Bar Yohai (and his son) became more persuasive, because Bar Yohai is the central figure in the Zohar and tradition
sees him as the author of the book. Another reason for the popularity of
the figure of Bar Yohai may have been that he, too, like the Jews expelled
from Spain, fled from persecutors in order to persevere in the study of
Torah. In any event, Yaári contends that Bar Yohai's burial place in the
Galilee soon took over the role of Ramah near Jerusalem. It has been an active pilgrimage site since then.

The coming-together of written kabbalistic tradition and popular pilgrimage practices was not a frictionless development. The Sephardi mystics were attracted to the Meron shrine as a place of prayer, personal devotion, and the study of kabbala carried out at times other than the
eighteenth of Iyyar, which was the date of the new popular celebration
there. They looked askance at the mass abandon in dance and probably objected to other "less desirable distractions," such as relaxed sociality between men and women or gambling, which often takes place at pilgrimage
sites.[38] They also took issue with the custom of giving boys their first haircut there.[39] Many mystics, in fact, refrained from cutting their hair during
the fifty-day period known as the 'Omer, which links Passover to Shavuót,
and within which the eighteenth of Iyyar falls.[40] This was because the
'Omer is considered to be a time of semi-mourning; for example, marriages
are not conducted during most of the 'Omer period.[41]

The background for mourning customs during the 'Omer is not clear,
but the Talmud states that during this period, thousands of students of
Rabbi Akiba (the mishnaic sage who was the teacher of Bar Yohai) died at
the same time (BT *Yebamot* 62b). A medieval source that sees their death
as caused by a plague explains that on the thirty-third day of the 'Omer,
which is the eighteenth of Iyyar, the plague ceased. Among the students of
Akiba who survived was Shimón Bar Yohai, and he thus was able to continue the study of Torah. Some scholars have given these legends a historical interpretation and suggested that the "plague" causing the death of
these students was in fact the second-century Roman persecution of Rabbi
Akiba and his students. Historians further speculate that some positive
event occurred in the struggle of the Jews against the Romans that explains
how the thirty-third day of the 'Omer became a festive day. Learned kabbalists, however, saw no relation between the legends and the festive visits
to the grave of Bar Yohai that were common on the eighteenth of Iyyar.[42]
In the sixteenth century, they still distanced themselves from these celebrations. Despite the lack of a clear story setting out its origin, and despite
the learned skepticism of the kabbalists, the thirty-third day of the
'Omer—Lag ba-'Omer—eventually came to be widely interpreted as a feast

marking the death of the author of the Zohar. How did the close link between Lag ba-'Omer and the sainted hero of the Zohar emerge?

The Lag ba-'Omer pilgrimage is a case in which the reasoning of learned elites succumbed to popular logic, which itself had textual moorings. Bar Yohai became a revered figure, particularly in the Sephardi Diaspora. One expression and cause of his popularity was a hymn by a sixteenth-century kabbalist who lived in North Africa that compares Bar Yohai to the high priest, praises him for studying Torah, and lavishes mystical qualities on him. This paean became popular among many Sephardi communities, and among eastern European Hasidim, as part of the ritual around the Friday night (Sabbath) table.[43] No ancient source claims that Bar Yohai died on Lag ba-'Omer, but the widespread attachment to the figure of the author of the Zohar and the symbolism of the reinvigorated pilgrimage to Meron partook of other allusions within rabbinic tradition that led to this linkage.[44]

The term attached to the emerging pilgrimage festival was *hillula*, a word appearing in the Talmud in connection with the celebration of a wedding. We encountered that word in the story of the rabbi who broke a glass at his son's wedding when he found that his guests had gone too far in their merriment.[45] The term could thus carry opposing meanings. The thirteenth-century Zohar uses it to indicate a celebration assigned to the occasion of Bar Yohai's death.[46] Another section of the Zohar remarks that it is a joyous occasion when the soul of a tzaddik seeks to "go out [of his body]."[47] Neither source, however, refers to the date of Lag ba-'Omer. The first text that makes a connection between the pilgrimage and the date of his death is from the sixteenth century and cites a story in which a man is criticized for mourning Jerusalem excessively rather than partaking in the joy of Bar Yohai.[48] As in the visits to the tomb of Samuel on his death day, which I have surmised was also his birthday, occasions of mourning and joy became intertwined in the hillula at Meron onLag ba-'Omer.

The reasoning that became widespread with regard to the pilgrimage was that it is appropriate to treat the death of a righteous person as a marriage, because his soul then returns and is "wedded" to its original divine source.[49] In later generations, this was sometimes expressed at the funerals of old and respected or venerated men. In Jerusalem, it could take the form of singing from the biblical Song of Songs (replete with wedding imagery) during a funeral cortège, even with the accompaniment of music. In North Africa, the deceased might be accompanied by the popular and joyous Bar Yohai hymn.[50] Learned kabbalistic opinion thus eventually accepted the merging of images from the Zohar with the mass Meron gatherings. The book *Ḥemdat Yamim* that appeared in Izmir, in Turkey, in the eighteenth century, which Gershom Scholem calls "one of the most beautiful and affecting works of Jewish literature," cites Lag ba-ʿOmer as the day of Bar Yohai's death and mentions ritual readings appropriate to the occasion.[51]

HILLULOT AND THE ZOHAR IN MOROCCO: SANCTITY AND EVERYDAY LIFE

Pilgrimages, and the search for contact with sainted personages, testify to people's desire to bring sanctity into their individual lives. This is not only a spiritual search; it reflects the will to mobilize sacred figures and forces in pursuing life's bounties. The material expression of this search in pilgrimages can even result in conflict, as people and groups compete over access to, or ownership of, places and objects that are considered a source of blessing.[52] The notions and practices defining the relationship to tzaddikim are thus interwoven with daily personal concerns and social processes. This may be seen clearly in the case of Morocco where the veneration of sainted persons and their graves was salient in the social and religious lives of both Muslims and Jews.

One of the features of traditional Morocco was the prominence of intermediaries in social life. In the mountainous regions and deserts, where the central government was only partially effective, disputes between groups were often worked out with the help of mediators who had a special religious status. The ability of these go-betweens to bring about compromise stemmed from the fact that they themselves were not contestants in the political arena. As mediators, they were endowed with an aura of sanctity and were believed to have the ability to curse and to bless. People who did not accept their influence risked suffering the consequences of their religious power. Just as they served as "go-betweens" between humans, so they came to be perceived as links between the ordinary villager or tribesman and God. Islamic mystical tradition provided theological underpinnings for the claim that such mediators, known as marabouts, were closer to God than the rank-and-file Muslim. Even after their death, they could be petitioned with personal requests at the places where they were buried, and could perform miracles to the benefit of their devotees. Their graves might be visited on an individual basis, or people might petition them on pilgrimages along with thousands of other visitors.[53]

The Jews living in the small villages of southern Morocco partially absorbed these notions from the culture in which they participated, but also placed their own interpretations on that culture. Far from the central government, the Jews depended on local strongmen for their safety and ability to travel around the countryside as merchants and craftsmen. The local reality, that everyone was dependent on a patron more powerful than himself, bolstered the religious notion of protection by patron saints who served as intermediaries between ordinary Jews and the Almighty. Just as Muslims had marabouts, Jews had powerful *tzaddikim* who were buried in the region. One of the central tasks of sainted rabbis, in Jewish eyes, was to protect them from wanton Muslims who might exploit the Jews' political weakness. Like those of Muslim saints, the graves of tzaddikim could be visited not only at pilgrimage times but on any occasion. The Jewish conception of sainthood was shaped by notions from the kabbala, and festive pilgrimages took place on the anniversary of the death of a tzaddik, known as his hillula. Use of this term from the Zohar shows that the archetype of sainted rabbis, Shimon Bar Yohai, provided general legitimization for the veneration of tzaddikim, which became a central feature of Jewish religious life in southern Morocco.[54]

Tzaddikim, or more properly their graves (Jews in Morocco did not differentiate between the two in their speech), were also the sites of ritual and celebration. A person could come to the cemetery at any time if he or she wanted to be close to the tzaddik and make a personal request and vow, in addition to attending the annual hillula. Hillulot brought together the whole community; it was often explained to me that "men, women, and children" all participated. People would visit the graveside and even sleep next to it overnight, light candles, pray, sing hymns in honor of the tzaddik, contribute to the poor who gathered at these events, and share a festive meal, involving the ritual slaughter of animals, creating an atmosphere that combined solemnity and festivity.

The activities and moods associated with visits to tzaddikim differed from synagogue routines that conformed to norms followed by Jewish communities everywhere. As suggested above, the salience of tzaddikim in the lives of women, and women's religious activities in relation to tzaddikim, were one aspect of this difference. Women frequently invoked the name of a tzaddik in everyday life, particularly with regard to the health and safety of members of their families. During hillulot, which are neither enjoined nor closely regulated by rules found in the Bible or Talmud, women could, in principle, do everything that men did. Norms dictated that women not approach a graveside along with men, but there was no class of behavior from which women were formally barred. They could, at appropriate times, come as close to a tzaddik as men, a situation substantially different from synagogue worship, in which formal ritual roles are not open to women.

The religious emphasis associated with tzaddikim may not only relate to women, however, but give greater religious recognition to *the individual* than is normally expressed in the synagogue. Synagogue life is highly structured and shaped by rules that allow minimal room for innovation or individual expression. In addition, there were clear status markers in synagogue life, in seating arrangements and in the allotment of ritual honors, which separated the learned from the ordinary Jew and the wealthy from the poor. In contrast, pilgrimages in North Africa, whether to a faraway shrine or to the local cemetery, were not as encumbered by complex requirements and prohibitions. During hillulot, one should obviously observe proscriptions governing daily life, and women were expected to refrain from visiting a tzaddik at times of menstrual impurity, but the observance of normal rules did not keep pilgrimages from serving as congenial settings for individual men and women of humble social station to express their religious desires and personal wishes.[55]

It should not be surprising that cemeteries are locales of individual expressions of religiosity. Death highlights the biological separateness of the individual, no matter how successful a society is in impressing a group identity on its members. In many societies, funeral rites seek to repair the social fabric of the group, which has lost a member, and therefore to suppress the sense of individuality.[56] In the setting we are considering, however, burial ceremonies appear to valorize the individual within an overall set of shared cultural ideals.[57] The tzaddik in the cemetery of each small community in southern Morocco was a metaphor for individual distinction in general. The literature of the kabbala, and in particular the Zohar, also played a role in cultivating a sense of individuality.

In Jewish communities everywhere, there is an association of individuals responsible for preparing a dead body and organizing funerals. The most common name for this association is *hevra kadisha*, the "holy society" concerned with the serious matter of organizing the termination of a human life in this world.[58] In many areas of Morocco, the burial association had a more specific name: *hevrat rebbi shimᵒn*—the society of Rabbi Shimᵒn[59]—referring to Bar Yohai. The connection with Rabbi Shimᵒn was made through activities of the association in addition to their burial tasks and rituals. Members of the association met at least once a week (typically on Saturday night) for readings and study of the Zohar. Normally, they read from the Idra Zuta, the part of the Zohar that describes the death of Bar Yohai. In larger communities, the *hevra* of Rabbi Shimᵒn consisted of a Zohar reading group that was not necessarily identical with the burial society, but the connection between the tradition of Bar Yohai and the local tzaddikim was apparent in other ways. Often the date of the hillula of a local tzaddik was Lag ba-ᵒOmer.[60] The Zohar and traditions growing up around it thus played a role in the lives of all the Jews, beyond the concern with death and burial, whether or not they were capable of reading or understanding its contents.

The small communities in southern Morocco were linked to wider Jewish tradition, but direct access to sacred texts was usually limited. Young boys learned to read in the synagogue, but some of them never completely achieved literacy, and women were normally given no schooling. Knowing how "to read," meant the ability to link a written text to the correct sounds, but not necessarily to understand its meaning. In every community, there were some individuals with a broader and deeper knowledge and understanding of these texts, but for most, the world of the text was a remote one, beyond the horizon of everyday involvement.[61]

The few books that played a role in these communities were religious texts, whose sanctity was enhanced by their rarity.[62] Every adult male would acquire a personal prayer book (purchased in a city like Marrakesh) upon becoming bar mitzvah, to be used on a daily basis, along with his prayer shawl and tefillin.[63] The central texts in communal life were the Torah scrolls in the synagogue, housed in the heikhal, and also a set, or sets, of the Zohar. It is instructive to compare the two.

The Torah scroll was "*the* book" in the synagogue, as reference to it as "the sefer" implies.[64] Torah scrolls, while utilized in a communal context, were, in many North African communities, the property of individuals who had paid the money to have them written by a scribe. This was a major financial undertaking. A scroll would be ordered from a scribe in a major faraway town, who completed the task over a period of many months. Contributing to the community by providing a Torah scroll was, therefore, a source of both social prestige and religious merit. It enabled both the donor and the community to have a sefer in its midst.

It was a major communal event when a new Torah scroll was brought to a synagogue.[65] In a sense, this was a reverse pilgrimage, in which the sefer came to the home and community of the pilgrim. Often the scroll would be kept in the house of the donor for a while, awaiting an appropriate occasion for its ceremonial transfer to the synagogue. During this time, an order might be placed with a carpenter to make a decorative case for the scroll.[66] There was also a notion that the presence of a Torah scroll in the house was propitious, which tended to prolong its "residence" there.[67] When the scroll and its case were ready, men conveyed it slowly in procession, with singing and chanting, from the home of the donor to the synagogue. Because of the merit associated with the occasion, many different men would take turns at carrying the sefer, which thus gradually arrived at the synagogue. Women followed behind, also contributing to the festivity with their ululations. These events also might include a religious lesson, and there would certainly be a festive meal provided by the donor for all the participants.

The basic description of the accompaniment of a Torah scroll to a synagogue applies to all traditional Jewries. The Jews of southern Morocco, however, engaged in a similar round of ceremonies when a new set of Zohar books was brought into their communities. The Zohar is not written on parchment, but is used ritually in its printed form. In other ways, however, the form of reverence paid to the Zohar directly parallels the honor bestowed upon Torah scrolls. When a new set of the Zohar reached a village, it was a time for celebration.

The members of the community were aware that a Zohar was scheduled to arrive, and it was greeted by the villagers at the outskirts of the settlement, from whence the procession of bringing it into the synagogue began. The honor of carrying the Zohar was auctioned, like a ritual honor in the synagogue. It was placed in a specially prepared container during the procession, and people took turns carrying it, each several steps, amidst chants fitting the occasion. The Zohar also had a fixed place where it was ceremoniously situated in the synagogue, although the location differed from one synagogue to the next. There were also occasions in some communities, such as Saturday nights at the end of the Sabbath, when the Zohar would be taken from the heikhal and treated like a Torah taken out for a ritual reading during prayer service.

There was a major difference, however, in the treatment of the Torah scroll and the Zohar book. Once brought into the synagogue, the Torah scroll was never removed from it. This was only done when the scroll was no longer fit for ritual reading and could not be repaired. It then simply stood in the heikhal, sometimes even for many years, but eventually, according to standard Jewish law, it would be buried in a cemetery in a manner analogous to the burial of a human being.[68] When Moroccan Jews left the villages in the south during the 1950s and 1960s to immigrate to Israel, they took care to bury the unusable scrolls or those that they could not take with them. Others were dismantled from their wooden cases and brought with the immigrants when they left their villages.

In contrast to the Torah scroll, which remained permanently in the synagogue, the Zohar book could be removed from the synagogue to individual homes, "reside" there for a day or so, and then be returned to the synagogue. Standard occasions for "visits" by the Zohar, and ritual reading from it, were cases of difficult sickness, the anniversary of a death, or the eve of a circumcision, as described earlier.[69] These were occasions to invite members of hevrat rebbi shimón, as well as other guests. There was a sense that the presence of the Zohar in the house, and perhaps the implicated presence of Rabbi Shimon Bar Yohai, might benefit an ill person or protect the newborn.

There was thus a contrast between the Torah scroll and Zohar book, against the background of the overall similarity in attitudes towards them. The Zohar was more accessible, even in terms of its purchase price, and could be brought into the lives of individuals at times of personal crises. The Torah remained "remote," in its own place. People could make personal requests "in the presence of" the Torah scroll, or women could utter prayers on behalf of themselves and their families, when the sefer was raised for viewing during regular synagogue worship, as already discussed.[70] But people had to come to the Torah scroll; the Torah would not "come to" individual people. From this point of view, the Zohar is clearly of lower status than the Torah, even though they are both objects of veneration.[71]

The logic of ritual practice with regard to the two books directly parallels the claim that attachment to saints "satisfies within a monotheistic religion a polytheistic need to fill the enormous gap between men and their god."[72] A Muslim marabout, a Jewish tzaddik, or a Catholic saint helps fill that gap, for these mediate beings can relate to ordinary individuals on the one hand and to the All-Powerful on the other. In both Judaism and Islam, mystical thought supplies the rationale for acknowledging the existence of individuals who, while human like everyone else, have a certain closeness to God. The Jews of Morocco, steeped in a culture of sainthood, have taken that logic one step further. Reluctant to be overly intimate with the Torah, which is the direct word of God, and only able to make a pilgrimage from time to time, they more comfortably brought the Zohar into contact with their individual lives.

BRINGING CLOSE THE DIVINE: PORTRAITS, PRAYERS, AND IDENTIFICATION

Jews in Morocco, while influenced by their surrounding culture, found a very Jewish way of bridging the "insurmountable barrier [that] divides an infinite and unapproachable Godhead from weak and finite humanity."[73] This sort of creativity was not confined to the Jews of North Africa. Attempting to bring close the divine is a recurring religious tendency, appearing in different forms and historical periods. I shall briefly cite examples from Europe and India and illustrate with regard to one group of Jews from North Africa how this religious thrust may undergo transformation in new circumstances.

Richard Cohen has shown how Jews in modern Europe who felt threatened by the ideas and lifestyle associated with the advancing Enlightenment began to purchase portraits and medallions with images of venerated rabbis to hang in their homes and carry on their persons.[74] The portraits were of Orthodox rabbis with widespread reputations for talmudic learning, but their visual images were used as amulets to attain well-being or to prevent misfortune in facing everyday travails and life-cycle events. Bringing a venerated rabbi "close" was thus a different, but parallel, strategy to that of striking out on pilgrimage. The spread of a popular iconography of rabbis was also distinct from another practice at that general period among Hasidim in eastern Europe of devotees traveling distances to visit and be physically present at the court of a living tzaddik (see below).

The petitioning of tzaddikim, or any sanctified mediators, is an aspect of "local religion."[75] Its immediate purpose is not to reach new heights in a relationship with the sublime but to solve the worldly problems of the petitioner. There has always been concern on the part of the religious elite that rank-and-file pilgrims might pray directly to a saint, rather than view him as a meritorious intercessor who can help bring a personal request before God (for only God can answer prayer).[76] Rabbis have sought to ensure that popular acts of veneration do not violate essential rules and tenets of the formal tradition. Prayers composed in the Middle Ages to be recited at the grave of the prophet Samuel were careful to guard this distinction.[77] The Zohar formulates a difference between visiting the grave of a Jewish tzaddik and ostensibly parallel practices in other religions. For example, it claims:

> For the other peoples, when they visit their dead, approach them
> with magic to arouse forbidden forces. But when Israel approach the
> deceased within their graves, see with what repentance they come
> before the Holy One, Blessed-be-He, with what contrite heart and
> fasting, all in order that the sainted souls will seek compassion from
> the Holy One, Blessed-be-He, and the Holy One, Blessed-be-He, has
> mercy upon the world for their sake![78]

With regard to the amulets among European Jews just mentioned, ways were found to justify the use of rabbinic portraits, despite opposition to them based on the prohibition against making "graven images."[79]

It is rarely possible to sort out neatly which aspects of a ritual act or a belief are "merely local," directed towards meeting life's challenges, and which are "sublime," made of pure "religious" stuff. This distinction is meaningless to participants in a pilgrimage. To increase the chances that a request will be granted, the supplicant undertakes acts of devotion that reflect broader religious values. For example, to prove that he or she is deserving, a petitioner will give charity to the poor. Prayer at a pilgrim site, while directed to prosaic ends, may also express refined religious sensibilities. These two aspects of prayer are not necessarily antithetical. As mentioned, the biblical Hannah's pouring out her soul at Shiloh when requesting a child was treated by the rabbis as the prototype of correct prayer in general.[80]

Pilgrimage visits not only bring the worshiper into physical proximity with a concrete representation or representative of the deity but separate the pilgrim from his or her mundane routine. Entering a mode of "liminality," to use Victor Turner's term for this separation, enables the pilgrim to reflect not only upon the normal social situations shaping his or her life but also on interior thoughts and feelings.[81] In an awe-inspiring setting, the pilgrim is likely to reflect upon his own worthiness. One translation of the Hebrew word to pray, *le-hitpallel*, might be "to seek a judgment for oneself."[82] Praying entails bearing oneself before God, with the confidence that God will decide in your favor. In prayer, an individual relates to his or her private being in an idiom taken from a recognized and highly defined public arena.

The connection (and tension) between the personal and spontaneous, on the one hand, and the social and firmly structured, on the other, emerges from Moshe Greenberg's discussion of biblical prayer. He argues against seeing a sharp difference between prayer expressed as the "outpouring of the heart" and prayer forms that are "the studied composition of the expert which might be appropriated for individual, private use." Greenberg claims that "this dichotomy fails to appreciate the mixture of spontaneity and prescription in all social behavior."[83] The mixture he cites is particularly prominent in pilgrimages, described by Victor Turner as "an interval between two distinct periods of intense involvement in structured social existence out of which one opts to do one's devoirs as a pilgrim."[84] A pilgrim is not only able to reflect on the normal social constraints from which he or she is temporarily removed but typically rubs shoulders with many other pilgrims, who in some ways are similar and in some ways different. This experience may provide new cultural materials for self-assessment, and a reformulated image of one's own persona. If personal prayer is a self-conceived courtroom, prayer during pilgrimage encourages the individual to feel unchained from the past and that more than one road is open for the future.

How does this courtroom image relate to the centrality of tzaddikim in pilgrimages? One would think that venerating a sainted person leads to a diminution of individuality, rather than its repair or enhancement. It is not difficult, however, to locate the tzaddik—an intercessor—in the courtroom metaphor. If prayer means self-assessment while aware of an awesome and judging God, then it is understandable to want to mobilize a tzaddik, whether on a pilgrimage or in a domestic setting, as a "legal" intermediary on your side. In fact, this is the way women from the Indian Bene Israel community speak about Elijah, in reference to a ceremony named after him that marks many life-cycle events. While some have criticized the excessive celebration of Elijah in this group, claiming that it is as if the Bene Israel worship a human being, women explain their link to the sainted prophet as being like the connection to a "lawyer working on your behalf."[85]

The relationship to sainted figures may thus entail a variety of attitudes. While singing hymns in honor of a tzaddik, or placing his portrait on the wall of your home, psychological processes akin to identification may take place. This occurs in the case of both women and of men, even though the symbolic intricacies may not be the same in each instance. Among Jews from North Africa, tzaddikim often serve as the source of names given to children, and women often play an active role in assigning names to their offspring.[86] Relating to saints in an identificatory mode takes on new import when ancient traditions of veneration come up against contemporary institutions and challenges.

I once attended the celebration of a hillula in honor of Rabbi Meir Ba'al ha-Ness ("the miracle worker"), which falls four days before the hillula of Bar Yohai.[87] This event did not take place at the tomb of Rabbi Meir in Tiberias but was organized in a small synagogue in the Tel Aviv area that served a group of Jews originating from former Spanish Morocco. Many of them came from Tetuan or Tangier, the two cities in which European-type schools for Jews were first set up in Muslim countries by the Alliance Is-raélite Universelle in the 1860s.[88] The participants in the hillula had therefore long been exposed to both North African religious forms and many aspects of European culture. As part of the celebration, the organizer, who was a high school teacher, selected six other figures from Jewish tradition, assigned them saintly status, and included them in the event. Among those selected (in addition to Rabbi Meir) were Rabbi Akiba, Maimonides, and Rabbi Isaac Luria.

Parts of the hillula were similar to other celebrations of North African Jews, whether at a pilgrimage site, in a home, or at a synagogue. Large candles were lit in honor of the tzaddik, and the privilege of lighting a candle was auctioned off. The person awarded this privilege received a public blessing, and those gathered in the synagogue responded by singing "Length of days and years of life and peace, They will add to you."[89] This hillula differed from others I have witnessed, however, because a special role was given to children. Parents bid for the privilege of lighting the candles, and those who won the bidding sent their sons or daughters to the front of the hall for the actual lighting. At this point, the teacher added an instructive element. Before a child lit the candle, the teacher read a brief statement describing the merits of the saint in whose honor the lighting took place. This created a public forum in which the child was temporarily attached to an individualized verbal portrait of a saint, and it was an explicit hope that the sense of attachment would last. Particularly impressive was the depiction of Maimonides, which merged the halo surrounding a physician serving the royal household in twelfth-century Cairo with the prestige of the medical profession in twentieth-century Israel. Visual portraits of Maimonides, known for his intellectual activities in both Jewish and general fields, were also very popular in nineteenth-century Europe.[90] The ceremony, a reworking of older practices, suggests that processes of identification may have been an aspect of the traditional veneration of tzaddikim, and also points to ways in which time-honored forms take on new meanings as individuals are faced with new challenges, options, and choices.

CONTEMPORARY TRAVEL AND IDENTITY

The veneration of tzaddikim was widespread among Jews in North Africa but it was not confined to that region alone. Parallel practices and ideas were part of Jewish life in the Middle East and in eastern Europe. Rabbi Yosef Ḥayyim, who lived in Baghdad a century ago, published prayers to be recited at the graves of tzaddikim. These appear both in a book in Judeo-Arabic addressed to women and in a Hebrew publication for male users.[91] In eastern Europe, people prayed at the graves of rabbis in local cemeteries, hoping that they would serve as intercessors in individual or communal matters, and women in particular visited the graves of their relatives. Such prayers were part of normal religious life and eventually took the form of supplicatory formulas, published in Yiddish, to be recited by women on appropriate occasions.[92] Within the Hasidic movement, which developed in the eighteenth century, it became common for men to travel long distances in order to spend time in the courts of Hasidic rabbis, also known as tzaddikim. The graves of several early Hasidic leaders are sites of pilgrimage today, as is the grave of the last rabbinic leader of the Habad movement, who was buried in Montefiore cemetery on Long Island, New York, in 1994. A broad look at Jewry today quickly shows that travel and tourism to locations that have been given sacred or special cultural meanings is a major contemporary form of Jewish expression and identification. What characterizes today's situation is the ability of individuals to select different centers according to their backgrounds and inclinations.[93]

Travel to Israel is a major form of tourism mixed with pilgrimage (or for some, pilgrimage mixed with tourism), and it is undertaken by Jews from all over the world (as well as by many Christians and some Muslims). It assumes a range of forms, such as teenage summer trips (as mentioned earlier), year-long study, volunteering for auxiliary service in the Israeli army, United Jewish Appeal "missions," or ordinary tours that include visits to archeological sites, historical monuments, and holy places. A number of Israel tours include travel to countries whose recent history has been tied to that of Israel, such as visits to the Nazi death camps in Poland, or visits to Egypt after the peace agreement between Israel and that country was signed in 1978. Some Jewish educators and philanthropists now attach so much importance to these trips that they hope that a trip to Israel for young people "will be another rite of passage of Jewish life."[94]

Israelis too visit sites within their country like the Western Wall, or join the pilgrimage to Meron on Lag ba-'Omer, discussed above, which today draws between 100,000 and 200,000 visitors each year.[95] Meron attracts people of both Ashkenazi and Sephardi backgrounds, while some less well-known pilgrimages within the country are connected mostly with one ethnic category.[96] Examples are the site of a Moroccan tzaddik from the Atlas Mountains that has been transferred, based on a "message" in a dream, to the city of Safed, and a synagogue built outside of the town of Lod modeled on a prototype on the coast of Libya that was believed by the Jews who once lived there to have miraculous powers.[97]

Another example is the annual *sigd* ceremony of Ethiopian Jews, which essentially is a pilgrimage. That day-long rite takes place once a year on a hill selected for the purpose by the religious leaders of the community. The location may vary according to changing circumstances. It is a day of fasting and prayer and includes a procession carrying the Five Books of Moses to the top of the hill, which among the Jews of Ethiopia are in the form of a hand-written codex called the Orit.[98] The religious leaders, or *kessotch*, ascend the hill in traditional garb, surrounded by followers from among the community. After lengthy prayers at the summit, there is a ceremonial descent and a festive meal at the conclusion. The occasion has been interpreted as renewing the covenant of the Israelites with God, similar to the renewal celebrated by those who returned to Judea under Persian rule, as recorded in Nehemiah 9–10.[99] It now has the additional meaning of asserting Ethiopian Jewish identity in Israeli society.

Pilgrimage sites may have special appeals to different groups on the basis of religion or politics, as well as ethnic background. Some are highly specialized, such as the red-brick building outside of Tel Aviv that is a replica of the headquarters of the Habad movement in Brooklyn in the United States.[100] Others have more general relevance in Israeli life. A recent and tragic instance is the grave of Prime Minister Yitzhak Rabin, assassinated in 1995, on Mt. Herzl in Jerusalem. The sharply diverse sentiments regarding Rabin in Israeli politics are reflected in the fact that two different major sites have become shrines to his memory and the ideas associated with it. The second is the square in Tel Aviv where the assassination took place, which is now called by his name.[101]

Some Israelis have ties to other countries and travel abroad on outward pilgrimages as well. Moroccan Jews seek their "roots" and visit the graves of tzaddikim in North Africa. Jews from Tunisia recently have been able to reconnect to the community of Jerba in that country, and Hasidim pray at graves in Poland or in Ukraine, such as at the burial place of Rabbi Nachman of Bratslav.[102] Poland is also visited by Israeli high school students, and in recent years some of them have linked up with American and European youngsters in a "March of the Living" that takes them from the sites of the World War II death camps to Israel. Both these trips convey powerful and highly orchestrated messages about the importance of Israeli national existence.[103] Israeli young people, after service in the army, and even up to the age of thirty, often take extended trips to Asian countries like India. Reflecting different backgrounds within Israeli life, these travelers see the trips as meaningful in relation to various aspects of Israeli society and culture.[104] The content and atmosphere of different forms of cultural and religious travel thus vary greatly, but a number of features appear in these enterprises with regularity.

In a world where identity itself is pieced together or consciously created, pilgrimage-like travel brings into focus and reinforces aspects of people's sense of who they are and their self-definition.[105] American Jewish teenagers are aware of the range of options they face between stressing Jewishness or ignoring it. Jewish youth organizations are attuned to this possibility. In the early 1960s, the United Synagogue Youth organization, linked to the Conservative movement, initiated a program called "USY on Wheels," in which youngsters traveled by bus throughout the United States visiting other teenagers in Conservative congregations. More recently, many Reform temples have made a visit to the Holocaust Museum in Washington a standard part of their confirmation program after bar or bat mitzvah. What impact these programs have on American young people when they move into their college years and adulthood is a matter of debate, but these trips do bring young people to consider the nature of their Jewish attachments intensely while in their teenage years.

One aspect of travel may be a reorientation of what Benedict Anderson calls a person's or group's "imagined community."[106] An American traveling to Israel may for the first time meet Jews from Baghdad or Buenos Aires. North African Jews visiting Rabbi Shim'on Bar Yohai at Meron see black-garbed Hasidim standing out at a shrine they view as part of "their" tradition. Notions of what "being Jewish" implies may be challenged. A young man from Iowa describing the beginning of an Israel trip said that at first he had thought it would be like "Sunday brunches at the synagogue" because when his group boarded the El Al plane, he was served bagels and lox. Whether the meeting of other "kinds" of Jews leads to an expanded sense of solidarity, to confusion, or to feelings of alienation cannot always be predicted in advance. Individuals may find themselves experiencing all these responses. Others may tour former Jewish centers, such as New York's Lower East Side, precisely to "forget" their Judaism, that is, to limit it to circumscribed nostalgic experiences.[107] Whatever the outcome, travel provides the setting of a potential reshuffling of one's sense of who "we" are.

The impressions and ideas absorbed during a pilgrimage are very much conditioned by what a person has been taught to expect before setting out on the journey. In addition, the process of travel itself is shaped by intense exposure to and discussions with other people. On a flight to Israel, American youths from outside the large urban centers may for the first time see Orthodox males donning tefillin for morning prayer and swaying vigorously (*shuckling*). Conversely, ultra-Orthodox Jews may witness the organized prayer of Conservative or Reform youngsters, in which women participate on an equal basis with men. Even the hours spent together on bus trips in Israel can shape the outcome of a pilgrimage.

Shifra Epstein has participated in bus rides from Jerusalem to the shrine of Rabbi Jonathan ben Uzziel in the north of Israel, on the slopes descending eastward from Safed in the direction of the Huleh Valley.[108] Ben Uzziel is a mishnaic sage traditionally credited with a translation of the Bible into Aramaic in the first century C.E. In the Middle Ages, a grave in the Galilee at a site called Amuka was identified as his burial place.[109] In general, any saint can be visited by a person praying for any matter, but in some instances, saints have developed specialized reputations for certain kinds of requests. Jonathan ben Uzziel has become known as the intercessor for the marriage of young people. His grave is visited today both by people who firmly believe that the merit of saints can help their children find a spouse, and by younger people, less devout than their parents, who nevertheless do not exclude the possibility that a tzaddik might bring some luck in that realm.[110]

Epstein's trips to Amuka were with the older people. The bus rides were organized by "The Torah from Sinai Society," which posts notices on billboards in Jerusalem stating that it provides day trips to saints in the north of the country. The notices appear in neighborhoods such as the Mahaneh Yehudah market, or near the ultra-Orthodox Meah Shearim, where they will catch the attention of the society's main target population: tradition-oriented Middle Eastern Jews. The society hopes to bring participants on the trips to higher levels of religious observance. People come on the trips as individuals, and the society will accept anyone paying the fare. Notices state that the graves of many tzaddikim will be visited during the trip, particularly those in the Galilee (see figure 16), and recent signs often place Amuka at the top of the list, even before Meron. Everyone understands that the main saint on people's minds is Ben Uzziel, and that visiting him to find a spouse for a close relative is extremely popular.

Participating in the trip also entails adhering to strict religious norms, even if a person does not ordinarily fully do so. Men wear skullcaps, and women dress modestly. On the trip north, women sit in the back of the bus and men in the front. They all are harangued with religious messages by the pilgrimage leader, in addition to his pointing out and giving the background to the graves of the tzaddikim. On the bus, interaction takes place not only between the supplicants and the saints, and between them and the group leader, but among the participants themselves. They get to know one another during the day. The separation of men and women is less strict when picnicking off the bus, and it slackens even more during the night trip back, after a tiring day of appointments with many saints. People relax, show pictures of their children and grandchildren, and exchange phone numbers and addresses. In some instances, the children or grandchildren of these people do marry subsequent to a trip to Amuka. Returning later to fulfill the vow they made, such pilgrims will be able to say, like those they heard before the first trip or on the bus ride north, that within a year of visiting Jonathan ben Uzziel, a relative or friend was married. These various activities make the visits to Ben Uzziel "self-fulfilling pilgrimage prayers," energizing the process of matchmaking, which is also an aspect of pilgrimage culture generally.[111]

The intensity and peculiarity of cultures that emerge in the course of pilgrimage or identity-seeking tourism are dramatically shown in the mental maps and perceptions of the landscape that these trips create. Both American Jews and young Israelis traveling in organized groups to Poland relate to that country as a background to the Holocaust, hardly noticing

Figure 16.   Gathering at the purported tomb of Bena-
yahu ben Yehoyada (one of King David's generals) in
the Galilee on a Tu be-Av Visit pilgrimage. The tour
leader is sounding the shofar. Courtesy Shifra Epstein.

Poles and Polish society as a contemporary arena of ordinary life.[112] During the travel of Israeli high school students to the same land, today's Poles
are sometimes conceptually merged with those guilty of the suffering of
the Jews during World War II.[113] Hasidim traveling to Poland visit concentration camp and death camp sites, but are also guided by another map: the
routes leading to the dozens of graves of former Hasidic leaders that lace
the southeastern part of the country. These highly structured perceptions
are not unique to eastern European Jews. Israelis of Moroccan origin began
to be able to visit their native country in the early 1980s. For many of
them, barred from the land of their birth for over a generation, "Morocco"
had mainly come to have meaning as the source of their ethnic culture in
the context of Israeli society. Some of them, visiting there after many years
of absence, were surprised to find it "such an Arab country."[114]

In the world of highly organized travel and tourism, selective perception of
one's surroundings is not only a function of heavy indoctrination before
and during travel. With adequate funds and knowledge of the right channels, the environment can accommodate itself to images being sought by
tourists and pilgrims. Youngsters traveling through Poland on the "March
of the Living" have no sense of the tremendous effort made by the Polish

police, who keep very much in the background, to assure that there are no security mishaps.[115] The American teenagers from the Reform organization NFTY (National Federation of Temple Youth) with whom I traveled in Israel during the summer of 1994 provide another example. This was in reference to one of the best-known tourist spots in Israel: the fortress of Masada, perched high above the shores of the Dead Sea, which was a site of confrontation between a militant group of second-century Jews and the legions of the Roman Empire.[116]

The program experienced by participants in the trip was the result of a curriculum in which "Israel" became a resource in implementing NFTY educational goals. This orientation was salient during an eighteen-hour period known as "the NFTY event." At the center of this event was a climb up Masada from the west, beginning about 4:30 A.M., culminating in a dramatic view of the Dead Sea and Transjordan Mountains, behind which the sun rose an hour later. In preparing the youths for this intensive journey, their counselors spoke of the activity as "the NFTY event," and not as "climbing Masada" (although after the fact, participants usually referred to their visit "to Masada"). Other elements of the event included a gathering with other NFTY groups at Mt. Herzl, where Theodore Herzl (the founder of political Zionism) is buried, which is also a military cemetery, and a march through Jerusalem streets to the Hebrew Union College campus, the institutional center of Reform Judaism in Israel. The Masada phase of "the NFTY event" began with a nocturnal bus ride to the western side of the mountain fortress and a midnight barbecue there, followed by a sound-and-light show at 2:30 A.M. depicting the ancient drama of the site. Many elements of the subsequent climb and tour are common to other Masada trips, and NFTY utilized familiar means of getting messages across to young people. Among them was the use of "fire inscriptions," borrowed from the repertoire of Israeli youth movements and army induction ceremonies.[117] A well-known text presented to soldiers finishing basic training, presented in the form of flaming letters on the mountain top, is MASADA SHALL NOT FALL AGAIN. NFTY's attempt to assimilate the drama of the site to its own goals appeared in a blazing predawn fire inscription, NFTY IN ISRAEL, that aimed to create a firm linkage between a peak emotional experience and the American youth organization.

This, and some other examples I have cited, point to an irony that often appears in identity-molding travel. One travels afar, with the result that the trip affects personal identity at the place of origin. Leaders of NFTY want Israel trips to encourage youngsters to become committed Reform Jews in the United States.[118] American Jews visit Holocaust sites in Poland in order to reinforce ethnic identity back home by highlighting a feature of

Jewish ethnicity distinguishing it from other ethnicities in the United States. André Levy has shown that Moroccan Israelis who travel to Morocco in order to explore their North African roots return home realizing how Israeli they have in fact become.[119]

Such ironies reflect the perspective of an outside observer. The incongruities are not felt by those who are caught up in the flow of the organized identity travel. Barbara Kirshenblatt-Gimblett has commented on the comparison between the trips of American teenagers to Israel, generically known as "The Israel Experience," and theme parks. "The Israel Experience" is modeled on precisely those features of theme parks that make them so successful, including careful planning, attention to detail, a high degree of managerial control, an emphasis on experiential and immersive opportunities, an appeal to imagination, the use of narrative to evoke feeling, and a thematic handling of complex subjects."[120] A sense of identity is the crux of the matter in these situations, not careful sober reflection. The youngsters in such programs are "embarked on an emotional itinerary that serve[s] as a training ground for how to feel Jewish."[121]

The victory of feeling and wish-fulfillment over logic and facts also characterizes the symbolism of pilgrimages, where paradox and reversal may be built into the beliefs about the sainted figures involved. One example is provided by the biblical Joseph, who tradition claims is buried in a tomb outside the Palestinian city of Nablus, corresponding to the Shechem of the Bible (Josh. 24:32). Joseph has become prominent in both Jewish and Muslim tradition because of his ability to resist the sexual advances of Potiphar's wife (Gen. 39:7–13), but mention of a biblical blessing including his name (Gen. 49:22–26) has become a standard incantation in seeking to bring about fertility.[122] Jonathan ben Uzziel, the saint of matchmaking, is viewed as having been celibate.[123] Reverse logic may also appear in the designation of Elijah as the "angel of circumcision," according to one interpretation of a midrash discussed earlier.[124] Because Elijah claimed that the children of Israel had "abandoned the covenant," God delegated him to be present at every circumcision to witness the loyalty of Jews to the covenant of circumcision. These examples fit a popular logic of remedying situations by the application of opposites.[125] As noted, a component of contrast, and even opposition, that appears in contemporary pilgrimage is that a person comes into contact with others of distinct and competing backgrounds.[126] This may bring the pilgrim or tourist to realize or decide what he or she is *not*. It may also be the basis of tension developing at pilgrimage sites.

Alex Weingrod has studied the development of a pilgrimage in the Beersheba cemetery where a rabbi who was well-known in southern Tunisia, and died in Israel, is buried. A hillula developed around his death date, which was at first formally organized by members of his family and others close to him from Tunisia, but later attracted many devotees from among Moroccan Jews.[127] Today, the Moroccan presence overwhelms that of the Tunisians by weight of numbers, causing some unease among the latter, even though they still are accorded the merit of initiating the celebration.

I have mentioned the contrasting prominence of people born in North Africa and Hasidim at Meron. This occurs elsewhere as well. On one of her visits to Amuka, Shifra Epstein noted a group of Hasidim arriving there while Sephardi Jews were engaged in a ritual, special to them, of encircling the tomb seven times. The Hasidim distanced themselves from this, one of them making a remark about "Sephardi nonsense" (*narishkeit*) in Yiddish.[128] In 1983, along with other anthropologists, I witnessed an angry exchange on the roof of Bar Yohai's tomb between Hasidim and a North American rabbi discussing kabbala with a group of followers that included both men and women.[129] The North American rabbi has since shifted the base of his kabbala operations and, among other programs, now provides lessons in midtown Manhattan.[130] Whether unintentionally or wittingly, the search for personal meaning or salvation at a shrine may lead individuals into wider social currents and conflicts.

THE PERSONAL AND THE POLITICAL

The difference between the perspectives of various groups of pilgrims to the same shrine can entail significant tension when one group has formal control of a sacred site and bars others from access to it. Conservative and Reform Jews who wish to celebrate a bar or bat mitzvah at the Western Wall, including the participation of women in worship, have not been allowed to do so because the Kotel is administered by the Orthodox Israeli rabbinate. Some non-Orthodox Jews have organized services for these celebrations in one or another secluded corner near the Western Wall, outside of the formally designated Kotel Plaza. Lately, they have been more insistent in demanding the right to worship near the Kotel, arguing that historically the site has been sacred to all Jews. Exclusive control by an organized rabbinate, they correctly claim, is only a recent phenomenon.

This issue has been linked in the public eye, and in Israeli politics, with that of the worship of women at the Kotel. A group calling itself "Women of the Wall" has insisted upon the right to have a women's minyan and read from the Torah when they come to pray at the Kotel. Women from abroad have been prominent in this effort, and while "Women of the Wall" includes many Israelis, their "foreignness" is commonly cited by the rabbinate, which rejects their demands. Another image of the group is that it is mostly made up of Reform and Conservative members, but the local group consists of mainly Orthodox women seeking halakhically acceptable ways of religious expression in accordance with recent trends.[131] Their demand that the state-organized rabbinate provide an adequate solution for their legitimate religious needs first came before the courts in 1989, and in May 2000, the Israel High Court directed the government to come up with arrangements that would allow them to pray according to their custom in the Kotel plaza within six months. The ultra-Orthodox political parties then quickly proposed legislation that would override the decision of the High Court. Since then, the government has changed, and how the issue will develop is uncertain.[132]

The international nature of these disagreements has brought them to the attention of the media. In the summer of 1997, Conservative Jews praying in the plaza behind the Kotel synagogue were physically accosted by ultra-Orthodox Jews. The reaction of the police was to remove those praying, making relatively few arrests among the aggressors. The approach of the police reflected the attitude that such prayer was a "provocation" that should be prevented, just as there is a policy of preventing Jewish prayer on the Temple Mount, which is also holy to Muslims.[133] The following summer, however, the police were more protective of the prayer of Conservative Jews. In the wake of these and other events, such as the debates over conversion in Israel, a moderate Orthodox member of the cabinet attempted to find paths of compromise among the different parties and positions relating to prayer at the Wall. No agreed-upon results emerged. In May 2000, an agreement was reached in which the government accorded a limited right to Conservative Jews to pray, on designated occasions, in an archeological garden at the southernmost tip of the Western Wall, but various parties still opposed this agreement[134]

The Western Wall is built up against the area that Jews call the Temple Mount and Muslims refer to as *al-Ḥaram ash-sharif*. This area, sacred to two religions, has long been a site of tension, outright conflict, and carefully managed coexistence.[135] In 1996, violent demonstrations by Palestinians erupted when the Israeli government opened an excavated water tunnel, built in Maccabean times, under the Temple Mount, and the current armed conflict with Palestinians has been linked to a visit by Ariel Sharon, before he became Israel's prime minister, to *Ḥaram ash-sharif*. Another well-publicized dispute over a pilgrimage site concerned the Auschwitz death camp, where Catholic nuns established a convent, expressing Auschwitz's meaning in their religious view. The presence of the convent was opposed by many Jewish groups, yielding a vigorous international debate.[136]

The cases discussed show that travel to religious or cultural shrines may be thickly intertwined with political developments. When, in the early 1980s, Sultan Hassan II of Morocco wanted to take a step in the direction of normalizing relations between his country (and other Arab states) and Israel, he invited Israelis born in Morocco to tour their country of birth. These tours entailed visiting relatives, former neighborhoods, and cemeteries where tzaddikim were buried. That Jews wanted to visit their tzaddikim was perfectly comprehensible to local Muslims, and the king sent representatives to address pilgrims gathering at one of the well-known shrines on Lag ba-'Omer.

The sigd of the Ethiopian Jews was also used politically in their country of origin (see figure 17). It brought together many people and, at an earlier period, members of the community who had ties to the Jewish Agency would address those congregated seeking to inspire excitement about Israel. After the 1974 revolution that replaced the ancient monarchy, government officials appeared at the sigd and spoke to those gathered, stressing how well off they were in Ethiopia itself.[137]

Within the Land of Israel, the structure built over the tomb of Joseph became the site of a yeshiva inspired by the Gush Emunim settler movement when the area around the Palestinian town of Nablus was under Israeli control.[138] This movement, formed by religious Israelis of European background, espoused an activist religious nationalism different from the popular nationalism of most Middle Eastern Jews in Israel. In the context of this difference, it is noteworthy that among the North African tzaddikim symbolically transferred from Morocco to Israel, none have "settled" on the West Bank; all have remained within the pre-1967 borders of Israel.[139] The tomb of Joseph has thus taken on very different political connotations than it had as a popular shrine approached with life's problems by local Arabs and Jews.

One indication of the link between pilgrimages and politics is the way pilgrimage sites change historically. Traditionally, the most prominent sainted figure associated with the Jewish people was the matriarch Rachel. According to the Bible (Gen. 35:19–20), she is buried on the road to Bethlehem, coming from the north, and a prophetic verse (Jer. 31:14–15) depicts Rachel, centuries later, weeping for her children as they march into exile. Today, a building with a cupola by the side of the road between Jerusalem and Bethlehem is recognized as Rachel's tomb.[140] In earlier centuries, when religious institutions in Palestine sent emissaries abroad to collect funds for those living, praying, and studying Torah in the holy city of Jerusalem, their appeal was often presented as a request to support "the grave of Rachel, our mother." Female saints are virtually absent in the learned mys-

Figure 17. Jews in Ambober, Ethiopia, celebrating the sigd pilgrimage festival, using Torah scrolls sent from Israel, rather than their traditional Orit. Courtesy Hagar Salamon.

tical tradition, and are also rare in popular conceptions of sainthood, so Rachel stands out in Jewish consciousness as a glaring exception. The image of a weak and subdued woman, however, was a historically appropriate representation of the scattered Jewish people who lacked political power.[141]

From about the mid nineteenth century on, the Western Wall began to replace the centrality of Rachel's tomb in Jewish folk art. For example, in Israel Zangwill's play *The Melting Pot,* a Jewish home in early twentieth-century New York is presented with a picture of "Jews at the Wailing Place" on the Wall.[142] Embodying memories of destruction while also indicating the ability to survive and the possibility of reconstruction, the Western Wall emerged as a persuasive symbol with the growth of Jewish national consciousness. Political events, such as the Israeli conquest of the Old City of Jerusalem in 1967, reinforced its power. Rachel's tomb has not disappeared from the scene, however, but has become specialized. It became a shrine for women and concerns associated with women, such as matchmaking and fertility.[143] Today, the border between the Israeli city of Jerusalem and the Palestinian Authority runs very close to Rachel's tomb, making it a candidate for conflictual political events and new meanings.[144]

Parallel to the fluctuation of shrines' political symbolism is the fluidity of their meanings to individuals. Jews in the Middle East often included a visit to a shrine as part of mundane travel for trade.[145] One reason for the popularity of hillulot among North African Jews in Israel is that they allow expressions of piety on the part of people who no longer adhere to many religious rules.[146] American Jews who reject the religiosity of their homes but seek ethnic and cultural links to Judaism have also found pilgrimages and pilgrim-like experiences to be an accessible way of making a connection to their heritage.[147] Individuals and specific groups shaping their own pilgrimages sometimes find innovative ways of using the Jewish past for this purpose. A conference of gay and lesbian Jews in 1987 selected Amsterdam as their venue. Seventeenth-century Amsterdam had been open to Marranos who previously had to hide their Jewishness, and the contemporary city had a reputation of accepting different lifestyles.[148] From the earlier period, a Hebrew word—*maqom*—meaning "place" had entered local Dutch slang as a term referring to the city. Amsterdam thus became a special "place" as an "impromptu pilgrimage site" in the late twentieth century.[149]

Precisely because pilgrimage sites are foci of personal prayers and hopes, they are easily mobilized as symbols of group identities and ideological claims. Such "mobilization" may serve obvious political interests, but collective structuring may emerge as a slow incremental process that preserves collective identity above and beyond any immediate political program. Such patterning may be discerned by taking an overall view of major shrines that developed and still are prominent in the Land of Israel.

During the Ottoman period, Jews in Palestine were concentrated in the towns that were known as the four holy cities: Jerusalem, Hebron, Safed, and Tiberias. Communities from all over the Diaspora sent funds to these cities to support the study of Torah there.[150] There is a correlation between the four well-known shrines found in these cities and four formative but distinct periods in Jewish history. Hebron is the locality of *me'arat ha-makhpela,* the burial cave of the biblical matriarchs and patriarchs, and currently a focus of tension between Israel and the Palestinian Authority.[151] King David moved the seat of his rule from Hebron to Jerusalem, which became the enduring spatial and spiritual capital of Judaism. The Western Wall, close to the site selected by David for the Temple to be built in the future, is now the symbolic center of that "eternal city" (see figure 18). Two other sites that rival the shrines in Hebron and Jerusalem in terms of the number of pilgrims they attract are the tombs of Rabbi Meir Ba'al ha-Ness in Tiberias and Rabbi Shim'on Bar Yohai in Meron. The historical identity of the former rabbi, called "Master of the Miracle," is unclear, but Tiberias is associated with the talmudic era from the late second century C.E. on.[152] Safed and Bar Yohai are salient in the mystical tradition, with particular reference to the sixteenth century, bridging medieval and early

Figure 18.   The men's section of Synagogue Plaza at the Western Wall (Kotel).
Photo Edith Turner.

modern times. A pilgrim visiting any of the shrines can, therefore, assign a
given act of devotion to a conceptual scheme that encapsulates a vast time-
space constellation of Jewish life.

   This overarching structuring of Jewish history and geography still
leaves room for a variety of understandings of each shrine and for individuals to approach these sites with personal prayers and feelings. This is
strikingly evident in the case of the Western Wall. The meanings attached
to the Kotel affect both Jews, like the American youngster cited above who
discovered that she had "two homes," and non-Jews who have become enmeshed in its public symbolism. I have seen non-Jewish tourists at the
Western Wall adopt the pose of the secular Israeli paratrooper, made famous in a photograph from the 1967 war, who, leaning against the Wall
that had become an object of both national and personal yearning, buried
his head in his arm in a moment of deep emotion. Sometimes an individual first encountering the Wall undergoes a temporary psychological collapse, and even severe disorientation, a phenomenon known to psychia-
trists in local hospitals as the "Kotel syndrome." Similar reactions are
known with regard to Christian visitors to other parts of Jerusalem. Research interviewers have discovered that when asking questions about the
religious and national orientations of individual Israelis, reference to the
Kotel often stimulates detailed reflection on the unique worldview that
each interviewee has constructed for him- or herself.[153]

The Kotel thus serves as a symbolic center for individuals of many backgrounds, countries, and religious or ideological commitments, and it is appropriated by each according to their inclinations and identities. It is a spot where heaven and earth may be joined in the eyes of the faithful, or of people on the path to seeking faith. It can also connect past, present, and future for those, like secular Israelis, with little interest in the supernatural. In this setting, opposites and contrasts—young American Jews, a family from Bukhara celebrating a bar mitzvah, a Yiddish-speaking Hasid engaged in daily prayer—may be brought together in harmony or in uneasy tension. Religion and secular nationalism, often at odds, may be linked, as in the torch-light swearing-in ceremonies of Israeli paratroopers that often take place on the site.[154] Local histories, carried in the memories of pilgrims from disparate lands, may merge with Jewish and Israeli myths through the parallel collapsing of time and space. The tourist becomes a pilgrim, and the pilgrim an onlooker; and the cycle of individual lives may be harnessed to the expression of collective identities. Emotional catharsis after having reached a long-dreamed-about place and communion with the ineffable stand side by side. Memory, consolation, and hope are bound up in a single act. Just as these diverse elements are brought together, and glance off one another, so they may be sorted out and isolated in accordance with private wishes and communal sentiments. Jews, the "people of the Book," have transformed the stones of the Kotel into a giant writing tablet, upon which distinct individuals and groups, at times in conflict and at times in coordination, inscribe their own stories.

Pilgrimage, as a notion and practice in Jewish culture, has itself undergone a long voyage over the course of history. It appears in the Pentateuch in formal hierarchical garb, limited to males visiting the society's sacred center controlled by priests, but has evolved into a popular form engaging men and women who select the place, timing, and meaning of travel that might connect them to the Divine or reinvigorate their sense of connection to a people and tradition. Perhaps it is precisely because the formal rules relating to the ancient Temple are not in force that pilgrimage has became a ritual form par excellence for expressing the religious trajectory and sense of group identity of many different individual lives.

6   Death, Mourning, and Remembering

Reference to death routinely emerges within the ceremonial cycle of Jewish life. We have already encountered several examples. In traditional education, pupils who were trained to sing hymns at circumcisions also chanted psalms and dirges at funerals. Breaking the glass at weddings may resonate with the rending of a garment at a burial. Chapter 5 discussed saints' graves as the foci of pilgrimages during which people ask for the blessings of life.[1] Several years ago, I witnessed another event that surprisingly but vividly showed this association.

The event was the laying of the cornerstone for a projected apartment house in Ashkelon. The ceremony, which took place in 1996, included important figures such as the developer, the mayor, and other local dignitaries. The surprise, however, was the person who headed the list of honored guests: Rabbi Yitzhak Kedourie.

Rabbi Kedourie was born in Baghdad and moved to Jerusalem in the 1930s. He was then an unobtrusive individual who supported himself by bookbinding, and devoted his time to reading and studying kabbalistic texts. In recent years, however, public attention was directed at him, stressing his great age and designating him as "the eldest kabbalist." The public also began to associate him with another Baghdadi rabbi, Ovadiah Yosef, who once served as the Sephardi chief rabbi of Israel and now was the leader of Shas (the Sephardi ultra-Orthodox political party). In the elections in the spring of that year, Kedourie had been mobilized to lend his religious prestige to the candidate of the Likud party, Benjamin Netanyahu. The latter visited him and received his blessing, while the Labour party was not able to arrange a visit to Kedourie by the rival candidate, Shimon Peres. Netanyahu won and became prime minister. Among Israelis for whom the blessings of rabbis form a vital element of their daily world, Kedourie's power was dramatically affirmed. What better choice could there be to bless the new building venture in Ashkelon?

Kedourie's name headed the list of honored guests featured in the invitation to the event, but his actual place in the ceremony was at the end, after all the speeches. He offered a blessing composed of well-known biblical and rabbinic phrases, shaped for the specific occasion and for the development company, and penned his signature to a scroll on which the blessing was written. After being signed by the project managers and many in the audience, the scroll was inserted into an empty *maḥia* (Moroccan arak or ouzo) bottle, which was placed in a foundation hole of the apartment house. The hole then began to be filled with concrete, and the spectators were given the chance to pour some into it. Although the overall ceremony was novel, those who participated in filling the foundation hole did so with an air of familiarity.

A vat of concrete stood next to the hole, and people lined up to take turns in troweling concrete into it. The spontaneous organization on the spot was strikingly similar to the way people at a funeral take turns in sprinkling soil on a coffin that has been lowered into a grave. The analogy was precise in that when one person had finished, he did not hand the trowel to the person behind him, but stuck it into the vat of concrete, from which it was then taken by the next in line. This precisely parallels the protocol at funerals, where those adding soil to the open grave leave the shovel in the pile of dirt when they are finished, rather than handing it directly to the next in line. The inauguration of a new building thus mimed the form of a human burial.

This striking parallel brought some historical references and classic texts to mind. In medieval Egypt, when a body was entombed under bricks or flagstone, the term "build" was used of burials.[2] In Genesis 2:22, the verb "build" describes the creation of woman from Adam's rib, and the Mishna states that a man's "house" means "his wife."[3] The use of "build" in Genesis is echoed in wedding blessings, for it is the joining of men and women that perpetuates humankind.[4] In the Ashkelon ceremony celebrating the start of a group of new homes, symbols of life and death were closely intertwined and suffused the act of "building." Jewish forms of death can only be understood in terms of the pathways of life that they mark and help sustain.[5]

DEATH IN THE BIBLE: EMPHASIZING LIFE ON EARTH

The Bible portrays a number of features of burial and mourning in ancient Israel, some of which have become incorporated into standard Jewish practice. The rending of a garment was an act that accompanied news of death, or other fateful changes.[6] Tearing a garment does not appear as a requirement in the Pentateuch, but became part of the rabbinic codes. There was probably a norm of rapid burial, reflected in the rule that executed criminals be buried without delay (Deut. 21:22–23).[7] The most dire biblical curses speak of corpses being left unburied and exposed (2 Kings 9:34–37; Isa. 66:24). With regard to mourning, narrative and prophetic materials refer to the wearing of sackcloth, and stories of David tell of, or imply, not washing and not rubbing oil on one's skin.[8]

The account of the ill-fated son stemming from the first union of David and Bathsheba portrays the king's refusal to eat when the child was dying. His eventual acceptance of a meal, offered by others, signaled his reconciliation with death. The term used there was linked to the practice of *seʿudat havraʾah*, the "meal of condolence" that is given a mourner upon return from the cemetery. The chanting of laments by women was also part of biblical bereavement (Jer. 9:16), and seven days was the mourning period after the death of Jacob (Gen. 50:10). Visiting the bereaved is depicted in the story of a pious non-Jew, Job. The book bearing his name is the source of a phrase in the first part of the standard burial service (Job 1:21): "The Lord gave, and the Lord hath taken away: blessed be the name of the Lord."[9]

The Bible does provide several specific negative injunctions concerning the dead, in addition to the law forbidding the exposure of the body of an executed criminal. Tithe contributions must not be used in rituals connected to death (Deut. 26:14). Priests are not to come into close proximity with the dead, except in the case of their closest relatives (Lev. 21:1–3), and the high priest may not defile himself through contact with the dead even when his parents pass away (Lev. 21:11). Laypeople are also encouraged to act in priestly fashion and are forbidden to gash their skin in mourning (Deut. 14:1–2). In reality, this practice could be observed until recently in some Jewish groups. Women in Kurdistan have been described as scratching their faces in mourning, and in the 1960s, I witnessed such acts among women from Tripolitania in Israel.[10] Perhaps the transformation of the ancient custom of rending a garment into an explicit rabbinic requirement reflects an attempt to sublimate the urge to rend one's flesh.[11]

Various biblical rules and practices relating to the death of individuals had implications for group existence. Thus the prohibition against self-flagellation, or puncturing one's skin as part of mourning, was subjected to linguistic maneuvering by the rabbis and interpreted as a warning to society not to break up into factions.[12] Keeping the human body intact became an expression both of the wholeness of the individual person and of the solidarity and order desirable within the "body politic."[13] The value of wholeness may also inform the prohibition against tattooing (Lev. 19:28).[14]

The integrity of the physical body implied by these rules is part of a general pattern in both biblical and rabbinic literature, which stresses the clarity of religiously defined boundaries.

Biblical rules convey a worldview that as far as possible keeps the realm of "life" separate from that of "death." Israelite worship, too, kept these spheres apart, as did the rules relating to impurity discussed earlier.[15] The Bible assumes that it is possible to have contact with those who are dead, and thereby obtain occult knowledge, but this sort of contact is forbidden to Israelites, who should rely only on God (Deut. 18:9–15). This perspective appears in the story of Saul, who, in despair, sought to reach the dead prophet Samuel through the magic of a medium, after he himself had tried to obliterate occult practitioners from the land of Israel (1 Sam. 28:3–25).

The ancient Israelites conceived of a nether world, Sheol, where the dead reside, but its nature is not elaborated in the Bible.[16] Archeological remains suggest that people brought food to graves, supposedly for the shadowy beings in Sheol. The realm of the dead, however, had negligible religious importance compared to God's expectations and actions in the world of the living. This orientation is often noted in quoting Psalms 115:17: "The dead will not Praise Yah [God], nor will those who descend to the grave." Isaiah also presents Sheol as a realm removed from God (38:10–11, 18).

While the Bible is primarily concerned with life on earth, the attention paid to graves in Genesis is striking. We explicitly learn that all of the patriarchs and matriarchs, save one, Rachel, were buried in the Machpelah cave near Hebron.[17] The value of being buried "with one's fathers" appears in various passages (2 Sam. 19:38; Neh. 2:3). In its original social setting, this probably reflected the centrality of a kinship group and rights to land that were transmitted in the paternal line beyond the lifetime of any single individual. The Bible utilizes these immediate social connotations to elaborate claims with reference to the continuity, and the claims to land, of all of Israel. Two figures in Genesis, Jacob and Joseph, are not buried immediately, but are first mummified in Egypt (Gen. 50:1–3, 26). Ultimately, however, the Land of Canaan was to be their resting place.[18] Their individual tales are linked to the story of the whole people; biblical "afterlife" is a collective survival.

Hebron, the burial place of the fathers and mothers of the nation, becomes the place in which David first established his monarchy. The figure of David is often associated with the salvation of Israel (Ps. 18:51; Ezek. 37:24). Rachel is the only matriarch not interred in Hebron, but where she is buried, on the way to Bethlehem (Gen. 35:19–20), evolves into a symbol of maternal concern over all "her" children, the children of Israel. According to Jeremiah 31:14–16, she weeps over their exile but is also promised that they will eventually return.[19] Subsequent to Jeremiah, Ezekiel's vision of dry human bones coming together and being revived (Ezekiel 37) is a vivid metaphor of national redemption. Burial places and practices, directly associated with the deaths of individuals, are forged anew into a vocabulary encoding a society's ideals and hopes for the future.

THE RABBIS, THE SOUL, AND RESURRECTION

The biblical assumption of the importance of "this world" is linked to the lack of a clear distinction between "body" and "soul." Both what we now call spiritual existence, on the one hand, and bodily functions, on the other, were seen as aspects of the single whole person. The future redemption to which Jeremiah and Ezekiel alluded was that of a people whose national and religious integrity would be restored. It did not entail a notion of life after death, focusing on the individual, in which a spiritual component became separated from a person's corporeal existence. This developed only later, at which time Ezekiel's vision of the dry bones also came to imply individual resurrection.[20]

A distinct conception of "soul" as opposed to "body" emerged within Jewish life in antiquity only slowly.[21] Ideas of this nature first appear in the Apocrypha and in literature from the late Second Temple period associated with sectarian groups living in the Judean Desert. They also reflect the influence in Jewish life of Platonic philosophy, which envisages a realm of "pure ideas" separate from material reality, as illustrated in the writings of Philo of Alexandria in the first century. The early rabbis of the Mishna, however, still held views in which the body and the soul were closely linked.

It was only after the failed Bar-Kokhba rebellion against the Romans in 132–35 C.E., and the massive destruction of Jewish life that ensued, that fuller attention to the soul as a separate entity emerged. Perhaps the need to answer the question: "Why does suffering befall those who follow the Torah?" pushed the later rabbis of the mishnaic period to elaborate notions of the reward the soul reaps after its sojourn on "this earth." Eventually, ideas about the soul were linked to the belief that God would resurrect each person, a religious theory that also developed only after the biblical period. Its later centrality is evident from its inclusion in the opening benedictions of the Amidah, the central prayer of daily worship.[22] The overall view was that at the end of days, people's bodies would be resurrected and rejoined to their souls.

After the mishnaic period, the soul continued to concern the sages of the Talmud. They speculated about the soul and its relation to the body. What happens to the soul when a person sleeps, or after death? How does the soul enter the body when a child is conceived? Views on these questions are scattered in talmudic literature and do not coalesce into a doctrinal set of ideas about life after death. One talmudic portrayal of the soul as leaving a sleeping person and returning to the body upon wakening was incorporated into the morning prayer.[23] Interest in the soul, however, did not entail denigration of the body. Morning prayer also thanks God for the body's normal functioning.[24] With regard to death, the rituals and rules respectful of the body continued to have force.

Some scholars have cited archeological evidence from ancient Palestine as pointing to new beliefs about the separate existence of the soul and eventual resurrection after death. Archeologists discovered that from the first century B.C.E. until the third century C.E., there was a practice among Jews of reinterring the bones of a body after its flesh had disintegrated.[25] At times, the bones were gathered together and reburied in a new spot, in a tract of land owned by a family for that purpose. Sometimes the bones were placed in a special container—an ossuary—and then inserted into a family vault dug into a hillside. The notion, according to this hypothesis, was that reburial prepared the individual for ultimate resurrection.

These findings of a secondary burial are striking, especially in light of the objection of contemporary ultra-Orthodox Jews to disturbing Jewish graves. These modern groups express their objection in mass demonstrations in Jerusalem, protesting the reburial of Jewish skeletal remains, even when it is necessary to move them for projects like building new roads. Their protests ignore the fact that there can be rabbinic sanction for reburial. Contemporary religious conflicts aside, it is not easy to determine from the physical findings alone what the meanings of ancient reburials were. It is likely that they were basically an accommodation to a lack of land for burial, a fact reflected in the frequent discovery of graves when excavation—for any purpose—takes place in Jerusalem today. Once the practice of reburial became established, new religious interpretations may have been attached to it. For example, if bones were dug up after a year, and the basic skeleton was intact, it could be claimed that this showed the merit of the dead person, who had emerged successfully from the trials of Gehenna (a Jewish version of what emerged in Christianity as "Hell"), and had thereby atoned for his sins.[26] While at this period, Jewish beliefs in life after death were becoming more elaborate, there is no convincing connection between them and the actual practices involved in burial and mourning.

Scholars often note that talmudic eschatological ideas concerning the "end of time" or personal resurrection lack clarity and systematization.

The phrases that appear most frequently, in addition to references to "the soul," distinguish between "this world" and "the next world" and allude to the days of the Messiah and the revival of the dead.[27] Even lacking full precision, these notions have been incorporated into the morning service of the Sabbath liturgy.[28] Perhaps more instructive than an exact outlining of each of these ideas is the fact that they merge into one another: that the fate of individual souls is enmeshed, in Jewish thought, with Messianic redemption and the fate of the people.

Belief in individual life after death may have provided some compensation for extensive personal and collective suffering on earth, but this did not exclude hopes for national revival. Not only that, some rabbinic writings protest God's actions against His people. Examples are found in the midrashic commentary on Lamentations, the biblical book bewailing the destruction of Jerusalem and the Temple.[29] Written after the destruction of the Second Temple (70 C.E.), this Midrash interweaves experiences from that event with texts and figures from the exile of the Ten Tribes (eighth century B.C.E.) and the sacking of the First Temple (sixth century B.C.E.), combining individual stories of death, loss, and mourning with these national tragedies. One set of stories concerns Rachel.[30] Far from being weak and submissive, the matriarch stands up to God, citing her own deeds and suffering, and pleads for His sons (who are also her sons) whom He has destroyed and exiled.[31] Her pleas succeed where those of Abraham, Isaac, Jacob, and Moses failed. Her arguments move God to promise, in the words of Jeremiah 31:14–16, that Israel will return to their land. This story may also reflect the kernel of an idea, discussed more fully in the next section, that the words of people "on earth" about those who have suffered and died have the power to make an impression "on high."

THE MIDDLE AGES: MEMORIALIZATION
AND THE KADDISH

The linkage between individual deaths and national calamities continued to characterize Jewish thought and practice in the Middle Ages. The slaughter of Jewish communities during the Crusades, which first occurred in 1096 in the Rhineland, had an impact upon Judaism that still reverberates today. A new form of literature emerged in the shape of memorial books containing lists of those who had been martyred, which assumed a ritual function. Outside of the European orbit, there was a tradition on ritual occasions of reading aloud the names of noted predecessors of the Jewish world generally, and of the ancestors of local notables. In Jewish practice in Muslim realms, ancestor lists included only males, whose names were recited at times of mourning or on Yom Kippur.[32] These lists featured noted ancestors whose names brought honor to living family members, but certain names were remembered because their bearers had died young or as the result of persecution.[33] This suggests a popular perception, if not an elaborate precept, that the public recitation of the names of the dead counteracts the suffering associated with their untimely demise.[34]

Within Europe, the Crusades resulted in the slaughter of large numbers of people, and women were prominent among the martyrs too.[35] The names of all the martyrs, not only prominent males, were enshrined in the communal books. As the historian Sylvie-Anne Goldberg has emphasized, these lists of martyrs, and, after the Crusades, memorial books including the names of all the departed, became central features in the definition of community in the Ashkenazi world.[36] The memorial books were not items stored on a shelf, but were integrated into ritual. Customs regarding the dead emerged that eventually became codified as requirements.

The dead were remembered, as individuals and as a community, four times during the year: on the Day of Atonement and on the final day of the festivals of Sukkot, Passover, and Shavuot. At these times, individuals lit memorial candles at home for the departed in their families, and also joined the communal memorial service in the synagogue. This service, known by the term *yizkor*, the opening word of a prayer asking for God's remembrance of a departed person, calls for the mention of every dead relative, and after that all the martyrs of Israel are recalled. Concern for the souls of individuals to whom one had been individually attached when they were alive became inextricably linked to a sense of community. This linkage also appears in another prayer that makes no mention of death but has become a symbol of Jewish mourning—the kaddish.

The kaddish prayer, beginning with the words "Yitgadal ve-yitqadash shmeh rabbah" ("Magnified and sanctified be His great name"), praises God and proclaims His holiness.[37] The opening statement in Aramaic concludes with a sentence to be said in unison aloud by all present: "May the name of God be blessed forever and ever." It derives from parallel expressions in the Bible, appearing both in Hebrew (Ps. 113:2) and Aramaic (Dan. 2:20). The communal response, historically, is the kernel and raison d'être of the kaddish. Today, it is followed by additional verses, in both Aramaic and Hebrew, which were appended later (and of which there are different versions). An extratalmudic compilation, the tractate Soferim (10:7), mentions the requirement that the kaddish prayer be said in a prayer quorum of ten men (a minyan). This was the norm in Babylonia; seven men were sufficient to constitute "a community" in Palestine.

The importance of the communal response within the kaddish is mentioned several times in the Babylonian Talmud. The rabbis attribute to it the power of "tearing up" an evil decree against an individual and of arousing God's compassion for His children, whom He exiled.[38] A medieval mystical text asserts that a group's response to the kaddish can stimulate God to raise the righteous souls from Gehenna.[39] This tradition assigned theurgic power, the ability to have an impact upon God and His actions, to the group recitation of the formula. It did not, however, explicitly place the recitation of the kaddish in the context of mourning.

The occasion envisioned in the mystical text was the study of Torah. It was customary to recite the kaddish at the end of a public lesson based on Aggadah: stories and legends taken from the Midrash or narrative sections of the Talmud. [40] Such lessons typically ended with statements of hope for collective redemption, setting the stage for a prayer that asserted God's eternity and kingdom over the world.[41] This became known as the "scholars' kaddish" (*kaddish de-rabbanan*). Another version of the kaddish (also a scholar's declaration) is recited when a group finishes studying a tractate of the Talmud.[42] This special kaddish is also recited at burials. It mentions resurrection and the rebuilding of Jerusalem. Both these notions invoke hope for the future, but the kaddish itself makes no reference to rituals related to death. In its more common forms, the kaddish eventually evolved into a marker of the divisions in the daily liturgy. How did it, then, become so intimately linked to individual mourning?[43]

To grasp this linkage, even without knowing the precise historical events that brought it about, it is necessary to attend to textual traditions and also to appreciate the communal contexts in which they took on meaning. A community is a corporate unit that persists beyond the lives of its individual members; a person may thus achieve some sort of perpetuity by belonging to a social body that outlives his or her own personal existence. The public recalling of individual members of a group who no longer are alive establishes a sense of unity over the generations. It is noteworthy that a single word—"remember" in English, or *zakhor* in Hebrew—can describe both individual recollection and the intergenerational transmission of memory. The Israelites were commanded to "remember what Amalek did to you" (Deut. 25:17–19), just as Texans are enjoined to "remember the Alamo." The same verb is applied to both those who directly experience a historical event and those of later generations who make it their own "experience." When, during the yizkor prayer, Jews call upon God to remember the departed, they invoke the intertwined modes of personal and communal memory.

Similar social factors operated with reference to the kaddish, and these merged with its textual history. This combined process coalesced in medieval Ashkenaz, but evidence of it may be seen earlier. A legend with roots in the Geonic period depicts Rabbi Akiba teaching a boy to recite the public praise of God, to which the congregation responds, and thereby brings about the movement of the boy's father from Gehenna to Paradise.[44] The legend is cited as the basis of a custom in which a person who is an orphan leads the prayer on Saturday night so that he can recite kaddish and delay the return of his parents to Gehenna at the end of the Sabbath.[45] The legend builds upon talmudic traditions that assert the "redeeming power, for the parent, of the orphan's recital of prayers to which there were congregational responses."[46] These talmudic statements do not all refer to the kaddish per se, but they provide the background for creating communal occasions upon which a mourner could act on behalf of the soul of his departed parent. What began as a custom in response to a common sentiment gradually became a fixed pattern that spread to other communities and eventually emerged as an obligation. The kaddish became *the* prayer appropriate to recalling parents and to mourning. It proclaims an acceptance of God's will but also implies belief in His ultimate act of redemption. The first part of the communal response, "may the name of God be blessed," was uttered by Job (1:21), the biblical paragon of acquiescence to a harsh divine decree. But, as indicated, that response also has been attached to human wishes that the Eternal be mobilized to overcome individual and communal difficulties.

With the trauma of the Crusades, the kaddish emerged as a "natural" spiritual antidote; it could not bring back individual dead people, but perhaps its public utterance could bring eternal life to those who had passed on. The rule that it be recited in a minyan meant that the kaddish was "ready-made" to merge communal will and the personal sentiments of those still alive. As notions of the trajectory of the afterlife of individuals took shape and spread, the kaddish came to be viewed as a prayer that, when recited by descendants, contributed to the progress of the soul of a parent as it left the body and, over the course of a year, made its way to an eternal reward. The view that the kaddish had an effect on those who had passed on was criticized by Sephardi scholars in the Middle Ages, but the link of kaddish to mourning eventually became universal in Jewish life.[47] In recalling and assisting their dead through the kaddish, individuals found the resolve, and communities the strength, to reaffirm their own existence. This process continues today, as people who have lost a relative commit themselves to "say kaddish" daily for eleven months, along with other members of a prayer community, thereby reinforcing intertwined social and religious bonds.[48]

THE INDIVIDUAL AND THE ORGANIZATION OF DEATH

Just as the kaddish, based on beliefs and text-based practices in antiquity, took on new significance in the Middle Ages, so other aspects of burial, mourning, and memorialization evolved from ancient times, were regulated in medieval communities, and underwent new changes at the end of that period. These were not isolated shifts of meaning but had to do with comprehensive changes in communal life. Focusing on the case of Prague, Sylvie-Anne Goldberg has shown that the breakdown of the medieval community there was succeeded by the rise in prominence of the burial society, the *hevra kadisha*.[49] We have already encountered that institution in connection with the reading of the Zohar and the veneration of tzaddikim in Morocco.[50] The first known development of a hevra kadisha, however, took place in Ashkenaz, when one was established in Prague in 1564.[51]

Although initially organized to handle matters of burial and mourning, the hevra kadisha in Prague, and others like it, came to deal with a range of matters such as visiting the sick, collecting and distributing charity, and providing funds for the dowries and weddings of orphans. These activities touched all members of the community, even though not everyone was a member of the burial society and only those with the proper religious and moral credentials could attain high rank within it. All were affected by the activities of the burial society, however, because "daily life was organized around everything that constituted the end of the individual, and this became in a sense the motivating force and catalyst of communal life."[52] The hevra kadisha became "the chosen vehicle for the spiritual growth of the whole community."[53]

Details of burial and mourning are found in the bylaws of burial societies, as well as in religious literature of the time. Some of the practices, described above, go back to the biblical period. Others are based on rabbinic writings, in particular the extratalmudic tractate Semahot, "Rejoicings," a euphemistic title for a composition the Talmud seems to refer to as Evel Rabbati, "The Major [Tractate of] Mourning."[54] That work, for example, defines the intense period of mourning for a week after burial—*shivah*—and a less intense period of thirty days. During shivah one should stay at home and refrain from washing, anointing oneself, wearing shoes, or engaging in sexual intercourse. During the subsequent thirty-day period—*shloshim*—a man is permitted to leave his house but should leave himself ungroomed. Certain ancient practices, such as closing the eyes of the deceased once there are no signs of life, may have been absorbed from the culture of the Greco-Roman world.[55] Still others, contained in the books used by burial societies, first appeared in the Middle Ages, such as covering mirrors in a house of mourning, or walking around the grave of a man seven times, discussed below.

The laws of burial and mourning outline different phases of the process of dying and refer to different categories of people. Some rules relate to representatives of the hevra kadisha who gathered around the dying person, along with members of the family. These people guided the sick individual in reciting a confessionary prayer and the Shma' Yisrael when they thought he or she was about to die. Anyone in the room at the time of death was to rend a garment when death took place. Another practice was to spill out all the drawn water from the house after a death. This was viewed by some as removing "dangerous" water, tainted with the impurity of death, but it also had the function of providing a public sign that a death had occurred. In some cases, water was thrown out of the houses of immediate neighbors as well.

Members of the burial society followed a detailed routine for preparing a corpse, a process called *taharah,* or purification, which entailed closing the orifices, washing the body, grooming it (cleaning its nails and combing its hair), and dressing it for burial. The notion was that it ultimately would be resurrected in the clothes in which it was interred. Until the actual burial, members of the family of the deceased are in a special status of *aninut.* They are exempt from positive religious demands (those that require action rather than refraining from deeds), such as reciting the Shma' Yisrael twice daily.[56] One reason for this is that in ancient times, the heirs of the deceased had the responsibility of quickly arranging the burial. A more psychological reason is that in the Shma' Yisrael prayer, an individual accepts "the yoke of the Heavenly King," and the exemption takes into account the fact that before burial, a person has not yet acquiesced to, or even fully grasped, the divine judgment. It is only after burial that the week of mourning—*evel*—begins. Those relatives required to mourn are fathers and mothers, daughters and sons, brothers and sisters, and spouses. There are also norms incumbent upon members of the community. It is a meritorious act to attend a funeral, even if it involves simply walking after the bier a short distance, no matter how many other people are there. It also is incumbent upon a Jew to visit the house of mourners and console them during shivah.

Historically, there have been some constants in practices concerning death that are linked to Jewish worldviews, such as the basic valuation of life. The tractate Semaḥot opens with the assertion that a person who is dying (a *gosses*) is to be considered alive in every respect. Those attending a gosses should do nothing to hasten death or take actions (such as closing the eyes) that hint that death is imminent. To participate in ending a life, even in a minor fashion, is equivalent to the spilling of blood.[57]

In other ways however, new ideas began to affect Jewish understanding of, and practices concerning, death. As noted, early Jewish tradition outlined rules on how to deal with burial and mourning, but did not provide elaborate reasons for the correct behavior or explain them in terms of an afterlife. This changed in the late Middle Ages, partially under the influence of mystical traditions. Nahmanides, a thirteenth-century Spanish rabbi and kabbalist (d. ca. 1270), wrote an important book of rules relating to death and burial, and the contemporaneous Zohar also deals with burial practices. One book of the Zohar, the Idra Zuta, deals with the death of the "hero" of the Zohar, Rabbi Shimʾon Bar Yohai.[58] Kabbalistic notions relating to death and the soul spread from Spain, and some of them had an impact on Jewish communities in central Europe. Developments within the burial societies of late medieval Ashkenaz were paralleled by the growing elaboration of notions of the fate of souls in the hereafter that were derived from kabbala.[59]

Notions that first appeared in the Zohar receive prominent attention in works on death and mourning, some of which existed both in complete and in abridged forms. The former were used by members of the burial society, as specialists, and the latter by laymen.[60] Although from a contemporary standpoint, these mystical ideas now appear very "medieval," their diffusion precisely at the end of the Middle Ages may have stemmed from a growing sense of the individual that is reflected in musings over the fate of the soul.

Kabbalistic ideas about the trajectory of the soul reshaped ancient notions. Kabbalists perceived the individual soul as struggling to return to a state of purity and move close to its Divine source, but threatened, in the period right after death, with satanic forces of "impurity." Impurity (*ṭumʾah*) is not presented in an articulated cosmology in the Bible, and certainly is not associated there with personified beings such as souls or demons. While it is connected directly and profoundly with death, the biblical concern with impurity takes the form of prohibitions and rules for reattaining a state of purity among the living.[61] In fact, the ancient rabbinical justification for erecting a grave marker was not to preserve the name of the deceased, for at that time people were buried on family land and it was known who was buried where.[62] The function of markers was, rather, to provide a warning to priests (kohanim) to keep away from a place defiled by human remains.[63] After the destruction of the Second Temple and the cessation of its cult activities, ṭumʾah stemming from death was not relevant to the ordinary Jew, and therefore less of an issue. Kabbalistic writings, however, reworked the concept of impurity into a scene of struggle between a soul detached from its body and a series of forces that tried to punish it, capitalizing on its individual religious imperfections during its earthly sojourn.

These ideas about the soul became widespread in Jewish life. They may have reached Yemen, for example, where the burning of frankincense was a common way of counteracting the odors of a corpse. There, a house with a strong smell of that spice was identified as a "house of death" and clearly distinguished from a dwelling with the aroma of myrrh, which characterized a home where a birth had taken place. Frankincense may originally have been seen as an aspect of purification and atonement vis-à-vis dead bodies, parallel to biblical precedents in which incense and spices are mentioned (Num. 17:12; 2 Chron. 16:14). Referring to the custom as practiced in Sanʾa, Yemenite Jews in Israel now explain that the aroma of frankincense was "intended to repel ghosts, believed to be anxious to snatch the dead person's soul."[64]

Consciousness of death and the afterlife of an individual soul began to pervade everyday activities and rituals in various parts of the Jewish world. One indication of this process is the insertion of religious introspection into prayer books. Individual confession was introduced into the weekly cycle of prayer after the main Amidah prayer in the morning service.[65] Previously, confession had been a communal activity that took place only on the High Holidays; its individual recitation was confined to the setting of a deathbed.[66]

Another way that consciousness of death entered daily life was through the widespread use of the proverb "Charity saves from death" (Prov. 10:2, 11:4). A dying person was encouraged to give alms, and funerals were an occasion for people to drop some coins into a collection box.[67] Such boxes often were decorated with the words of the verse (see figure 19).

The sense of charity as protecting against death, or other misfortunes, appeared in other contexts too. Wedding festivities were particularly appropriate times to make material gestures of concern for the poor. It was common in both Europe and North Africa for a table to be set aside for the poor as part of a wedding feast. In nineteenth-century Tripoli, wealthy families prepared a meal for the indigent the evening before they celebrated a marriage, and this was also a Hasidic tradition.[68] The constancy of almsgiving was one way in which the life transitions of individuals echoed one another, and this last example is of particular interest because of the

Figure 19.   Alms box, carried in the cemetery by shoulder strap, inscribed "Charity Saves from Death." Poland, twentieth century. Courtesy Center for Jewish Art, Hebrew University, Jerusalem. Sc 469, no. 19.

link between death and marriage that it implies. We already have discussed some parallels between marriage and death rituals.[69] Another example is found in the so-called *danse macabre,* or "dance of death."

The danse macabre is alluded to in European Christian poetry and drama, and depicted in art, from the late thirteenth and fourteenth centuries on. The "dance" is a procession, which includes both living people and the dead, pictured as skeletons or as dwellers of the cemetery. Its theme is to remind people of their fated end, and its purpose is to bring them to seriousness and repentance. Some suggest that the French word *macabre* derives from "Maccabee," with reference to the apocryphal book 2 Maccabees (6:7), which tells of the gruesome martyring of seven brothers. Another suggestion is that the French word comes from the Hebrew (in Yiddish intonation) *mekabber,* gravedigger.[70] Whatever the origin, there is evidence that a "dance of death" became part of Jewish weddings in some areas. As we have seen elsewhere, the joy of marriage directly brings in its wake a consciousness of life's end.[71]

The symbolic linkage of marriage (entailing sex) and death is both widespread and ancient, but at the end of the Middle Ages, that association may have become tied to an awareness of the individual in new ways. One example is what came to be known as a *dibbuk,* or "evil spirit," which possessed a victim, making her or him ill, requiring exorcism. The phenomenon of possession had earlier been attributed by Jews to anonymous "demons," but the new formulation of "evil spirits" identified the possessing beings as the souls of specific people who had died. The ideological basis for this idea, which implied a belief in the transmigration of souls, also derived from Spanish and Provençal kabbala in the twelfth and thirteenth centuries. The soul of an individual who had sinned egregiously while alive often did not find peace in the upper realms and might return to earth, entering the body of a living individual. As in the case of other kabbalistic ideas, it was around the sixteenth century when these beliefs emerged from the limited circles of those familiar with esoteric texts.[72] They became embodied in the behavior of possessed individuals and in social institutions reacting to that behavior.

Reports of dibbuk possession first appear in Mediterranean lands and later in eastern Europe.[73] Yoram Bilu has analyzed these accounts of possession and exorcism from a psychological perspective and has shown that sexual matters were a major concern to those entering into a possession trance.[74] Most of the documented cases involved male spirits entering females. Those possessed were typically young, recently married women, but unmarried males were sometimes also affected. During exorcism, a dibbuk was pressed to identify himself (and in a few cases herself) by the rabbi leading the ceremony. Upon being identified, an evil spirit was shown to belong to a gallery of sinners, many of whom had transgressed sexually while alive. Exorcism thus made "visible" the strength of sexual impulses, and highlighted the strain between individual desires and communal norms. One of the purposes of exorcism was to impress upon the onlookers the dire consequences of transgressing these norms, for sometimes exorcism did not work and the victim eventually died. At the same time, the ritual procedure underlined sexuality as an expression of internalized motivation, differing with the character of the person in question. This reinforced the growing sense of individuality.[75]

A similar set of links, among sex, death, and individuality, may be seen in the custom of *haqqafot,* and in the kabbalistic ideas supporting it. This was a practice at the funerals of males in which men circumambulated a grave seven times.[76] The kabbalistic theory was that ejaculated sperm that was not aimed at procreation (as a result of masturbation, a nocturnal emission, or withdrawal during intercourse) turned into bodiless demonic beings who were the offspring of their father and the she-demon Lilith. These beings, never having received an inheritance from their father, were attracted to his funeral to attempt to claim what was theirs, or to harm him. The act of circling a grave protected the deceased from such demons. In Ashkenaz, the practice was found in a few regions, and money was sometimes placed in the grave.[77] In Sephardi contexts, I have seen bits of gold dust scattered about during the haqqafot, explicitly to divert the attention of demons.[78] This custom, and its full explanation, rarely fail to seize the attention of those previously unfamiliar with it, which at one time included the famed student of kabbala Gershom Scholem.[79] The perception of dangerous demons descended from a man was so strong that the parallel custom emerged of not allowing the actual living sons of a deceased male to follow his bier to the graveside in the cemetery. This practice continues in many Jerusalem funerals today. When the kabbalistic rationale behind these acts was widely known, these customs invoked intimate concern with the personal life of the departing soul, even as the process of his departure was under the strict control of the hevra kadisha.

Growing individuation at the end of the Middle Ages may also be seen in memorial practices that took place after the first week of mourning, or even the full year of mourning after the death of a parent. It is appropriate to remember the departed on the anniversary of their death, and a custom deriving from sixteenth-century Lurianic kabbala was to read sections of the Mishna as part of the memorial ritual.[80] This is based on wordplay with the written Hebrew consonants of the word Mishna, *M Sh N H*, which may be rearranged as *NeShaMaH*—Hebrew for "soul." The ritual emerged of reading a section from the Mishna, the first letters of which would form an acrostic spelling out the name of the deceased. This ritual reading highlighted each person singly, even as it placed the individual in a field of texts that encompassed all Jews. Thus, various practices of burial, mourning, and memorialization constituted communal scenarios upon which the profiles of individual lives were sketched with increasing, although cautious, clarity.

DEATH, DISTINCTION, AND DESCENT

An old adage states that death is the great leveler, stressing the essential equality of the end of all human lives. In Judaism, there is a long tradition of concern that burial and memorial customs should not ostentatiously display the differences between rich and poor. Relating to instances in which such differences were glaring and led people to spend exorbitant amounts on burials, the Talmud recounts how Rabban Gamliel of Yavneh decided that he "would make light of himself" and insisted that he be buried in simple flax garments.[81] One interpretation of the requirement for rapid burial is that it does not allow for the elaborate planning of a showy funeral. Today, however, funeral arrangements are normally handled by professionals, and the expectation of a quick burial can be misused in pressuring a family to make quick decisions that will cost them more than necessary.

There has always been tension between the ideal of equality and social reality, not only with regard to differences in wealth. The struggle between strict equality and individual distinction has arisen in realms such as grave markers in the Israeli army, which has formulated uniform rules to apply to all soldiers, while often the family of a fallen soldier insists on including something unique on the gravestone.[82] Another sphere where equality in death has not been the norm is that of gender. Burial practices and memorial rites often have separated men from women.

Medieval memorial books, as stated, included both women and men, but in other ways they were kept apart. Women left the room when a dying man confessed.[83] They were not allowed to carry a bier and had to follow behind the men in processions to the cemetery. The kaddish, during the year after death and on death anniversaries (known in Yiddish as yahrtzeit), was normally recited only by sons, for both mother and father.[84] The connection between saying kaddish and males was so strong that the Yiddish language came to refer to a son as a person's "kaddish."[85] This perception changed in America in Reform and Conservative synagogues, but also showed remarkable persistence. In the 1980s, with regard to women who wished to recite kaddish in Orthodox synagogues, it was noted that "kaddish is *the* synagogue experience that awakens women to their exclusion from an important component of Jewish ritual." A recent trend in some Orthodox kibbutzim in Israel that women recite kaddish is considered a development worth noting.[86]

The fact that women in traditional Jewish societies did not participate in memorial rituals in the same manner as men did not mean that this was a sphere that was closed to them. In most societies, the life expectancy of women is longer than that of men. This creates a natural situation for them to be concerned with matters connected to the end of life in their later years. Elderly Sephardi women in Jerusalem, as depicted by Susan Sered, became "ritual experts" in "domestic religion."[87] Many of them were widowed and spent their time "attending to" their children and grandchildren by lighting candles at appropriate times, or visiting the graves of ancestors and tzaddikim, when they prayed on behalf of the members of their families. Their special religious roles in old age reflected their defined task when younger: lavishing care on those who were close to them. This care was not limited to their families alone, for they also offered prayers for others, such as soldiers in the army. Being freed from the domestic demands of their earlier adult life, they became leaders in this religious realm.

Memorializing may be linked to inequality in other ways. Sephardi tradition, in its memorial prayers (*hashkavot*), distinguishes between scholars or (former) leaders and ordinary members of the community.[88] The anthropologist Meyer Fortes once remarked that "death by itself does not confer ancestorhood."[89] Where there is no practice of creating a written record of all who died, people may be memorialized so long as those who knew them personally are still alive, but move into oblivion once close relatives no longer keep up memorial prayers.

The widespread custom of lighting an oil lamp in the synagogue for a deceased relative has been described for the community of Jerba, in southern Tunisia.[90] In nearby Tripoli, in order to make sure a lamp was lit throughout the year of mourning, some men joined a mutual aid society that made funds available to members for this purpose and others, such as purchasing burial shrouds. To maintain memorial practices required both personnel and financial resources. Those who "became ancestors," lasting over generations, had the support of either an enduring family, a community, or a special group.

Memorialization in Jewish life continues to be a basis of community organization even though traditional ideas of the soul in the afterlife are preserved only by some sections of contemporary Jewry. Synagogues in the United States (and elsewhere) contain bronze memorial boards with individual plaques naming dead relatives, which can be illuminated with a small electric bulb when appropriate (see figure 20). In recent decades, many synagogues in the urban areas where immigrant Jews first settled have been disbanded, but their memorial boards were often preserved and moved to newer suburban synagogues. Stratification is found in this setting as well. Everyone's name may be placed on a memorial board, but those who have made special contributions ensure that they become "ancestors" by having their names inscribed with extra prominence elsewhere in the building as well. This is sometimes also done by the person's descendants after his or her death. In such cases, memorialization may be more of a social statement on the part of the living than a direct reflection of the life of the deceased. As in earlier periods, the Kol Nidre service, at the onset of the Yom Kippur fast, continues to be the occasion on which such prominence is demonstrated.

Even those with modest means may seek immortality through the transmission of names. It is common for Jews to name children after grandparents or other forebears. In Ashkenaz, it became forbidden to name a child after a grandparent who was still alive, but some Sephardi groups assign the name of a living grandparent if the latter agrees. This practice, like many others concerning the afterlife, was originally enmeshed in kab-

Figure 20.   Memorial board in an Israeli synagogue
bearing individual plaques forming the design of a
candelabra. Photo Harvey E. Goldberg.

balistic theory, and it could be interpreted in opposite ways. Naming a child
for a live grandparent who had reached an old age could represent the wish
that the baby, too, attain longevity. On the other hand, there was a perception that giving the name transferred the soul of the older person to the
younger, so that when the former passed away, the child might die too.[91]
This concern may be compared to the insistence of many Ashkenazi Jews
that a child whose parents are both alive should not stay in the synagogue
while the yizkor prayer is being recited. Many time-honored Sephardi and
Ashkenazi practices relating to parents continue today among people who
have no knowledge of the beliefs to which they once were linked.

   Another way in which people could work for immortality was by the
contribution of a Torah scroll to the synagogue.[92] This type of contribution
was of special meaning to childless couples who, using the Yiddish expression, left no "kaddish." The values implied were not merely Ashkenazi,
however, and were also found among Middle Eastern Jews.[93] The practice
also implies a more general cultural association between Jews and their
Torah books. Earlier, I mentioned the processions accompanying the intro-

duction of a sefer Torah or a set of the Zohar into a synagogue.[94] In many places, such a procession is known as a *levayah*—an "accompaniment," which is also the common Hebrew-derived term for "funeral."

Ashkenazi sources liken carrying a bier to bearing the ancient ark that housed the "tablets of the covenant." Jews in Morocco took turns in carrying a bier, just as they sought the honor of being part of the levayah of a sefer Torah. The same symbolic association is inscribed in the general Jewish norm of burying sacred books in a manner parallel to the burial of humans.[95] Some book burials took place on the occasion of the funeral of a learned individual. In Morocco, they were organized on the day after Shavuʿot, the holiday commemorating the giving of the Torah.[96] Among the Jews of Georgia, there formerly was a practice of burying a woman's ketubba with her, although this was opposed by rabbis.[97] Even when women were illiterate, the ketubba was a personally relevant text in their lives. A rabbi in America today tries to include children in book burials, separate from actual funerals, so that they become familiar with cemeteries before they are forced to encounter them in difficult personal circumstances.[98]

Values based on Torah also introduced distinctions into funeral procedures. In Ashkenaz, if a dead man was a reputed scholar, the last ritual preparations before leaving for the cemetery took place in the room where he studied.[99] In Yemen, a normal funeral entailed seven stops between the city gate and the graveyard, during which words of eulogy would be said, while for Torah scholars additional stops were made, sometimes as many as twenty.[100] The value of Torah was given expression in mass funeral processions for rabbinic leaders in early twentieth-century New York City. Tens of thousands of people, and rabbis from out of town, attended the funeral of Rabbi Jacob Joseph, an eminent leader of Orthodox Jewry, which lasted for over five hours as it moved from the Lower East Side of Manhattan to a cemetery in Brooklyn.[101]

Beyond the context of a specific community, Jews could set their sights on an afterlife in the framework of the broadest Jewish collectivity and its spatial center. Ancient beliefs, linked to Zechariah 14:4, associate the Mount of Olives in Jerusalem, where there have been Jewish graves since Second Temple times, with the messianic era. A talmudic statement claims that at the end of days, all the bodies buried in the Diaspora will make their way to the Land of Israel.[102] This belief was the basis of an old custom of collecting earth from the Land of Israel to place over the eyes of a dead person, as if his or her journey were already under way. A parallel expression of the importance of "the Land," as it was known in rabbinic parlance, was having a person reburied there, in spite of the reluctance to rebury in other instances.[103] Yet another way to connect with the Holy Land was to move there in one's old age to await the end of one's days. In recent centuries, many Jews settled in one of four "Holy Cities"—Jerusalem, Hebron, Tiberias, or Safed—so as eventually to be buried in "the Land."[104] Zionism, in contrast, sought to make Palestine a land in which Jews came to live, rather than to die.

MODERN DEATH

Modern conditions have led people to place eschatological expectations in the background and to focus on life in "this world." The celebration of birthdays was unusual in traditional Jewish culture; the anniversaries of people's deaths were marked, rather than the date of birth. The Talmud does mention that Rabbi Yosef organized a festive day for his colleagues when he reached the age of sixty. The reason was that when death arrived after that age, it was not considered unusual and could not be interpreted as divine punishment. Another eminent scholar was skeptical about R. Yosef's initiative, but the incident does suggest what "life expectancy" was in ancient times.[105] A practice noted in several places in Europe in the twentieth century was that a man reaching the age of eighty-three would celebrate his "second bar mitzvah" in the synagogue. Contemporary trends, while encouraging longevity, have also shaped the way people die.

Developments of the past two hundred years, including the emancipation of the Jews in Europe, affected the way Jews died and treated death, just as they had an impact on birth and circumcision. Jewish tradition had always called for rapid burial. In the last decades of the eighteenth century, this practice was confronted with a growing concern over the phenomenon of "false death": the possibility that a person would appear to be dead, but then unexpectedly "come to life." Death might be declared prematurely, and a person might be buried alive. The ancient Jewish norm was criticized both by some Jews and by Gentiles who wanted Jews to be subject to the same "progressive" laws as other citizens of the states into which Jews were being incorporated.

The issue of delaying burial in order to check that a person was really dead before interment yielded a vigorous debate. It touched upon basic issues such as the relationship between Jewish law (halakha) and science. To what extent and in what circumstances should rabbis seek the expertise of doctors? Developments in medicine could challenge the legitimacy of rabbinic authority. The debate over delaying burial became emblematic of the views of the radical Hebrew Enlightenment (*haskala*) in Berlin, which sought to create a new culture free from traditional customs.[106]

Jews were also, of course, exposed to factors affecting the health of the general population. Vaccines and the establishment of public health measures reduced infant mortality and raised the average life expectancy. Jews in eastern Europe, whose numbers increased dramatically during the eighteenth and nineteenth centuries, underwent what has been called "the demographic transition." Population grew rapidly because more people survived early childhood diseases. This meant larger families and overall population growth. Eventually, changes in patterns of mortality led to changes in natality. Parents learned that it is not necessary to have many children to ensure that a few will survive. Those aspiring to middle-class styles of life knew that a great deal had to be invested in each child in education and economic resources. Smaller families became the norm. These demographic changes were evident among eastern European Jews migrating to America or western Europe at the end of the nineteenth century and among Middle Eastern Jews migrating to Israel after 1948.

The medical and demographic trends had echoes in Jewish tradition. The development of vaccines brought about debates about their permissibility, in particular, over whether it was permissible to administer them on the Sabbath.[107] More basically, there were shifts in the perception of the imminence of death during life, during both childhood and adulthood. In the Mzab, in southern Algeria, there was a synagogue ceremony on the holiday of Shavuot that marked the initiation of little boys into the study of Torah.[108] An account I was given of the ceremony by Mzab Jews living in Strasbourg indicated that it also marked the youngsters' having survived the dangerous years of childhood illness. Presumably, this aspect of the custom lost its poignancy as infant diseases came under control. It also came to be taken for granted that adults, too, lived with less of a threat of unexpected death, as can be seen from a rabbinic verdict handed down in Egypt.

The Babylonian Talmud states that a person who meets a friend after not seeing him for twelve months should utter the blessing "Barukh mehayeh metim" ("Blessed be the Reviver of the dead").[109] This rule, reflecting the uncertainties of life when people traveled great distances, was encoded in the *Shulhan Arukh,* and the practice became common in many regions. With nineteenth-century steamship and rail travel, however, people came to view long journeys as routine and could maintain contact with one another even when far apart. When Rabbi Eliahu Ḥazan of Alexandria was asked about the trend among Jews in Egypt of neglecting the "Reviver of the dead" blessing, he said that uttering the blessing whenever one saw a person one had not seen for twelve months was no longer warranted.[110]

Modern travel technology is, of course, a mixed blessing. It provides the setting for new types of violent death, such as car accidents, while these in turn are now utilized as a source of organ transplants. In the past, rabbinic tradition was hesitant to authorize invading a dead body for postmortem examinations, but if it is likely that another person's life will be preserved by a transplant, there is little question but that halakha may justify it.[111] Still, in comparison to European countries, Israel has a low percentage of organ donors, and some explain this by the widespread perception that donating part of one's body is contrary to Jewish law. In recent years, attempts have been made to bring together rabbinical councils and representatives of the Israeli medical establishment to find ways of encouraging traditional Jews to list themselves as potential donors. One suggestion is that they carry donation cards stating that they are "willing to donate organs as authorized by a halakhic authority."[112] A major concern of some rabbis is that doctors may use criteria for determining death that are not acceptable from a rabbinic viewpoint. Other interesting questions, aside from those linked to religion, arise in Israel from the consciousness of the continuity of part of one person's body in another individual. It is newsworthy when the organ of a Palestinian is transplanted into an Israeli Jew, or vice versa.

Longevity, another result of the advance of medicine and health policies, is also a blessing that brings its own dilemmas. People now live longer, but many spend more years in a state of dependence, of physical and mental limitation, or of painful illness.[113] A growing sense of individual autonomy leads some people to demand that they should be able to make decisions with regard to death, just as they made decisions in life. Jews concerned with their tradition ask how their religious culture relates to decisions, often entailing "abetted suicide," in which one human is asked to participate in ending the life of another. Judaism condemns suicide, claiming that no one has a right to take human life, harming that which is "owned" by God.[114] Those who do so are not supposed to be buried in a cemetery along with other Jews. Rabbinic law, however, has found ways of modifying that stark position. It is claimed in cases of apparent suicide that it is not always possible to know a person's motives, or that a person may have repented at the last minute but have been unable to stop the process of self-destruction, so on the basis of that possibility she or he should receive a standard burial.[115] Some rabbis who are strictly opposed to actively contributing to ending a life nonetheless recognize the right to refuse "heroic" measures: medical intervention that keeps alive a suffering person who appears to have no chance of recovery.[116]

As pointed out by Leon Kass, the language people use is a profound factor in how they view issues like euthanasia. One position argues that the value of "human dignity" may justify taking a life that has entered a "protracted state of reduced humanity." Kass's analysis of that term leads to the opposite conclusion.[117] Yoel Kahn, struggling with the same problem, offers the idea that *hillul ha-shem,* the desecration of God's name, which was offered as a motive for Jews' martyring themselves in the past, might be applied in such circumstances to make sense of ending a life from which the semblance of holiness has departed. He sees himself as moving towards this new interpretation while still having feelings of loyalty to the traditional viewpoint.[118] In modern Hebrew, "mercy killing" has been translated as *hamatat hesed,* delivering death as an act of grace. According to one's stance, this term is either a creative reworking, or a distortion, of the traditional phrase applied to those who deal with the preparation and burial of the dead—*hesed shel emet* (true grace).[119] Voluntary acts of grace towards the dead were seen as "true," because there could be no expectation of reciprocity from them. This vocabulary, in contrast to the contemporary emphasis on individual autonomy, envisions a dead person as still enmeshed in a series of social relationships.

In traditional society, people saw themselves as having ongoing ties to those no longer in "this world," while one result of the improvement of medical technology and treatment is the creation of relationships with those yet to be born. A fetus in a mother's womb was always a focus of attention and of many popular practices, but devices like ultrasound, the high rate of successful pregnancies leading to live births, and the careful planning that leads to decisions to have a baby create an atmosphere in which parents relate to a child still developing in utero as an individual personality.[120] When a modern pregnancy is not successful, whether through miscarriage or a stillbirth, a sharp sense of loss ensues. This presents a challenge both to young couples and to rabbis, for traditional law provides no rituals relating to a miscarriage nor mourning practices for a baby who dies when less than thirty days old.[121] Innovations in this regard have taken on a variety of forms, some drawing upon the traditional mitzvah of visiting the sick in the former instance, and others suggesting ceremonies drawing from funeral ritual for the latter.[122] One suggestion incorporates the father into the category of the sick after a miscarriage.[123] Others draw upon traditional acts and concepts such as giving charity, saying kaddish, having an abbreviated shivah, and acts of remembrance.

CONTEMPORARY SOCIAL AND CULTURAL DILEMMAS

Demographic and scientific developments present social and cultural challenges, as well as individual dilemmas of medical ethics. Elderly people are a more salient feature of society than they were in the past. Many, no longer engaged in economic production but still healthy, look back on their lives, gathering up and structuring their memories. Life reviews may become especially significant when images of an afterlife are no longer central in a culture. Barbara Myerhoff has depicted this process among Jews in Los Angeles, born in shtetls in eastern Europe, who had lived most of their lives in America and, in old age, spent much of their day together in a center for the aged.[124] She shows how childhood memories from eastern Europe, shared by the elderly and summed up by them in the term *yiddishkeit* (Yiddish-ness), formed a reworked culture that energized their individual and group lives while they were old. They were confronted with problems common to all old people in America (and elsewhere), and utilized their memories of a vanished culture to face these challenges in their own idiom. Elsewhere, a Jew born in Belarus in 1881 recorded audiotapes, narrating his childhood memories, several years before his death in 1977. He wished to transmit these memories to his family, perhaps like the ethical wills of earlier generations.[125]

The concern for the perpetuation of memories reflects not only the individual facing his or her own demise, but the tremendous dislocations that have affected Jewish communities over the course of the past century and a half. Not only did mass migration obliterate life in eastern European shtetls, it threatens the pasts of Jews who moved from North Africa and the Middle East as well. In recent years, with continual Jewish out-migration from South Africa, some Jews there have chosen to be cremated after death—despite traditional rabbinic opposition to the practice—because they know their graves will not be visited by their descendants. Migrants have reached diverse destinations in western Europe, North America, and Latin America, where ethnographers have found them eager to give recorded shape to their personal stories, which also are collective memories.[126] On more than one occasion, researchers have found personal significance in becoming the vehicles for the perpetuation of these memories.[127]

In addition to large-scale migrations, the destruction of one-third of the Jewish people in the Holocaust, in the various regions of Europe, gives powerful impetus to the cultivation of Jewish memory.[128] The enormity of that organized attack on Jews and other groups targeted by the Nazis raises many questions, including issues of human understanding and of memory. There are also matters of a personal, "practical" nature that arise from this mass destruction. Often, those wishing to say kaddish annually for relatives who died in the gas chambers do not know a date of a family member's death and can only recite the kaddish on occasions of communal memorial, such as on the festivals when yizkor is said or on the tenth of the

Hebrew month of Tevet, a fast day marking the siege of Jerusalem in the sixth century B.C.E.[129] That date was selected by Israel's Chief Rabbinate for the recital of kaddish on behalf of all Holocaust victims whose date of death is not known. The selection not only links an intimate loss with that of the nation but also ties together various calamities in the Jews' long history. In addition to a common date for Holocaust victims, in 1950, Israel established an official "place of memory," the Yad Vashem Holocaust memorial, both for Israelis and for visitors from abroad.[130] I encountered an unsettling case of interaction among Holocaust "scripts" in 1994, when I visited Yad Vashem with youngsters from the United States, many of whom had been to the Holocaust Museum in Washington, D.C. After walking through the section of Yad Vashem that presents its story through photographs (and some film), one girl commented that she was disappointed, saying, "the Holocaust Museum did much more for me."

Merging individual deaths with that of a vast collective creates dilemmas. One is the relegation of the event to a vast anonymous reality, which loses intimate meaning with time. In the attempt to maintain sensitivity to this reality, recourse is often had to individual stories. An early example was the publication of the diary of the Dutch Jewish teenager Anne Frank, a book that was later made into a play and a movie and translated into dozens of languages.[131] More recently, the Yad Vashem memorial created a hall in which visitors hear the solemn recitation of the names of single victims. Today, trips to the death camps by Israel teenagers include an elderly survivor of the Holocaust as a "witness," who tells a personal story, and in doing so makes the youth with whom he travels part of that story.[132] Most recently, reports of the frequent deaths of and mourning for individuals as the result of the Palestinian-Israeli conflict have been flashed across television screens not only in that region but throughout the world. It is debatable whether this highlights individual sensitivity or ultimately serves to numb collective awareness.

Another dilemma of linking individual and group perspectives of death is that a person may be faced with alternative or competing collectives with which he or she might "merge," each with its own interpretations. In Israel, the national memorial day for victims of the Holocaust precedes Independence Day (the fifth day of the month of Iyyar) by one week, with that holiday following immediately upon a memorial day for the fallen soldiers of Israel's wars. The Holocaust thus becomes linked to the creation of a modern Jewish state. For some American Jews, the Holocaust, dramatized through visits to Auschwitz, has become a central part of their Jewish ethnicity.[133]

Interpreting and reinterpreting the Holocaust is an ongoing process, as illustrated by Steven Spielberg's 1993 film *Schindler's List*. Its interactive impact on other forms of remembrance may be seen in Yad Vashem at the tree planted in honor of Otto Schindler in the grove of Righteous Gentiles, non-Jews who risked their lives to save Jews during the war. Today, a pile of stones, spontaneously placed there by visitors, surrounds the tree, which has thus become a folk monument "in conversation with" the Hollywood production. The Ashkenazi custom of placing a stone on a grave, which is now a widespread Israeli gesture when visiting a cemetery, has turned the memorial tree into a surrogate burial spot (Schindler is actually buried in a Christian cemetery in Jerusalem's "Old City").[134]

Yad Vashem is perhaps the most effective and meaningful instance in Israel of calling upon memory in relation to collective identity, but the Israeli landscape is marked by hundreds of other graves, monuments, and memorial sites from different periods, representing a range of views about what being Jewish and Israeli signifies (several were mentioned in chapter 5 in connection with travel in search of identity). The identities maintained and bolstered by these sites vary considerably. Some are secular Zionist memorials, like those that highlight the patriotic death of Yosef Trumpeldor at Tel Hai in the early part of the twentieth century;[135] and others are religious self-definitions within the framework of the Israeli state. An example of the latter is the limited attempt to develop David's putative grave on Mt. Zion as a national shrine.[136]

There has been extensive discussion of the way official bodies seek to shape the meaning of death, and "dictate" group memory.[137] An example concerns the fort at Latrun, off the Tel Aviv–Jerusalem highway, the site of a bloody and unsuccessful battle during Israel's War of Independence. Latrun now houses the official museum and memorial monument of the Israel Defense Force's armored corps. Among those who fell, and are now remembered as heroes, were immigrants who had arrived in Israel only a short time before the battle. They included World War II survivors, and some claim that they were treated as expendable in the process of building the new state. Historically, this is a complex question, but the issue shows the growing contestation of national collective memories.[138] Other post-state newcomers have challenged the map of national memory by claiming that they were excluded from it, and have also succeeded in making a place for themselves upon it. After many years, Moroccan Jews were able to bring the remains of countrymen who drowned in an unseaworthy ship on its way to Israel to be buried there in the national cemetery on Mt. Herzl.[139] This illustrates the growing trend for memorialism to reflect individual and group initiatives, and not only official decisions "from above."[140] Beyond that trend, there is the growing challenge to the claim of Israeli culture that everyone in the society "shares in" the losses of individual families whose children die as the result of war.[141]

DEALING WITH DEATH: PERSONAL
AND COMMUNAL EMPHASES

In Israel, the state is involved, not only in the defining of collective memory, but in the concrete arrangements of funerals and burial. In this regard, as in other spheres of life, the range of Judaic religious expression is narrower in Israel than it is in Diaspora communities. The majority of Jewish Israelis, whether they like it or not, are buried according to the procedures of a hevra kadisha, whose conduct is often foreign to them.[142] Almost all burials, except those on kibbutzim, involve rabbinic supervision.[143] This may entail conflict over meaningful details. For example, a Jerusalem hevra kadisha tried to prevent a man who had immigrated from the United States from inscribing the Gregorian date of his wife's death on her tombstone, along with the Hebrew date. Eventually, a court upheld his right to do so.[144] Elsewhere including Gregorian dates on Jewish tombstones is a widespread practice (see figure 21).

The existing arrangements are becoming less satisfactory with regard to a growing number of Israelis. One category consists of people with Jewish fathers and non-Jewish mothers (often, but not only, from the former Soviet Union), who are not Jewish from the standpoint of rabbinic law.[145] This is particularly problematic in the case of young soldiers who have given their lives for the country or those who were killed in terrorist attacks along with other Israelis. The Orthodox rabbinic monopoly also disturbs ideologically committed secular Jews or those who want a non-Orthodox rabbi to preside over a funeral. As a result of a high court decision, and a law passed in 1996, the Ministry of Religions was required to develop special cemeteries for those needing or preferring alternative forms of interment. The ministry dragged its feet. One cemetery was established in Beersheba in 1999, and some small municipalities have followed suit. There are now (December 2002) plans for others in Haifa and in Jerusalem, but their implementation remains slow.[146]

In the United States, even without a reaction against the arbitrary intervention of official agencies, there is a trend towards making burial, and rituals connected to mourning, a more personal and communal experience. Leon Wieseltier describes how he was "furious" at the suggestion, made to

Figure 21.   Grave in cemetery of Fez, Morocco. Photo
Harvey E. Goldberg.

his mother, that reciting kaddish for his father be assigned to a paid "kaddish sayer," who was sure to be in the synagogue at every prayer service,
even though this way of meeting the obligation of kaddish was once quite
common in America. "It is *my* obligation," he emphasizes.[147] Citing a
number of instances in different parts of the United States in which people
have joined or organized volunteer groups to perform the purification and
burial of bodies, Jack Riemer comments: "Who would have thought that
the hevra kadisha, of all things, would make a comeback?"[148] Although
there is anxiety and awkwardness in approaching a mitzvah that in recent
generations has been given over to "professionals," there are also the rewards of attending to this task of ḥesed shel emet—true grace.[149]

There seems to be a parallel between this trend and a rediscovered concern with the idea of the resurrection of the individual dead person. Neil

Gillman notes a change from the mid twentieth century to the present in this regard.[150] Two or three generations ago, most liberal Jewish leaders did not take the idea of bodily resurrection very seriously. They were prepared to accept a metaphorical understanding of the soul living beyond the physical existence of the body, but to believe that the individual body would rise again, as suggested in the language of the daily Amidah prayer, appeared to make little sense in the modern scientific age.[151]

Some recent thinkers, however, have engaged the traditional notion precisely because focusing on the body lends importance to specific individuals, in their full personhood, rather than viewing them as statistics. In addition, the hope of returning to an existence in which the soul is rejoined to the body may be interpreted as reinforcing the value on action in "this world," as opposed to some disembodied future time. The willingness and readiness to deal with the corpse of someone who has just died, evident in participation in a hevra kadisha, may partake of similar concerns.

Something of this shift of perception, attendant upon exposure to concrete expressions of death, may be sensed in the following meditation on death and burial, written in a group diary by an American teenager who spent a few days on an Israeli kibbutz.[152] The aim was to give the youngsters an experience of "working on a kibbutz." Near where they worked, however, were the graves of kibbutz founders who had fallen in its defense during Israel's War of Independence. This led the young woman to pen the following words:

> I firmly believe that the body is no more than earthly packaging for
> the soul; and that upon death, the soul moves on to another place.
> Therefore, we should dispose of the packaging in a way as ecologi-
> cally sound as possible. Until today, I thought all those gravestones
> and plots were no more than a waste of land. [Our guide's] haunting
> stories of land made me realize that the stones serve as a memorial to
> those who have died for our people. The people may have perished
> and been forgotten by the living, but the stone stands as an eternal
> reminder of their existence. I want to work in the cemetery here to
> preserve the memory of the men and women who died. I feel I
> should do something to remember those before us who died so that
> we could be here today. *Am Yisrael Chai* [the Jewish people lives].

This teenager did not explore the idea of resurrection, but her thinking and feeling were affected by direct contact with specific human graves.

Her meditation is a contemporary expression of the theme we have explored: that much as the biological death of a human organism highlights the individuality of human existence, the meaning attached to persons and their limited existence is always enmeshed in communities with their ways of life and traditions. We may diagnose a historical trend within Jewish culture in which, over time, greater recognition has been given to the individual, but collective expression of and input into the meaning of death is never absent. The story of a single life is also a group saga.

How does one conclude a chapter on death? I am reminded of an interview I conducted on the cycle of festivals with a rabbi who came from Jerba in Tunisia. My set of questions began with the New Year (Rosh Hashanah) season in the fall, and ended with queries about the fast day of Tish'ah be-Av, which commemorates the destruction of the Temple and occurs in late summer. When he saw that I had finished, the rabbi expressed dissatisfaction. "You should end *be-khi ṭov* [with something positive]," he admonished. "Ask me another question about Rosh Hashanah!" I was pleased that he had not only tolerated my inquiries but thought them significant enough to wish to place his stamp on the way I carried them out. Anthropologists are the students of those whom they interrogate. The rabbi taught me both about Jewish life and about my own discipline. To end *be-khi ṭov,* I next turn to the topic of community.

7 Bonds of Community and Individual Lives

In the preceding chapters, we have seen how life-cycle events entail the presence of a community. During the Middle Ages, there was a tendency to move circumcisions from the home to the synagogue.[1] With regard to weddings, in many places the sum of money entered into a ketubba depended on how local notables assessed the value of a dowry. Those starting out on pilgrimages would enjoy enhanced status within their communities upon return. When death affected a family, mourners obligated to recite kaddish could only do so in a minyan, a prayer quorum of ten men.[2] Both travel and death provided occasions for a heightened sense of individuality, but the new perceptions of the early modern period emerged within a cultural field still suffused with traditional norms. The inevitable gap between personal wills and group norms notwithstanding, a focus on individual Jewish lives implies a communal setting.

There are other reasons as well why a discussion of life-cycle events naturally leads to the topic of community. Inclusion in, or exclusion from, communal Jewish life was itself often framed by a life-cycle event. The receipt of the Torah by the People of Israel was frequently pictured as an act of marriage.[3] On the contrary, when a community saw that an individual was threatening shared norms and decided to prohibit contact with him, he was treated like a mourner, and his social life was severely restricted. In addition, the very act of becoming Jewish, conversion, was sometimes seen in life-cycle terms: the Talmud states that a proselyte is like a newborn child.[4]

Today, against the background of over two hundred years of emancipation, the issue of the linkage between an individual's life course and communal involvement gains in poignancy. If Jews join Jewish communities, especially in the Diaspora, it is because they choose to do so. They can opt not to be enmeshed in Jewish life at all, and if they do choose Jewish social and religious connections, they can select among a range of ways of creating them. Moreover, such choices may vary over time, and they often become salient on the basis of questions raised by life's milestones: what kind of wedding with what category of rabbi should I have, or what sort of Jewish education should I provide for my children? Choice is also becoming evident in Israeli life, even though the government there has made Orthodox rabbis the gatekeepers to events like marriage or burial. As described below, a growing number of young couples in Israel take steps to avoid this compulsion by marrying abroad. To what extent they will or will not relate to Jewish tradition thereafter is up to them. In the contemporary world, Jewish communal life is often an aspect of individual life cycles.

This fact appears troublesome to many people who are concerned about future forms of Jewish life, particularly with reference to Diaspora communities. There is a growing tendency for people to live out their Jewish lives "primarily in the intimate spaces of love and family, friendship and reflection—the spaces in which late twentieth century individuals are in their own eyes 'most themselves.' "[5] This fits into another trend wherein American Jews seem to be maintaining their attachment to Judaism in religious terms, while becoming less involved in communal and organizational forms of Jewish life: community centers, fund-raising efforts, or the political support of Israel.[6] Such a trend is puzzling to those who always have assumed that the religious aspects and communal or ethnic sides of Judaism, which still constitute the most widespread criteria by which Jews define themselves, are inextricably intertwined.[7] But there are clear indications of this development, such as the growing number of cases of intermarriage in which one partner maintains his or her Jewish involvement while the other does not.

Troubling or puzzling as these trends may be, it is worthwhile reflecting upon them, as we have with regard to our other topics, within a broad overview of Jewish religious and cultural expression. A number of themes, some of which we have already explored, such as the emerging sense of the individual, are worth highlighting.[8] Among them is the fact that Jewish life has always been conceived of as taking place in multiple registers. Between the family and its members on one side, and the entire people on the other, there have been intermediate levels such as "tribes" during biblical times and "communities" developing in the Middle Ages. The nature of these intermediate levels always has been dynamic, undergoing historical changes.

Transformations in national and communal structure have, of course, implied shifts in the shape of authority. These have ranged from biblical kings and priests, through "exilarchs" and the Geonim (heads of religious academies) in Iraq under Muslim rule, to later forms of communal organization in the Middle Ages. Alongside these official patterns, there has been the reality of informal communal "authority," what Jews expected of one another and the nature of their daily interaction in the light of those expectations. As contemporary Jewish life becomes more dependent upon voluntary affiliation, an understanding of the nature of the mutual involvement and commitment of "ordinary" Jewish men and women becomes fundamental.

Not only has history brought change to Jewish life, but it has resulted in diversification. It was easy for diversity to exist so long as varied practices and different understandings of the authority of rabbinic law were confined to separate geographical regions. But since early modern times, and certainly within the past century, there has been significant geographical movement within the Jewish world, bringing Jews with distinct traditions into contact with one another. In addition, some Jews migrating to Palestine (later Israel) explicitly forged lifestyles that explicitly rebelled against the past. At the same time, new religious ideologies that arose in Europe in the nineteenth century, and later spread both to the United States and to Israel, added to the potential for conflict between different Jewish ways of life. Paradoxically, the success of Israel in bringing Jews from many different countries and traditions under one roof has created a formally single nation and symbolic unity, on the one hand, but intense competition over the same cultural "turf," on the other.

Life-cycle events, both in Israel and in the Diaspora, are one realm in which such differences and tensions are keenly felt. Which Jews will court and marry one another? Which will be prepared to eat the food at the others' celebrations? And, as noted in chapter 6, who may make decisions concerning the proper procedures of burial? Indeed, there are currently strident debates and opinions even about who is to be considered Jewish, particularly in the case of conversions. Individual Jewish lives cannot long be separated from these communal questions.

THE BASES OF COMMUNAL LIFE

The Bible highlights the collective experience of the Jewish people and also gives us portraits of family life such as those in the Books of Genesis and Ruth. Notions of community do not appear saliently in the biblical text, although there are obvious structures of social organization between that of the family and that of the nation. One level of organization, the "tribe," is central in the way the Book of Judges portrays ancient Israel before the monarchy that began with Saul and his successor, David. The stories in Judges rotate among different tribal areas in the Land of Israel, stressing the problems that arose in each region and how local leaders—judges inspired by God—arose to deal with them. The book as a whole includes the stories of twelve judges, an allusion to the twelve tribes that in principle made up the Israelite polity. At times, there was great tension among certain tribes; towards the end of the book, the tribe of Benjamin is ostracized for a period of time, and marriage into it is forbidden (Judges 19–21). Even when national unity was at an ebb, the literary account of the period seeks to remind us of the ideal structure.[9]

The strain towards national unity, working against forces that split the united monarchy, is evident in the biblical insistence that there be only one center in which God is worshipped (as noted in the chapter on pilgrimage). This ideal is prominent in Deuteronomy and first became a historical reality under King Josiah in the last quarter of the seventh century B.C.E., when he took steps to unify worship in the Temple in Jerusalem. In earlier periods, Israelites had carried out sacrificial worship at local "high places." Some biblical literature severely criticizes this practice, but it may not always have consisted of the worship of "foreign gods." In some instances, it may have represented the normal tendency to give ritual expression to local and regional social life, while also participating in the cultic forms established in Jerusalem.[10]

Tribal structure lost its relevance towards the end of the sixth century B.C.E., when the province of Judah was restored by the Persian empire. One feature of the tribal structure remained, however. Members of the priestly tribe, the kohanim, were still in charge of worship in the Temple. At the same time, there was a parallel development in which features of the Temple cult and priesthood became models for behavior in the life of ordinary Israelites. We have already examined examples of this process in biblical literature with reference to the fringes on men's garments and the phylacteries to be placed on the arm and between the eyes.[11] It was later given explicit expression in the Mishna (Avot 3:3):

> Rabbi Shimon said, "If three have eaten at a table and have spoken there no words of Torah, it is as if they had eaten of sacrifices to the Dead. . . . But if three have eaten at a table and have spoken there words of Torah, it is as if they had eaten at the Table of the All-Present, to which the verse may be applied 'And he said unto me: "this is the table that is before the Lord." ' " (Ezek. 41:22)

The "Table of the All-Present" is the altar in the Temple upon which sacrifices were offered. Many aspects of the ritual life advocated by the Pharisee sages, and by the rabbis who were their successors, stemmed from this metaphorical principle. The destruction of the Temple in 70 C.E. served as a catalyst to further shaping everyday individual and group life on priestly models.

The use of the Temple as a model is prominent with regard to the synagogue. No one knows how synagogue life began. Often it is traced to the phrase *miqdash meʿaṭ* ("miniature Temple") used by Ezekiel, who was a priest (Ezek. 11:16). This is a homiletic, but not necessarily historical, understanding of the phrase, which makes a direct connection between Temple and synagogue.[12] We hear of actual synagogues only in the last centuries before the Common Era. There is evidence of their existence both in the Diaspora and in the Land of Israel. It is difficult to speak of "the synagogue," for both the physical structures and the activities that took place in them varied widely. In Roman Judea, the synagogue seems to have been an all-purpose communal building that was not only, or even necessarily, a place of worship.[13] Women may have had active roles in synagogue leadership.[14] It was used for the public reading and the study of the Torah and the Prophets before it was used for prayer.

Public prayer may have become part of synagogue life only after the Temple was destroyed, although there are diverse scholarly views on this matter.[15] After its destruction, activities that took place in the Temple, such as the daily reading of the Shmaʿ Yisrael and the recitation of the "Psalm of the Day," were transferred to the synagogue.[16] These developments, too, were probably gradual. Knowledge of synagogue life comes from a variety of Jewish, pagan, and Christian writings, as well as from archeology. "All ancient synagogues had a cult based on communal study or prayer, but the diversity possible within this general definition was so great that the term is not always helpful," Shaye Cohen observes.[17]

The sources testify to a wide range of forms in the organization of communal life, and to the discretion exercised by individuals and small groups. When the synagogue developed, the Pharisees, and later the rabbis of the Mishna, were in active competition with other groups claiming to represent the religious life ordained by God for the Children of Israel. By the Middle Ages, however, Judaism had become a separate religious tradition followed by a distinct ethnic minority living in scattered communities under either Christian or Muslim rule. Both of these civilizations accorded Jewish communities internal autonomy, allowing them to run their own affairs.[18] Earlier internal Jewish variety was partially reduced as the standard religious and communal forms characterizing rabbinic Jewry in the Middle Ages came to hold sway. Rabbinic tradition provided the ideological underpinnings for that way of life, with the only salient exception being the Karaite schism.[19]

Until the eleventh century, some degree of centralization existed in the religious life of Jews despite their wide dispersion. Externally, the framework of this centralization was based upon the appointment of a Jewish exilarch by the caliph of the far-flung Arab empire. This "Head of the Exile" represented all the Jewish communities under the caliph's rule.[20] Internally, central authority among Jews was constituted by the rabbinic academies (yeshivot) in Iraq, still referred to by them as "Babylonia," that provided guidance in religious matters both in that region and in distant lands.[21] At the same time, active local communal life developed under this ideological umbrella, as was the case in Kairouan in North Africa.[22]

When the yeshivot in Baghdad waned in importance, Jewish centers developed in North Africa (Egypt and Tunisia), in Spain (then under Muslim rule), and elsewhere in western Europe, with the Italian peninsula being a point of partial contact among these disparate regions.[23] Communities in these areas found ways of establishing their authority on rabbinic principles. Rabbinic law embraced many aspects of daily life, and medieval communities assumed extensive powers.[24] Not only did they tax individuals under their jurisdiction and were they able to summon them to court, but they sometimes had the power of deciding who was able to reside in a given town. In some matters, they controlled relations with non-Jews. The houses in which Jews lived were often owned by Gentiles but laws developed that protected the stability of residence of Jewish lessees in these dwellings.

Jews who flagrantly disobeyed rabbinic ordinances, or violated ritual rules, were subject to various degrees of ostracism or even excommunication. These included not circumcising the newborn son of the banned individual so long as the ban was in effect. In general, a person upon whom a ban was placed underwent "social death." Many of the rules he was forced to observe, such as staying home with his family, were parallel to the rules imposed upon mourners. These sanctions were all-powerful, because in the medieval world there was no "social life" for the individual outside of an established religious community.

Along with the powerful control they exercised, medieval communities also provided means for individuals to mobilize public support to redress wrongs they felt they had suffered. One salient mechanism of this nature was anchored in synagogue life. An individual wishing to press a claim who did not succeed in bringing his adversary before the communal authorities could interrupt prayers in the synagogue until such time as his grievance was addressed or until he was told that the community leaders would relate to his situation seriously. One communal ordinance stipulated that an individual had to state his complaint publicly on three occasions at the end of the services; only then did he have the right to interrupt the prayers until he was granted a hearing. Such ordinances were common in medieval Ashkenaz, and, though less formalized, the practice of stopping prayers to appeal to the community as a "judge" took place in communities in the Islamic orbit too.[25]

As stated, communities were also the stage upon which the drama of personal lives and familial cycles unfolded. Usually, this was based upon a clear division of gender roles. Earlier, in connection with differential access to Torah, it was suggested that the adoption of the priestly model as an inspiration to rabbinic authority might have been a factor in clearly delimiting the religious roles of men and women.[26] The model of the Temple and the priesthood continued to influence worship in the Middle Ages.[27] How such intertwined logic is expressed in practice may be seen in customs that are observed to this day. In many North African synagogues, when the kohanim face the congregation and bless the lay members with the words of the priestly blessing, it is common for sons to gather around their fathers (whatever their ages), while the latter spread a prayer shawl over their offspring as if constituting a link in the transmission of the blessing.[28] Women do not take part in this ceremony either as priests or as parents. Normally, they also are not among the direct recipients of the blessing. The expression of intergenerational transmission via males is made clear in the description of this practice in Tripoli. A grandfather places his prayer shawl over the heads of his sons, who simultaneously place their own shawls over the heads of their children.[29]

The same account, however, notes that when the priestly blessing was recited in this manner at the culmination of the Day of Atonement, women would look on from the upper gallery and pour forth their own blessings on their children and grandchildren. In nearby Tunisia, on that occasion, all members of the family—including women—gathered under the prayer shawl of the father when the priestly blessing was recited.[30] In the Italian synagogue in Jerusalem, I have also seen fathers extend their prayer shawls over daughters during the priestly blessing on Sabbath morning, while standing outside the main prayer hall. If it is permissible to extrapolate from these recent observations to the situation of medieval communities, religious life then was not as uniform as is sometimes assumed.

Individual religious expression and speculation always existed along with the standard communal forms. One mode of personal expression was reading from the Book of Psalms in times of distress and crisis. Whether or not the individual understood the poetic Hebrew of these ancient compositions, his private wishes were attached to their ritualized recitation. Women lighting candles on the eve of the Sabbath, or attending the synagogue when the Torah scroll was taken from the ark, uttered their prayers for themselves and the families under their care. In the former instance, we know from the early modern period that some women dared liken their position to that of the biblical high priest.[31] Further basing ourselves on recent ethnography, it seems that in these spheres, women might be viewed as the "ritual experts."[32]

There was a constant interplay between the standardized demands of communal life and the search of individuals for religious expression, a search in which women could join. A highly regulated perception of relations between the genders is found in Rabbi Jacob ben Asher's classic halakhic codification of laws concerning marriage and related subjects, written in Spain early in the fourteenth century. The introduction to that work compares the fashioning of humans in Genesis, in which woman is taken from man's rib, to the story of the creation of animals, in which male and female appear simultaneously. In the animal world, Ben Asher notes, the female does not accept the rule of the male, while the idea among humans is that a man should rule over a women, just as he controls the limbs of his body.[33] There was other literature in the Middle Ages, however, which offered different views of women, both socially and religiously.

MYSTICISM, THE GENDERS, AND THE INDIVIDUAL

We have already seen in the contexts of pilgrimage and the rituals surrounding death that mystical tradition (kabbala) provided textual bases for an individual link to the divine.[34] The Zohar was written in Spain in the last quarter of the thirteenth century, around the same time as Jacob ben Asher's halakhic codification, although it is presented as the inspired product of the second-century mishnaic sage Rabbi Shimon Bar Yohai.[35] When it was written, and for several centuries thereafter, the Zohar and other mystical writings were kept within the limited domain of adepts who were also steeped in the established branches of religious knowledge.[36] Their mystical insights and practices were confined to the realm of *sod*, or "secrecy," an attitude expressed in the dictum that one should not begin to study kabbala until the age of forty.

Among the reasons for restricting access to the kabbala was probably the motive of limiting it to those who had proven their commitment and responsibility to the community. Even as communal norms were highly effective, mystical literature provided the opportunity to explore realms of human existence beyond those ordinarily expressed in public life. Kabbala consisted of religious territory within which the complexities of the human psyche were plumbed and a heightened sense of "the individual" could be cultivated.

An example of mystical exploration challenging common conventions appears in the realm of relations between the genders. At one level, the Zohar presents speculation concerning feminine aspects of the divinity.[37] At another, it delves into the apparently privileged position of men in relation to women. It does so by elaborating earlier midrashic material discussing the relationship between the sun and the moon, a topic discussed earlier with reference to the opening section of the Bible.[38]

The biblical stories of Genesis hint at imagery in which man is compared to the sun and woman to the moon. This is made explicit in one talmudic story that tells how the two luminaries were at first equal in size, but the moon was then "diminished."[39] The Zohar builds upon this talmudic and midrashic material and maintains that the inherent equality of the moon is preserved at some "higher" level, even though in daily reality she may appear subordinate to the sun:

> The great light rules by day; the small light rules at night. From this we learn the secret that the masculine dominates during the day to fill the house with everything that is needed, meats and grains. When night falls, the feminine takes everything, and only the feminine dominates in the home, since this is her time to rule as it is written: "She rises while it is still night, and supplies provisions for her household" (Prov. 31:15), she and not he. The masculine rules by day, the feminine by night.[40]

The Zohar also cites the Sabbath as the period when the masculine and feminine are conjoined and their light is equal, while during the six days of the work week, the apparent ascendancy of the sun over the moon is maintained. Clearly, social and personal matters relating to the genders are reflected in these texts, in addition to religious ones.

Mystical speculations like these, which contain hidden glimpses of a more perfect cosmos and human nature, were restricted to circles of mystics for many generations. In the sixteenth century, however, we find ideas from the Zohar being formulated in ways that impinged upon the behavior of the individual male and his family, as well as on the community. A central figure in this transformation was R. Isaac Luria who was active among the mystics living in the city of Safed in Ottoman Palestine.

We have already encountered the mystics of sixteenth-century Safed in connection with the image of the Sabbath bride in the Lekha Dodi hymn, which became part of the standard liturgy of the Friday night service that welcomes the Sabbath.[41] That hymn passionately portrays the restoration of Jerusalem as a symbol of all of Israel. Other liturgic innovations from this period also became widespread within the Jewish world.[42] Some of them also related to the Sabbath and particularly the Friday night meal in the home.

Friday night ritual has long involved a division of religious labor linking synagogue and home. Since the time of the Mishna, lighting a Sabbath candle has been presented as the duty of women (even though rabbinic law requires a man to light candles if no woman is in a household). Most of the preparation of Sabbath food was done by women (but the Talmud does praise men for carrying out special tasks in expectation of the Sabbath),[43] and men, returning home after Friday evening prayers would expect a set table to await them so that they could begin the ritually structured meal. All this existed well before the sixteenth century, but the Safed kabbalists further embellished the Friday night repast. They introduced the recitation of Proverbs 31:10–31, from which the verse about women cited in the Zohar (above) is taken. That recitation, beginning with the words "A woman of valor," displays an ideal of women's virtuosity. While originally its ritual reading was not formally connected to the woman in each household, it is now often declaimed by the husband (and in some contemporary houses by children) while the whole family is around the table.[44] This takes place just before the recitation of the *kiddush* that sanctifies the Sabbath at the beginning of the meal. The "woman of valor" custom both accords recognition to the contribution of women, which perhaps was publicly overlooked before the practice was institutionalized, and at the same time provides a picture of a firm division of labor and of social roles within the family.

Why did these new customs, linked to esoteric kabbalistic texts, begin to take root in wider circles at that time and place, and what explains their movement from Safed to communities around the Mediterranean and into Europe? It is possible to attempt an answer by looking at broad changes taking place in the sixteenth and seventeenth centuries that affected Jewish life in many spheres: community, gender roles, opportunities for personal choice, and the sense of individuality.

SEEDS AND SOCIAL SITES OF THE MODERN JEWISH WORLD

The city of Safed, tucked away in the mountains of the Upper Galilee, seems (even now) to be an ideal retreat for study and contemplation, but its place in Jewish history must be understood in terms of the general expanse of trade of that period and the migrations of Jewish groups. At the end of the fifteenth century, tens of thousands of Jews had to leave the Iberian Peninsula. They went to various parts of the Ottoman Empire, North Africa, Italy and other parts of western Europe, and the New World. The rabbis settling in Safed were mostly from this background and were well connected with cultural and historical currents elsewhere in the Diaspora.[45] There developed an active Jewish connection between Safed and Venice, which was still the hub of a far-reaching trading empire. In Venice, as in other Italian cities, one could find Jews of German (Ashkenazi) background, Sephardim, Marranos who had returned to Judaism (see below), and Jews from the Levant, as well as Italian Jews with ancient roots in the country. All of them had been exposed to the influence of the Renaissance and more recently to the Catholic Counter-Reformation. Italy was the scene of diverse and interacting cultural and religious currents, and there is evidence there since the thirteenth century of a "general shift of interest toward the individual, the single human personality, in preference to the social group."[46] The growing prominence of kabbala and kabbala-based practices must be viewed against this background.

A special situation was created by the Marranos of Spain and Portugal, who lived secret Jewish lives in the Iberian Peninsula and later returned openly to Judaism when taking up residence in other areas of Europe or in Muslim lands. These Marrano families had led double lives as Catholics and Jews for many years, and sometimes for generations. They were deeply familiar with Christian culture and assumed a full Jewish life on their own volition. Some may have felt that they had options vis-à-vis rabbinic authority not available to ordinary members of the community.[47] Jewish life was still quite separate from that of the non-Jews, and traditional forms of authority seemed to function, but in subtle ways, some people were beginning to become "Jews by choice."[48]

Robert Bonfil has discussed some of the paradoxes of Italian Jewish life in the sixteenth century.[49] It was in that period that a walled-off area was built in Venice separating the Jews from the rest of the population. The area was called the ghetto (from an Italian word meaning foundry), and this was the historical origin of the word, which has since spread to many other urban contexts. The building of ghettos in Italy now seems paradoxical because it occurred at a time when there was growing contact between the Jewish and Christian worlds. Bonfil sees the ghetto as a compromise between expelling the Jews, as had occurred often in Europe in preceding centuries, and accepting them more fully as members of local society. He diagnoses the whole period as one of shifting cultural ideas. Kabbala provided one mechanism by which notions that had been foreign to Jewish life were absorbed into Jewish culture and "domesticated."

The process of more contact with the non-Jewish world, more choice, and then reactions to these developments was an ongoing dynamic. Marranos who returned to Judaism were not only a source of potential innovation, but could also be zealous in upholding their refound faith and way of life. They were among the members of the Sephardi community of Amsterdam who excommunicated Benedict (Baruch) Spinoza in the seventeenth century. Spinoza later became the prototype of the freethinking individual unshackled by religious rules and dogmas. Those who opposed him show that choice could lead to a reaction of strictness, as well as in the direction of greater "openness" for individuals.

An interesting example of the relationship between choice and strictness also can be found in sixteenth-century Safed, where there were not only masters of mysticism, such as Isaac Luria, but leading rabbinic authorities, including R. Yosef Caro, author of the *Shulhan Arukh*, which in later generations became the standard code of Jewish orthodoxy.[50] Safed was a city of "legists and mystics," to use the title of Solomon Schechter's essay on the topic.[51] In addition to the religious sensibilities that these virtuosos brought from the Diaspora, living in the Land of Israel added extra dimensions to their observance. It is instructive to see how rabbinic authority reacted to this new situation.[52]

There is a class of religious commandments dealing with agricultural produce known as the "mitzvot [commandments] dependent on The Land." These commandments are in force only within the Land of Israel: an example is the requirement to separate a tithe offering from produce when it is harvested and designate it for the Levites. This must be done before a person is allowed to consume what has grown on his land (Deut. 14:22–29). There are, however, exemptions to the rule: if produce grows on land owned by a Gentile, even in the Land of Israel, the tithing requirement does not hold. At the same time, there is a minority opinion that produce grown on Gentile-owned land within the Land of Israel must be tithed as well. A person of stringent halakhic standards who is offered food from produce grown on non-Jewish land might refuse to eat it in order to conform with the stricter position. Some individuals in Safed began to adopt this ritual position.

One might think that the concentration of devout scholars in Safed at the time would encourage the acceptance of strict religious norms, but in fact an opposite reaction took place. No less a figure than Yosef Caro strongly opposed the new stricture with regard to tithes and threatened to issue a ban against whoever adhered to it. He argued that introducing new rules of this sort brought divisiveness into the community and also claimed that following the new norm challenged the authority of "our ancestors," who had seen no need to be so stringent.[53] The inclusiveness of community, expressed in rules about what was and was not permissible to eat, was valued over the sincere religious desires of pious individuals.

It is interesting to consider another instance of an attitude of inclusiveness, this time taken from the periphery of the Jewish world, in India. Jews were found in India from the Middle Ages. They are mentioned briefly in a letter by Maimonides, which says that they "know nothing of the Torah and keep no laws except that they rest on the Sabbath and circumcise at eight days."[54] We do not know who the Jews to whom Maimonides referred were. In recent times, indigenous Jewish communities existed in two distinct areas of India: along the Konkan coast near the city of Bombay and in the town of Cochin on the Malabar coast in the south (see figure 22). Both were heavily influenced by their local milieus, but the Jews of Malabar were more exposed to Jews in Europe and the Middle East than were those further north. Portuguese expansion to southern India brought Cochin Jews into contact with Sephardim in the sixteenth century, and this influence was reinforced after the Dutch took control of the area in the 1660s. Jews in the Konkan area came to the attention of Europeans upon their "discovery" by a Danish missionary in 1738.

The missionary's account depicts these Jews as knowing neither the Bible nor Hebrew. They did, however, observe some form of Rosh Hashanah, Yom Kippur, and other holidays, and refrained from work on the Sabbath. Hindus referred to them as the "Saturday oilmen" because they did not do the work associated with their caste-like status—oil pressing—on Saturdays. They had a minimal liturgy, knowing how to say the Shma' Yisrael, which they used as a prayer in different situations such as circumcisions, weddings, and at the end of mourning. Outsiders recognized them as Jews, and British officialdom in India assigned them the name Bene Israel.

During the eighteenth century, the Judaic content of Bene Israel life was reinforced through contact with outsiders. Among them were Cochin Jews who took the role of educators, reflecting the input of Jewish influence in their own lives. Late in the century, with the expanding trade of the British Empire, Jews from the Middle East began to settle in the area, and they too had an impact on the Bene Israel. Another unexpected source of Judaic influence came from missionaries who wanted to make better Jews out of the Bene Israel, hoping they would eventually convert to Christianity. As the Bene Israel moved from rural communities to Bombay, and also learned English, they began to acquire Jewish prayer books and Bibles translated into that language.

The above developments show the Bene Israel becoming "better Jews" by virtue of greater knowledge, but there were other sides to the story of

Figure 22.   Interior of a synagogue in Nevatim, Israel, replicating one in Cochin, India. The proximity of the women's gallery *(above)* to the dais from which the Torah is read on the level below was common in the synagogues in that region. Photo Harvey E. Goldberg.

their reconnection to their ancient roots. According to local legends that emerged, the group's return to Judaism was linked to an individual named David Rahabi, who "discovered" the Bene Israel and decided to reeducate them. According to an account by a member of the community:

> Although David Rahabi was convinced that the Bene Israel were the real descendants of the Hebrews, he still wanted to test them further. He therefore, it is said, gave their women [ritually] clean and unclean fish to be cooked together; but they promptly singled out the clean fish from the unclean ones, saying that they never used fish that had neither fins nor scales.[55] (cf. Lev. 11:12; Deut. 14:9–10)

We do not know the historical basis, if any, of this legend; the name Rahabi may reflect a Cochin Jew who was active among the Bene Israel.[56] The message the story conveys is that an important component of Jewish continuity was the observance of food rules on the part of women. Dietary observance was a basis for including the Bene Israel among the Jewish people, expanding the overall collectivity, not creating divisions within it.

Returning to the more densely inhabited realms of Jewish life, from the sixteenth century on, we witness new activities for and perceptions of women, and not only as ritual experts regarding food. Women began to appear with greater visibility in public. This demanded attempts to redefine their roles. The new Friday night table rituals may have been part of this process. Evidence of changing relations between women and men may also be seen in other spheres, including that of social dancing.

Zvi Friedhaber has surveyed forms of dance among Mediterranean Jewish communities in the period after the expulsion from Spain in 1492. Documentation on the subject is scattered, but much of the literature consists of rabbis writing about local customs. Rabbis often react to practices of which they disapprove, either forbidding them or defining which aspects of a custom are acceptable and which are not. We know that these guidelines were not always followed, because some rules and ordinances were restated over the years.[57]

It seems that the custom of mixed dancing emerged as part of court life in Spain, with which some members of the Jewish elite were familiar. Social dancing continued in the sixteenth century among Sephardim who migrated to northern Italy. There, learning to dance became a set part of education, and we even hear of Jewish dance teachers. One of the common settings in which dancing took place was at weddings. The approved form was for men to be separate from women. There is clear evidence, however, that men and women danced together in Italy, and documentation of this is similarly available from Ashkenazi communities in Alsace and Germany.

Most rabbinic authorities objected to men and women dancing together, although there is one opinion encouraging the public singing of young women at wedding celebrations in order "to endear young men [to them], so that they then will then court them."[58] Restrictive rules said that men and women had to wear gloves if they danced together, or insisted that a man could only dance with his wife or another member of his family (e.g., a daughter). Practices and rabbinic comments in Greece and other Balkan countries to which Sephardi Jews migrated were generally similar to those in Italy.[59] In the Sephardi communities of the Ottoman Empire, in contrast, we find no evidence of mixed dancing. Most likely, the norms of Muslim culture kept Jews from following this custom. It was known in Ottoman lands, however, for Muslim musicians to be employed in Jewish weddings, or for Jewish entertainers to appear in the courts of Muslim rulers. This sometimes included Jewish woman dancers, along with entertainers from Christian minorities.

The rabbis' concern over contact between the sexes in social dancing was not an isolated phenomenon. At the same period of time, there appeared a new form of culturally patterned psychological stress and therapeutic practice, discussed in chapter 6: possession by a dibbuk and corresponding exorcism. Both the rabbinic rules restricting mixed dancing and the exorcism of evil spirits may have stemmed from historical developments that created the possibility of greater public contact between men and women.[60] In sixteenth-century Cairo, for example, rabbis criticized both the invitation of Muslim women musician-dancers to Jewish weddings because they attracted young Jewish men, and the behavior of male Jewish musicians at such weddings who acted improperly towards the girls who were present.[61] In the next century (1666), in the same city, the son of the kabbalist Hayyim Vital exorcised an evil spirit from the body of a young married woman. Judging from her name, she was a member of the small Ashkenazi community in the city.[62] The spirit first identified himself as a Gentile who had possessed the woman because he lusted after her.[63] Both dancing and the dibbuk reflect new social realities in the contact between women and men, and concomitant individual awareness arising from this.

Another indication of the growing consciousness of personal lives appeared in less dramatic forms as well: that of autobiographical writing. A forerunner to this style was found in the tradition of composing ethical wills. In these works, authors sought to extract lessons from their life experiences and pass them on to members of their families.[64] They contained some degree of reflection upon the self in the effort to communicate life messages to children and descendants. One beneficiary of such a will in sixteenth-century Italy was Abraham Yagel (1553–ca. 1623), whose writings about his own misfortunes show a growing awareness of self.[65] Another work approaching the modern conception of autobiography was by Leone de Modena (1571–1648) from the Venice ghetto, the first Jewish author of a book on Judaism written for European Christians.[66] In his *The Life of Judah*, he reflects on his life, not only his religion.[67]

Following upon Modena's period we find a Yiddish-speaking woman, Glueckl of Hameln (1646–1724), writing her memoirs. These were intended for the members of her family, not for wider publication, but they also tell a story of broader social trends. Natalie Davis points to Glueckl's active decision-making and management in economic matters along with her husband, and her sense of ultimate reliance on God, even more than on members of her family.[68] Both Glueckl and Modena express parallels between their personal dramas and the tribulations that characterize the story of the Jewish people. Neither of them engaged in highly intricate introspection, but both still represent a new valuation of individual experience that had not received expression in medieval Jewish culture.

The trends beginning in the sixteenth century continued to develop. Contact between Jews and Gentiles became more common. Poorer Jews had little choice but to be involved with non-Jews in order to make a living, while wealthier ones, moving to positions of leadership, often found themselves in roles mediating between the Gentile and the Jewish worlds. In central Europe, "court Jews" provided financial services to local rulers and sometimes were granted privileges in Christian society that were not given to other Jews. They therefore were less subject to rabbinic supervision than typical members of the "Jewish street."[69] In Morocco, well-to-do merchants with connections to powerful Muslims enjoyed leverage and leeway not available to the rank-and-file Jew, and this situation could impinge upon developments within the Jewish community.[70] The "traditional" Jewish community at this period was far more varied and dynamic than we usually imagine it to be.

During these centuries, Jews faced many situations somewhat parallel to what we experience today. There was widespread migration, and Jews from various lands came in contact with one another. Questions of the boundaries of the Jewish collectivity arose. Not only were Jews in India reconnected to larger Jewish centers, but it was in the sixteenth century that R. Ben Zimra in Egypt issued a decision that Jews in Ethiopia were descended from the tribe of Dan, an opinion that formed the basis for Ethiopian Jewry immigrating to Israel in recent decades.[71] During this period, communities both dissolved and were (re)created. Authority was challenged, reasserted, and reformulated. The roles of men and women were modified, and a sense of individuality both grew in potency and was simultaneously harnessed by communal forces. Towards the end of the eighteenth century, the new dimensions of enlightenment and emancipation were added to this complex picture.

EMANCIPATION AND ITS IMPLICATIONS

The expressions of greater choice for the individual Jew that began to appear in the early modern period were bolstered by Enlightenment thought in Europe, which carried implications that Jews could participate in society on the same basis as all other persons. Within Judaism, there developed the Haskala (Enlightenment) movement, which encouraged the cultural, linguistic, and social integration of Jews into the societies of which they were a part. The emblematic representative of Haskala was Moses Mendelssohn (1729–1786). It is symptomatic of the new forms of Jewish life he envisioned that he advocated abolishing rabbinic excommunication.[72] Both the general Enlightenment and the Jewish Haskala reflected the diminished scope of religion as the central factor providing collective meaning and societal legitimacy. They were paralleled by the emergence of nation-states as frameworks of encompassing identification and loyalty, whatever an individual's religious outlook might be. These trends first received political expression in 1791 when France emancipated the Jews, making them full citizens of the state.[73]

Emancipation in France initially applied to the well-to-do Sephardi communities in Bordeaux and the southwest and only later was granted to the rural Ashkenazi Yiddish-speakers of Alsace. This illustrates the hesitancy and complex attitudes accompanying emancipation as it extended eastward in Europe, with uneven vigor, throughout the nineteenth and twentieth centuries. There was no one-time emancipation for Jews in the Middle East. In the Ottoman Empire, policies of reform sought to turn all subjects, including Christians and Jews, into loyal and identified members of society, but these met with only partial success. Both in Europe and the Middle East, the character and policies of emerging states created frameworks for new forms of Jewish communal life and new sets of choices for individual Jews.[74]

Under these conditions, religion became less central in the lives of many Jews, and observance slackened. Patterns of secular life emerged gradually and selectively. Certain aspects of tradition were abandoned, others were maintained, and yet others were reinvigorated. New religious ideologies and social identities emerged, along with various orientations to Judaism's religious and cultural heritage, which often were not expressed as consistent principles.[75] Traditionalist leaders felt threatened by new ideas and by the possibility of Jews freeing themselves from communal scrutiny. Nevertheless, the inability of rabbis to exercise control and apply sanctions within communal frameworks did not bring about a wholesale abandonment of Jewish culture and religion.

In the sections that follow, I explore a number of ways in which Jews followed, revised, abandoned, or strengthened traditions from the past. The examples are not, of course, exhaustive, but they serve to highlight the variety of reactions that led to the panorama of Jewish life that we witness today. The illustrations come from various parts of the world and show distinctive investments in and commitments to the individual/familial, communal, and national levels of Jewish existence. These differing emphases receive expression in various spheres, including life-cycle events. Developments in all these realms reflect the new structure of choices available to Jews as individuals and in groups during the past two hundred years.

FAMILY, COMMUNITY, AND FOOD

Judaism is not only a matter of ideology and doctrine. It consists of many patterns of life acted out in the context of family and community.[76] These did not wither away in the nineteenth and twentieth centuries in the wake of the new intellectual developments or as a result of new political and legal statuses accorded to Jews. It may even be that, in some ways, the attenuation of external structures stimulated the emergence of communal life in the synagogue, and family life at home, as renewed loci of loyalty and continuity.

In several studies of North African Jews in France, Joëlle Bahloul has shown how the family became a bastion of ethnic and religious identity.[77] As Jews became integrated into spheres of French life such as the world of work, customs and rules concerning food were invested with additional meanings linked to Jewish identity. Preparing Sabbath meals in a family setting, even more than before, was viewed as an act contributing to Jewish continuity. Even in cases of intermarriage with Christians, the participation of non-Jewish spouses in family celebrations such as bar mitzvahs and weddings, and their ingestion of North African Jewish delicacies, was perceived as incorporating them into a Jewish way of life. Preserving kitchen and table habits from North Africa within the confines of the home did not impede social mobility or economic success, so the realm of food came to carry an extra burden of cultural associations hitherto shared with other life domains. This development added social and religious importance to the domestic activities of women, although their contribution was often not explicitly recognized.[78]

The processes depicted by Bahloul had parallels among Jewish immigrants from eastern Europe to the United States at the turn of the twentieth century. In reflecting upon his own experience in Poland in the first part of the twentieth century, the linguist and cultural historian Max Weinreich expresses the earlier situation in terms of the family taking a subordinate role in relation to religion. He surmises that "the Jews themselves did not recognize this predominant place of the family as the real nucleus of the community. Everything Jewish being rationalized in terms of religion, the family seemed to be only the carrier of some phases of religious life."[79] In America, "the Jewish family" took on some of the meanings and roles depicted by Bahloul for North African Jews in France, but this was often the subject of criticism, particularly on the part of subsequent generations. Philip Roth's portrayal of Alexander Portnoy's romance with liver is an example in a humorous vein.[80] From my teenage years in New York City in the 1950s, I remember rabbis criticizing "culinary Jews" whose "only" connection to Judaism was through food and castigating "coronary Jews" who claimed that they were good Jews "in their hearts." These religious spokesmen wanted wider involvement in the "serious" aspects of Jewish life, such as study and ritual observance. They usually did not appreciate how deeply domestic culture was linked to communal aspects of Judaism. One way of gaining such appreciation is by further considering the Bene Israel of India.

Among the Bene Israel, there was a custom called Eliahu ha-Nabi, "Elijah the Prophet."[81] Its centrality is obvious to all who are familiar with the Bene Israel in Israel, where most of them now live. It seems to have replaced the reciting of Shma' Yisrael as an omnibus ritual and is used on life-cycle occasions such as circumcisions, moving into a new home, and weddings.[82] In the last instance, it is sometimes juxtaposed with other prenuptial festivities, like the henna ceremonies of Middle Eastern Jews. Eliahu ha-Nabi also is performed in fulfillment of a vow, usually made by a woman as part of a personal prayer. In Israel, new situations have been added to the list of occasions that call forth Elijah the Prophet, such as a child's induction into or discharge from the army.

The structure of the ceremony consists of two phases. The first is the preparation and presentation of food: a plate with a mixture of rice flour and sugar, to which nuts, raisins, and coconut may be added, and a tray with five whole fruits—pears, apples, oranges, dates, and bananas. Both are prepared with great care and placed on a table in a room where the second side of the ceremony takes place. The second, textual, phase consists of reciting blessings over the fruits, and reading liturgical selections that mention Elijah the Prophet. Women organize the preparation of food, while a man leads the reading. It is proper that this be done by a man from outside the celebrant family.

We do not know how Eliahu ha-Nabi developed, but it is clear that the textual side of the ceremony is an overlay on the ritual presentation of special foods within the family context.[83] Some members of the community who have memories from India are aware of this. In fact, the celebration is often called *malida*, which is the word for the dish of rice flour and sugar. Bene Israel women explain that such a dish figures in the domestic ceremonies of Muslims and Hindus, as well as of Jews.[84] The number five has significance in Hindu culture, and the fruit tray hints at a ritual offering. With regard to the textual side of the rite, one man claimed that when Cochin Jews encountered the Bene Israel, they saw that the latter only knew about Eliahu ha-Nabi within Jewish tradition and therefore encouraged them to enrich their ritual life based on the little they knew. H. S. Kehimkar tells of a Cochini who criticized the excessive celebration of Elijah on the fifteenth of the month of Shvat, saying that it seemed as if he were worshipped by the Bene Israel.[85] Harnessing Eliahu ha-Nabi to accepted textual frameworks was one way of counteracting this tendency.

Eliahu ha-Nabi ceremonies in Israel today feature both culinary and textual aspects. The latter has been reinforced by the rabbinate, which has made available further explanations on the importance of Elijah, thereby according legitimacy to the total ritual. This development notwithstanding, the domestic side of the celebration is still the main bearer of its meaning within the community. It is initiated by women, they commit the major energies in its preparation, and they also remember past celebrations in detail, much more so than men. The way the ritual has been maintained and its partial reshaping combine to preserve the identity of the Bene Israel and secure them a place under the larger umbrella of Jewish life in Israel.

ORTHODOXY AND SEPARATION

A link between food and group identity is very ancient in Judaism. Ever since rules sorting animals into those that could be eaten and those that were forbidden were set forth in the Bible, laws concerning food have served to distinguish Israelites, and later Jews, from other peoples and religions with whom they were in contact.[86] At times, they mark differences among Jews as well. In chapter 5, I mentioned the difference between haverim, who were strict about only eating food from which tithes had been separated, and àm ha-àres, whom the former regarded as negligent in this regard. The rabbis decided, nevertheless, that in the pilgrimage situation of visits to Jerusalem, this distinction be overlooked.[87] Rules concerning food, or the realm of *kashrut*, are a marker of Jewish identity today and also serve to separate one "kind" of Jew from another. Understanding this requires a glimpse of the roots and dynamics of Orthodoxy.

Emancipation established the relation of an individual to the state as separate from the realm of religious dictates. This did not happen all at once. In many European countries, Jewish communal life continued to take place in frameworks that were formally recognized and backed by the state, even after Jews were emancipated. With time, however, the link between state administration and Jewish religious life was loosened or eliminated. We usually associate the weakening of compulsory membership in the Jewish community with a decline in religious observance. This indeed was the general tendency, but the opposite trend—greater observance—took place as well. This socioreligious phenomenon among Jews is known as

"Orthodoxy," and its development also stems from the situation of emancipation.

There are various blends of Orthodox Jewry, but what they have in common is the claim that they keep Judaism as it was observed over the generations. Other religious movements, in their view, such as Conservative or Reform Judaism, represent unacceptable innovations vis-à-vis the traditions of the past. What they do not acknowledge is that Orthodoxy also developed in nineteenth-century Europe. One aspect of Orthodoxy was the self-conscious attempt to articulate a systematic ideology countering religious reform and its appeal to Jews who became more involved in Gentile society. In preemancipation settings, such explicit ideologies were not necessary. Even with the increasing variation in the behavior of Jews through contact with Gentile society in the early modern period, there were no challenges to the conceptual underpinnings of the traditional way of life until the late eighteenth century.

A second new aspect of Orthodoxy emerged at the organizational level. In many parts of Europe, Jews modified their ritual behavior in line with evolving circumstances. Insofar as Jewish life took place in state-sponsored frameworks, new ritual modes adopted by the majority of Jews also implicated those wishing to adhere to older religious norms. Reinforced by Orthodox ideology, traditionalists demanded that they be released from the obligation to follow the majority trend and be accorded the right to organize religiously based on their own beliefs and practice. Emancipation, and the recognition of the rights of individuals, made this a reasonable expectation. Such demands were acceded to by the governments in Hungary in the 1860s and Prussia in the 1870s. In these countries, there came to exist two recognized Jewish organizations, one "liberal" and the other "Orthodox." The age-old assumption of the intertwined unity of Judaism and the Jewish people was undermined by principled differences among Jews over matters of religion. Emancipation thus brought about a situation quite different from the one faced by Rabbi Caro in Safed 300 years earlier.

Menahem Friedman, citing the sociologist Peter Berger, calls the new setting a "market situation" with regard to religion. The freedom granted by democratic states meant that Jews could practice any version of Judaism they pleased, no version at all, or even convert to another religion. While this freed them "from" religious compulsion, it also provided the opportunity for those committed to a specific religious way of life to set up their own synagogues, schools, and communal institutions. Orthodoxy, including the haredi way of life often described as "ultra-Orthodoxy," thus has the ability to operate successfully in contemporary society. Not only can

these ways of life function in the modern context, but they flourish because they only have to attend to the needs and desires of like-minded individuals. They need not be concerned that the style of religious life that
they hold dear is of minimal consequence to many other Jews. In the postemancipation West, the overall Jewish community, in the traditional sense,
no longer exists. Were he alive today, Yosef Caro would not be able to "keep
in line" the super strict and prevent Jews from splintering into different
groups. Whether he wished to or not, he would have to identify with one
"party" or other. It would be interesting to know which one he would
choose!

This process began in the nineteenth century and is still going on today.
The contemporary trend can be illustrated in the sphere of food with reference to the concept of *glatt kosher,* or *glatt kashrut,* which has become
salient only in the past generation or so. On the East Coast of the United
States in the first half of the twentieth century, people used to say, "If his
name is Mendel, You can eat from his *fendel* [pot]," situating the observance of kashrut within the framework of community membership recognized by everyday signs widely familiar among Jews. By contrast, insistence upon the norms of glatt kashrut depends upon the judgment of a
religious elite who see themselves as very separate from the majority of
the Jewish people.

Glatt is a Yiddish word meaning smooth. It refers to the inspection of the
lung of a slaughtered animal to see whether or not it shows signs of a disease that would render the animal not kosher (see figure 23). Beyond its
substantive meaning, the term *glatt kosher* has come to signal standards of
kashrut stricter than those followed by "ordinary" Jews. Individual men
and women might take it upon themselves not to eat the meat of an animal
regarding which a question has been raised. Thus, if a rabbi were to check
the lung of an animal and not find it smooth, but still—upon further inspection—reach the decision that the animal was kosher, those individuals
would still refrain from eating its meat. At first, in the Ashkenazi world,
this appeared as an act of personal piety and zeal in devotion to ritual law.
With time, however, and in the context of competition among versions of
Judaism, the glatt kosher concept became an emblem setting one group of
Jews off from another. With reference to the haredi community, it went
along with special dress and residential concentration to mark them off
from Jews whom they saw as giving in to the modern world.

In addition to a field of open competition among religious ways, Friedman sees the Holocaust as contributing to the continued emergence of new
strictures in the haredi way of life.[88] In wiping out communities and fami-

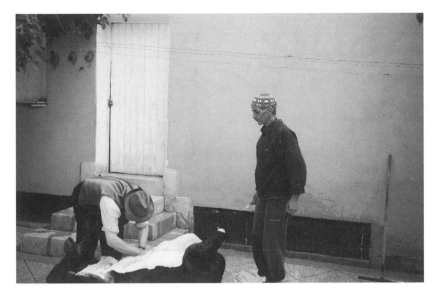

Figure 23. Checking the lung of a slaughtered cow in the courtyard of a Jewish home in Marrakesh to see if it is kosher. A Muslim assistant stands by. Photo Harvey E. Goldberg.

lies, the Holocaust also severed the threads of tradition that linked children to parents or bound up neighbors in a mutually taken-for-granted way of life. When, after World War II, religious communities were reconstituted by haredi Jews in Israel or the Diaspora, living models, such as a grandparent or a pious but practical neighbor, were no longer on hand for imitation. In place of that, written texts were scrutinized as to what constituted correct behavior, providing the opportunity of constantly selecting the most severe option found within them. Thus modern haredi Jews follow rules that would have been foreign to the traditional behavior of their recent forebears, including many rules as to what it is permissible or forbidden to eat.[89]

In recent decades, some of the strictures of ultra-Orthodoxy in ritual matters have been adopted by much of the Orthodox world generally.[90] While Orthodox Jews plumbed rabbinic writings for details of religious correctness, the majority of Jewry ignored most texts and forged ways of life that seemed, in a commonsense way, to mix what they knew of Judaism with modern reality. They made no pretense at learnedness and did not advertise their religious styles as authentic representations of the Jewish past. In any "market situation," those who persuasively claim to have the highest-quality product have an advantage. In this manner, the glatt kosher concept, once a notion relevant to a pious few, has captured the market and now appears to be the basic norm for many of those who keep kashrut laws at all. This includes people new to Orthodoxy who are not aware of the many options within rabbinic law and have never experienced older styles of observance that were not shackled to ideologies of escalating strictness. The term *glatt kosher* seems to have become synonymous with "kosher by the highest standards," and it is sometimes used quite inappropriately from the point of view of its origin, such as when people employ the term in reference to vegetarian meals. One Israeli settlement in the Gaza Strip specializes in *glatt* green-grocery, growing and selling lettuce and scallions guaranteed to be free of worms. The phrase "glatt-kosher greens," historically, is about as logical as "fat-free orange juice." The recency and dynamism of this process may be gauged by checking the *Encyclopaedia Judaica*, published in 1971, which makes no mention of glatt kosher in the entries dealing with kashrut.[91] Their claim to preserve Judaism as it always was notwithstanding, ultra-Orthodox Jews are often extreme innovators and have devised intricate ways of promoting their way of life, while both drawing upon and remaining separate from the rest of Jewry.

KIBBUTZ

Another modern attempt to establish Jewish communities around clearly articulated ideologies was the kibbutz movement. Like ultra-Orthodoxy, the kibbutz entailed a residentially distinct community. It focused on economic and social goals, however, stressing the equality of its members. Against the background of life in eastern Europe, those settling in kibbutzim reacted against religion, which they felt sustained ignorance and backwardness. They rejected rabbinic authority and communal control. But they held a deep sense of peoplehood and saw themselves as fulfilling Jewish values, especially those of social justice. They perceived the links among individual, family, community, and a Jewish nation differently from those who followed Orthodoxy.[92]

The first kibbutz, Degania, was established in 1909 at the southern end of the Sea of Galilee. It was settled by young adults, mostly unmarried, who fervently believed that only by tilling the soil and "returning to the land" would Jews become a normal people and extricate themselves from the persecution and economic exclusion they had experienced in Europe. They undertook this project in conjunction with officials of the Jewish National Fund, which had purchased land in Ottoman Palestine. In 1914, soon after the collective settlement of Degania took root, World War I broke out and many of the Jewish immigrants to the country left. After the war ended in 1918 and the British Mandate was established in Palestine in 1920, another wave of young pioneers made their way to the country, generally known as the "third *aliya.*" Many of them came on the basis of socialist ideals, and some were specifically oriented to taking up life in the collective kibbutzim. As young people searching for a new life, they spent much time in personal and ideological reflection intimately tied to the question of the kind of community they wanted to form.

One of the third *aliya* groups that came into being was the Sharon *kvutza* (a word related to kibbutz). Like other *kvutzot*, it took a number of years for this group to crystallize and be assigned a place on which it could build its own settlement. During that time, members of the group hired themselves out working in construction or in paving roads, and underwent agricultural training. At this period, they faced many problems, such as selecting new members and coping with the fact that some people left the kvutza. Throughout, they debated their ideals, but they also had to take practical decisions. From 1922, before they had a permanent locale, the kvutza kept a group diary in which they could make entries to be shared with all other members. That diary provides a picture of the internal struggles of individual young people in the context of forging a commitment to a community and collective living.[93]

Most of the people in the kvutza came from smaller towns in eastern Europe, rather than from big cities, but had no experience in agriculture. They each had to undergo a personal transformation to learn a new way of life. They saw the new collective forms as closely linked to that transformation: "repairing the soul of the individual will bring about the redemption of the community." To partake in such change, it was important that people share their thoughts frankly; open discussion "purified and sanctified" the community. The focus on the quality of internal relationships sometimes left them little emotional energy to invest in new or potential members of the group. This, too, was a matter upon which they reflected and over which they anguished.

The processes characterizing these highly ideologized groups can be described in general sociological terms applicable to other utopian communes.[94] Their rhetoric stressed the emergence of new social forms and human relationships rather than the continuation of Jewish life as it was organized in the Diaspora. While seemingly totally rejecting their past, their goals in fact reflected trends in the societies from which they came. One model that influenced them was a religious commune in Russia founded in 1886 on the shores of the Black Sea, which had also produced a group diary, translated into Hebrew in the 1920s.[95] Later, some aspects of kibbutz life, particularly the collective raising of children, attracted the attention of social scientists abroad.[96] The stress on "universal" questions notwithstanding, the influence of Jewish culture and religion was apparent in many of the activities and aspirations of the kvutza.

Particularly obvious was their use of Hebrew. Most members of the kvutza, including women, had learned Hebrew and classic Jewish sources while growing up abroad. Some described themselves as "zealots" of the Hebrew language and criticized other immigrants who continued to speak Yiddish. Diary entries are in Hebrew and have allusions to biblical and other religious texts; some passages possess a literary quality. One member depicted his room and the mixture of religious and secular books found on the bookshelf.

The group also sang Hasidic songs whose melodies expressed "longing for the hidden and the unseen." In the discourse on the new life that they were shaping, terms that originally had religious meanings took on novel associations. The words "purity" and "holiness" appear often with reference to their cherished values. The above-cited passage about "repairing the soul" builds upon the kabbalistic notion of *tikkun,* or mending, which originally referred to a cosmological process in which individuals mystically were entailed in messianic redemption.

The Sabbath and the cycle of festivals continued to be the framework for the tempo of their lives, even as they were given new content. The days preceding Passover in 1925 prompted some of the members to contribute long statements summarizing their "personal journey" in the context of the group's history. They consciously selected that holiday as a period of self-reflection and self-criticism. One contributor dwelled on what the pioneers had lost in abandoning the old forms of the holidays and on the still unmet imperative of creating new ones.

In Israel today, one of the images associated with "the kibbutz," particularly on the part of Orthodox Jews, is "anti-religiosity." The abandonment of rituals such as the rules of kashrut, sometimes taken to the extent of deciding to raise pork, makes kibbutzim the emblem of anti-Judaism in the eyes of haredim. The founders of kibbutzim, however, even those who were not as steeped in Jewish sources as were the members of the Sharon kvutza, saw themselves as creating a new form of *Jewish* life. They intuitively felt the connection between the practice of Judaism they had known in childhood, on which they had turned their backs, and the one they sought to forge, but they only partially transmitted the same sense of connection to the next generation.

As we have seen with regard to Orthodoxy, the ritual life of a contemporary generation is rarely the precise replica of the one that preceded it. The same is true of the kibbutz, and may be seen in the realm of dancing.

The "horah" circle dance, which concluded many evening discussion sessions, seemed to function as a persuasive ritual through which the kvutza energized its members for the tasks of collective work on the morrow.[97] This link between ideological soul-searching and the organization of everyday life was apparent to kibbutz founders. A poem in the diary, the first line of which includes words from the Sabbath liturgy asking God to "purify our hearts," suggests the connection. That liturgical phrase, the poem declares, is "carried to the wild song of the dancers." The same verse concludes:

> As an electric flow
> Heart and soul are transferred
> Through the arms linked to the shoulders
> Of brothers and sisters.
> They dedicate themselves and are elated
> In the joy of the original dance
> Of the Land of Israel
> Hasidic . . .
> The lines of difference are blurred
> That distinguish "nuances" and ideologies
> Oh, Ah! . . . "And purify our hearts!"
> We shall not separate ourselves
> From flesh—my flesh—our flesh!!![98]

The "dancing out" of their ideological commitments arose spontaneously in the context of the kvutza, but perhaps the message of the horah was too general to successfully condense and convey the highly specific qualities of the founders' ideology. Powerful as it may have been in their own lives, the dance did not provide the same symbolic linkages in the experience of their children.

Kibbutz members did attempt to give ritual expression to the life they shaped. They stressed the agricultural aspects of holidays such as Passover or Shavuot, which marked the beginning and end of the grain harvest, over the religious and historic meanings of those festivals. The new celebrations they composed might have had great meaning to those who themselves had wrought a personal revolution by turning to a life of agriculture, but was less existentially compelling for the next generation, to whom farming constituted the taken-for-granted world of work. There were yet other reasons, too, why the rituals and the way of life that generated them, which had been created by the kibbutz, changed relatively rapidly in the succeeding generations.

Most kibbutz celebrations highlighted the community as a whole, rather than personal or family events.[99] The first wedding in the Sharon kvutza was arranged to coincide with the festival of Shavu̇ot, as if a general communal occasion were needed to celebrate the formation of a new family unit. If, as suggested above, symbols grounded in family life (such as food) may contribute to the construction of communal attachments as well, the weakening of the family in the kibbutz may have unintendedly deprived community rituals of some of their power.[100] In one sense, a developing kibbutz became a family in itself; members of the Sharon kvutza often referred to their group as "our family" in the diary. Ultimately, the growth of real families in the group presented a challenge to the collective norms. One diary entry expresses concern that "the family commits all the resources of the two members to ends that are special to them to the extent that it leaves nothing available for the general good beyond their private happiness."[101]

The majority of the entries in the group diary stem from the years before the kvutza settled in a permanent location. Once it was established, new realities monopolized the thoughts and activities of its members. Economic tasks and communal organization demanded that regular roles be assigned to people, and differences in influence among the members emerged in spite of the values of equality. With marriage and the growth of families, emotional ties between individuals competed with those of the kvutza. These processes took place in all kibbutzim; the founders had not envisioned the new kinds of ambivalent relationships between family and collective life that would eventually emerge.

But the changes in, and decline of, the kibbutz way of life have to be understood on a much broader canvas as well. After the State of Israel was established (1948), additional forces challenged these forms of collective living. The kibbutz ceased to be the main embodiment of the central values of the society. Kibbutzim no longer played a major role in defense, and industry, rather than agriculture, became the major economic challenge facing the country. Those choosing kibbutz life no longer held a monopoly of esteem in the eyes of the rest of the society, and this weakened motivation to adhere to the collective values cultivated so conscientiously by the generation of founders. In recent decades, many kibbutzim have undergone far-reaching changes based on compromises between collective norms and the values of middle-class society now firmly entrenched in contemporary Israel.

The decline of collectivism in the kibbutz has one other source, which was inherent in the kibbutz way of life from the outset: the emphasis on personal choice. Kibbutz education stressed collective values, but kibbutz children were simultaneously imbued with a free and even rebellious spirit. Indeed, the freedom enjoyed by these children was seen as representing the independence sought by the Jewish people in returning to its land. The commitment of kibbutz founders to a collective way of life was no less deep than the commitment of Orthodox Jews to their norms, but the former insisted that the younger generation join that way of life out of choice, not as the result of education that excluded other options. Children were not formally members of the kibbutz but joined at the age of eighteen, and some kibbutzim adopted the policy of not inducting young people as members until after they had finished their army service. Given this emphasis on choice, and the changes both within the kibbutz and the society at large, it is not surprising that many young people today decide to leave the kibbutz they were born on upon reaching adulthood.

In evaluating the history of the kibbutz, an attempt to build a special type of community in a national Jewish setting, it is important to view its peaks as well as its problems. The number of people living on kibbutzim was never large, but the kibbutz way of life was held up as an example by many Jews in Mandate Palestine. Teenagers from the cities spent time working on kibbutzim in the framework of ideological youth movements. Whether or not they decided to stay there, this was considered an important phase of their education and maturation. Parallel to this, some of the values, such as "return to the land" and the importance of the individual, which received symbolic expression in other sectors of the society, took on concrete institutional form in kibbutz life.

Tsili Doleve-Gandelman has analyzed this process with reference to kindergarten birthday celebrations.[102] As noted, birthday parties were not part of traditional Jewish culture. One setting in which birthday celebrations developed in Palestine were kindergartens established by the Jewish community. The Hebrew word for kindergarten preserves the sense of the German original: a children's garden. More generally, attitudes towards the young were shaped by metaphors comparing children to plants. This is seen in the term "sabra"—the cactus plant widespread in Palestine—which became the designation for Jewish children born there. These metaphors inscribed upon daily life gave expression to the notion of the Jews finding a place in nature (space), as well as having a history (time). Kindergarten birthday celebrations formed part of the curricula supplied by the education department of the Jewish National Fund, the organization that purchased national land. They embellished fully the symbolism linking the growth of the individual child to the blossoming of plants and trees in the Land of Israel.

The innovation of birthday parties thus points to the new valuation of the single person. At the same time, Jewish National Fund–inspired individualism was immediately mobilized for national purposes. Jewish National Fund–structured ritual may not, in fact, have been part of kibbutz life itself. There, children were socialized directly into a life of agriculture with little need to have this value presented in focused ceremonies. In one kibbutz, birthday celebrations varied in form and were not occasions of giving presents to the birthday boy or girl. Rather, the parents of the child would provide gifts, and these would be shared by all the children, including the celebrant.[103] The mode of balancing individual and collective orientations differed in kibbutz and urban settings, but the basic dilemma was common to the whole Jewish population during the prestate period. Pedagogical birthday celebrations continue to be part of Israeli kindergartens today, but they now feature other themes.[104] Half a century after the establishment of Israel, the society still ponders the optimal blend of individual fulfillment and group loyalties.[105]

HAVURA AND OTHER AMERICAN FORMS

The subtle interplay of individual aspirations and group identities has taken many forms in modern Jewish life. Another example, of which brief mention has been made already, was the emergence of havura prayer and study groups in America.[106] Like the founders of kibbutzim, those who created *havurot* were young people seeking new forms of Jewish organization and expression. The pioneers in Palestine had rebelled against the dependent situation of Jews in the European Diaspora, while the creators of the havura movement rebelled against the formality and passivity of synagogue life in post–World War II American suburbia. Like the members of kibbutz, the latter spent a good deal of time discussing and sometimes writing about the forms of organization with which they were experimenting.

The havura movement arose against the background of what is now called "the sixties" and the questioning of American politics and values that characterized that period. Developments within the wider society had reverberations that affected Jews and Judaism.[107] The growing political consciousness and assertiveness of American blacks brought the issue of "ethnicity" to the foreground. Overseas, the Vietnam War exposed U.S. postcolonial interference in the affairs of other regions. The resulting perception of U.S. foreign policy as a form of imperialism created a basis for sympathy with Palestinian Arabs who had come under Israeli military occupation as the result of the 1967 war. Many young Jews, while sharing a critical view of U.S. policy with other middle-class Americans of their age, were sensitive to having Israel cast in the role of an oppressor. In this crucible of ideological and ethnic crosscurrents, heightened by the new technology of videotapes appearing on color TV, young Jews had to forge viable personal and ethnic identities.

One tactic was to focus on a realm in which realities seemed to consist of simple contrasts, with Jews cast in the role of the "good guys." Such an arena was provided by the Soviet Union and its policies of suppressing religious life and prohibiting emigration. The situation of Soviet Jewry first became the rallying cry of the Jewish Defense League (JDL), which reflected the atmosphere of the 1960s in advocating "Jewish Power."[108] The leader of the JDL, Meir Kahane, and many of his followers came from lower-middle-class sections of New York City where tensions between Jews and blacks were common.[109] Kahane later moved to Israel, reformulating his blend of religious and ultranationalistic views in that setting, and succeeded in being elected to the Knesset.[110] At the same period of time, young Jews from middle-class milieus who sought involvement in Jewish life tried out new forms of communal worship and study in an American context.

Havura comes from a Hebrew stem (*ḤVR*) with many associations signifying sociality. The stem yields words translated as friend, comrade, company, gang, member of a group, and so forth. In the context we are discussing, *havura* is often translated as "fellowship," but when it became prominent in the late 1960s, it covered several kinds of groupings. One kind featured young people, including many who had solid Judaic educations, who were looking for more intense and intimate ways of expressing and deepening their knowledge and commitments. Another included people of diverse ages, many of whom had had a limited Jewish background in their childhood, but, for various reasons, were interested in strengthening the Jewish components in their lives.[111]

Havura Jews were concerned with all levels of Jewish life, and they challenged the existing priorities of organized Judaism. They addressed the way people studied, the extent and meaning of ritual observance, and the nature of worship. The latter included both the content of the liturgy and the atmosphere of interaction among those praying.[112] In the latter sphere, they wished to break the pattern in which a rabbi was "the expert" and formal leader of prayer, distant from the congregation in style of dress and his place on an elevated dais. They adopted a model whereby prayer engaged all members of a group who shared in worship as equals. At one level, this involved "going back" to forms of "davening" that prevailed in eastern Europe.[113] In other ways, however, havurot were bold innovations. In them, women assumed ritual roles that in the past had only been assigned to men. As indicated, some members of the havurot had experienced participatory worship in summer camps, but it still was unusual in the synagogues most of them had known as children.[114]

Among the leaders of the havura movement were a number of former rabbinical school students, mainly from the Conservative Jewish Theological Seminary and to a lesser extent from Reform institutions. These individuals were prominent in Havurat Shalom, which organized itself in the Boston area in 1969. In fact, they constituted themselves as an alternative framework for studying Judaism and training rabbis.[115] They sought to counter the academic approach to Judaism that stressed philological precision and historical objectivity in the analysis of ancient texts as the essence of rabbinic training.[116] Instead, they wanted to link the study of Judaism to spiritual depth and social relevance. This entailed encouraging individuals to seek a personal relationship to classic texts, as much as mastering the scientific tools of historical analysis.

The havura ideal spread rapidly in certain settings. It flourished on university campuses and in communities close to them. Its growth coincided with another new trend: that of the spread of Jewish studies in American academia. Before the 1960s, Jewish studies existed in only a handful of American universities; most people interested in advanced training had to attend a rabbinical seminary.[117] As more universities provided positions and programs in Jewish studies, more avenues were available to become acquainted with Jewish religion and culture in an atmosphere of personal choice. A local havura might include some individuals with a strong Judaic background, along with people finding their way in new forms of worship and realms of knowledge.

The havura was a comfortable setting for those groping towards a new involvement. Dress and seating arrangements were informal. One could begin participating by learning simple ritual activities, such as lifting or dressing the sefer Torah, before attempting a role requiring knowledge of Hebrew. Another form of participation might be making an object to enhance the ritual atmosphere, such as a table-covering to be used when reading from the Torah. Contributions, and advances in involvement, on the part of individuals were publicly acknowledged by the havura. Open discussions of the values and development of the group provided access to its culture and ethos.

The havura also entailed a revision of notions of authority. Some early havurot, citing historical precedent, experimented with having people commit themselves to further ritual observance.[118] This, however, did not become a widespread or lasting feature of their religious style. While havurot might include rabbis or rabbinical students, the basic purpose was to move past the role of a rabbi as a religious decider. Every member was to develop a personal connection to Jewish tradition and its textual sources and help shape the group's direction. At the same time, those who were particularly knowledgeable played an important role in both founding and leading early havurot. For members of a havura first finding their way, such an individual "symbolize[d] the group's roots in the Jewish past, and through his example, he is the group's guarantor that the journey taken into the future is feasible and worthwhile."[119] On the other hand, differential knowledge of Jewish tradition among members could cause stress when it came to deciding upon ritual matters.[120]

Tension also appeared between havurot and the wider Jewish community. Established congregations and rabbis criticized them for being separatist and elitist. Over time, however, ways were found of accommodating the existence of havurot and their innovations. Sometimes havurot operated within existing synagogues, working out a modus vivendi with the formal congregation. This took place in Reform congregations as well as in Conservative synagogues.[121] The turn towards smaller and more intimate prayer settings was a general phenomenon, developing among Orthodox Jews as well.[122] In some matters, congregations and rabbis ended up adopting modes of conducting prayer that first appeared in havura contexts.

The experimentation with and legitimation of new forms of worship, and of celebrating religious events, became taken for granted in America. One theme of continued religious exploration was, and is, gender. This is seen in the formation of Rosh Hodesh groups that meet monthly based on the traditional connection between the New Moon festival and women.[123] These have special importance among innovating Orthodox Jews (but are not exclusive to them) because they maintain gender separation while attaching value to women's religiosity. Another development is the formation of synagogues and communities based on homosexuality. These entail a new perception of possible links among gender, sexual norms, ethnicity, and religious commitment.[124] Even when gender and sexual preference are not at issue, Jews in America seek religious forms that are finely calibrated to their own values and tastes. An example may be found in a bat mitzvah celebration among Russian Jews in Brooklyn carried out in a restaurant with the assistance of a Reform rabbi.[125] The religious and material resources of American life allow an ever-burgeoning variety of ritual forms. In this situation, communal, ethnic, and religious affiliations appear as expressions of individual identity channeled and articulated in myriad ritual patterns.[126]

RELIGION IN ISRAELI SOCIETY: BUREAUCRACY AND FAMILY MILESTONES

The diverse paths discussed in the previous sections do not only reflect varying beliefs and practices. They also imply distinct ways in which the different realms within which Judaism is articulated—individual and family, school and community, and broad identification with the Jewish people—are linked to, or separated from, one another. The ultra-Orthodox rejected the nationalist ideology of Zionism. This left them free, even those moving to the Land of Israel, to cultivate tightly integrated family, educational, and communal institutions, with little concern for other Jews who understood themselves in terms of a broad ethnic definition of Jewishness that did not entail detailed rules of behavior applicable to everyone. In addition, the democratic rights enjoyed by the ultra-Orthodox, in both the United States and Israel, have been utilized by them to closely shape and scrutinize the behavior of their own community's members.

Secular Zionists assumed that a Jewish state would replace the role that religion had played in the Diaspora. They did not foresee that once the main concrete tasks of Zionism were achieved (establishing a state and army, developing an economy), people would want some place for ritual and spirituality as part of normal life. Other trends we have described, less involved with encompassing ideologies, portray looser and more flexible connections among the different levels of Jewish expression. They may shift among the Jewish registers of communal commitments, private and familial concerns, or mobilization for broad national purposes. In its creative phases, Jewish culture and religion (through education and ritual) have been able to find ways of making these levels feed into one another, rather than pull in independent or clashing directions.

While these and many other developments have been taking place, there have been major demographic transformations in Jewry over the past half century. Only 600,000 Jews lived in Israel when the state was established, but soon half of the world's Jews will reside there. Two countries, Israel and the United States, will probably contain (as they do now) about four-fifths of all Jews. Our discussion thus far and popular images see these two countries as providing very different contexts for Jewish ritual life: extreme variety in North America in contrast to an Orthodox monopoly in Israel, along with a sharp gap there separating Jews who are "religious" from those who are not. In a broad and official way, this image has much truth, and I shall now sketch some of the historical background to it. A closer look at current developments, however, will show that there also are certain parallels between trends in America and Israel, as well as emerging realities that are bringing some Jews in both countries to deal with overlapping concerns.

Many Israelis see Judaism and Orthodox rabbinic authority as depriving them of personal freedom within their own society. This condition has many historic sources. Among them is the linking of Orthodox ideologies to national politics, a phenomenon with historic roots in Europe. Both within the Zionist movement and outside it, in particular in interwar Poland, Orthodox groups felt they had to organize politically to ensure their ability to maintain an observant way of life while large numbers of Jews around them were moving away from it. This political pattern was transferred to Mandate Palestine. One of its implications, after Israel gained independence, was the setting-up in 1953 of two distinct national school tracks, one general and one religious, along with small ultra-Orthodox tracks separate from the national education system. This has resulted in the socialization and entrenchment of disparate world views regarding religion in Israeli society. Along with these developments, there was the tendency for Israeli Jews to take up residence in areas and housing projects of like-minded neighbors along the religious/secular divide, thereby limiting contact among sectors. All this encouraged a view of Israeli society as being divided into two nonoverlapping categories, religious and secular, even though individual variation in ritual behavior was always wider than suggested by this dichotomy.[127]

An important aspect of this trend was the failure of, and even lack of interest in, attempts to formulate substantive approaches to Judaism and Jewish culture on the part of secular Jewish Israelis. This failure or oversight partially had to do with the weakness of community in the development of Jewish society in Palestine and the State of Israel. Young pioneer immigrants had separated themselves from both family and community abroad, creating frameworks such as political parties and the General Federation of Jewish Workers (Histadrut). These were multipurpose organizations that also concerned themselves with health services and leisure activities. They appropriated functions in which, under other circumstances, family and community might play a part. Post-1948 immigrants from Europe who were Holocaust survivors also were typically devoid of familial and communal connections.

Immigrants from Middle Eastern countries at that period mostly arrived as families along with others from the same social background but were unfamiliar with Israeli institutions and too dependent economically to create their own communal structures. Even their family life was subject to criticism in the new setting. The notion of the "generation of the wilderness," referring to the biblical Israelites who had died in the desert while their children entered the Promised Land, gave a message driving a wedge between the adult immigrants and their children. Much of Israeli culture, including aspects of religion, was processed through governmental bodies, as illustrated by the incident of the circumcision inspector discussed in chapter 2. This dampened initiatives to recreate religious life according to norms familiar from abroad. Slowly, as the immigrants established themselves, they were able to reassert older patterns in the new setting. The ultra-Orthodox Sephardi party, Shas, which was the third largest in the country after the 1999 elections, adopted some ideological forms that originated in eastern Europe and succeeded in expanding its influence by cultivating values related to family life and by building schools and community-like institutions with the aid of governmental budgets.

The formal link between state and religion continues to be firm in Israel today (although it is now subject to much public debate). It is expressed in several spheres that other societies relegate to the individual and family realms. For example, all food served by public institutions such as the army or the national air carrier must be kosher. In another realm (as mentioned), the Ministry of Religions resisted the right of families to engrave dates using the generally accepted Gregorian year on tombstones, although the courts eventually upheld this right. With regard to marriage, no mechanism for civil marriage within Israel exists, although there is partial recognition of common law marriage for purposes of inheritance. Marriages are carried out under the supervision of established religious authority, Jewish, Muslim, or Christian, as the case may be. With regard to Jews, this means that the Ministry of the Interior will only register marriages carried out under the supervision of the Orthodox rabbinate. It also means, for example, that all women are required to undergo ritual immersion in a miqveh before their weddings, whether they wish to or not. In addition, coalition politics typically places the Ministry of Interior in the hands a religious political party (a recent exception was the short period after the 1999 elections). All these factors combine to give many Israelis the feeling that the form of wedding ceremony they "undergo" is alien to their personal experience and worldview and imposed upon them by the laws of the state and by coalition politics.

Menachem Friedman has characterized the rabbinic bureaucracy that developed in Israel as a supplier of religious services, a phrase highlighting the difference between this situation and the celebration of life-cycle rituals within the flow of familial and communal traditions.[128] Bureaucrats are notorious for the way they act as gatekeepers, often seeking to enhance their importance beyond the sphere of their defined task. This is not new in Jewish life, of course. Sylvie-Anne Goldberg's analysis of the hevra kadisha shows how members of the burial society, who were perceived to hold the key to an individual's entrance to the world to come, extended their influence into all realms of life. This took place, however, when both officials and "clients" shared basic assumptions about the world (both this one and the "next"), and what was important in it.[129] In Israel, where the control of religious officials derives from the power of the state, the meeting of religious bureaucrats with ordinary citizens is as likely to create tension as it is to reflect consensus.

Given this situation, Israelis seek ways of getting around state-imposed religious rules. For example, Israeli law, tied into international agreements, recognizes marriages performed outside of the country, irrespective of their religious or nonreligious quality. Some Israelis go abroad and marry, which enables them to be listed according to their new status in the official Population Registry. This option has been especially convenient for categories of Israelis such as recent immigrants from Russia who were born of non-Jewish mothers and are therefore not recognized as Jewish by the rabbinate. Another category is those prohibited from marriage by rabbinic law, such as a male who is a kohen (priest), who is not allowed to marry a divorcee.[130] In the past, those who had a specific "problem with the rabbinate" had recourse to civil marriage abroad, but today trips to Cyprus or some other foreign venue by Jewish Israelis with no obvious halakhic difficulties who simply want to avoid that institution are increasingly common.[131] Couples who do so can subsequently, if they wish, be married after they return home in "alternative" wedding ceremonies that might involve a Conservative or Reform rabbi, even though they have no legal standing in Israel. This trend has been growing in recent years.

Some of those entrenched in the religious bureaucracies grasp the extent of alienation between themselves and the nonreligious public and realize that they are beginning to face a "market situation." Recently, the Ministry of Religion has advertised its services in the media with respect to rituals like bar mitzvah, which has no formal legal implications. The sense of a religious "market" appears in other realms as well and is now cultivated by a variety of individuals and groups. In a column in the Jerusalem weekly *Qol Ha'ir*, Ya'aqov (Jackie) Levi has written humorous reviews of local synagogues, rating them like a restaurant reviewer. A 1996 publication similarly gives the historic and religious background of the traditional wedding ceremony and then explains in practical terms the alternatives, given the laws of the state, open to Israelis who wish to marry.[132] More recently, there have been legislative changes that enlarge the scope of choice with regard to divorce. A series of family courts in the general court system are now empowered to handle matters of alimony, child support, and division of property for couples who seek their guidance and decisions, leaving only the technical matters of conveying a bill of divorce (get) to the rabbinate.[133] Another development has been an annual "Torah study fair," in which various groups participate, each demonstrating and thus advertising its particular approach to grasping Jewish tradition. There is every indication that within both Israel and world Jewry abroad, people will press for additional alternatives in these matters.

ISRAEL AND DIASPORA LINKS:
THE CASE OF CONVERSION

Israel, where legislation, governmental bureaucracy, and politics impinge directly on some life-cycle events, is a special situation in modern Jewish life, but there is now a growing engagement between committed Jews there and in the Diaspora with regard to these questions. Contact between different centers of Jewish life has grown through widespread travel, along with developments in electronic communication. We live in an era of the globalization of Jewish issues.[134] One example, cited above, is the network of people concerned with problems of the agunah, a woman unable to re-marry because of halakhic bonds to a husband that are not easily broken, even when in reality a marriage is defunct.[135] Another concerns the debates surrounding conversion.

The question of conversion has recently become prominent because of immigration to Israel from the former Soviet Union, on the one hand, and the approaches to Jewish religion growing out of American historical experience (Conservative, Reconstructionist, and Reform Judaism), which seek to make an impact on Israeli society, on the other.[136] Among the approximately one million "Russian" immigrants are many men and women who are not Jewish but who have become citizens of the state along with their Jewish spouses. For the most part, they have not sought to convert to Judaism in terms of religion. This situation adds many individuals to the Israeli population who appear to be Jewish from the perspective of everyday practical life but are not in terms of traditional rabbinical law or in the categories of the Ministry of the Interior, which refer to that law.

From the viewpoint of traditional law, the children of Gentile women are not Jewish, a norm that further increases the section of the Israeli population with which Jews who follow halakha will not intermarry. If Israelis not born as Jews were to convert to Judaism, the predicament would be alleviated, but the attitude of the established rabbinate has been to treat prospective converts with skepticism, being suspicious of their motives for turning to a new religion. At the same time, the leaders of Orthodoxy have refused to acknowledge other paths to conversion, such as those offered by Reform or Conservative rabbis, that might prove more congenial to some immigrants who have minimal previous experience with Jewish life. They argue that Reform rabbis do not carry out conversions that include circumcision and ritual immersion, which are basic in halakha, but they also withhold recognition from Conservative conversions that do include these elements. Within Reform Judaism, decisions regarding individual conversions are typically made by individual rabbis, so that there is variation with regard to the actual process in individual cases. Recently, the leadership of Reform Judaism in the United States has advocated restoring circumcision and immersion to the conversion procedure.[137]

This issue in Israel came to a head in 1997–98. In 1995, the Conservative movement in Israel had taken a case dealing with conversions it had carried out on babies legally adopted from abroad by Jewish Israeli parents to the high court. The request was that the court order the Ministry of the Interior to recognize the conversions and enter the children into the Population Registry as Jews. This request was later joined by parallel petitions concerning conversions by the Reform movement. In response to the possibility that the court might grant these requests, Orthodox political parties in the coalition demanded that the government support legislation giving Orthodox rabbis a formal monopoly on conversion (in contrast to the current de facto administrative monopoly). The call for such legislation stimulated vociferous opposition from many Israelis and large segments of Diaspora Jewry. In the absence of a stable political resolution to the conversion dilemma, the court decided in 2000 to create a special panel of eleven justices to deliberate the question.[138] In February 2002, the court handed down a decision requiring the minister of the interior to register twenty-four people as Jews who had been converted under the auspices of the Conservative and Reform movements.[139] The ministry subsequently did so, but entered the information into the Population Registry in a manner that would indicate that a person was a non-Orthodox convert. In response to that, the Conservative movement returned to the court, and it still appears (as of December 2002) that a "solution" to this issue will not be reached soon.

This dilemma, which has been in the making for many years, invites a discussion of the development of the rules and practice of conversion to Judaism.[140] While not an inevitable phase of the "life cycle," conversion ritual can be viewed as a rite of passage and has a long history, like the other rituals we have discussed. The Bible envisions the possibility of foreigners joining the Israelites and participating in Israelite rituals but does not provide a single marker of that process. It insists that foreigners residing with the Israelites be circumcised in order to partake of the Passover sacrifice and also specifies the way a woman captured in war may become a legitimate wife.[141] The Mishna does not include a special tractate dealing with proselytes (*gerim*), but talmudic literature does incorporate various discussions of conversion rituals.[142]

One passage in the Talmud presents different opinions over what act constitutes the basic ritual of conversion: circumcision or immersion (in a miqveh or an appropriate natural body of water). Another view is that both are necessary.[143] Yet another source states that the proselyte must be informed about some of the weightier mitzvot, along with some less central ones, but there is not a great stress on understanding the motivations of the individual proselyte when carrying out the ritual acts of conversion.[144] The notion of examining the motives of a potential convert emerged only in the Middle Ages, and doing so is not mentioned by the standard authorities.[145] Although we know of Jews proselytizing in antiquity, for much of the medieval period the actual likelihood of Christians or Muslims converting to Judaism was minimal, so for many centuries the rabbinic legal tradition in this area was not tested by the crucible of historical experience. When, with emancipation, issues of intermarriage and potential conversion arose in modern Europe, a range of options in the conditions for accepting converts was available within rabbinic sources.

From a broad historical view, Moshe Samet has compared the development of conversion ritual to that of the wedding ceremony, as discussed in chapter 4. Ancient law suggests alternative options for getting married (monetary payment, *or* a contract, *or* sexual congress), and for becoming Jewish (circumcision *or* immersion), but with time, the developing ritual requirements incorporated all the elements simultaneously.[146] Avi Sagi and Zvi Zohar liken the final shape of the conversion process to a classic rite of passage, as described by Arnold van Gennep. Circumcision and the removal of the foreskin separate the male from his previous status and immersion marks the entry into the new status of belonging to the Jewish people. Shaye Cohen suggests a different perspective. He compares the process of becoming a convert to the steps taken when a Jew took upon himself extra obligations with regard to the laws of purity in order to join the circumscribed fellowship of haverim. The ceremony is a vehicle "by which society affirms that the initiate has undergone a change of the legal status based on the performance of, and stated obligation to continue performing, certain legal norms." Both points of view downplay conversion as a personal religious transformation and stress the affiliation with a new collectivity and its norms.[147]

Sagi and Zohar see the talmudic prescriptions, in the first instance, as incorporating a person into descent-based Jewish peoplehood, which is a status that entails the obligations of following the Torah's commandments based on the ancient covenant between God and the Jews as a group. With their rites-of-passage perspective, they claim that conversion ritual may be understood as changing the "essence" of a person so that he or she is permanently Jewish, whether or not he or she ultimately continues to follow the traditional religious rules.[148] This point of view plays down intentionality in the making of converts and stresses their becoming part of "the body" of the Jewish people.

The different ways conversion is understood, both in terms of the technical requirements and in terms of cultural perceptions that accompany them, have implications for marriage and for the status of children. The latter, of course, affect inclusion in or exclusion from full participation in Jewish life. There long has existed among some Jews a sense that membership in the religion or people is transmitted almost biologically.[149] Some of these notions have seemed close to racist in formulation.[150] The fact that birth into a Jewish family has been the main source of recruitment to Judaism helps sustain this feeling. This sentiment has been utilized in the rhetoric of religious leaders seeking exclusive control over marriage, and over conversion to Judaism. Their claim is that without this control, there would be large categories of people who "appear to be Jews" but "in fact" are not. Marriage to these people by "kosher" Jews would increase the number of unmarriageable mamzerim, they argue, creating unbridgeable gaps within the Jewish collectivity.[151]

On the other hand, the Jewish past also shows that what is viewed as "biology" can be altered by human action and social facts. A well-known query directed to Maimonides by a scholarly proselyte in Baghdad asked whether it is correct for a convert to recite the phrase "our God and God of our fathers" in the Amidah prayer, when his own ancestors were not Jewish.[152] Maimonides' response was that as someone who "unifies the name of the Holy One as it is written in the Torah, . . . Abraham, peace be on him, is your father."[153] This suggests that too much emphasis on genealogy is misplaced, even though the response does not challenge the role of descent in the way Jews usually define themselves. Across Jewish history, many problematic cases of "unmarriageable" individuals were solved discreetly when those facing that dilemma moved to a distant community, presented themselves straightforwardly as Jews, and slid into normal communal life. The ability of a rabbinic establishment today, aided by modern record keeping and data processing, to efficiently track vast numbers of individuals and sort out those who halakhically are problematic with regard to marriage, is a new and questionable development in Judaism. History also reveals shifting reasoning and practice with regard to groups who have at certain times been considered unmarriageable but who at other times have reconnected to rabbinic tradition and communities. A notable example is the ancient category of Karaite Jews, who in modern times were found in Crimea and Egypt, and who currently reside in Israel as well.[154]

The claim that conversions and marriages outside the control of a monolithic rabbinate would sever the unity of the Jewish people also faces another question: how many marriages are likely to take place between haredi Jews and secular or Reform Jews (for example) anyway? The original "Who is a Jew?" issue, aiming to establish a legal Orthodox monopoly over conversion, entailed a handful of cases of Jews in the Diaspora who underwent non-Orthodox conversions and then considered moving to Israel. The controversy did not, therefore, address a social reality experienced by a significant number of Jews, but dramatized the way different ultra-Orthodox groups competed with one another in their demands for greater vigilance. By contrast, the recent immigration of non-Jews from the former Soviet Union does create a socioreligious reality of serious proportions for Israeli society. The weight of the question is reflected in the fact that it is discussed in a book by a major secular Israeli politician, with a broad Jewish perspective in mind.[155] The issue has also been taken up by prominent people in the "national religious" sector of Israeli society who both seek to uphold Orthodox rabbinic norms and are also committed to the Zionist ideal of creating a new and unified modern Jewish society. This led to the creation of new schools for potential converts that include teachers from Conservative and Reform backgrounds, while the actual power to convert was left in the hands of Orthodox rabbinic courts. This arrangement has been in place for several years and has dealt with relatively small numbers of converts, and whether it will be a satisfactory long-range solution is still not clear.[156]

COMMUNITIES, TEXTS, AND AN ANTHROPOLOGICAL PERSPECTIVE

The conversion question is one example of a global Jewish issue relevant to those who embrace a broad view of Jewish existence and attach importance to the differing segments of contemporary Jewry. The substantive kernel of the issue deals with the lives of single individuals, but the existence of a Jewish state in which there is an established rabbinate, along with traditional linkages among individual, family, and community in Judaism, makes it an existential question of wide concern. As indicated in the introductory chapter, rituals concerning single individuals at times touch upon matters of broad principle that potentially affect Jewish groups everywhere. Also, as suggested there, an anthropological perspective provides a means of bringing into view these various levels of Jewish existence and their interactions.

One current conundrum implied by various topics considered throughout this book concerns the place of "the individual" among those attached to halakha. For example, "modern Orthodox" Jews in America, whose ideologies overlap with those of "national religious" Jews in Israel, face the dilemma of recognizing value both in religious authority and in personal autonomy. The growing sharpness of this problem is seen in publications over the past decade or so. In America, it was the focus of a conference at Yeshiva University in 1989.[157] In Israel, a volume of essays (in Hebrew) entitled *Between Authority and Autonomy in Jewish Tradition* was published on the second anniversary of the assassination of Prime Minister Yitzhak Rabin, an act that was carried out in the name of religious values and with reference to rabbinic authority.[158] It is perhaps a new development in Jewish thought that the issue of personal autonomy is addressed as an explicit Jewish theme and not just an empirical fact of life. While facing different daily challenges, both the Israeli and American versions of modern Orthodoxy struggle with the religious competition of the haredi world, and this social and spiritual confrontation is found in other countries, like France, as well.[159] The interrelatedness of such trends across different communities, and the way they entail the very definition of Jewish collective life, invite general reflections on balancing a commitment to tradition and to some sort of religious authority with an acknowledgment of the plurality of Jewish perspectives and ways of life.

We have seen that there are many ways in which Jews define an attachment to the past as they carry out their lives today and envision a Jewish future. Among Orthodox Jews, and some streams of Conservative Judaism, following halakha—text-based rabbinic law—is the major Jewish anchor. Departing from this view, some nineteenth-century ideologies in Europe, the cultural ground from which today's Reform and Conservative Judaism grew, examined the Jewish past with scholarly eyes and cited history as the arbiter of what features of the Jewish past would prove important for the future.[160] Another approach, which received less prominent philosophic articulation, was to look to Jewish "folklore," the Judaism of "ordinary Jews," or the ongoing practices of a community for inspiration as to what was worth preserving. This outlook was implied in some strands of Zionist thought and in ideologies hoping for continued Jewish national existence in the eastern European Diaspora.[161] This book is predicated on the assumption that all these thrusts—halakha, history, and ethnography—now have relevance for engaged Jews.

Many Jews today are attuned to these three components of Jewish culture, albeit in strikingly different proportions and combinations. Some thinkers have defined the Jews as a people who stand in a shared relationship to revered Jewish texts. One major task of a community positioning itself vis-à-vis Jewish tradition would be to nurture that relationship. The notion of "relationship" implies two distinct partners, who sometimes will be close to one another and sometimes pulled apart. Extreme Orthodoxy represents the demand for a monopoly over the right to interpret sacred texts, distancing itself from the mass of the Jews. On the other hand, those wishing to select only texts that "speak to us today" face the dilemma that a sense of peoplehood may be undermined by reading texts so that they readily collapse into the peculiarities of each group. Selectivity with regard to texts, taken to the extreme, leads to a multiplicity of Jewish peoples. An overly user-friendly and tailored text loses its ability to inform us of alternatives in Jewish life or to inspire people to think beyond their present situations. Key texts must be accorded their own integrity.

At the same time, most Jews today realize that the rules, norms, and perspectives embodied in such texts have changed over the course of history. In earlier times, Jewish communities could convince themselves that shifts in rabbinic norms were divinely preprogrammed into the original meanings of classic texts. Today, even for those taking such a "fundamentalist" view, it is hard to erase the awareness that their stance is one that they themselves have chosen. Most contemporary approaches to Judaism exhibit, if only implicitly, some consciousness of history. This means that modern scholarly (in addition to traditional rabbinic scholarly) readings of how Jewish culture and Jewish lives were actually lived, whether offered by historians, anthropologists, or specialists in other disciplines, enter into the tool kit of ideas and modes of thought by which all Jews understand themselves and pass on that understanding to future generations.

Along with a consciousness of history, coupled with being conscious of that consciousness, is the growing appreciation that all Jewish groups today are expressions of the contemporary world. If, in the past, the "modern world" was seen as eroding "traditional" Judaism, it is now understood that sometimes factors of modernity (or "postmodernity") can abet the adoption and preservation of ancient ritual forms that have meaning for individuals and families. Consider the trend in America, evident from the 1960s, of a growing number of young people wearing skull caps in public. This gesture of piety reflects many factors, including an enlarged tolerance within the wider society of ethnic and religious differences, which also includes the acceptance of saffron robes and "exotic" hair styles.[162] Another example of the contemporaneity of tradition comes from the innovations in the technology of reproduction over the past few decades. The new procedures have had an impact on basic assumptions about "the body" that cut across the boundaries of cultural and religious groups. Today, ultra-Orthodox families avail themselves of such technologies in pursuance of the religious (and personal) goal of bearing children, and do so on the basis of what seems to be a "natural," commonsense, religious position that it is acceptable. Halakhic reasons can be marshaled to discourage or to prohibit taking advantage of the new procedures, but religious leaders adopting that position would find themselves at odds with deeply rooted sensibilities of what people want and assume they should be able to have.[163]

Given this dual avenue of heightened awareness, of both how the past has been made and how all Jews are affected by contemporary developments that appear to them as self-evidently legitimate, it is inevitable that there will be perceived gaps between ideal forms of religious life projected by those enveloped in rabbinic learning and emerging norms of behavior holding sway in any given communal setting. All leaders claiming to represent the authority of sacred texts, as well as communities following versions of Judaism that partake of tradition, face the task of negotiating the shifting tension between text and community. Their challenge is to do so while maintaining a respectful position towards both parties in that relationship, even as it is obvious that there will be episodes of strain along with periods of comfort.

As in many current marriages, the link between community and text may at times require the input of "counseling." Perhaps this is one way to phrase the contribution of academic work to broader Jewish self-understanding. When formerly unquestioned rules and customs no longer make sense to members of a community, an "outside" point of view may prove capable of supplying a perspective within which the pained parties can move beyond their impasse. Scholarly research itself does not provide normative answers, but it can be an ingredient in the struggle of mutually committed partners to assess their situation, give it new interpretations, and then move forward together.

In viewing the ties between a Jewish community and its textual heritage in terms of a romantic involvement, I am, of course, borrowing from an ancient metaphor. Aside from its appearance in the Bible and in rabbinic literature, the picture of the relationship between God and Israel as that of a groom and bride has been salient in mystical tradition. Kabbala and its tropes, as seen in our discussion of the growing recognition of "the individual," have sometimes served as lubricants smoothing the relationship, potentially fraught with friction, between Jewish communities and cultural orientations gaining momentum in the wider society.[164] This suggests that the self-conscious embrace of Jewish tradition by today's Jews might be eased, not only by the findings of fastidious research, but by poetic imagination and insight as well.

Finally, even when a productive modus vivendi between a community and aspects of Jewish tradition is achieved, there remains the awareness of other "couples" who have worked out different kinds of relationships. It is normal that in a complex and stressful world, people want to realize their religious lives in homogeneous surroundings where they don't have to repeatedly bother themselves with the perspectives of other Jews. This can lead to a situation, however, in which each Jewish group grows complacent in the rectitude of its own habits. Confrontation with textual treasures, *along with* an understanding of how different Jewish groups have read them and lived them, can be an antidote to insularity. An openness to different aspects of and claims to the Jewish past, and an appreciation of how the lives of women and men have been played out in relation to it, should engender a sense of continuity of a broad and dynamic Jewish tradition, along with the possibility of discourse among the diverse strands of present-day Jewry.

MARRIAGE AND COMMUNITY: A MODERN MIDRASH

This chapter began by recalling the Israelite tribes. "Tribe" is a term that points in opposite directions; it evokes images both of solidarity and of divisiveness. Both these tendencies have always been present in Jewish history. In the contemporary era, there may be more factors than existed previously that shape Jewish diversity, but, at the same time, the opportunity for different groups of Jews to be in contact with one another is also very impressive. Contact, however, does not automatically entail unity: it can also lead to conflict. The dynamic is open-ended. How Jewish society and societies will evolve cannot be predicted in advance. We can be sure, however, that Jews will continue to monitor these trends closely, and that some will do so with an attentive ear to the trends and tropes of the Jewish past.

In Jewish life, with its emphasis on family, patterns of marriage have always been central to the transmission of culture. I note, in conclusion, an ancient discussion of marriage in relation to the tribes of Israel. The Mishna presents the following statement by Rabban Shimón ben Gamliel: "There were no happier days for Israel than the fifteenth of Av and the Day of Atonement, for on them the daughters of Jerusalem go forth in white raiments. . . . And the daughters of Jerusalem went forth to dance in the vineyards and what did they say? 'Young man, lift up your eyes and see

Figure 24.   Sign at the entrance to a kibbutz announcing a Tu be-Av festival.
Photo Harvey E. Goldberg.

what you would choose for yourself.' "[165] Both the Day of Atonement and the fifteenth of the month of Av, or Tu be-Av, appear as a kind of Sadie Hawkins Day (in addition to their other meanings), on which engagements are brought about at the instigation of young women. Why Tu be-Av is important is not made clear in the Mishna, and the rabbis of the Talmud offered various reasons.[166] Two of them refer to specific biblical events, over a thousand years earlier. In both biblical episodes, the selection of a mate was restricted to certain tribes. One incident, in Numbers 36, refers to the daughters of Zelophehad and the limitation of their marriage choice in order to preserve inheritance within the tribal line. The other, in Judges 21, is the prohibition of marrying into the tribe of Benjamin, a rule that was later rescinded. Tu be-Av was interpreted as the date upon which these limitations were repealed and marriage could take place between all segments of society. These interpretations recognize the contribution of an open marriage arena to overall Jewish solidarity.[167]

This recognition is not inappropriate to Israeli society today, where marriages between partners whose families are from different countries and continents is increasingly common. This pattern serves to lower the barriers separating original ethnic groups, even while in-marriage along the lines of social class, which is partially correlated with ethnicity, continues to exist.[168] The general trend in the country is for young people within a given social milieu to increasingly ignore the "tribal" past of their parents when choosing a mate. Without examining talmudic literature, many young Israelis select the date of Tu be-Av, usually in August, for their weddings, as it carries the aura of a colorful tradition that is not surrounded by rules of rabbinical law (see figure 24). In the week before that date, merchants feature gifts similar to those sent on Valentine's Day in America, newspapers announce concerts for young people celebrating the "holiday of love" and hotels advertise special rates for couples.

The accounts that the Talmud offers for the origin of Tu be-Av also raise the question of how united Israelite or Jewish society has actually been over the course of its long history. Current slogans evoking "the wholeness of the Jewish people" assume a stability and homogeneity of Judaism in the past, a view that does not stand up to historical scrutiny.[169] As has been often noted, biblical Ruth, who came from another society to join the people and the God of ancient Israel, was an ancestress of David; and did not Esther rescue the Jews of the Persian empire through her marriage to a Gentile king? Marriage links have been important in bringing together different kinds of people in Jewish life, and the ways in which differences have emerged and have been overcome have constituted a story far more complex than the consistent application of a single set of norms.

It is now clear that the establishment of modern Israel and its development over five decades has yielded diversity rather than the uniform society earlier imagined. Internal divisions reflect a host of factors including class, ethnicity, and—most blatantly—religious ideology. Parallel to that, Diaspora Jewries continue to evolve in directions that reflect both their local milieus and global trends. Contemporary Jewry, both in and out of Israel, faces the challenge of forming meaningful communities, with their own institutions and personal styles of life, while remaining concerned about, and involved with, other Jews of different cultural and religious orientations. In dealing with these challenges, some Jews will undoubtedly turn to their venerable library of scholarly and religious books. But I also suggest, as in the case of Tu be-Av and other popular expressions seeking a link to tradition, that attention also be paid to what "ordinary Jews" have done, and are now doing and saying, in their personal and collective lives.

Outline of a Circumcision Ceremony (*Brit Milah*)

The child is brought into the room where the circumcision will take place and those present at the ceremony say:

> Barukh Ha-ba (Blessed is he that arrives).

The mohel (circumciser) takes the child and places him on a seat, saying:

> This is the seat of Elijah (*kise shel eliyyahu*)—may he be remembered for good!

The mohel places the child on the knees of a person, the sandek, who holds the infant in the course of the circumcision. The mohel then recites the following blessing:

> Blessed art thou, O Lord our God, King of the universe, who hast hallowed us by thy commandments, and hast given us command concerning the Circumcision.

The mohel cuts the foreskin and carries out the acts of periah (removal of the prepuce) and meṣiṣah (sucking blood from the wound), and the father of the child recites the following:

> Blessed art thou, O Lord our God, King of the universe, who hast hallowed us by thy commandments, and hast commanded us to make our sons enter into the covenant of Abraham our father.

Those present at the ceremony then say:

> Even as he has entered into the covenant, so may he enter into the Torah, the nuptial canopy and into good deeds.

The mohel recites the following:

> Blessed art thou, O Lord our God, King of the universe, who createst the fruit of the wine.

Blessed art thou, O Lord our God, King of the universe, who didst sanctify the well-beloved from birth setting thy statute in his flesh, and sealing his offspring with the sign of the holy covenant. On this account, O living God, our Portion and our Rock, give command to deliver from destruction thy dearly beloved People, for the sake of the covenant thou hast set in our bodies. Blessed art thou, O Lord, who dost establish thy covenant.

This is followed by another paragraph during which the child is named:

Our God and God of our fathers, preserve this child to his father and mother, and let his name be called in Israel____the son of____. Let the father rejoice in his offspring, and the mother be glad with the fruit of her body; as it is written [Prov. 23:25] "Let thy father and mother rejoice, and let her that bare thee be glad." And it is said [Ezek. 16:6] "And I passed by thee and I saw thee weltering in thy blood and I said unto thee 'In thy blood, live.' Yea, I said unto thee 'In thy blood, live.'. . ." This little boy [name is mentioned again], may he become great. Even as he has entered into the covenant, so may he enter into the Torah, the nuptial canopy and into good deeds.

The wine is then drunk, typically by the sandek, and the cup of wine is often passed to the mother.

SOURCE: Adapted from Joseph Hertz, *The Authorised Daily Prayer Book*, rev. ed. (New York: Bloch, 1948), pp. 1024–29.

Ceremony for Naming a Daughter (*Zeved Ha-bat*)

FROM THE SONG OF SONGS (2:14)

> Oh my dove in rocky clefts,
> In the covert of terrace high
> Let me hear thy countenance
> Let me hear thy voice
> For sweet is thy voice
> And thy countenance comely.

IF THE CHILD BE THE FIRSTBORN, ADD (SONG OF SONGS 6:9)

> One alone is my dove, my perfect one,
> The darling of her mother;
> The choice one of her that bore her;
> Daughters saw her, they acclaimed her,
> Queens and consorts, they sang her praises.

May He who blessed Sarah, Rebecca, Rachel, and Leah, and Miriam the prophetess, and Abigail, and Esther the queen the daughter of Abihayil, bless this darling babe. In happy augury may her name be called . . . daughter of . . . May He bless her to grow up in weal, health and happiness. May He give to her parents the joy of seeing her happily married, a radiant mother of children [literally, male children], rich in honor and joy to a ripe old age. May this be the will of God, and let us say, Amen.

SOURCE: Adapted from David de Sola Pool, ed. and trans., *The Book of Prayer: According to the Custom of the Spanish and Portuguese Jews* (New York: Union of Sephardi Congregations, 1941), p. 417. A more literal translation is found in Moses Gaster, ed., *The Book of Prayer and Order of Service According to the Custom of the Spanish and Portuguese Jews* (London: Henry Frowde, 1901), p. 180.

Tefillin and the Shma‘

The black leather boxes and their contents that constitute tefillin include four
short sections of the Torah written on pieces of parchment. These sections are
listed and briefly described below:

(1) Exodus 13:1–10 first states that all firstborn, of humans and of
domestic beasts, must be treated as holy. It later mentions the Exodus and the Passover festival, indicating that on that holiday
one should explain the Exodus to sons. Immediately thereafter,
the text, whose plain meaning is not fully clear, refers to something that should be a sign upon your hands and for memory between yours eyes "in order that the Torah of the Lord be in your
mouth."

(2) Exodus 13:11–16 repeats the above themes, and specifically requires the ritual redemption of the firstborn when the Israelites
reach the Land of Canaan. In v. 16, the Hebrew word *totafot*
(usually translated "frontlets"), between the eyes, appears instead of the word "memory" as in v. 9 (above).

(3) Deuteronomy 6:4–9 is the well-known Shma‘ Yisrael—Hear, O
Israel, the Lord is our God, the Lord is One—followed by verses
stressing constant rehearsal and instruction.

(4) Deuteronomy 11:13–21 outlines a system of reward and punishment in God's relation to Israel. After the promise and the
warning, this paragraph stresses the importance of repeating
God's teachings and of placing them on the hand and between
the eyes.

The last two sections from Deuteronomy also are included in daily prayer, both
in the morning and at night. In fact, they constitute a part of one of the two

central elements of the service. Together with a third passage taken from Numbers 15:37–41 (see below), these passages have become collectively known as the Shma.' The selection from Numbers requires Israelites to wear fringes on the corner of their garments in order to remember the commandments of God. Scholars have made comparisons between these fringes (tzitzit), to be worn by every man, and the garments worn by kohanim (priests) as a sign of their holy status.

NUMBERS 15:37–41

The Eternal spoke to Moses, saying: Speak to the Israelite people and instruct them to make for themselves fringes on the corners of their garments throughout the ages; let them attach a cord of blue to the fringe at each corner. That shall be your fringe; look at it and recall all the commandments of the Lord and observe them, so that you do not follow your heart and eyes in your lustful urge. Thus you shall be reminded to observe all my commandments and be holy to your God. I the Lord am your God, who brought you out of the land of Egypt, to be your God; I, the Lord your God.

The following table summarizes textual parallels and differences between ancient practices and the contemporary contents of tefillin and the Shma' Yisrael prayer, as discussed above and in chapter 3.

I	II	III	IV
Recitation of Kohanim in Temple (partial)	Ancient Tefillin (from Qumran)	Current Tefillin	Shma' Yisrael Prayer
Shma' Yisrael Prayer (IV)	Same as Current Tefillin (III)	Exod. 13:1–10	Deut. 6:4–9
Ten Commandments	Ten Commandments	Exod. 13:11–16	Deut. 11:13–21
		Deut. 6:4–9	Num.
		Deut. 11:13–21	15:37–41

Elements of the Marriage Service and Blessings

Some opening declarations and verses:

> Blessed be he that cometh in the name of the Lord; we bless you out of the house of the Lord.
>
> He who is mighty, blessed and great above all things, may he bless the groom and the bride.

Blessings of erusin (betrothal):

> Blessed art Thou, O Lord our God, King of the universe, who createst the fruit of the vine.
>
> Blessed art Thou, O Lord our God, King of the universe, who hast hallowed us by thy commandments, and hast given us command concerning forbidden marriages, and hast disallowed unto us those that are betrothed, but has sanctioned unto us such as are wedded to us by the rite of ḥuppah and the sacred rite of matrimony. Blessed art thou, O Lord, who hallowest thy people Israel by the rite of ḥuppah and the sacred rite of matrimony.

The groom and bride drink from the first cup of wine.
The groom then places the ring upon the forefinger of the bride's right hand and declares:

> Behold thou art consecrated unto me by this ring, according to the Law of Moses and of Israel.

The ketubba or a portion of it is read aloud:
The seven blessings of nesuin (matrimony) are recited:

> Blessed art thou, O Lord our God, King of the universe, who createst the fruit of the vine.
>
> Blessed art thou, O Lord our God, King of the universe, who hast created all things to thy glory.

Blessed art thou, O Lord our God, King of the universe, Creator of mankind.

Blessed art thou, O Lord our God, King of the universe, who hast made mankind in thine image, after thy likeness, and hast established through him, out of his very self, a perpetual edifice of life.

Blessed art thou, O Lord, Creator of mankind.

May she who was barren [Zion] be exceedingly glad and exult, when her children are gathered within her in joy. Blessed art thou, O Lord, who makest Zion joyful through her children.

Make these loved companions greatly to rejoice, even as of old thou didst gladden thy creatures in the garden of Eden. Blessed art thou, O Lord, who makest groom and bride to rejoice.

Blessed art thou, O Lord our God, King of the universe, who hast created joy and gladness, groom and bride, mirth and exultation, pleasure and delight, love, brotherhood, peace and companionship. Soon may there be heard in the cities of Judah, and in the streets of Jerusalem, the voice of joy and gladness, the voice of the groom and the voice of the bride, the jubilant voice of grooms from their canopies, and of youths from their feasts of song. Blessed art thou, O Lord, who makest the groom to rejoice with the bride.

The groom and bride drink from the second cup of wine.
The groom breaks the glass.

SOURCE: Adapted from Joseph Hertz, *The Authorised Daily Prayer Book,* rev. ed. (New York: Bloch, 1948), pp. 1008–13.

Notes

CHAPTER 1. BEING JEWISH

1. Stuart Schoenfeld, "Integration into the Group and Sacred Uniqueness: An Analysis of Adult Bat-Mitzvah," in *Persistence and Flexibility: Anthropological Perspectives on the American Jewish Experience*, ed. Walter P. Zenner (Albany: State University of New York Press, 1988), pp. 117–35; Joëlle Bahloul, "The Sephardi Family and the Challenge of Assimilation: Family Ritual and Ethnic Reproduction," in *Sephardi and Middle Eastern Jewries: History and Culture in the Modern Era*, ed. Harvey E. Goldberg (Bloomington: Indiana University Press; New York: Jewish Theological Seminary of America, 1996), pp. 312–24.

2. Steven M. Cohen and Arnold M. Eisen, *The Jew Within: Self, Family and Community in the United States* (Bloomington: Indiana University Press, 2000).

3. Baruch Kimmerling, *The Invention and Decline of Israeliness: State, Society, and the Military in Israel* (Berkeley: University of California Press, 2001).

4. See the discussion of "experience-near" in Clifford Geertz, " 'From the Native's Point of View': On the Nature of Anthropological Understanding," in *Local Knowledge: Further Essays in Interpretive Anthropology* (New York: Basic Books, 1983), ch. 3.

5. William Robertson Smith, *Lectures on the Religion of the Semites: The Fundamental Institutions* (London: Black, 1914), pp. 16–18; Émile Durkheim, *Les formes elementaires de la vie religieuse* (Paris: Alcan, 1912). A similar stance was adopted by Franz Boas, *The Mind of Primitive Man* (New York: Macmillan, 1916), pp. 229–30.

6. About thirty years ago, Clifford Geertz, *The Interpretation of Cultures* (New York: Basic Books, 1973), p. 10, suggested that ethnography was akin to reading a manuscript. At that time, anthropologists had begun to focus more regularly on the place of texts in societies, as exemplified in J. Goody, ed., *Lit-*

eracy in Traditional Societies (Cambridge: Cambridge University Press, 1968) and R. K. Jain, *Text and Context: The Social Anthropology of Tradition* (Philadelphia: Institute for the Study of Human Issues, 1977). Another collection, Harvey E. Goldberg, ed., *Judaism Viewed from Within and from Without: Anthropological Studies* (Albany: State University of New York Press, 1987), demonstrated the varied functions of texts in ongoing Jewish life. More recently, the field of cultural studies has highlighted textual analysis and has been placed in conjunction with Jewish life by Jonathan Boyarin and Daniel Boyarin, eds., *Jews and Other Differences: The New Jewish Cultural Studies* (Minneapolis: University of Minnesota Press, 1997).

7. See "On Judaism and Islam: The Antipathetic Symbiosis," *Judaism* 16, 4, special issue (Fall 1968).

8. Lancelot Addison, *The Present State of the Jews (More Particularly Relating to Those in Barbary)* (London, 1675). For a discussion of the context of the book, see Elliot Horowitz, " 'A Different Mode of Civility': Lancelot Addison on the Jews of Barbary," *Studies in Church History* 29 (1992): 309–25.

9. Abraham J. Heschel, *The Prophets* (Philadelphia: Jewish Publication Society of America, 1962 [orig. 1936]), p. 324.

10. William Robertson Smith, *The Prophets of Israel and Their Place in History. To the Close of the Eighth Century B.C.* (Edinburgh: Black, 1895); T. O. Beidelman, *W. Robertson Smith and the Sociological Study of Religion* (Chicago: University of Chicago Press, 1974); Harvey E. Goldberg, "The Voice of Jacob: Jewish Perspectives on Anthropology and the Study of the Bible," *Jewish Social Studies*, n.s., 2 (1995): 36–71.

11. James G. Frazer, *The Golden Bough* (London: Macmillan, 1890).

12. James G. Frazer, *Folklore in the Old Testament: Studies in Comparative Religion, Legend and Law*, vol. 1 (London: Macmillan, 1918), p. xi.

13. Louis Ginzberg, *Legends of the Jews* (Philadelphia: Jewish Publication Society of America, 1909–38), and Eli Ginzberg, *Keeper of the Law: Louis Ginzberg* (Philadelphia: Jewish Publication Society, 1966), p. 181.

14. Jacob Z. Lauterbach, *Studies in Jewish Law, Custom, and Folklore*, ed. B. J. Bamberger (New York: Ktav, 1970). His study of the custom of breaking a glass at weddings is discussed in chapter 4 of this volume.

15. Raphael Patai, *On Jewish Folklore* (Detroit: Wayne State University Press, 1983), p. 17; originally published in Hebrew in *Edoth* 1 (1945): 1–12.

16. Thomas Trautmann, *Aryans and British India* (Berkeley: University of California Press, 1997).

17. John Efron, *Defenders of the Race: Jewish Doctors and Race Science in Fin-de-Siècle Europe* (New Haven, Conn.: Yale University Press, 1994); B. Massin, "From Virchow to Fisher: Physical Anthropology and 'Modern Race Theories' in Wilhelmine Germany," in *Volkgeist as Method and Ethic: Essays on Boasian Ethnography and the German Anthropological Tradition*, ed. George Stocking Jr. (Madison: University of Wisconsin Press, 1996), pp. 79–154; Mitchell Hart, *Social Science and the Politics of Modern Jewish Identity* (Stanford, Calif.: Stanford University Press, 2000).

18. Franz Boas, *Race, Language and Culture* (New York: Macmillan, 1940).

19. Dov Noy, "Dr. Max Grunwald—The Founder of Jewish Folkloristics," in Max Grunwald, *Tales, Songs and Folkways of Sephardic Jews*, Folklore Research Center, 6 (Jerusalem: Magnes Press, 1982), pp. ix–xiv; Barbara Kirshenblatt-Gimblett, "Problems in the Early History of Jewish Folkloristics," *Proceedings of the Tenth World Congress of Jewish Studies*, Division D, 2 (1990): 21–31.

20. Efron, *Defenders of the Race.*

21. While hardly any scientific researchers would today defend racial theories, the concern with "race" and racism as social and cultural phenomena has, of course, not disappeared.

22. I later was to learn much more about the background of the moshav residents. See Mordecaï Ha-Cohen, *The Book of Mordechai: A Study of the Jews of Libya*, trans. and ed. H. E. Goldberg (London: Darf, 1993 [orig. 1980]).

23. Jacob Katz, *Tradition and Crisis: Jewish Society at the End of the Middle Ages* (New York: Free Press, 1961).

24. Bronislaw Malinowski, *Argonauts of the Western Pacific* (London: Routledge & Kegan Paul, 1950 [orig. 1922]).

25. Ruth Benedict, *Patterns of Culture* (London: Routledge & Kegan Paul, 1945 [orig. 1934]).

26. Umberto Cassuto, *Biblical and Oriental Studies*, 2 vols., trans. I. Abrahams (Jerusalem: Magnes Press, 1973–75); Yehezkel Kaufmann, *The History of the Israelite Religion: From Early Times until the End of the Second Temple Period*, 8 vols. (in Hebrew) (Jerusalem: Bialik; Tel Aviv: Dvir, 1948).

27. Goldberg, *Judaism Viewed*, ch. 1 (Introduction).

28. Mark Zborowski and Elizabeth Herzog, *Life Is with People: The Culture of the Shtetl* (New York: Schocken Books, 1996 [orig. 1952]); see the introduction by Barbara Kirshenblatt-Gimblett.

29. Melford Spiro with the assistance of A. G. Spiro, *Children of the Kibbutz* (Cambridge, Mass.: Harvard University Press, 1958).

30. Alex Weingrod, *Reluctant Pioneers* (Ithaca, N.Y.: Cornell University Press, 1966); Dorothy Willner, *Nation-Building and Community in Israel* (Princeton, N.J.: Princeton University Press, 1969); Shlomo Deshen and Moshe Shokeid, *The Predicament of Homecoming* (Ithaca, N.Y.: Cornell University Press, 1974).

31. Joëlle Bahloul, *Le culte de la table dressée: Rites et traditions de la table juive algerienne* (Paris: Métailié, 1983). The passage quoted is translated in Goldberg, *Judaism Viewed*, pp. 9–10.

32. Goldberg, *Judaism Viewed*; Jack Kugelmass, *Between Two Worlds: Ethnographic Essays on American Jewry* (Ithaca, N.Y.: Cornell University Press, 1988); Zenner, ed., *Persistence and Flexibility.*

33. For an overview of anthropological work in Israel, see Orit Abuhav, Esther Hertzog, Harvey E. Goldberg, and Emanuel Marx, eds., *Yisrael: Antropologia Meqomit* [A Reader in Israeli Anthropology] (Tel Aviv: Tcherikover, 1998).

34. James Boon, *Other Tribes, Other Scribes: Symbolic Anthropology in the Comparative Study of Cultures, Histories, Religions, and Texts* (Cambridge: Cambridge University Press, 1982).

35. Eric R. Wolf, *Peasants* (Englewood Cliffs, N.J.: Prentice-Hall, 1966).

36. Robert Redfield, "The Social Organization of Tradition," *Far Eastern Quarterly* 15 (1955): 13–22.

37. E. E. Evans-Pritchard, *Nuer Religion* (Oxford: Oxford University Press, 1956); Meyer Fortes, *Oedipus and Job in West African Religion* (Cambridge: Cambridge University Press, 1959); Edmund Leach, "Lévi-Strauss in the Garden of Eden," *Transactions of the New York Academy of Sciences* 23 (1961): 386–96; Victor Turner, *Chihamba: The White Spirit: A Ritual Drama of the Ndembu*, Rhodes-Livingstone Papers, no. 33 (Manchester: Manchester University Press on behalf of the Rhodes-Livingstone Institute, 1962); id., "Muchona the Hornet, Interpreter of Religion," in *The Company of Man: Twenty Portraits of Anthropological Informants*, ed. J. Casagrande (New York: Harper, 1960), pp. 333–55, esp. p. 338; Mary Douglas, *Purity and Danger: An Analysis of Concepts of Pollution and Taboo* (New York: Praeger, 1966).

38. On the ancient period, see Jacob Neusner, *The Idea of Purity in Ancient Judaism, with a Critique and Commentary by Mary Douglas* (Leiden: Brill, 1973); Gillian Feeley-Harnik, *The Lord's Table: The Meaning of Food in Early Judaism and Christianity* (Washington, D.C.: Smithsonian Institution Press, 1994); Howard Eilberg-Schwartz, *The Savage in Judaism: An Anthropology of Israelite Religion and Ancient Judaism* (Bloomington: Indiana University Press, 1990); Nissan Rubin, *The Beginning of Life: Rites of Birth, Circumcision, and Redemption of the Firstborn in the Talmud and Midrash* (in Hebrew) (Tel Aviv: Hakibbutz Hameuchad, 1995); and Lawrence A. Hoffman, *Covenant of Blood: Circumcision and Gender in Rabbinic Judaism* (Chicago: University of Chicago Press, 1996). The latter study also deals with the medieval period, as does Ivan Marcus, *Rituals of Childhood: Jewish Acculturation in Medieval Europe* (New Haven, Conn.: Yale University Press, 1996). A very recent contribution to that period is Alick Isaacs, "An Anthropological and Historical Study of the Role of the Synagogue in Ashkenazi Jewish Life in the Middle Ages" (Ph.D. diss., Hebrew University, 2002). Sylvie-Anne Goldberg, *Crossing the Jabbok: Illness and Death in Ashkenazi Judaism in Sixteenth- through Nineteenth-Century Prague*, trans. Carol Cosman (Berkeley: University of California Press, 1996 [orig. 1989]), reflects a French approach to the study of *mentalités* in early modern Europe.

39. S. D. Goitein, *A Mediterranean Society: The Jewish Communities of the Arab World as Portrayed in the Documents of the Cairo Geniza* (Berkeley: University of California Press, 1967–93), vol. 3: *The Family*, p. ix; vol. 5: *The Individual*, pp. 498–501; Orit Abuhav, "E. Brauer and R. Patai: Pioneer Ethnologists and the Anthropological Study of Jews in Palestine" (in Hebrew), *Jerusalem Studies in Jewish Folklore* 22 (2002): 155–73.

40. Laurence Loeb, *Outcaste: Jewish Life in Southern Iran* (New York: Gordon & Breach, 1977); Shlomo Deshen, *The Mellah Society: Jewish Community Life in Sherifian Morocco* (Chicago: University of Chicago Press, 1989); Harvey E. Goldberg, *Jewish Life in Muslim Libya: Rivals and Relatives* (Chicago: University of Chicago Press, 1990); Joëlle Bahloul, *The Architecture of Memory: A Jewish-Muslim Household in Colonial Algeria, 1937–1962* (New York: Cambridge University Press, 1996); Shlomo Deshen and Walter P. Zenner, eds.,

Jews among Muslims: Communities in the Precolonial Middle East (New York: New York University Press; Houndmills, Hants, U.K.: Macmillan, 1996); Walter P. Zenner, *A Global Community: Jews from Aleppo* (Detroit: Wayne State University Press, 2000).

41. Hoffman, *Covenant of Blood*.

42. The term *yoreh de'ah* implies deciding and instructing.

43. The term *even ha'ezer* is reminiscent of the phrase *'ezer ke-negdo* in Gen. 2:18 describing woman as a helpmate to man.

44. TB *Soṭah* 14a.

45. Midrash *Shir ha-Shirim Rabbah* 1:10. All these books were written much later than the period of Solomon even though the texts link themselves to him. See also, in this volume, chapter 6, "Modern Death," on the case of the talmudic Rabbi Yosef who initiated a celebration when he reached his sixtieth year.

46. *Avot*, Ethics of the Fathers 5:21, quoted in Marcus, *Rituals of Childhood*, pp. 43–44. The inserted passage is also ancient, but its inclusion in *Avot* is medieval.

47. Harvey E. Goldberg, *Cave-Dwellers and Citrus Growers: A Jewish Community in Libya and Israel* (Cambridge: Cambridge University Press, 1972).

48. Adiel Schremer, "Men's Age at Marriage in Jewish Palestine of the Hellenistic and Roman Periods" (in Hebrew), *Zion* 61 (1996): 45–66.

49. Aaron Berechia de Modena, *Ma'avar Yabboq* (Vilnius: Ram, 1896). See also the discussion in chapter 6 of this volume of S.-A. Goldberg, *Crossing the Jabbok*.

50. This, of course, is a simplified portrait. Spanish Jews were heavily influenced by the Muslim presence in Spain before the Christian reconquest, and the Muslim Ottoman Empire ruled over large Christian populations in southeastern Europe.

51. On the Karaites, see Salo W. Baron, *Social and Religious History of the Jews*, 2d ed., rev. (New York: Columbia University Press; Philadelphia: Jewish Publication Society of America, 1952–83), 5: 209–85; Zvi Ankori, *Karaites in Byzantium: The Formative Years, 970–1100* (New York: Columbia University Press, 1959); Gerson D. Cohen, trans. and ed., *The Book of Tradition (Sefer ha-Qabbalah)* by Abraham Ibn Daud (Philadelphia: Jewish Publication Society of America, 1967), pp. xliii–l. Except for a few brief mentions (chapter 4, "Marriage, Women, and Menstruation"; chapter 6, n. 32; chapter 7, "Israel and Diaspora Links"), this book does not deal with the Karaites.

52. Goldberg, *Jewish Life in Muslim Libya*, pp. 92–94. On the Great Festival in general, see Gustave Von Grunebaum, *Muhammedan Festivals* (New York: Henry Schuman, 1951).

53. Based on Gen. 17:12 and 25. There is no set required time for Muslim circumcision; it may take place any time during childhood.

54. David Cohen, *Le parler arabe des Juifs de Tunis: Textes et documents linquistiques et ethnographiques* (Paris: Mouton, 1964), pp. 131–32.

55. For an analysis of such practices in a Christian context, see Hagar Salamon, *The Hyena People: Ethiopian Jews in Christian Ethiopia* (Berkeley: University of California Press, 1999).

56. Susan Sered, " 'She Perceives Her Work to Be Rewarding': Jewish Women in Cross-Cultural Perspective," in *Feminist Perspectives on Jewish Studies*, ed. Lynn Davidman and Shelly Tenenbaum (New Haven, Conn.: Yale University Press, 1994), pp. 169–90.

57. Frazer, *Folklore*, vol. 1.

58. It might be noted that the term "patriarchy" had almost disappeared from anthropology as analytically useful, because it had been defined as the opposite of "matriarchy" and researchers concluded that there is no evidence that matriarchal societies ever existed. The current revival of the term reflects feminist consciousness.

59. Carol Delaney, "The Meaning of Paternity and the Virgin Birth Debate," *Man*, n.s., 21 (1986): 494–513. The literature on monotheism and women is vast. An argument that the Hebrew Bible typically treats men and women in the same moral-religious framework is found in Tikva Frymer-Kenski, *In the Wake of the Goddesses* (New York: Free Press, 1992).

60. Ilana Pardes, *Countertraditions in the Bible: A Feminist Approach* (Cambridge, Mass.: Harvard University Press, 1992), ch. 6.

61. Mordechai Friedman, "Tamar, a Symbol of Life: The 'Killer Wife' Superstition in the Bible and Jewish Tradition," *AJS Review* 15 (1990): 23–62.

62. Eilberg-Schwartz, *Savage in Judaism*; Hoffman, *Covenant of Blood*.

63. Jacob Milgrom, *The Anchor Bible: Leviticus 1–16* (New York: Doubleday, 1991).

64. See in this volume chapter 4, "Marriage, Women, and Menstruation," and the study of Judaism in the Roman period by Miriam Peskowitz, *Spinning Fantasies: Rabbis, Gender, and History* (Berkeley: University of California Press, 1997).

65. A *geniza* is a storage place in which ritual texts or other documents containing God's name are stored until they are properly buried. See in this volume chapter 6, "Death, Distinction, and Descent," and the Goitein citation in n. 39 above.

66. Goitein, *Mediterranean Society*, vol. 3.

67. Shaye J. D. Cohen, "Purity, Piety, and Polemic: Medieval Rabbinic Denunciations of 'Incorrect' Purification Practices," in *Women and Water: Menstruation in Jewish Life and Law*, ed. Rahel R. Wasserfall (Hanover, N.H.: Brandeis University Press, 1999), pp. 82–100, states: "The Judaism of Jewish women of pre-modern times is hidden from us." He also notes that occasionally "the veil of secrecy is lifted somewhat" (p. 83).

68. Chava Weissler, *Voices of the Matriarchs: Listening to the Prayers of Early Modern Jewish Women* (Boston: Beacon Press, 1998).

69. Joseph Chetrit, *The Written Judeo-Arabic Poetry in North Africa* (in Hebrew) (Jerusalem: Misgav Yerushalayim, 1994), pp. 33–35.

70. Susan S. Sered, *Women as Ritual Experts: The Religious Lives of Elderly Jewish Women in Jerusalem* (New York: Oxford University Press, 1992).

71. Rahel Wasserfall, "Introduction," in *Women and Water,* ed. id., pp. 1–18.

72. Bahloul, *Le culte de la table dressée.*

73. Harvey E. Goldberg, "Family and Community in Sephardic North Africa: Historical and Anthropological Perspectives," in *The Jewish Family: Metaphor and Memory,* ed. D. Kraemer (New York: Oxford University Press, 1989), pp. 137–38.

74. Tamar El-Or, *Educated and Ignorant: Ultraorthodox Jewish Women and their World* (Boulder, Colo.: Lynne Rienner, 1994), ch. 2; id., "Rabbi Akiva and Rabbi Ben Zakkai in an Israeli Classroom," in *The Life of Judaism,* ed. Harvey E. Goldberg (Berkeley: University of California Press, 2001), pp. 213–25.

75. See also Steven M. Cohen and Paula E. Hyman, eds., *The Jewish Family: Myths and Reality* (New York: Holmes & Meier, 1986).

76. Grace Harris, "Concepts of Individual, Self, and Person in Description and Analysis," *American Anthropologist* 91 (1989): 599–612.

77. Arjun Appadurai, *Modernity at Large: Cultural Dimensions of Globalization* (Minneapolis: University of Minnesota Press, 1996), ch. 2.

78. Marcus, *Rituals of Childhood.*

CHAPTER 2. BEGINNINGS

1. Benedict de Spinoza, *The Chief Works of Benedict de Spinoza,* trans. and with an introduction by R. H. M. Elwes (New York: Dover, 1951), pp. 55–56. The significance of circumcision to Marranos in Amsterdam in the seventeenth century is discussed by Miriam Bodian, *Hebrews of the Portuguese Nation: Conversos and Community in Early Modern Amsterdam* (Bloomington: Indiana University Press, 1997), pp. 33, 97–99, 112–13.

2. A circumcision in a similar setting is described in M. Y. Ohel, "The Circumcision Ceremony among Immigrants from Tripolitania in the Israeli Village of Dalton," *Israel Annals of Psychiatry and Related Disciplines* 11 (1973): 66–71.

3. Arnold van Gennep, *The Rites of Passage,* trans. M. B. Vizedom and G. L. Caffee (London: Routledge & Kegan Paul, 1960 [orig. 1909]), p. 10.

4. Henri A. Junod, *The Life of a South African Tribe,* vol. 1: *Social Life* (New Hyde Park, N.Y.: University Books, 1962), pp. 71–94.

5. Ibid., p. 80.

6. Below I use the name that accords with the portion of the story discussed (and similarly with Sarai who becomes Sarah).

7. See *The Jewish Encyclopedia* (New York: Funk & Wagnalls, 1903), 4: 92–102, s.v. "Circumcision."

8. Michael Fox, "The Sign of the Covenant: Circumcision in the Light of the Priestly *'ot* Etiologies," *Revue biblique* 81 (1974): 557–96.

9. See, e.g., John Skinner, ed., *The International Critical Commentary: Genesis,* 2d ed. (Edinburgh: Clark, 1930), pp. lviii–lxv, 289–90.

10. Fox, "Sign," p. 595; emphasis in the original.

11. See Howard Eilberg-Schwartz, *The Savage in Judaism: An Anthropology of Israelite Religion and Ancient Judaism* (Bloomington: Indiana Univer-

sity Press, 1990), who makes this argument stressing the patrilineal organization of the priesthood. For another perspective, see Harvey E. Goldberg, "Cambridge in the Land of Canaan: Descent, Alliance, Circumcision, and Instruction in the Bible," *Journal of the Ancient Near Eastern Society* 24 (1996): 9–34.

12. This discussion follows Shunia Bendor, *The Social Structure in Ancient Israel: The Institution of the Family (BEIT'AB) from the Settlement to the End of the Monarchy* (Jerusalem: Simor, 1996).

13. See the story of Noah (Gen. 9:8–17) and the first covenant with Abram (Gen. 15:7–21).

14. 1 Sam. 20:29, 42.

15. Mary Douglas, *Natural Symbols: Explorations in Cosmology* (New York: Vintage Books, 1973).

16. Claude Lévi-Strauss, "Exode sur *Exode*," *L'Homme* 28 (1988): 13–23; Jacob Lassner, "The Covenant of the Prophets: Muslim Texts, Jewish Subtexts," *AJS Review* 15 (1990): 226.

17. Chapter 24 of Genesis describes in detail how Rebecca was found for Isaac, and we learn in Gen. 26:34–35 that Esau's marriage to Hittite women was a "source of bitterness" to his parents.

18. After the selection of Jacob, Esau moves closer to the central line of Abraham, taking a daughter of Ishmael as an additional wife (Gen. 28:9). See also N. Wander, "Structure, Contradiction, and 'Resolution' in Mythology: Father's Brother's Daughter Marriage and the Treatment of Women in Genesis 11–50," *Journal of the Ancient Near Eastern Society* 13 (1981): 89.

19. For example, Gen. 30:2 and Ruth 4:13.

20. Following J. P. Fokkelman, "Genesis," in *The Literary Guide to the Bible,* ed. Robert Alter and Frank Kermode (Cambridge, Mass.: Harvard University Press, 1987), p. 43. For a different view of Abraham, and the understanding of conception and birth, see Carol Delaney, *Abraham on Trial: The Social Legacy of Biblical Myth* (Princeton, N.J.: Princeton University Press, 1998).

21. Baruch M. Bokser, *The Origins of the Seder: The Passover Rite and Early Rabbinic Judaism* (Berkeley: University of California Press, 1984).

22. Goldberg, "Cambridge in the Land of Canaan."

23. The phrase "good deeds" may have been added after the first two items. See Nissan Rubin, *The Beginning of Life: Rites of Birth, Circumcision and Redemption of the Firstborn in the Talmud and Midrash* (in Hebrew) (Tel Aviv: Hakibbutz Hameuchad, 1995), p. 107 n. 176; Lawrence A. Hoffman, *Covenant of Blood: Circumcision and Gender in Rabbinic Judaism* (Chicago: University of Chicago Press, 1996), p. 122.

24. There are other versions of this passage, particularly within Sephardi groups, such as thanking God for *brit ve-torah,* "the covenant [of circumcision] and Torah." Some recent Sephardi liturgical books instruct women to omit the passage "for the covenant which You have sealed in our flesh." See also the discussion of the link between circumcision and the ability to study Torah in chapter 5, "Popular Pilgrimage," in this volume.

25. E. Mary Smallwood, "The Legislation of Hadrian and Antoninus Pius against Circumcision," *Latomus* 18 (1959): 334–47, and her addendum, *Latomus* 20 (1961): 93–96. See also, more recently, Shaye J. D. Cohen, *The Beginnings of Jewishness: Boundaries, Varieties, Uncertainties* (Berkeley: University of California Press, 1999), p. 46.

26. Gal. 3:27.

27. Rubin, *Beginning*, pp. 101–2.

28. TB *Yebamot* 64b.

29. Gal. 3:28–29.

30. Hoffman, *Covenant*, ch. 8.

31. Herbert Dobrinsky, *A Treasury of Sephardic Laws and Customs* (Hoboken, N.J.: Ktav, 1988), p. 5.

32. David Cohen, *Le parler arabe des Juifs de Tunis: Textes et documents linquistiques et ethnographiques* (Paris: Mouton, 1964), pp. 21–25.

33. Peninnah Schram, *Tales of Elijah the Prophet* (Northvale, N.J.: Jason Aronson, 1991).

34. *Pirqei de-Rabbi Eli'ezer*, trans. and ed. G. Friedlander (New York: Hermon, 1965), ch. 29.

35. *Pirqei de-Rabbi Eli'ezer*, p. 214.

36. Victor Turner, "Myth and Symbol," in *International Encyclopedia of the Social Sciences*, 10: 576–81.

37. TB *Pesaḥim* 101a, comment of the *Tosafot*, ad loc. (beginning with *de-akhalu*).

38. TB *Qiddushin* 29a.

39. I presume the trend to perform circumcisions in the synagogue was not always an ironclad norm. Jacob Katz has, for example, shown the impact of climate on the norms of Sabbath observance.

40. I am indebted to Elisheva Baumgarten for guidance in the following discussion. For a recent analysis of women in relation to circumcisions in the medieval period, see her "Mothers and Children: The Medieval Jewish Experience" (Ph.D. diss., Hebrew University, Jerusalem, 2000), pp. 104–53. See also Hoffman, *Covenant*, pp. 198–207, and Avraham Grossman, *Pious and Rebellious: Jewish Women in Europe in the Middle Ages* (in Hebrew) (Jerusalem: Shazar Center, 2001), pp. 321–23.

41. Herman Pollack, *Jewish Folkways in Germanic Lands (1648–1806)* (Cambridge, Mass.: MIT Press, 1971), pp. 23–24, 215 n. 52.

42. Daniel Sperber, "The Custom of Drinking Wine during Circumcision" (in Hebrew), *Milet* 1 (1983): 221–29.

43. The Hebrew for "send," *shager*, suggests that the mother is at some distance from the main proceedings.

44. Understanding the separation of the activities of men and women into the public and private spheres, respectively, has provided basic insights into the determinants of the status of women. See Sherry Ortner, "Is Male to Female as Nature is to Culture?" in *Woman, Culture, and Society*, ed. M. Rosaldo and L. Lamphere (Stanford, Calif.: Stanford University Press, 1974), pp. 67–87, and Michelle Rosaldo's introduction to that volume, pp. 1–15. More recent work

has refined the lines of thought presented therein. With regard to Jewish societies, see Lynn Davidman and Shelly Tenenbaum, eds., *Feminist Perspectives on Jewish Studies* (New Haven, Conn.: Yale University Press, 1994), pp. 10–12, 14 n. 12, and the article in that volume by Judith Hauptman, "Feminist Perspectives on Rabbinic Texts," p. 45.

45. It seems that the term *ba'alat ha-brit* disappeared from usage, and the male term *ba'al brit* came to be applied to the sandek, the mohel, or the father.

46. Elliot Horowitz, "The Eve of Circumcision: A Chapter in the History of Jewish Nightlife," *Journal of Social History* 23 (1989): 45–69; Uriel Weinreich, "Mapping a Culture," *Columbia University Forum* 6, 3 (1963): 17–21; H. Pollack, *Jewish Folkways*, pp. 19–20.

47. Cited in Horowitz, "Eve," p. 47.

48. In which the commandment of circumcision appears.

49. See chapter 3 in this volume, "Adult Study."

50. Mordecaï Ha-Cohen, *Higgid Mordecaï: Histoire de la Libye et de ses Juifs* (in Hebrew), ed. and annotated by H. E. Goldberg (Jerusalem: Institut Ben-Zvi, 1978), p. 272.

51. Aaron Berechia de Modena, *Ma'avar Yabboq* (Vilnius: Ram, 1896 [orig. 1626]), p. 255. On the *Ma'avar Yabboq*, see chapter 6 in this volume.

52. Horowitz's analysis may be relevant to the custom of having a celebration in connection with the Friday night meal on the Sabbath before a circumcision. Described in some sources as *shabbat zakhor*, the "Sabbath of remembrance," and in others as *shalom zakhor*, "greetings, male!" (Pollack, *Jewish Folkways*, pp. 20, 102–3), it was also designated in Yiddish in recent times as *sholem zukher*. There may be some connection between the latter terms and the talmudic statement (TB *Niddah* 31b) that when a male (*zakhar*) comes to the world, peace (*shalom*) comes to the world. See also the mention of the unusual celebration in Tunis, in chapter 3 in this volume, "Other Torah Education Ceremonies."

53. Hoffman, *Covenant*.

54. See the discussion on the study of women in chapter 1 of this volume.

55. See above, "Circumcision after the Bible." A fifteenth-century Haggadah from southern Germany has an illustration of Zipporah circumcising her son (Second Nuremberg Haggadah, p. 13b, Schocken Library, Jerusalem, Ms. 24087). There is a halakhic basis for permitting women to act as circumcisers, and in the Middle Ages in Ashkenaz, this actually took place. See Rubin, *Beginning*, pp. 88–89; Maimonides, *Yad ha-Ḥazaqah*, *Ahavah* (Love of God), *Milah* (Circumcision) 2:1; Grossman, *Pious and Rebellious*, pp. 331–32.

56. Elliot Wolfson, "Circumcision, Vision of God, and Textual Interpretation: From Midrashic Trope to Mystical Symbol," *History of Religions* 27 (1987): 189–215, pp. 201–2; Daniel Boyarin, " 'This We Know to be the Carnal Israel': Circumcision and the Erotic Life of God and Israel," *Critical Inquiry* 18 (1992): 474–505; Gil Anidjar, "On the (Under)Cutting Edge: Does Jewish Memory Need Sharpening?" in *Jews and Other Differences: The New Jewish Cultural Studies*, ed. Jonathan Boyarin and Daniel Boyarin (Minneapolis: University of Minnesota Press, 1997), pp. 360–96.

57. Dobrinsky, *Treasury*, p. 7.

58. Bleeding from the male sex organ consciously or unconsciously evokes associations of menstruation. Bruno Bettelheim, *Symbolic Wounds: Puberty Rites and the Envious Male* (London: Thames & Hudson, 1955); Robert V. Burton and J. W. M. Whiting, "The Absent Father and Cross-Sex Identity," *Merrill-Palmer Quarterly* 7 (1961): 85–95.

59. Hoffman, *Covenant*, pp. 90–92.

60. David Wachtel, " 'In Your Bloods Live': The Exegetical, Ritual and Liturgical History of Ezekiel 16:6 in Medieval Ashkenaz" (paper presented at the Twelfth World Congress of Jewish Studies, Jerusalem, 1997).

61. For example, Isa. 1:21; Lam. 1:1.

62. A targum often constitutes a commentary or a midrash on a text and not only a translation.

63. That interpretation appears in other rabbinic sources as well. See Wachtel, " 'In Your Bloods Live.' "

64. Gillian Feeley-Harnik, *The Lord's Table: The Meaning of Food in Early Judaism and Christianity* (Washington, D.C.: Smithsonian Institution, 1994). See also Bokser, *Origins*, pp. 25–28.

65. Hoffman, *Covenant*, ch. 8.

66. Yosef Tabory, *The Passover Ritual throughout the Generations* (in Hebrew) (Tel Aviv: Hakibbutz Hameuchad, 1996).

67. Israel Yuval, *"Two Nations in Your Womb": Perceptions of Jews and Christians* (in Hebrew) (Tel Aviv: Am Oved, 2000).

68. Avraham Grossman, "The Blood Libel and the Blood of Circumcision: An Ashkenazic Custom that Disappeared in the Middle Ages," *Jewish Quarterly Review* 86 (1995): 171–74.

69. See Yuval, *"Two Nations in Your Womb,"* p. 116, who also states that the practice of spilling out wine began in the Ashkenazi Middle Ages. For a modern example, from Egypt, of linking the ancient Egyptians to contemporary Gentiles, see Jacqueline Kahanoff, *Essais* (in Hebrew) (Tel Aviv: Hadar, 1978), pp. 20–23. Kahanoff recalls how, as a child, she hesitated to tell a non-Jewish friend about the ten plagues.

70. Hillel J. Kieval, "Representation and Knowledge in Medieval and Modern Accounts of Jewish Ritual Murder," *Jewish Social Studies*, n.s., 1 (1994): 52–71; Daniel Sperber, *Minhagei Yisrael: Meqorot ve-toladot* [Jewish Customs: Sources and History] (Jerusalem: Mosad Ha-Rav Kook, 1989–95), 3: 81–82. Joseph Guttman points out that near the verse "Pour out Thy wrath . . ." in a fourteenth-century Sephardic Haggadah (a book with the Passover seder liturgy), "a winged angel, or simply a hand, pouring a cup full of blood on a group of assembled people" appears. See his "The Messiah of the Seder: A Fifteenth-Century Motif in Jewish Art," in *Essays in Honor of Refael Mahler*, ed. Shmuel Yavin (Tel Aviv: Merhaviah, 1974), pp. 35–36.

71. Menahem Kasher, *Haggadah Shelemah* (Jerusalem: Torah Shelemah, 1955), p. 180.

72. Joseph Kafih, *Jewish Life in Sanʿa* (in Hebrew) (Jerusalem: Ben-Zvi Institute, 1969), pp. 22–23.

73. The verse that immediately follows (Ezek. 16:7) became part of the Haggadah earlier, seemingly to supplement another Bible-based explanation. It is likely, however, that its insertion was a way of hinting at verse 16:6—with the words "in your bloods live"—without putting them down "on paper." The technique of citing one verse in order to bring another verse in its immediate vicinity to the reader's (or listener's) attention is employed in the Midrash. See Yonah Fraenkel, *Darkei ha-aggadah ve-ha-midrash,* 2 vols. (Givatayyim: Masada, 1991), pp. 247–48.

74. Vital resided in various places such as Safed, Jerusalem, and Damascus. A disciple of the renowned kabbalist Isaac Luria, Vital was one of those who helped turn Luria's innovations into widespread Jewish practice. See chapter 3, n. 80.

75. Daniel Lasker, "Transubstantiation, Elijah's Chair, Plato, and the Jewish-Christian Debate," *Revue des Études juives* 143 (1984): 31–58.

76. See Hoffman, *Covenant,* pp. 17–22, on the difference between official and public meanings of rituals.

77. A. J. Wensinck, "Circumcision," in *The Encyclopedia of Islam,* 2d ed. (Leiden: Brill, 1986), 5: 20–22; van Gennep, *Rites,* pp. 70–71.

78. A. Cesàro, *L'Arabo parlato a Tripoli* (Rome, 1939), p. 207; Harvey E. Goldberg, *Jewish Life in Muslim Libya: Rivals and Relatives* (Chicago: University of Chicago Press, 1990), pp. 91–92. Among Islamic scholars an opinion exists that one should circumcise on the seventh day, and this is interpreted by some as the seventh day not counting the day of birth, namely, the eighth day. See Wensinck, "Circumcision," p. 20.

79. Jacob Katz, *Halacha in Straits: Obstacles to Orthodoxy at Its Inception* (in Hebrew) (Jerusalem: Magnes Press, 1992), pp. 123–83.

80. Stephen Sharot, *Judaism: A Sociology* (New York: Holmes & Meier; Newton Abbot, U.K.: David & Charles, 1976), pp. 77–78.

81. Katz, *Halacha,* p. 123.

82. Michael A. Meyer, "*Berit Milah* within the History of the Reform Movement," in *Berit Milah in the Reform Context,* ed. Lewis Barth (New York: Central Conference of American Rabbis, 1990), pp. 141–51.

83. Even though Christianity rejected circumcision, the awareness that Jesus, as a Jew, was circumcised was the focus of some religious attention in Europe. See Marc Shell, "The Holy Foreskin; or, Money, Relics, and Judeo-Christianity," in *Jews and Other Differences,* ed. J. Boyarin and D. Boyarin (Minneapolis: University of Minnesota Press, 1997), pp. 345–59.

84. Katz, *Halacha,* pp. 150–52.

85. Mark Zborowski and Elizabeth Herzog, *Life Is with People: The Culture of the Shtetl* (New York: Schocken Books, 1996), p. 319.

86. David Gollaher, *Circumcision: The World's Most Controversial Surgery* (New York: Basic Books, 2000).

87. Meyer, "*Berit*"; Rachel Michaeli, "Painful Choice," *Haaretz,* Features, 2 November 1997, p. 5. Although it is rare, opposition to circumcision exists among some Israeli Jews as well.

88. Thomas Goldenberg, "Medical Issues and *Berit Milah*," in *Berit Milah in the Reform Context*, ed. Lewis Barth (New York: Central Conference of American Rabbis, 1990), pp. 195–96, cites the relevant literature.

89. Mary Douglas, *Purity and Danger* (London: Routledge & Kegan Paul, 1966), p. 29. The quip is not far-fetched: see Gollaher, *Circumcision*, and Mitchell Hart, "Moses the Microbiologist: Judaism and Social Hygiene in the Work of Alfred Nossig," *Jewish Social Studies*, n.s., 2 (1995): 72–97.

90. Shulamit Magnus, "*Simḥat Lev:* Celebrating a Birth," in *Lifecycles: Jewish Women on Life Passages and Personal Milestones*, ed. Debra Orenstein (Woodstock, Vt.: Jewish Lights Publishing, 1994), pp. 68–75; Margaret Sandel, "*Brit Milah:* An Inscription of Social Power," *Reconstructionist* 61, 2 (1996): 49–58.

91. Lisa B. Moss, "A Painful Case," *Tikkun* 5, 5 (1990): 70–72; id., "Circumcision: A Jewish Inquiry," *Midstream* 38, 1 (1992): 20–23; Daniel Landes and Sheryl Robbin, "Gainful Pain," *Tikkun* 5, 5 (1990): 72–74; Esther Raul-Friedman, "Rebuttal—Circumcision: A Jewish Legacy," *Midstream* 38, 4 (1992): 31–33.

92. Michael Herzbrun, "Circumcision: The Pain of the Fathers," *CCAR Journal* 38, 4 (1991): 1–13.

93. Hagar Salamon, *The Hyena People: Ethiopian Jews in Christian Ethiopia* (Berkeley: University of California Press, 1999). See also Steven Kaplan, *The Beta Israel (Falasha) in Ethiopia: From Earliest Times to the Twentieth Century* (New York: New York University Press, 1992).

94. On conversion, see chapter 7 in this volume, "Israel and the Diaspora."

95. Ruth Westheimer and Steven Kaplan, *Surviving Salvation: The Ethiopian Jewish Family in Transition* (New York: New York University Press, 1992).

96. Esther Hertzog, *Bureaucrats and Immigrants in an Absorption Center* (in Hebrew) (Tel Aviv: Tscherikover, 1998).

97. N. Grisaru, S. Lezer, and R. H. Belmaker, "Ritual Female Genital Surgery among Ethiopian Jews," *Archives of Sexual Behavior* 26 (1997): 211–15.

98. Karungari Kiragu, "Female Genital Mutilation: A Reproductive Health Concern," Supplement to *Population Reports* [Meeting the Needs of Young Adults, ser. J, no. 41] 23, 3 (1995): 1–4; Christine J. Walley, " 'Searching for Voices': Feminism, Anthropology, and the Global Debate over Female Genital Operations," *Cultural Anthropology* 12 (1997): 405–38.

99. Jonathan P. Berkey, "Circumcision Circumscribed: Female Excision and Cultural Accommodation," *International Journal of Middle East Studies* 28 (1996): 19–38. Engaging in speculation, it is possible to understand Genesis 17 as intending to exclude female circumcision. This speculation assumes that the female and male procedures were then seen as parallel (and spoken of similarly), for which no evidence exists one way or the other. Rabbinic literature considers the theoretical possibility of female circumcision. See Rubin, *Beginning*, pp. 100, 179 nn. 131–34. See also Shaye J. D. Cohen, "Why Aren't Jewish Women Circumcised?" *Gender and History* 9 (1997): 560–78.

100. Berkey, "Circumcision," pp. 35–36, n. 27.

101. Jomo Kenyatta, *Facing Mt. Kenya: The Tribal Life of the Gikuyu* (New York: Vintage Books, n.d.), p. 128.

102. Abdellah Hammoudi and Lawrence Rosen, "Islam Doesn't Sanction Female Circumcision," letter, *New York Times*, 5 February 1993.

103. "Egypt to Appeal Ruling on Genital Cutting," *New York Times* (International), 12 July 1997, p. L5.

104. Orenstein, *Lifecycles*, pp. 1–15.

105. Raphael Patai, *On Jewish Folklore* (Detroit: Wayne State University Press, 1983), ch. 21; Susan Sered, "Religious Rituals and Secular Ritual: Interpenetrating Models of Childbirth in a Modern, Israeli Context," *Sociology of Religion* 54 (1993): 101–14.

106. Sperber, *Minhagei Yisrael*, 3: 126–31, cites this custom from the writings of Ḥ. Y. D. Azulai, a Palestinian rabbi who traveled widely in the Jewish world in the eighteenth century. See also Miriam Russo-Katz, "Childbirth," in *Sephardi Jews in the Ottoman Empire: Aspects of Material Culture*, ed. Esther Juhasz (Jerusalem: Israel Museum, 1990), p. 256.

107. Chava Weissler, *Voices of the Matriarchs: Listening to the Prayers of Early Modern Jewish Women* (Boston: Beacon Press, 1998), p. 40. The etrog, a lemon-like fruit, is one of the "four species" that are part of the celebration of the festival of Sukkot (*EJ*, 6: 1448–50). Their use ends on the culminating day known as Hoshana Rabba.

108. See also the custom of giving a Torah scroll to hold to a woman experiencing difficult childbirth, cited by Howard Adelman, "Italian Jewish Women," in *Jewish Women in Historical Perspective*, ed. Judith Baskin (Detroit: Wayne State University Press, 1991), pp. 146–47. Somewhat parallel is the case of an antique hand-written Bible discovered in a village in Libya at the turn of the nineteenth century, and kept in the home of one of the notables in Tripoli. It was wrapped in a manner parallel to a Torah scroll, and was brought into the home of a woman experiencing difficulty in childbirth. See Ha-Cohen, *Higgid Mordecaï*, p. 266.

109. Weissler, *Voices*, ch. 6.

110. Ester Muchawsky-Schnapper, "Symbolic Decorations for a Woman after Childbirth in Sanà," *Israel Museum Journal* 7 (Spring 1988): 61–74.

111. Ibid.; Pierre Bourdieu, "The Berber House," in *Rules and Meanings*, ed. M. Douglas (Harmondsworth, U.K.: Penguin Books, 1973), pp. 98–110.

112. This was not the case throughout all of Yemen. See Laurence Loeb, "Gender, Marriage, and Social Conflict in Habban," in *Sephardi and Middle Eastern Jewries: History and Culture in the Modern Era*, ed. Harvey E. Goldberg (Bloomington: Indiana University Press; New York: Jewish Theological Seminary of America, 1996), pp. 259–76.

113. Muchawsky-Schnapper, "Symbolic," p. 62.

114. See also Exod. 34:20; Num. 18:15.

115. Rubin, *Beginning*, pp. 123–25.

116. Fred E. Greenspahn, *When Brothers Dwell Together: The Preeminence of Younger Siblings in the Hebrew Bible* (New York: Oxford University Press, 1994).

117. Rubin, *Beginning*, p. 140.

118. Cohen, *Le parler*, pp. 25–26; Dobrinsky, *Treasury*, pp. 17–18.

119. TB *Bekhorot* 50a.

120. Dobrinsky, *Treasury*, pp. 17, 23, 28.

121. When he reaches religious maturity, a firstborn is obligated to fast on the eve of Passover, commemorating "his" being saved in Egypt during the tenth plague, but can circumvent that obligation by engaging in study. See chapter 3 in this volume, "Adult Study and Rituals."

122. A. Demsky, J. A. Reif, and J. Tabory, eds., *These Are the Names: Studies in Jewish Onomastics* (Ramat Gan: Bar-Ilan University Press, 1997).

123. Cohen, *Le parler*, pp. 21, 23–24.

124. Mavis Hyman, *Jews of the Raj* (London: Hyman Publishers, 1995), pp. 108–9.

125. Dobrinsky, *Treasury*, pp. 3, 11, 20, 25.

126. Toby F. Reifman, eds., *Blessing the Birth of a Daughter: Jewish Naming Ceremonies for Girls* (New York: Ezrat Nashim, 1978), p. 27, cites an unpublished paper by Marc Angel. See appendix 2 for an example of the text of the zeved ha-bat ceremony.

127. The background and evolution of the custom are unclear. See Pollack, *Jewish Folkways*, pp. 27–28; Paul Wexler, *The Ashkenazic Jews: A Slavic-Turkic People in Search of a Jewish Identity* (Columbus, Ohio: Slavica Publications, 1993), pp. 119–20. In some cases it may have been part of a Sabbath celebration in which the mother of an infant ended her house confinement. See the beginning of chapter 3 and Elisheva Baumgarten, *Mothers and Children*, pp. 165–87.

128. See Jonathan Sacks, "Creativity and Innovation in *Halakhah*," in *Rabbinic Authority and Personal Autonomy*, ed. Moshe Sokol (Northvale, N.J.: Jason Aronson, 1992), pp. 123–68, who mentions the comment of the nineteenth-century authority, Y. M. Epstein, that "the birth of a girl does not bring much joy."

129. See, for example, Susan W. Schneider, *Jewish and Female: Choices and Changes in Our Lives Today* (New York: Simon & Schuster, 1984); Anita Diamant, *The New Jewish Baby Book: Names, Ceremonies and Customs: A Guide for Today's Families* (Woodstock, Vt.: Jewish Lights Publishing, 1993); Sacks, "Creativity," pp. 149–55; Daniel Siegel, "Moon: White Silver of *Shekhinah's* Return," in *Worlds of Jewish Prayer*, ed. Shohama Harris Wiener and Jonathan Omer-man (Northvale, N.J.: Jason Aronson, 1993), pp. 231–55. Much relevant material may be found in publications like *Lilith; The Second Jewish Catalogue: Sources and Resources*, ed. and comp. Sharon Strassfeld and Michael Strassfeld (Philadelphia: Jewish Publication Society, 1976), pp. 17–23; or the birth ceremonies guide: *Brit Banot: Covenant of Our Daughters* (New York: Jewish Women's Resource Center, National Council of Jewish Women, 1985).

130. *Brit Banot*, pp. 1–2.

131. Maimonides, *Yad ha-Ḥazaqah*, *Shofṭim* (Judges), *Avel* (Mourning), 1:6.

132. See chapter 4, "Marriage, Women, and Menstruation."

133. See Penina Adelman, "A Drink from Miriam's Cup: Invention of Tradition among Jewish Women," *Journal of Feminist Studies in Religion* 10 (1994): 151–66. Meira Josephy called my attention to this development.

134. TB *Giṭin* 57a.

135. Tsili Doleve-Gandelman, "The Symbolic Inscription of Zionist Ideology in the Space of Eretz Israel: Why the Native Israeli Is Called *Tsabar*," in *Judaism Viewed from Within and from Without: Anthropological Studies*, ed. Harvey E. Goldberg (Albany: State University of New York Press, 1987), pp. 257–84.

136. Midrash *Shir ha-Shirim Rabbah* 1:24.

137. Sacks, "Creativity," pp. 149–55.

138. See appendix 4.

139. See Judith Seid, *We Rejoice in Our Heritage: Home Rituals for Secular and Humanistic Jews* (Ann Arbor, Mich.: Kopinvant Secular Press, 1989).

140. See chapter 6, "The Individual and the Organization of Death."

141. See chapter 4, "Hoary Texts and Local Practices."

142. For a general perspective and new rituals in the lives of women, see Shulamit Magnus, "Re-inventing Miriam's Well: Feminist Jewish Ceremonials," in *The Uses of Tradition: Jewish Continuity in the Modern Era*, ed. Jack Wertheimer (New York: Jewish Theological Seminary of America with Harvard University Press, 1992), pp. 331–47.

143. Barth, *Berit Milah*.

144. See chapter 3, "Receiving the Torah and Access to It."

145. Laura Geller, "Brit Milah and Brit Banot," in Orenstein, *Lifecycles*, p. 63.

146. An example of a revision is found in Reifman, *Blessing*, pp. 26–27, where she suggests inserting: "sons and daughters." Another example is in the translation in appendix 2.

147. Purist norms do not permit a person to receive payment for the performance of a commandment (mitzvah), but tradition has found various acceptable ways of justifying remuneration in response to the realities of occupational specialization.

148. Daniel I. Liefer and Myra Liefer, "On the Birth of a Daughter," in *The Jewish Woman: New Perspectives*, ed. Elizabeth Koltun (New York: Schocken Books, 1976), pp. 21–30.

149. Faye Ginsburg, *Contested Lives: The Abortion Debate in an American Community* (Berkeley: University of California Press, 1989); Janet Dolgin, *Defining the Family: Law, Technology and Reproduction in an Uneasy Age* (New York: New York University Press, 1997).

CHAPTER 3. RITUALS OF EDUCATION

1. P. J. Abbink van der Zwan, "Ornamentation on Eighteenth-Century Torah Binders," *Israel Museum News* 14 (1978): 54–63; Barbara Kirshenblatt-Gimblett, "The Cut That Binds: The Western Ashkenazic Torah Binder as Nexus between Circumcision and Torah," in *Celebration: Studies in Festivity and Ritual*, ed. V. Turner (Washington, D.C.: Smithsonian Institution Press,

1982), pp. 136–46; Daniel Sperber, *Minhagei Yisrael: Meqorot ve-toladot* [Jewish Customs: Sources and History] (Jerusalem: Mosad Ha-Rav Kook, 1989–95), 2: 197. A somewhat contrasting pattern is presented by Cissy Grossman, "Womanly Arts: A Study of Italian Torah Binders in the New York Jewish Museum Collection," *Journal of Jewish Art* 7 (1980): 35–43.

2. In some instances, the wimpel was presented to the synagogue several weeks after birth, on the first Sabbath that a postpartum mother went out to the synagogue. The woman was honored in the synagogue and later, in her home, a holekreish naming ceremony might take place. See chapter 2, "Recognizing Gender," and Elisheva Baumgarten, "Mothers and Children: The Medieval Jewish Experience" (Ph.D. diss., Hebrew University, Jerusalem, 2000), pp. 165–87.

3. Exodus 20 and Deuteronomy 5.

4. TB *Makkot* 23b–24a and *Menaḥot* 29b.

5. Jay M. Harris, *How Do We Know This? Midrash and the Fragmentation of Modern Jewry* (Albany: State University of New York Press, 1995).

6. See Daniel Boyarin, *Carnal Israel: Reading Sex in Talmudic Culture* (Berkeley: University of California Press, 1993).

7. Exod. 19:22 and the comments by Rashi and Ibn Ezra, ad loc. The appointment of the sons of Aaron as kohanim only takes place in chapters 28 and 29 of Exodus.

8. Exod. 32:15–16.

9. Aaron Demsky, "Writing in Ancient Israel and Early Judaism. Part One: The Biblical Period," in *Miqra: Text, Translation, Reading and Interpretation of the Hebrew Bible in Ancient Israel and Early Judaism,* ed. M. J. Mulder (Assen, Neth.: Van Gorcum; Philadelphia: Fortress Press, 1988), pp. 1–20.

10. In Hebrew, *tefillin shel rosh,* in contrast to the arm-tefillin, *tefillin shel yad.*

11. See Rashi's comment on verse 37 and Exod. 39:30. See also Maimonides, *Yad ha-Hazaqah, Ahavah* (Love of God), *Tefillin* 4:14.

12. See chapter 2, "Recognizing Gender."

13. See also the contents of the "Nash papyrus" found in Egypt and dating from the second century B.C.E., in *EJ,* 12: 833–34.

14. In contrast to tefillin, the mezuzah, the container affixed to an entranceway in fulfillment of the rule of attaching "them to the doorpost of your house," contains only the verses from Deuteronomy, for that command appears only in them. It is curious however, that the word *mezuzah,* which originally meant only "doorpost" but came to be applied to the container of parchment on the doorpost as well, does appear in Exodus in the context of the paschal sacrifice (Exod. 12:7). The Children of Israel were to place the blood of the paschal lamb on their doorposts, and therefore ensure that the firstborns in their homes were not smitten. The "omission" of the first two passages (that are found in tefillin) from the mezuzah might also be a way of combating a perception of the mezuzah as possessing apotropaic powers. Cf. Jon Levenson, *The Death and Resurrection of the Beloved Son: The Transformation of Child Sacrifice in Judaism and Christianity* (New Haven, Conn.: Yale University

Press, 1993), ch. 1, on Deuteronomy not relating to the smiting of firstborn and paschal blood.

15. Num. 6:22–27. On the continuing practice in the synagogue, see Eric Zimmer, *Society and Its Customs: Studies in the History and Metamorphosis of Jewish Customs* (in Hebrew) (Jerusalem: Zalman Shazar Center, 1996), pp. 132–51. On pidyon ha-ben, see chapter 2 in this volume, "Recognizing Gender."

16. Lev. 21:1–3. See chapter 6 in this volume, "Death in the Bible."

17. Midrash *Vayiqra Rabbah* 7:3.

18. Demsky, "Writing"; Meir Bar-Ilan, "Writing in Ancient Israel and Early Judaism. Part Two: Scribes and Books in the Late Second Commonwealth and Rabbinic Periods," in *Miqra: Text, Translation, Reading and Interpretation of the Hebrew Bible in Ancient Israel and Early Judaism*, ed. M. J. Mulder (Assen, Neth.: Van Gorcum; Philadelphia: Fortress Press, 1988), pp. 21–38.

19. Eli Yassif, "Hebrew Prose in the East: Its Formation in the Middle Ages and Transition to Modern Times" (in Hebrew), *Pe'amim* 26 (1986): 58–59.

20. Joseph Tedgi, *Le livre et l'imprimerie hébraïque à Fes* (in Hebrew) (Jerusalem: Institut Ben-Zvi, 1994), p. 13.

21. Laurence Podselver, "Le don comme élément de l'hospitalité," in *Groupe de travail sur les formes de l'hospitalité* (Paris: Maison des Sciences de l'Homme, 1997), pp. 51–56. See now, Jonathan Brumberg-Kraus, "Meat-eating and Jewish Identity: Ritualization of the Priestly 'Torah of Beast and Fowl' (Lev. 11:46) in Rabbinic Judaism and Medieval Kabbalah," *AJS Review* 24 (1999): 227–62.

22. TJ *Berakhot* 5:4, 9a.

23. Hebrew Manuscript Division, Jewish National and University Library, Jerusalem, ARC 4° 1512, 20.

24. Yoram Bilu, "Sigmund Freud and Rabbi Yehudah: On a Jewish Mystical Tradition of 'Psychoanalytic' Dream Interpretation," *Journal of Psychological Anthropology* 2 (1979): 443–63.

25. Howard Eilberg-Schwartz, *The Savage in Judaism: An Anthropology of Israelite Religion and Ancient Judaism* (Bloomington: Indiana University Press, 1990), p. 133. See also chapter 4 in this volume, "The Marriage Ceremony."

26. Demsky, "Writing," and Bar-Ilan, "Writing."

27. The Hebrew phrase is *ha-yom harat 'olam.* The story of Sarah is included in the Torah-reading for that day, while the story of Hannah is in the reading from the prophets, the *haftara.*

28. On *se'udat mitzvah,* and when it is appropriate, see Herman Pollack, *Jewish Folkways in Germanic Lands (1648–1806)* (Cambridge, Mass.: MIT Press, 1971), pp. 103–4.

29. 1 Sam. 1:22–24.

30. The figure of two years is, at best, a rough estimate. See Rubin, *Beginning,* pp. 22–25; John Cooper, *The Child in Jewish History* (Northvale, N.J.: Jason Aronson, 1996), pp. 54–57. Isa. 28:9–13 also hints at a link between weaning and the beginning of learning. See Harvey E. Goldberg, "Cambridge

in the Land of Canaan: Descent, Alliance, Circumcision, and Instruction in the Bible," *Journal of the Ancient Near Eastern Society* 24 (1996): 27 n. 91.

31. Arnold van Gennep, *The Rites of Passage,* trans. M. B. Vizedom and G. L. Caffee (London: Routledge & Kegan Paul, 1960 [orig. 1909]).

32. The importance of toilet training is implicit in the criticism of a rabbi in Tripoli discussing the dismal situation of education in the city in the 1870s. See Eliahu Bekhor Hazzan, *Ta'alumot Lev,* pt. 1 (Leghorn: Ben-Amozegh, 1879), p. 14a.

33. Ivan Marcus, *Rituals of Childhood: Jewish Culture and Acculturation in the Middle Ages* (New Haven, Conn.: Yale University Press, 1996).

34. Rashi is the acronym of R. Solomon ben Isaac of Troyes (1040–1105). On the Tosaphists of the following generations, see *EJ,* 15: 1278–83.

35. See the discussion of circumcision, chapter 2, "Circumcision, Blood, and Passover."

36. This association is established textually in the French sources as well, even when the time for the ceremony is not set at Shavuot. It is expressed in the ritual prominence of a verse from Deut. 33:4: "Moses commanded us the Law, an inheritance of the congregation of Jacob."

37. See Exod. 12:1–2.

38. It might also be noted that Ezekiel was a priest. Before the destruction of the Temple and the exile to Babylonia, he would have been entitled to eat certain portions of the sacrificial offerings.

39. Evelyn M. Cohen, "The Teacher, the Father and the Virgin Mary in the *Leipzig Mahzor,*" *Proceedings of the Tenth World Congress of Jewish Studies,* Division D, vol. 2: *Art, Folklore, and Music* (Jerusalem: World Union of Jewish Studies, 1990), pp. 71–76.

40. The depiction of Moses as "nurturant" inspired a study of Moses by a political scientist. See Aaron Wildavsky, *The Nursing Father: Moses as a Political Leader* (Tuscaloosa: University of Alabama Press, 1984). It is quite possible that the illuminations in the *Leipzig Mahzor* were done by a Christian artist (I am indebted to Malachi Beit-Arié for this point). That possibility offers a different perspective on the similarity between the Jewish and Christian images.

41. Marcus, *Rituals,* p. 96.

42. Mark Zborowski and Elizabeth Herzog, *Life Is with People: The Culture of the Shtetl* (New York: Schocken Books, 1996), p. 88.

43. Chaim Nachman Bialik, "A Jewish Child Engaged in Torah": "Who are you, Shamir, who are you, flint, / Before a Hebrew youth who is occupied with the Torah?" See Steven L. Jacobs, *Shirot Bialik* (Columbus, Ohio: Aleph Publishing, 1987), pp. 40–41. The word *shamir* denotes both a very hard stone and a legendary worm able to cut stone, i.e., the hardest of substances.

44. Erich Brauer, *The Jews of Kurdistan,* completed and ed. Raphael Patai (Detroit: Wayne State University Press, 1993), p. 240. The language quoted by Brauer is Neo-Aramaic.

45. David Cohen, *Le parler arabe des Juifs de Tunis* (Paris: Mouton, 1964), pp. 79–80, 172, claims that this ritual is known only from Tunis, but there also was a celebration in Algeria during the same week, defined by the Torah-

reading cycle, although it seems to have related to adults rather than children. See J. D. Eisenstein, ed., *Ozar Yisrael* (New York: Eisenstein, 1909), 7: 176.

46. See chapter 2 in this volume, "The Eve of Circumcision Celebrations," and ibid. n. 52 on the *shalom zakhor* celebration.

47. Zborowski and Herzog, *Life*, pp. 348–49. A brief description of a more recent practice is found in Samuel Heilman, *Defenders of the Faith: Inside Ultra-Orthodox Jewry* (New York: Schocken Books, 1992), pp. 131–34. The connection between hair-cutting and entering "heder" among Jerusalem haredim was pointed out to me by Rachel Rabinowitch (personal communication). See now Yoram Bilu, "Mi-milah le-milah: Nituah psikho-tarbuti shel havnayat zehut gavrit be-tiksei yaldut ba-hevra ha-haredit," *Alpayim* 19 (2000): 17–45.

48. Cohen, *Le parler arabe*, pp. 27–34; Elizabeth Friedman, *Colonialism and After: An Algerian Jewish Community* (South Hadley, Mass.: Bergin & Garvey, 1988), p. 41. In the Tripolitanian moshav, on the morning of "donning tefillin," a young boy was dressed by his mother and female relatives, highlighting his departure from them as he marched off to the synagogue.

49. Van Gennep, *Rites*, pp. 71–72.

50. Cohen, *Le parler arabe*, pp. 24–25.

51. Aryeh Arthur Goren, "Sacred and Secular: The Place of Public Funerals in the Immigrant Life of American Jews," *Jewish History* 8 (1994): 269–305.

52. Irene Awret, *Days of Honey: The Tunisian Boyhood of Rafael Uzan* (New York: Schocken Books, 1984), pp. 38–39.

53. TB *Yoma* 82a.

54. Midrash *Bereshit Rabbah* 63:14.

55. *Yad ha-Ḥazaqah, Nashim* (Women), *Ishut* (Marital Relations) 2:9–10. See also Rashi to Mishna *Yoma* 8:4.

56. *Yad ha-Ḥazaqah, Shofṭim* (Judges), *Edut* (Testimony) 9:8.

57. This topic was made prominent by the work of Philippe Ariès, *Centuries of Childhood: A Social History of Family Life*, trans. R. Baldick (London: J. Cape, 1962), and explored with reference to Jewish history by John Cooper, *The Child in Jewish History* (Northvale, N.J.: J. Aronson, 1996).

58. S. D. Goitein, "Jewish Education in Yemen as an Archetype of Traditional Jewish Education," in *Between Past and Future: Essays and Studies on Aspects of Immigrant Absorption in Israel*, ed. Carl Frankenstein (Jerusalem: Szold Foundation, 1953), p. 114.

59. David Ben Kalifa, *She'elot u-teshuvot darkei David* (Jerusalem, 1980), pp. 14–16; Henry Toledano, "Les cérémonies de la *Bar-mitswah* dans la communauté de Meknès" (in Hebrew), in *Recherches sur la culture des Juifs d'Afrique du Nord*, ed. I. Ben-Ami (Jerusalem: Communauté Israélite Nord-Africaine, 1990), pp. 97–114.

60. See Roni Weinstein, "Rites of Passage in Sixteenth-Century Italy: The Bar-Mitzvah Ceremony and Its Sociological Implications" (in Hebrew), *Italia* 11 (1994): 77–98.

61. Shlomoh Luria, *Yam Shel Shlomoh, Baba Qama*, 7: 37. See also the discussion in Jacob Katz, "Traditional Jewish Society and Modern Society," in

Jews among Muslims: Communities in the Precolonial Middle East, ed. Shlomo Deshen and Walter P. Zenner (New York: New York University Press; Houndmills, Hants, U.K.: Macmillan, 1996), pp. 31–32.

62. Toledano, "Les cérémonies," p. 101.

63. Awret, *Days of Honey,* p. 110; I have heard bar mitzvah songs concerning work from Moroccan Jews. For an example of a song in Tunis, see Cohen, *Le parler arabe,* pp. 131–32. See also Toledano, "Les cérémonies," p. 98. On Habad Hasidim, see Lis Harris, *Holy Days: The World of a Hasidic Family* (New York: Summit Books, 1985).

64. Herbert Dobrinsky, *A Treasury of Sephardic Laws and Customs* (Hoboken, N.J.: Ktav, 1988), p. 35; Cohen, *Le parler arabe,* p. 28.

65. Laurence Loeb, *Outcaste: Jewish Life in Southern Iran* (London: Gordon & Breach, 1977), pp. 199–202.

66. On Jews in Cochin, see chapter 7, "The Beginnings of the Modern Jewish World."

67. David Mandelbaum, "The Jewish Way of Life in Cochin," *Jewish Social Studies* 1 (1939): 456–57; Nathan Katz and Ellen Goldberg, *The Last Jews of Cochin: Jewish Identity in Hindu India* (Columbia, S.C.: University of South Carolina Press, 1993), p. 242.

68. Bracha Yaniv, *The Torah Case: Its History and Design* (Ramat Gan: Bar-Ilan University Press; Jerusalem: Ben-Zvi Institute, 1997).

69. See Frank Talmage, "Apples of Gold: The Inner Meaning of Sacred Texts in Medieval Judaism," in *Jewish Spirituality from the Bible through the Middle Ages,* ed. Arthur Green (New York: Crossroad, 1985), pp. 313–55; Isaiah Tishby and Fishel Lachower, trans. and eds., *The Wisdom of the Zohar,* 3 vols. (New York: Oxford University Press, 1989), 3: 1084–85. Jeffrey Tigay has called it to my attention that the theme of comparing a Jew to a sefer torah was developed in lectures originally delivered in Yiddish by Rabbi Joseph D. Soloveitchik. See his "Ha-Yehudi mashul le-sefer torah," *Beit Yosef Shaul* [New York: Rabbi Isaac Elchanan Theological Seminary, Hebrew] 4 (1994): 68–100.

70. Ester Muchawsky-Schnapper, *The Jews of Yemen: Highlights of the Israel Museum Collection* (Jerusalem: Israel Museum, 1994), p. 114.

71. Abraham J. Heschel, *The Earth Is the Lord's* (New York: Henry Schuman, 1949), p. 47; Harvey E. Goldberg, "Torah and Children: Symbolic Aspects of the Reproduction of Jews and Judaism," in id., *Judaism Viewed from Within and from Without: Anthropological Studies* (Albany: State University of New York Press, 1987), pp. 113–14, 125; Riv-Ellen Prell, "Sacred Categories and Social Relations: The Visibility and Invisibility of Gender in an American Jewish Community," in *Judaism Viewed,* ed. H. E. Goldberg (Albany: State University of New York Press, 1987), p. 179; Marcus, *Rituals,* pp. 77, 150 n. 16.

72. The term "holy ark" is a translation of the Hebrew *aron qodesh,* which was widespread in Ashkenaz, while the word *heikhal,* a Hebrew term referring to the Temple, was common in many Sephardi regions.

73. Grossman, "Womanly Arts," and see below, "Torah and Women."

74. Goldberg, "Torah," pp. 112, 125, n. 9; Tedgi, *Le livre,* p. 16. See also below, chapter 5, "*Hillulot* and the Zohar in Morocco."

75. Marcus, *Ritual*, p. 77.

76. Mordecaï Ha-Cohen, *Higgid Mordecaï: The History, Institutions and Customs of the Jews of Libya* (in Hebrew), ed. and annotated by H. Goldberg (Jerusalem: Ben-Zvi Institute, 1979), p. 254.

77. Howard Adelman, "Italian Jewish Women," in *Jewish Women in Historical Perspective*, ed. Judith Baskin (Detroit: Wayne State University Press, 1991), p. 139.

78. David Weiss Halivni, *The Book and the Sword: A Life of Learning in the Shadow of Destruction* (New York: Farrar, Straus & Giroux), p. 9.

79. Tishby and Lachower, *Wisdom of the Zohar*, vol. 3, p. 1037. English translation in *The Zohar*, vol. 4, trans. M. Simon and P. Levertoff (London: Soncino, 1984), p. 199.

80. This happened through the influence of the sixteenth-century kabbalist Isaac Luria and his circle. See Gershom Scholem, *Major Trends in Jewish Mysticism* (New York: Schocken Books, 1941), ch. 7. Other examples of Lurianic influence are discussed in "Torah and Women" in this chapter; "Breaking the Glass" in chapter 4; "Popular Pilgrimages" and "*Hillulot* and the Zohar in Morocco" in chapter 5; "The Individual and the Organization of Death," in chapter 6; and "Mysticism, the Genders, and the Individual" in chapter 7.

81. The translation is from Philip Birnbaum, *Daily Prayer Book* (New York: Hebrew Publishing Co., 1949), pp. 365–66.

82. See the phrase in Dan. 3:25.

83. See chapter 5, "*Hillulot* and the Zohar in Morocco," and Harvey E. Goldberg, "The Zohar in Southern Morocco: A Study in the Ethnography of Texts," *History of Religions* 29 (1990): 233–58.

84. Nosson Scherman with Meir Zlotowitz, *The Complete ArtScroll Siddur: Weekday/Sabbath/Festival—Nusach Sefarad* (New York: Mesorah Publications, 1985), pp. 466–67.

85. Deborah Weissman, "The Education of Religious Girls in Jerusalem during the Period of British Rule: The Crystallization and Institutionalization of Five Educational Ideologies" (Ph.D. diss., Hebrew University, Jerusalem, 1993), pp. 3–8.

86. TJ *Soṭah* 3:4, 19a.

87. See Numbers 5. The image of "burning the words of Torah" may be a "mirror image" of that part of the biblical ordeal in which the words of an oath, written by a priest, are dissolved in the bitter waters (Num. 5:23).

88. Blu Greenberg, *On Women and Judaism: A View from Tradition* (Philadelphia: Jewish Publication Society of America, 1981), pp. 72–73, n. 35.

89. Boyarin, *Carnal*, pp. 170–80.

90. See Miriam Peskowitz, *Spinning Fantasies: Rabbis, Gender, and History* (Berkeley: University of California Press, 1997), pp. 73–76.

91. S. D. Goitein, *A Mediterranean Society: The Jewish Communities of the Arab World as Portrayed in the Documents of the Cairo Geniza*, vol. 3: *The Family* (Berkeley: University of California Press, 1978), p. 24. I have seen women purchase the honor of reciting blessings over the Torah for male members of their family in Sephardi synagogues in Israel and have been told that

the same practice existed in the Lower East Side of New York among Ashkenazi immigrants in the early part of the twentieth century.

92. Ivan Marcus, "Mothers, Martyrs, and Moneymakers: Some Jewish Women in Medieval Europe," *Conservative Judaism* 38, 3 (1986): 34–45.

93. Cohen, *Le parler arabe*, pp. 27–34.

94. Zborowski and Herzog, *Life*, p. 85. Their account also includes other lullabies.

95. Chava Weissler, *Voices of the Matriarchs: Listening to the Prayers of Early Modern Jewish Women* (Boston: Beacon Press, 1998).

96. Weissler, *Voices*, ch. 6.

97. R. Vulture, *"Hours of Devotion": Book of Prayer and Devotion for Israel's Women and Maids for Public and House Devotion as Well as for All Circumstances of Female Life* (Budapest: M. E. Loewy Son, n.d.). My guess is that this collection dates from the late nineteenth or early twentieth century. The ideal expressed represents a reaction to changing roles of women at that time, rather than a "traditional" tkhine. See Paula Hyman, *Gender and Assimilation in Modern Jewish History: The Roles and Representation of Women* (Seattle: University of Washington Press, 1995), ch. 2.

98. Weissler, *Voices*, ch. 5.

99. Ibid., p. 25.

100. Don Seeman, "The Silence of Rayna Batya: Torah, Suffering, and Rabbi Barukh Epstein's 'Wisdom of Women,' " *The Torah u-Madda Journal* 5 (Spring 1996): 91–128.

101. Matthias B. Lehmann, "The Intended Reader of Ladino Rabbinic Literature and Judeo-Spanish Reading Culture," *Jewish History* 16 (2002): 283–307. Judeo-Spanish, which originated as a communal dialect of Jews in Spanish-speaking realms, is also known as Judezmo or Ladino. See David Bunis, "Modernization and the 'Language Question' among Judezmo-speaking Sephardim of the Ottoman Empire," in *Sephardi and Middle Eastern Jewries*, ed. H. E. Goldberg (Bloomington: Indiana University Press; New York: Jewish Theological Seminary of America, 1996), pp. 226–39.

102. Tamar Alexander and Galit Hasan-Rokem, "The Multivalent Construction of Ethos in the Proverbs of a Sephardic Woman" (in Hebrew), *Jerusalem Studies in Jewish Folklore* 17 (1995): 63–87.

103. Prov. 31:10–31. For remarks on the significance of these verses in their original context, see Peskowitz, *Spinning Fantasies*, p. 96.

104. See chapter 7, "Mysticism, the Genders, and the Individual."

105. Examples of religious values within women's lives, transmitted orally while reflecting textual traditions, are found in Esther Schely-Newman, " 'The Peg of Your Tent': Narratives of North African Israeli Women," in *Sephardi and Middle Eastern Jewries*, ed. H. E. Goldberg (Bloomington: Indiana University Press; New York: Jewish Theological Seminary of America, 1996), pp. 277–87. The article discusses these stories in an Israeli setting.

106. Yosef Tobi, "The Flowering of Judeo-Arabic Literature in North Africa, 1850–1950," in *Sephardi and Middle Eastern Jewries*, ed. H. E. Goldberg (Bloomington: Indiana University Press; New York: Jewish Theological Seminary of America, 1996), p. 218.

107. On Beruriah, see David Goodblatt, "The Beruriah Traditions," *Journal of Jewish Studies* 26 (1975): 68–85; Tal Ilan, "The Historical Beruriah, Rachel and Imma Shalom," *AJS Review* 22 (1997): 1–17; Boyarin, *Carnal*, pp. 181–96. On Rashi's daughter, see Avraham Grossman, *The Early Sages of France*, 2d ed. (in Hebrew) (Jerusalem: Magnes Press, 1997), p. 142.

108. Renée Levine Melammed, "He Said, She Said: A Woman Teacher in Twelfth-Century Cairo," *AJS Review* 22 (1997): 19–36. The material has been interpreted in different ways. See Goitein, *Mediterranean Society*, 3: 344–46, 355–56.

109. Shirley Kaufman, Galit Hasan-Rokem, and Tamar S. Hess, *The Defiant Muse: Hebrew Feminist Poems, from Antiquity to the Present* (New York: Feminist Press of the City University of New York, 1999), pp. 5–6.

110. Judith Baskin, "Some Parallels in the Education of Medieval Jewish and Christian Women," *Jewish History* 5 (1991): 41–52; Weissman, "Education of Religious Girls in Jerusalem during the Period of British Rule," pp. 1–9. See now the articles in *Pe'amim* 82 (2000) discussing the study of Torah among women in Middle Eastern Jewish communities (in Hebrew).

111. Howard Adelman, "Rabbis and Reality: Public Activities of Jewish Women in Italy during the Renaissance and Catholic Restoration," *Jewish History* 5 (1991): 27–40; id., "The Educational and Literary Activities of Jewish Women in Italy during the Renaissance and the Catholic Restoration," in *Shlomo Simonsohn Jubilee Volume: Studies in the History of the Jews in the Middle Ages and the Renaissance Period*, ed. D. Carpi et al. (Tel Aviv: Tel Aviv University, 1993), pp. 9–23.

112. Goitein, *Mediterranean Society*, 3: 356.

113. Aron Rodrigue, *French Jews, Turkish Jews: The Alliance Israélite and the Politics of Jewish Schooling in Turkey, 1860–1925* (Bloomington: Indiana University Press, 1990).

114. Harvey E. Goldberg and Claudio G. Segrè, "Mixtures of Diverse Substances: Education and the Hebrew Language among the Jews of Libya, 1875–1951," in *Essays in the Social Scientific Study of Judaism and Jewish Society*, ed. S. Fishbane and J. Lightstone (Montreal: Concordia University Press, 1990), pp. 151–201; Rachel Simon, *Change within Tradition among Jewish Women in Libya* (Seattle: University of Washington Press, 1992).

115. The Hebrew term may mean either "polite behavior" or "gainful work."

116. Weissman, "Education of Religious Girls in Jerusalem during the Period of British Rule," p. 28.

117. See above in this chapter "Receiving the Torah and Access to It."

118. Weissman, "Education of Religious Girls in Jerusalem during the Period of British Rule," p. 30 n. 77. For the source see Hafetz Haim (Yisrael Meir Ha-Cohen), *Liqutei halakhot* (Petriakoff, 1918), *Soṭah* 21.

119. Greenberg, *On Women*, p. 28.

120. Tamar El-Or, *Educated and Ignorant: Ultraorthodox Jewish Women and Their World* (Boulder, Colo.: Lynne Rienner, 1994), ch. 2; id., *Next Pessach: Literacy and Identity of Young Religious Zionist Women* (in Hebrew) (Tel

Aviv: Am Oved, 1998); Lauren B. Granite, "Tradition as a Modality of Religious Change: Talmud Study in the Lives of Orthodox Jewish Women" (Ph.D. diss., Drew University, Madison, N.J., 1995).

121. Michael A. Meyer, *Response to Modernity: A History of the Reform Movement in Judaism* (New York: Oxford University Press, 1988), p. 39.

122. Sperber, *Minhagei Yisrael*, 1: 118–20.

123. Jack Wertheimer, *A People Divided: Judaism in Contemporary America* (New York: Basic Books, 1993), pp. 3–7.

124. Cherie Koller-Fox, "Women and Jewish Education: A New Look at Bat Mitzvah," in *The Jewish Woman: New Perspectives,* ed. Elizabeth Koltun (New York: Schocken Books, 1976), pp. 31–42.

125. Eisenstein, ed., *Ozar Yisrael*, 3: 170; *EJ*, 4:246. According to a communication by Gilad J. Gevaryahu of the H-Judaic list (h-judaic@h-net.msu.edu), 14 January 2001, he is preparing an article on the history of bat mitzvah. Other communications on that list between 8 and 15 January 2001 contain information and perspective on the topic.

126. Dov Sedan (Stock), "Bat Mitzvah" (in Hebrew), in *Dat u-Medina* [Religion and State], ed. E. F. Kaminka (Tel Aviv: Ha-oved Ha-dati, 1949), pp. 59–61. The implication of Sedan's short report seems to be that the time has arrived for religious Zionists in Israel to face the challenge of finding an appropriate ceremony for young women.

127. Yosef Ḥayyim, *Ben Ish Ḥai* (Jerusalem: Mansour, 1957), p. 186. R. Ḥayyim lived from 1835 to 1909. See also Louis Jacobs, "The Responsa of Rabbi Joseph Ḥayyim of Baghdad," in *Perspectives on Jews and Judaism*, ed. A. A. Chiel (New York: Rabbinical Assembly, 1978), p. 189.

128. Eliahu Ḥazzan, *Neveh Shalom* [Customs of Alexandria], 2d ed. (Alexandria: Ben Aṭar, 1930); the biographical introduction by B.-Z. Taragan (pp. 4–7) mentions the celebration taking place in 1970 [*sic*], most likely a typographical error instead of 1907. Ḥazzan died in 1908.

129. Edda Servi Machlin, *The Classic Cuisine of Italian Jews* (New York: Everest House, 1981), p. 69.

130. In Turkey today, a joint bat mitzvah is celebrated for all the girls in a congregation who turn twelve in a given year.

131. Weissman, "Education of Religious Girls in Jerusalem during the Period of British Rule," p. 23 n. 44.

132. Jenna Weissman Joselit with Karen S. Mittelman, *Worthy Use of Summer: Jewish Summer Camping in America,* with an Introduction by Chaim Potok (Philadelphia: National Museum of American Jewish History, 1993).

133. Jewish Theological Seminary of America, Ratner Center archives, Levi Soshuk to Seymour Fox, 30 March 1959, RG1-O 174/48. See also Michael Brown, "It's Off to Camp We Go: Ramah, LTF, and the Seminary in the Finkelstein Era," in *Tradition Renewed: A History of the Jewish Theological Seminary,* vol. 1, ed. Jack Wertheimer (New York: Jewish Theological Seminary of America, 1997), pp. 844–45.

134. Riv-Ellen Prell, *Prayer and Community: The Havurah in American Judaism* (Detroit: Wayne State University Press, 1989); Chava Weissler, "Mak-

ing Davening Meaningful: Worship in the Havurah Movement," *YIVO Annual* 19 (1990): 255–82. See also "Adult Study and Rituals" in this chapter and "Havura and Other American Forms" in chapter 7.

135. Janet Rosenbaum, H-Judaic list (h-judaic@h-net.msu.edu), 15 January 2001.

136. Boas Huss, "Sefer ha-Zohar as a Canonical, Sacred and Holy Text: Changing Perspectives on the Book of Splendor between the Thirteenth and Eighteenth Centuries," *Journal of Jewish Thought and Philosophy* 7 (1998): 257–307. On Ḥoq le-Yisrael, see p. 297.

137. A. Z. Idelsohn, *Jewish Liturgy and Its Development* (New York: Sacred Music Press, 1932), pp. 84–88. See also chapter 6 in this volume, "The Middle Ages."

138. Samuel Heilman, *People of the Book: Drama, Fellowship and Religion* (Chicago: University of Chicago Press, 1983).

139. See chapter 7, "Havura and Other American Forms."

140. See also Jonathan Boyarin, "Voices around the Text: The Ethnography of Reading at Mesivta Tifereth Jerusalem," *Cultural Anthropology* 4 (1989): 399–421.

141. Barbara Myerhoff, *Number Our Days* (New York: Simon & Schuster, 1978), p. 101.

142. Heilman, *People*, p. 272.

143. Pollack, *Jewish Folkways*, p. 103.

144. Heilman, *People*, p. 287.

145. *Yedioth Aharonoth*, 28 September 1997, p. 17. On the cycle of study called *daf yomi*, see Haym Soloveitchik, "Rupture and Reconstruction: The Transformation of Contemporary Orthodoxy," *Tradition* 28 (1994): 92.

146. See chapter 2, "Recent Developments."

147. See the discussion in David Weiss Halivni, *Midrash, Mishnah, and Gemara: The Jewish Predilection for Justified Law* (Cambridge, Mass.: Harvard University Press, 1986), ch. 7.

148. Examples of the varying involvement of scholars in halakhic decision-making, with reference to Conservative Judaism, are discussed in David Golinken, "The Influence of Seminary Professors on *Halakha* in the Conservative Movement, 1902–1968," in *Tradition Renewed*, vol. 2, ed. J. Wertheimer (New York: Jewish Theological Seminary of America, 1997), pp. 443–82.

149. Ismar Schorsch, "Emancipation and the Crisis of Religious Authority: The Emergence of the Modern Rabbinate," in *From Text to Context: The Turn to History in Modern Judaism* (Hanover, N.H.: Brandeis University Press and University Press of New England, 1994), pp. 9–50.

150. Jacob Z. Lauterbach, "Responsum on Question 'Shall Women Be Ordained Rabbis?' " *Central Conference of American Rabbis Yearbook* 32 (1922): 156–62; Beth Wenger, "The Politics of Women's Ordination: Jewish Law, Institutional Power, and the Debate over Women in the Rabbinate," in *Tradition Renewed*, vol. 2, ed. J. Wertheimer (New York: Jewish Theological Seminary of America, 1997), pp. 483–523; Pamela S. Nadell, *Women Who Would Be Rabbis: A History of Women's Ordination, 1889–1985* (Boston: Beacon Press, 1998);

Ezra Kopelowitz, "Shifting Boundaries of Religious Authority: A Comparative Historical Study of the Role of Religious Movements in the Conflict between Jews in Israel and the United States" (Ph.D. diss., Hebrew University, Jerusalem, 2000).

151. Elizabeth Sarah, "Rabbiner Regina Jonas, 1902–1944: Missing Link in a Broken Chain," in *Hear Our Voice: Women Rabbis Tell Stories,* ed. Sybil Sheridan (London: SCM Press, 1994), pp. 2–9.

152. Prell, *Prayer,* pp. 39–48.

153. See chapter 7, "Havura and Other American Forms."

154. Moshe Shokeid, *A Gay Synagogue in New York* (New York: Columbia University Press, 1995), ch. 7.

155. Stuart Schoenfeld, "Integration into the Group and Sacred Uniqueness: An Analysis of Adult Bat-Mitzvah," in *Persistence and Flexibility: Anthropological Perspectives on the American Jewish Experience,* ed. Walter P. Zenner (Albany: State University of New York Press, 1988), pp. 117–35.

156. Schoenfeld, "Integration," p. 131.

157. See chapter 7, "Religion in Israeli Society."

158. See website: www.acheret.co.il.

159. Ezra Kopelowitz, *Creating Jewish Unity in a Non-Traditional Way: An Evaluative Study of the Bavli-Yerushalmi Project* (Jerusalem: Kolot, 1999). See also the general discussion in chapter 7, "Israel and Diaspora Links."

160. See, e.g., a newspaper review of CD-ROMs: Judy Siegel-Itzkovich, "Learning Torah Has Never Been So Easy," *Jerusalem Post,* 19 May 1999, p. 9.

161. *A Proposal for the Seder: The Passover Haggadah—Tradition and Renewal,* compiled by Sh. Zarhi, R. Ahituv, E. Lin, B. Talmi, and M. Shapira (in Hebrew) (Tel Aviv: Yedioth Aharonoth and the Midrasha at Oranim, 2000). On the kibbutz, see chapter 7, "Kibbutz."

162. Mimi Feigelson, review of *The Book of Blessings: New Jewish Prayers for Daily Life, the Sabbath, and the New Moon Festival,* by Marcia Falk (Boston: Beacon Press, 1999), *Haaretz, Sefarim,* 25 April 2000, p. 1.

CHAPTER 4. MARRIAGE

1. See "Tensions in Marriage" in this chapter for an explanation of the possibly controversial nature of that ketubba, and also "Religion in Israeli Society" in chapter 7.

2. Abraham Chill, *The Minhagim: The Customs and Ceremonies of Judaism, Their Origins and Rationale* (New York: Sepher-Hermon Press, 1979), p. 275.

3. See chapter 2, "Birth, the Firstborn, and Naming."

4. Rahel Rosen [Wasserfall], "Le symbolisme féminin ou la femme dans le système de représentation judéo-marocain dans un mochav en Israel" (in Hebrew) (M.A. thesis, Department of Sociology and Anthropology, Hebrew University, Jerusalem, 1981); Lucette Valensi, "Religious Orthodoxy or Local Tradition: Marriage Celebration in Southern Tunisia," in *Jews among Arabs:*

Contacts and Boundaries, ed. M. R. Cohen and A. L. Udovitch (Princeton, N.J.: Darwin Press, 1989), p. 66.

5. TB *Ketubbot* 8a, and Rashi ad loc.

6. Jeremy Cohen, *Be Fertile and Increase: Fill the Earth and Master It: The Ancient and Medieval Career of a Biblical Text* (Ithaca, N.Y.: Cornell University Press, 1989).

7. Debra Orenstein, ed., *Lifecycles: Jewish Women on Life Passages and Personal Milestones* (Woodstock, Vt.: Jewish Lights Publishing, 1994), pp. 94–95.

8. Mark Zborowski and Elizabeth Herzog, *Life Is with People: The Culture of the Shtetl* (New York: Schocken Books, 1996), pp. 347–48; Elizabeth Ehrlich, *Miriam's Kitchen: A Memoir* (New York: Viking, 1997), p. 205.

9. Esther Schely-Newman, *Our Lives Are but Stories: Narratives of Tunisian-Israeli Women* (Detroit: Wayne State University Press, 2002), pp. 30–32; Alana Suskin, H-Judaic list (h-judaic@h-net.msu.edu), 22 January 2000.

10. Irene Awret, *Days of Honey: The Tunisian Boyhood of Rafael Uzan* (New York: Schocken Books, 1984), p. 156, also refers to the marking of menarche in the Tunisian community of Nabeul by a feast prepared by the mother. There is no mention of the use of oil. A study of Jerba in southern Tunisia states that there was no ceremonial recognition of menarche there, but notes that customs on that occasion were known in other North African communities. See Abraham Udovitch and Lucette Valensi, *The Last Arab Jews: The Communities of Jerba, Tunisia* (New York: Harwood Academic, 1984), p. 46.

11. Yehoshua Yonatan Rubinstein, *Zikhron Ya'aqov Yosef* (Jerusalem: n.d. [1930]), p. 54b. For other traditional remedies, some of which seem to fly in the face of human sensibilities and rabbinic rules, see Sylvie-Anne Goldberg, *Crossing the Jabbok: Illness and Death in Ashkenazi Judaism in Sixteenth-through Nineteenth-Century Prague,* trans. Carol Cosman (Berkeley: University of California Press, 1996 [orig. 1989]), pp. 151–58, and Raphael Patai, *On Jewish Folklore* (Detroit: Wayne State University Press, 1983), pp. 302–13.

12. On some traditional views of menstruation, see Chava Weissler, *Voices of the Matriarchs: Listening to the Prayers of Early Modern Jewish Women* (Boston: Beacon, 1998), pp. 68–70. See also Rahel Wasserfall, ed., *Women and Water: Menstruation in Jewish Life and Law* (Hanover, N.H.: University Press of New England, 1999), including articles cited in chapter 1 above.

13. Howard Eilberg-Schwartz, *The Savage in Judaism: An Anthropology of Israelite Religion and Ancient Judaism* (Bloomington: Indiana University Press, 1990); Nissan Rubin, *The Beginning of Life: Rites of Birth, Circumcision, and Redemption of the Firstborn in the Talmud and Midrash* (in Hebrew) (Tel Aviv: Hakibbutz Hameuchad, 1995); Lawrence A. Hoffman, *Covenant of Blood: Circumcision and Gender in Rabbinic Judaism* (Chicago: University of Chicago Press, 1996).

14. The "shekhina." See Moshe Idel, "Sexual Metaphors and Praxis in the Kabbalah," in *The Jewish Family: Metaphor and Memory,* ed. David Kraemer (New York: Oxford University Press, 1989), pp. 201–2.

15. Everett Gendler, "On the Judaism of Nature," in *The New Jews*, ed. James A. Sleeper and Alan C. Mintz (New York: Random House, 1971), pp. 235–38. For recent elaborations of this theme in contemporary rituals for women, see Arlene Agus, "This Month Is for You: Observing Rosh Hodesh as a Woman's Holiday," in *The Jewish Woman: New Perspectives*, ed. E. Koltun (New York: Schocken Books, 1976), pp. 84–93; Shulamit Magnus, "Re-inventing Miriam's Well: Feminist Jewish Ceremonials," in *The Uses of Tradition: Jewish Continuity in the Modern Era*, ed. Jack Wertheimer (New York: Jewish Theological Seminary of America with Harvard University Press, 1992), pp. 331–47; David M. Rosen and Victoria P. Rosen, "New Myths and Meanings in Jewish New Moon Rituals," *Ethnology* 39 (2000): 263–77.

16. The stem only appears once in the interim, with regard to Abraham's servant, the "ruler" of his household (Gen. 24:2).

17. Gershom Scholem, *On the Kabbalah and Its Symbolism* (New York: Schocken Books, 1965), pp. 151–53. The relevant sources are presented in Dan Siegel, "Moon: White Silver of *Shekhinah*'s Return," in *Worlds of Jewish Prayer*, ed. Shohama Harris Wiener and Jonathan Omer-man (Northvale, N.J.: Jason Aronson, 1993), pp. 231–55. See chapter 7, "Mysticism, the Genders, and the Individual," for further discussion of this imagery.

18. Rubin, *Beginning*, pp. 22–25.

19. Yedidyah Dinari, "The Impurity Customs of the Menstruate Woman— Sources and Development" (in Hebrew), *Tarbiz* 49 (1980): 302–34; Rubin, *Beginning*, pp. 38–70.

20. Hagar Salamon, *The Hyena People: Ethiopian Jews in Christian Ethiopia* (Berkeley: University of California Press, 1999), pp. 97–100; Rachel Qimur, "The Samaritan Family: Traditionality and Modernity" (in Hebrew), in *Families in Israel*, ed. L. Shamgar-Handelman and R. Bar-Yosef (Jerusalem: Academon, 1991), pp. 211–39.

21. Erich Brauer, *The Jews of Kurdistan*, completed and ed. Raphael Patai (Detroit: Wayne State University Press, 1993), pp. 158–59, 182.

22. Mordecaï Ha-Cohen, *The Book of Mordechaï*, trans. and ed. H. E. Goldberg (London: Darf, 1993), p. 120.

23. Ibid., p. 128.

24. Rahel Wasserfall, "Menstruation and Identity: The Meaning of Niddah for Moroccan Women Immigrants to Israel," in *People of the Body: Jews and Judaism from an Embodied Perspective*, ed. H. Eilberg-Schwartz (Albany: State University of New York Press, 1992), pp. 309–27.

25. Ha-Cohen, *Book*, p. 119.

26. This continues to be practiced today by many Karaites. See Sumi Colligan, "Religion, Nationalism, and Ethnicity in Israel: The Case of the Karaite Jews" (Ph.D. diss., Princeton University, 1980). The attitude can also be documented in Jewish communities. See Paula Hyman, *The Emancipation of the Jews of Alsace: Acculturation and Tradition in the Nineteenth Century* (New Haven, Conn.: Yale University Press, 1991), pp. 127–28.

27. See Yosef Caro's *Shulhan Arukh*, *Yoreh De'ah* 282:9, which presents the Sephardi rabbinic norm of the sixteenth century, and the glosses of Moshe Is-

serles ad loc., which cite variant Ashkenazi practice. For a historical survey of the issue, see Shaye J. D. Cohen, "Purity and Piety: The Separation of Menstruants from the Sancta," in *Daughters of the King: Women and the Synagogue*, ed. Susan Grossman and Rivka Haut (Philadelphia: Jewish Publication Society, 1992), pp. 103–15. For a recent rabbinic reiteration of Caro's rule, which suggests that popular norms may have been otherwise in North Africa, see Avraham Hai Adadi, *Ha-shomer emet* (Leghorn: Ben-Amozag, 1849), 4:24, 7:3; reprint, Tel Aviv: Vaàd Qehillot Luv Be-Yisrael, 1986, pp. 22, 35.

28. Awret, *Days of Honey*, p. 50; chapter 5, "*Hillulot* and the Zohar in Morocco."

29. Louis Jacobs, "The Responsa of Rabbi Joseph Hayyim of Baghdad," in *Perspectives on Jews and Judaism*, ed. A. A. Chiel (New York: Rabbinical Assembly, 1978), pp. 190–91 n. 3.

30. Judith Hauptman, "Feminist Perspectives on Rabbinic Texts," in *Feminist Perspectives on Jewish Studies*, ed. Lynn Davidman and Shelly Tenenbaum (New Haven, Conn.: Yale University Press, 1994), pp. 40–61. See also Judith Plaskow, *Standing Again at Sinai: Judaism from a Feminist Perspective* (San Francisco: Harper & Row, 1991), pp. 63–64.

31. See also Moshe Halbertal, *Interpretative Revolutions in the Making: Values as Interpretative Considerations in Midrashei Halakhah* (in Hebrew) (Jerusalem: Magnes Press, 1997), ch. 3.

32. The earliest known ketubba-like document linked to Jewish tradition is from the colony of Jewish mercenaries in Elephantine in southern Egypt (near contemporary Aswan), 5th century B.C.E. See Hayyim Schauss, *The Lifetime of a Jew: Throughout the Ages of Jewish History* (Cincinnati: Union of American Hebrew Congregations, 1950), pp. 139–41. An extensive study of the development of the ketubba is found in Mordechai Akiva Friedman, *Jewish Marriage in Palestine: A Cairo Geniza Study*, vol. 1: *The Ketubba Traditions of Eretz Israel* (Tel-Aviv: Tel-Aviv University; New York: Jewish Theological Seminary of America, 1980). For a broad view of marriage among Jews in ancient times, see Michael Satlow, *Jewish Marriage in Antiquity* (Princeton, N.J.: Princeton University Press, 2001).

33. TB *Qiddushin* 2b.

34. See "Tensions in Marriages" in this chapter.

35. Zeèv W. Falk, *Jewish Matrimonial Law in the Middle Ages* (London: Oxford University Press, 1966), pp. 43–44; S. D. Goitein, *A Mediterranean Society: The Jewish Communities of the Arab World as Portrayed in the Documents of the Cairo Geniza*, vol. 3: *The Family* (Berkeley: University of California Press, 1978), p. 70.

36. Yitzhak Avishur, *The Jewish Wedding in Baghdad and Its Filiations: Customs and Ceremonies, Documents and Songs, Costumes and Jewelry*, vol. 2 (in Hebrew) (Haifa: University of Haifa, 1990), p. 67.

37. For an analysis that seeks to decode overall conceptions of this part of the Mishna, over and above the specific rules, see Noam Zohar, "Women, Men and Religious Status: Deciphering a Chapter in Mishna," in *Approaches to An-*

cient Judaism, n.s., 5, ed. H. W. Basser and S. Fishbane (Atlanta: Scholars Press, 1993), pp. 33–54.

38. Joseph Kafih, *Jewish Life in Sana* (in Hebrew) (Jerusalem: Ben-Zvi Institute, 1969), p. 139.

39. Herbert Dobrinsky, *A Treasury of Sephardic Laws and Customs* (Hoboken, N.J.: Ktav, 1988), p. 44.

40. Yokhi Brandes and Ruhama Weiss-Goldman, *Lirqod 'al kamah ḥatunot* [To Dance at Several Weddings]: *The Complete Guide for Registering Marriages and Arranging Alternative Wedding Ceremonies* (Jerusalem: Ḥidush, 1996), pp. 33–34.

41. See appendix 4. Among Syrian Jews, there is a third blessing over spices.

42. The possible textual background to this custom is suggested in Daniel Sperber, *Minhagei Yisrael: Meqorot ve-toladot* [Jewish Customs: Sources and History] (Jerusalem: Mosad Ha-Rav Kook, 1989–95), 2: 222–26.

43. Dobrinsky, *Treasury,* pp. 44, 58. See "Tensions in Marriages" in this chapter.

44. Shalom Sabar, *Ketubbah: Jewish Marriage Contracts in the Hebrew Union College Skirball Museum and Klau Library* (Philadelphia: Jewish Publication Society, 1990); id., *Mazal Tov: Illuminated Jewish Marriage Contracts from the Israel Museum Collection* (Jerusalem: Israel Museum, 1993).

45. Schauss, *Lifetime,* pp. 162–64; Frija Zuaretz et al., eds., *Sefer Yahadut Luv* [Libyan Jewry] (Tel Aviv: Va'ad Qehillot Luv Be-Yisrael, 1960), p. 393; Joseph Guttman, "Jewish Medieval Marriage Customs in Art: Creativity and Adaptation," in *The Jewish Family,* ed. David Kraemer (New York: Oxford University Press, 1989), pp. 48–49.

46. TB *Qiddushin* 7a. See also TB *Yebamot* 63a: "A man who has no wife is not a man."

47. Midrash *Bereshit Rabbah* 68:4.

48. Harvey E. Goldberg, "Torah and Children: Symbolic Aspects of the Reproduction of Jews and Judaism," in *Judaism Viewed from Within and from Without: Anthropological Studies,* ed. Harvey E. Goldberg (Albany: State University of New York Press, 1987), pp. 113–14, 125; Dobrinsky, *Treasury,* p. 59. That is also current practice in the Etz Ha-hayyim synagogue in Ortakoy, Istanbul. The Sephardi custom, in various forms, was once more widespread than it is today, and also existed in some regions in Ashkenaz. See Naphtali Wieder, *The Formation of Jewish Liturgy in the East and in the West,* vol. 2 (in Hebrew) (Jerusalem: Ben-Zvi Institute, 1998), pp. 631–34.

49. See comment of Rashi on Gen. 25:20, citing *Seder Olam* [The Order of the World].

50. The image of Rebecca as being very young may be reinforced by reference to her nursemaid who accompanied her (Gen. 24:59).

51. Mishna *Qiddushin* 2:1; TB *Qiddushin* 41a.

52. See the comments of the *Tosafot* (previous note), ad loc. (beginning with the word *asur*). For a general discussion, see Avraham Grossman, "Child Marriage in Jewish Society in the Middle Ages until the Thirteenth Century" (in Hebrew), *Pe'amim* 45 (1990): 108–25.

53. I am indebted to Susan Sered for pointing out that a wedding ceremony may take place without the bride saying a word.

54. Gen. 38:11.

55. Shaul Stampfer, "The Social Implications of Very Early Marriage in Eastern Europe in the Nineteenth Century" (in Hebrew), in *Studies on Polish Jewry: Paul Glikson Memorial Volume,* ed. E. Mendelsohn and Ch. Shmeruk (Jerusalem: Institute of Contemporary Jewry, 1987), pp. 65–77; Steven M. Lowenstein, "Ashkenazic Jewry and the European Marriage Pattern: A Preliminary Survey of Jewish Marriage Age," *Jewish History* 8 (1994): 155–75.

56. Flower Elias Cooper and Judith E. Cooper, *The Jews of Calcutta: The Autobiography of a Community* (Calcutta: Jewish Association of Calcutta, 1974), p. 47.

57. Avishur, *Jewish Wedding,* pp. 32–35.

58. Aron Rodrigue, *Images of Sephardi and Eastern Jewries in Transition: The Teachers of the Alliance Israélite Universelle, 1860–1939* (Seattle: University of Washington Press, 1993), pp. 83–84.

59. For example: "Happy is he with male children, and woe unto him with female children" (TB *Qiddushin* 82b); "Whoever has no son, it is as if he is dead, as if he is destroyed" (Midrash *Bereshit Rabbah* 45:3). See also Blu Greenberg, *On Women and Judaism: A View from Tradition* (Philadelphia: Jewish Publication Society of America, 1981), p. 63.

60. See chapter 3, "Torah and Women."

61. See Rubin, *Beginning,* p. 38, citing TB *Niddah* 31b.

62. Avishur, *Jewish Wedding,* p. 28, citing a paper published by Baghdadi Jews in Calcutta. I have not been able to identify a rabbinic source for this; perhaps it is of Muslim origin. A parallel figure of speech appears in the Talmud with regard to divorce. See n. 105 below.

63. Mardocheo Cohen, *Usi, costumi e istituti degli Ebrei libici,* trans. M. M. Moreno, 2d ed. (London: Darf, 1987 [orig. 1924]), pp. 117–21.

64. Cooper and Cooper, *Jews of Calcutta,* p. 35.

65. Kafih, *Jewish Life,* p. 108.

66. Laurence Loeb, *Outcaste: Jewish Life in Southern Iran* (London: Gordon & Breach, 1977), pp. 224–30. On pilgrimages, see chapter 5.

67. Cooper and Cooper, *Jews of Calcutta,* p. 5, citing Alexander Russel, *The Natural History of Aleppo* (London: G. G. and J. Robinson, 1794); Azriel Qamon, ed., *The Duar and Seqel Families: Damascus Jews* (in Hebrew) (Ramat Efal: Yad Tabenkin, 1995), pp. 31–32.

68. Harvey E. Goldberg, "The Jewish Wedding in Tripolitania: A Study in Cultural Sources," *Maghreb Review* 9, 3 (1978): 1–6.

69. Avishur, *Jewish Wedding,* pp. 51–52.

70. Mordecaï Ha-Cohen, *Higgid Mordecaï: The History, Institutions and Customs of the Jews of Libya* (in Hebrew), ed. and annotated by H. Goldberg (Jerusalem: Ben-Zvi Institute, 1979), p. 275.

71. Maya Meltzer-Geva, "The Choice of a Mate among Georgian Jews" (in Hebrew) (M.A. thesis, Department of Sociology and Anthropology, Hebrew University, Jerusalem, 1983). The clash of values between modes of marriage

that were common among Georgian Jews and those widespread in contemporary Israel is the subject of Dover Kovashvili's film *Late Marriage* (2001).

72. Abraham Marcus, *The Middle East on the Eve of Modernity: Aleppo in the Eighteenth Century* (New York: Columbia University Press, 1989), p. 204.

73. See Mishna *Ketubbot* 6:5.

74. Mark Glazer, "The Dowry as Capital Accumulation among Sephardic Jews of Istanbul, Turkey," *International Journal of Middle Eastern Studies* 10 (1979): 373–80.

75. Joëlle Bahloul, *Parenté et ethnicité: La famille juive nord-africaine en France* (Paris: Mission du patrimoine ethnologique de la France, 1984), pp. 135–64.

76. Goldberg, "Jewish Wedding in Tripolitania"; Kafih, *Jewish Life*, p. 109.

77. Jacob Lauterbach, "The Ceremony of Breaking a Glass at Weddings," *Hebrew Union College Annual* 2 (1925): 377 n. 38.

78. TB *Pesaḥim* 49a.

79. Udovitch and Valensi, *Last*, p. 48.

80. The bedekn was also carried out in other manners, and sometimes linked to the blessing of children found in Gen. 24:60. A consideration of the custom from a rabbinic perspective is found in Sperber, *Minhagei Yisrael*, 2: 66 n. 34.

81. Kafih, *Jewish Life*, p. 123.

82. Mishna *Ketubbot* 1:2.

83. Ibid., 2:1.

84. TB *Ketubbot* 16b–17b.

85. Raphael Patai, *Sex and Family in the Bible and Middle East* (Garden City, N.Y.: Doubleday, 1959), pp. 66–70; Issachar Ben-Ami, "Le mariage traditionnel chez les Juifs marocains," in *Studies in Marriage Customs*, ed. I. Ben-Ami and D. Noy (Jerusalem: Magnes Press, 1974); Dobrinsky, *Treasury*, p. 54. Jeffrey Tigay, "Examination of the Accused Bride in 4Q159: Forensic Medicine at Qumran," *Journal of the Ancient Near Eastern Society* 22 (1993): 129–34.

86. Wieder, *Formation*, pp. 619–21. Saàdya Gaon (882–942) was born in Egypt, and headed one of the academies in Baghdad. Maimonides (1135–1205) was born in Spain and became head of the Jewish community in Cairo.

87. Robert Bonfil, *Rabbis and Jewish Communities in Renaissance Italy* (London: Littman Library, 1993), p. 77. Yehudah Mintz, *Teshuvot*, sec. 6. Italy, at the time, was a region in which Ashkenazi and Sephardi traditions met.

88. Gen. 1:10; Lev. 11:36.

89. An introduction to the topic of miqveh written from the perspective of modern American Orthodoxy is found in Norman Lamm, *A Hedge of Roses: Jewish Insights into Marriage and Married Life* (New York: Feldheim, 1966). Basic laws may be found in Isaac Klein, *A Guide to Jewish Religious Practice* (New York: Jewish Theological Seminary of America, 1979), pp. 513–22. See also Wasserfall, *Women and Water*.

90. Patricia Hidiroglou, "Du Hammam Maghrébin au *Mikveh* Parisien," *Journal of Mediterranean Studies* 4 (1994): 241–62; Susan Starr Sered with Romi Kaplan and Samuel Cooper, "Talking about Miqveh Parties, or Discourses of Gender, Hierarchy and Control," in *Women and Water: Menstrua-*

tion in Jewish Life and Law, ed. Rahel Wasserfall (Hanover, N.H.: Brandeis University Press, 1999), pp. 145–65.

91. The standard length of seven also appears in the Talmud, for example TB *Baba Batra* 145a. Examples of longer prenuptial periods are found in Valensi, "Religious," pp. 65–84, and Kafih, *Jewish Life*, pp. 110–53.

92. Marcel Cohen, *Le parler arabe des Juifs d'Alger* (Paris: Champion, 1912), pp. 504–5 n. 9.

93. Valensi, "Religious," pp. 76–77.

94. Kafih, *Jewish Life*, p. 128.

95. Goldberg, "Jewish Wedding in Tripolitania."

96. Valensi, "Religious," p. 77.

97. Eric R. Wolf, *Peasants* (Englewood Cliffs, N.J.: Prentice-Hall, 1966), pp. 97–98.

98. Ben-Ami, "Mariage," p. 92.

99. See also Isa. 50:1 and Jer. 3:8.

100. TB *Qiddushin* 5a.

101. Various symmetries between Jewish marriage and divorce are pointed out by Rivka Haut, "The *Agunah* and Divorce," in Orenstein, *Lifecycles*, pp. 188–200. Her discussion highlights similarities and differences in the two formal procedures.

102. The name of Gershom ben Yehudah—widely known as "Rabbeinu Gershom, Meor ha-Golah" ("Our Rabbi Gershom, Light of the Exile")—is associated with many rulings formative of communal life in the Ashkenazi communities of the Rhineland and France. See the discussion of polygyny in this chapter.

103. *Get* technically means a legal document, but commonly refers to a writ of divorce.

104. Some basic rabbinic principles of divorce are found in Klein, *Guide*, pp. 475–508.

105. TB *Giṭin* 90b.

106. *Shulhan Arukh, Even Ha-ʿezer* 1:3.

107. See the lists of forbidden relatives in Leviticus 18 and 20.

108. The rabbinic term reflects the usage in Ruth 1:13. A concise picture of legal aspects of the status of aguna is found in *EJ,* 2: 429–34.

109. For example, Goitein, *Mediterranean Society,* 3: 144; id., *Letters of Medieval Jewish Traders Translated from the Arabic* (Princeton, N.J.: Princeton University Press, 1973), pp. 316–19.

110. Zvi Zohar, "The Halakhic Teaching of Egyptian Rabbis in Modern Times" (in Hebrew), *Peʿamim* 16 (1983): 65–88; id., "Halakhic Responses of Syrian and Egyptian Rabbinical Authorities to Social and Technological Change," in *Studies in Contemporary Judaism,* vol. 2, ed. P. Medding (Bloomington: Indiana University Press, 1986), pp. 18–51.

111. For a fuller explanation see Klein, *Guide*, pp. 393–94.

112. Greenberg, *On Women*, pp. 35, 136.

113. Norma Joseph, H-Judaic list (h-judaic@h-net.msu.edu), 24–25 June 1997. See also *International Jewish Women's Human Rights Watch* (Jerusalem

Center for Public Affairs and the International Council of Jewish Women) newsletter, no. 11 (Fall 2001) and *Jewish Law Watch: The Agunah Dilemma* (Jerusalem: Schechter Institute of Jewish Studies, 2001). This is an example of a recent issue that brings together the religious concerns of Diaspora and Israeli Jews. See chapter 7, "Israel and Diaspora Links."

114. Haut, "*Agunah*," pp. 197–99.

115. Ronen Shamir, Michal Shitrai, and Nelly Elias, "Religion, Feminism, and Professionalism," *Jewish Journal of Sociology* 38 (1996): 73–88.

116. Mordechai Friedman, "Polygamy in Jewish Society—New Sources from the Cairo Geniza; the State of Research" (in Hebrew), *Pe'amim* 25 (1985): 3–12; A. Laredo, "Las Taqqanot de los expulsados de Castilla en Marruecos y su regimen matrimonial y successoral," *Sefarad* 8 (1948): 245–76.

117. Ha-Cohen, *Higgid*, p. 117.

118. Avishur, *Jewish Wedding*, p. 66.

119. Harvey E. Goldberg, *Cave-Dwellers and Citrus-Growers: A Jewish Community in Libya and Israel* (Cambridge: Cambridge University Press, 1972), pp. 24–25, 44. The venerated Moroccan rabbi Yisrael Abihatsira, popularly known as Baba Sali, was married to two wives when he migrated to Israel in the 1960s. On Yemen, see Laurence Loeb, "Gender, Marriage, and Social Conflict in Habban," in *Sephardi and Middle Eastern Jewries: History and Culture in the Modern Era*, ed. Harvey E. Goldberg (Bloomington: Indiana University Press; New York: Jewish Theological Seminary of America, 1996), pp. 267–68.

120. Reuben Ahroni, *The Jews of the British Crown Colony of Aden: History, Culture, and Ethnic Relations* (Leiden: Brill, 1994), p. 146, n. 1. On the kaddish prayer, see chapter 6, "The Middle Ages."

121. Udovitch and Valensi, *Last*, p. 49.

122. Israeli law, as it developed after statehood (in 1948), allowed existing plural marriages to remain intact, both among local Arabs and among Jews immigrating from the Middle Eastern countries. It did not allow new polygynous marriages to take place, but the law was sometimes discreetly ignored by certain groups.

123. Goitein, *Mediterranean Society*, 3: 149.

124. Loeb, "Gender," pp. 267–68.

125. Ibid., p. 273.

126. A description of a *tish* is found in Samuel Heilman, *Defenders of the Faith: Inside Ultra-Orthodox Judaism* (New York: Schocken Books, 1992), pp. 85–93. An example of a tish turning into a different kind of celebratory occasion is found in Shifra Epstein, "Drama on a Table: The Bobover Hasidim *Piremshpiyl*," in *Judaism Viewed*, ed. H. E. Goldberg (Albany: State University of New York Press, 1987), pp. 195–217.

127. Israel Yuval, personal communication.

128. Mishna *Berakhot* 2:5 and 3:1. On the Shma' Yisrael, see chapter 3, "Receiving the Torah and Access to It."

129. Edward Westermarck, *A History of Human Marriage*, 5th ed., rewritten (New York: Allerton, 1922), 2: 462. The work originally appeared in part as Westermarck's thesis (Helsingfors, 1889).

130. TB *Berakhot* 30b–31a. A zuz is a monetary unit.

131. Lauterbach, "Ceremony."

132. A perspective stemming from the classic study of Arnold van Gennep, *The Rites of Passage,* trans. M. B. Vizedom and G. L. Caffee (London: Routledge & Kegan Paul, 1960 [orig. 1909]). See also "Henna and Transitions" earlier in this chapter.

133. Ruth Gladstein-Kestenberg, "The Breaking of a Glass at a Wedding" (in Hebrew), *Studies in the History of the Jewish People and the Land of Israel* 4 (1978): 205–8.

134. TB *Ketubbot* 16b.

135. Lancelot Addison, *The Present State of the Jews (More Particularly Relating to Those in Barbary)* (London, 1675), p. 53. That Addison included material taken from the work of the Swiss author Johannes Buxtorf has been discussed by Elliot Horowitz, " 'A Different Mode of Civility': Lancelot Addison on the Jews of Barbary," *Studies in Church History* 29 (1992): 309–25. See the English translation of Johannes Buxtorf, *The Jewish Synagogue, or an Historical Narration of the State of the Jewes* (London, 1657), p. 292.

136. Benzion Meir Hai Uzziel, *Mishpetei Uzziel* [The Laws of Uzziel], 3 vols. (Jerusalem, 1950–1964), 2: 431–32; Maurice Lamm, *The Jewish Way in Love and Marriage* (San Francisco: Harper & Row, 1980), p. 230.

137. Guttman, "Jewish Medieval Marriage," p. 50.

138. The custom was known to an Ashkenazi rabbi in Italy; see n. 87 above.

139. See Valensi, "Religious," p. 76.

140. For other examples, and parallels among Muslims, see Ben-Ami, "Mariage."

141. Westermarck, *History,* pp. 456–64.

142. Jamil Hilal, "Meaning and Symbol in Some Marriage Ceremonies in Arab Rural Communities: A Case Study from Tripolitania, Libya," *A Monthly Journal and Record of the Departmental Societies of the Faculty of Arts and Education* 4 (1969): 14–17; John Mason, "Sex and Symbol in the Treatment of Women: The Wedding Rite in a Libyan Oasis Community," *American Ethnologist* 2 (1975): 649–61.

143. Dan Pagis, *A Secret Sealed: Hebrew Baroque Emblem-Riddles from Italy and Holland* (in Hebrew) (Jerusalem: Magnes Press, 1986), pp. 65–81.

144. Galit Hasan-Rokem, *Web of Life: Folklore and Midrash in Rabbinic Literature,* trans. Batya Stein (Stanford, Calif.: Stanford University Press, 2000), p. 65.

145. Edmund Leach, *Culture and Communication: The Logic by Which Symbols Are Connected* (Cambridge: Cambridge University Press, 1976), pp. 19, 27. There is some indication of a white-black contrast paralleling marriage and mourning in the Babylonian Talmud, *Shabbat* 114a.

146. Mishna *Berakhot* 3:1.

147. TB *Ketubbot* 7a–8b.

148. One text which may provide the basis of this association may be found in the Zohar. See Isaiah Tishby and Fishel Lachower, trans. and eds., *The Wisdom of the Zohar,* 3 vols. (New York: Oxford University Press, 1989), 1:

158–59. See also Michael Fishbane, *The Kiss of God: Spiritual and Mystical Death in Judaism* (Seattle: University of Washington Press, 1994), p. 37. For other customs that bring together weddings and the awareness of death, see Herman Pollack, *Jewish Folkways in Germanic Lands: Studies in Aspects of Daily Life* (Cambridge, Mass.: MIT Press, 1971), pp. 36–38; S.-A. Goldberg, *Crossing the Jabbok*, pp. 119, 145.

149. See chapter 5, "Popular Pilgrimages."

150. For example, Gen. 37:34, 2 Sam. 1:11, and Job 1:20.

151. Rabbi Joseph Brodie.

152. *Arba'ah Turim, Even Ha-'ezer* 65:3.

153. In Hebrew orthography, the wordplay simply entails the reversal of the first two letters of the words.

154. *Arba'ah Turim, Even Ha-'ezer* 65:3, Perisha commentary ad loc. citing the *Kol Bo*.

155. Kafih, *Halikhot*, p. 139.

156. Midrash *Eikha Rabbah*, ed. S. Buber (Vilnius: Ram, 1899), pp. 89–90 (on Lam. 1:16).

157. TB *Makkot* 24b.

158. I follow the logic of a story about Rabban Yohanan Ben-Zakkai who, after losing a son, criticized colleagues for trying to comfort him by mentioning the losses of biblical characters, an attempt at consolation that only compounded his own sorrow. See *The Fathers According to Rabbi Nathan* 14:6, trans. and ed. Judah Goldin (New Haven, Conn.: Yale University Press, 1955), pp. 76–77.

159. Solomon Schechter, "Safed in the Sixteenth Century," in *Studies in Judaism* (Philadelphia: Jewish Publication Society, 1958), pp. 231–97; Scholem, *On the Kabbalah*, pp. 138–45.

160. For the sources, see Isa. 49:19; 62:5. The Lekha Dodi hymn was translated into German by J. G. von Herder in the eighteenth century and Heinrich Heine in the nineteenth century.

161. Leone Modena, *Historia dei riti hebraici* (*The History of the Rites, Customs, and Manner of Life of the Present Jews throughout the World*), trans. E. Chilmead (London, 1650), pp. 178 ff.

CHAPTER 5. PILGRIMAGE AND CREATING IDENTITIES

1. Harvey E. Goldberg, Samuel C. Heilman, and Barbara Kirshenblatt-Gimblett, *The Israel Experience: Studies in Youth Travel and Jewish Identity* (Jerusalem: Andrea and Charles Bronfman Philanthropies Foundation, 2002), p. 79.

2. Arnold van Gennep, "The Pilgrimage of the Rabb," in *Time out of Time (Essays on the Festival)*, ed. Alessandro Falassi (Albuquerque: University of New Mexico Press, 1987), pp. 54–61. It was van Gennep who formulated the concept of "rites of passage." See his *The Rites of Passage*, trans. M. B. Vizedom and G. L. Caffee (London: Routledge & Kegan Paul, 1960 [orig. 1909]), and the discussion below (including n. 13).

3. Jack Kugelmass, "The Rites of the Tribe: The Meaning of Poland for American Jewish Tourists," *Going Home, YIVO ANNUAL* 21 (1993): 395–453; Jackie Feldman, " 'Roots in Destruction': The Jewish Past as Portrayed in Israeli Youth Voyages to Poland," in *The Life of Judaism,* ed. Harvey E. Goldberg (Berkeley: University of California Press, 2001), pp. 149–72.

4. Exod. 23:14–17, 34:23–24; Deut. 16:16.

5. The association between Shavuot and the "giving of the Torah" emerged in rabbinic tradition but is not mentioned in the Pentateuch. See chapter 3, "Entering the World of Torah."

6. See the references in n. 4 above.

7. See beginning of chapter 2 in this volume.

8. See also the discussion of Elijah in chapter 2, "Rabbinic Circumcision."

9. Van Gennep, "The Pilgrimage," p. 60.

10. See chapter 3, "Entering the World of Torah."

11. TB *Berakhot* 31a.

12. Victor Turner, *The Ritual Process: Structure and Anti-Structure* (Chicago: Aldine, 1969), pp. 126–27; Martin Buber, *I and Thou,* trans. R. G. Smith (Edinburgh: Clark, 1958).

13. Turner, *Ritual Process.* For the application of van Gennep's notion of rites of passage to pilgrimage, see Victor Turner, "The Center out There: Pilgrim's Goal," *History of Religions* 12 (1973): 191–230; Victor Turner and Edith Turner, *Image and Pilgrimage in Christian Culture: Anthropological Perspectives* (New York: Columbia University Press, 1978). Subsequent research has modified Turner's paradigm in various ways, while still recognizing that the shaping of personal identities within a cultural matrix is a major theme of pilgrimages and some kinds of tourism. See John Eade and Michael Sallnow, *Contesting the Sacred: The Anthropology of Christian Pilgrimage* (London: Routledge, 1991). One educational program that brings young American Jews to Israel was explicitly stimulated by Turner's ideas. See Charles Herman, "Nesiya—An Israel Experience," in *Studies in Jewish Education,* vol. 7 (Jerusalem: Magnes Press, 1995), pp. 158–81.

14. Jackie Feldman, "The Pull of the Center and the Experience of Communitas in Second Temple Pilgrimage" (in Hebrew) (M.A. thesis, Department of Religion, Hebrew University, Jerusalem, 1988); id., "Les pèlerinages rituel au deuxième Temple," in *La société juive au travers des siècles,* vol. 2, ed. Shmuel Trigano (Paris: Fayard, 1992), pp. 156–79. Feldman builds upon the study of Shmuel Safrai, *Haaliyah le-regel be-vayit sheni* [Pilgrimage during the Second Temple] (Tel Aviv: Am Ha-sefer, 1965; 2d rev. ed., Jerusalem, 1985).

15. Rabbinic discussions understand this rule in different ways. One line of reasoning is that Jerusalem was not among the territories allotted to the tribes by Joshua; it was annexed by David at a later time when he made the city his capital. For that reason, no Israelite can claim outright ownership of land in Jerusalem and each must share it with others. Another line of reasoning sees all of Jerusalem as sharing in the sanctity of the Temple, and therefore considered the property of God.

16. Strict observance of the laws of tithes and heave-offerings was also among the ritual issues stressed by Pharisees in Second Temple times to set themselves apart from the less punctilious "people of the land." See, e.g., Jacob Neusner, "Fellowship through Law: The Ancient Havurah," in id., *Contemporary Judaic Fellowship in Theory and in Practice,* (New York: Ktav, 1972), pp. 13–30. What the connection between people known as ḥaverim (members of a havura) and those called the *perushim,* or Pharisees, was is unclear. Shaye J. Cohen, *From the Maccabees to the Mishnah* (Philadelphia: Westminster Press, 1987), pp. 118–19, notes that much is unclear about the historical content of "the havura."

17. TJ *Ḥagigah* 3:6, 79d. See the further discussion in chapter 7, "Orthodoxy and Separation."

18. Elchanan Reiner, "Pilgrims and Pilgrimage to Eretz Yisrael, 1099–1517" (Ph.D. diss., Hebrew University, Jerusalem, 1988). For the previous period, see Moshe Gil, *A History of Palestine, 634–1099,* trans. E. Broido (Cambridge: Cambridge University Press, 1992), pp. 609–31.

19. Ignaz Goldziher, "Veneration of Saints in Islam," in *Muslim Studies,* vol. 2, trans. C. R. Barber and S. M. Stern (London: Allen & Unwin, 1971 [orig. 1890]), pp. 255–341.

20. Avraham Ben-Yaʿaqov, *Qevarim qedoshim be-bavel* [Sacred Graves in Babylonia] (Jerusalem: Mossad Har-Rav Kook, 1973), pp. 37–98; Zvi Yehuda, "The Jews of Babylon's Struggle for Control of the Tomb of the Prophet Ezekiel in Kifel in the Second Millennium C.E." (in Hebrew), in *Studies in the History and Culture of Iraqi Jewry,* vol. 6 (Or Yehudah: Babylonian Jewry Heritage Center, 1991), pp. 21–75.

21. S. D. Goitein, *A Mediterranean Society: The Jewish Communities of the Arab World as Portrayed in the Documents of the Cairo Geniza,* vol. 5: *The Individual* (Berkeley: University of California Press, 1988), pp. 19–24.

22. On Ha-Levi, see ibid., 5: 448–68. On Yehiel, see Israel Ta-Shema, "A New Chronography on the Thirteenth-Century Tosaphists" (in Hebrew), *Shalem* 3 (1981): 319–24. In Paris, Yehiel participated in a public disputation in which he was required to defend the Talmud against Christian charges.

23. See chapter 4, "Breaking the Glass."

24. Y. Elitzur, "Sources of the 'Nebi-Samuel' Traditions" (in Hebrew), *Cathedra* 31 (1984): 75–90. See the discussion of Samuel's birth in the previous section ("Pilgrimage in the Bible and Second Temple Times"), and in chapter 3, "Entering the World of Torah."

25. TB *Qiddushin* 38a; *Rosh Ha-shanah* 10b–11a. The latter source suggests that Samuel was born in the New Year months of Tishri or Nisan, and also, in trying to reconcile various text-based inferences with the fact that pregnancy normally lasts nine months, expresses an opinion that the sons of Sarah, Rachel, and Hannah (Samuel's mother) might have been born after seven months and survived. The discussion raises the possibility of different calculations with regard to Samuel's birth.

26. Later mystical literature in the Zohar provides a theory that makes circumcision a prerequisite for the study of Torah or the more rare experience of prophetic revelation. See Elliot Wolfson, "Circumcision, Vision of God, and

Textual Interpretation: From Midrashic Trope to Mystical Symbol," *History of Religions* 27 (1987): 189–215, esp. 211–13. This refined textual argument may perhaps reflect earlier popular ideas linking circumcision to the study of Torah and/or the experience of prophecy (which also applied to Samuel), notions that could have shaped tradition's determination of Samuel's death/birthday.

27. David ben Zimra, *She'elot u-teshuvot* [Responsa] (Warsaw, 1882), pt. 2, no. 608. See the discussion of hair-cutting in chapter 3, "Other Torah Education Ceremonies."

28. For a midrashic precedent linking the weight of an infant to the size of a religious donation, see Galit Hasan-Rokem, *Web of Life: Folklore and Midrash in Rabbinic Literature,* trans. Batya Stein (Stanford, Calif.: Stanford University Press, 2000), pp. 119–20, and her reference to Midrash *Eikha Rabba* 1:51 [in the edition by S. Buber (Vilnius: Ram, 1899), pp. 85–86].

29. Van Gennep, *Rites of Passage,* pp. 71–72, 167; Yoram Bilu, "Mi-milah le-milah: Nituah psikho-tarbuti shel havnayat zehut gavrit be-tiksei yaldut ba-hevra ha-haredit," *Alpayim* 19 (2000): 17–45.

30. Harvey E. Goldberg, "Cambridge in the Land of Canaan: Descent, Alliance, Circumcision, and Instruction in the Bible," *Journal of the Ancient Near Eastern Society* 24 (1996): 9–34.

31. See chapter 3, "Other Torah Education Ceremonies."

32. Ben Zimra, *She'elot u-teshuvot,* pt. 1, no. 513, refers to vows made by a woman with regard to her sick son.

33. Abraham Ya'ari, "History of the Pilgrimage to Meron" (in Hebrew), *Tarbiz* 31 (1961): 72–101.

34. Such collections of water are formed by percolation through porous limestone.

35. These sages, who came to represent competing "schools" or orientations within rabbinic Judaism, lived before the destruction of the Temple in 70 C.E. See Mishna *Avot* 1:12.

36. TB *Shabbat* 33b–34a.

37. Solomon Schechter, "Safed in the Sixteenth Century—A City of Legists and Mystics," in id., *Studies in Judaism,* vol. 2 (Philadelphia: Jewish Publication Society of America, 1908), pp. 182–285.

38. See, e.g., Goitein, *Mediterranean Society,* 5: 18–22, and the description of the modern pilgrimage in Meron in Y. Bilu and H. Abramowitz, "In Search of the Saddiq: Visitational Dreams among Moroccan Jews in Israel," *Psychiatry* 48 (1985): 83–92.

39. See chapter 3, "Other Torah Education Ceremonies."

40. *EJ,* 12: 1382–89.

41. There are many variations regarding this rule. In general, Sephardi traditions provide more days within the 'Omer period when one is allowed to marry than do Ashkenazi traditions. See Herbert C. Dobrinsky, *A Treasury of Sephardic Laws and Customs* (New York: Ktav, 1988), pp. 46, 63, 283–84, and Solomon Ganzfried, *Qizzur Shulhan Arukh* 120: 6–7. Both traditions allow marriages to take place on the 33d day of the 'Omer.

42. See Yael Zerubavel, *Recovered Roots: Collective Memory and the Making of Israeli National Tradition* (Chicago: University of Chicago Press, 1995), pp. 54–56, 96–116, on reinterpretations of the historical events in the background of Lag ba-'Omer.

43. See chapter 7, "Mysticism, the Genders, and the Individual."

44. Rabbi Shim'on Lavi, of Spanish origin, was active in Fez, Morocco, and in Tripoli, Libya. It is in fact possible that there were two Rabbi Lavis who have become merged in collective memory and documents. In any event, "he" is known for the Bar Yohai hymn, into which his name is woven as an acrostic, and was the author of a major commentary on the Zohar entitled *Ketem Paz* (*EJ*, 10: 1318–19). The Zohar does not see Lag ba-'Omer as the date of Bar Yohai's death. See Yehudah Libes, "Ha-mashiah shel ha-zohar," in *Ha-ra'ayon ha-meshihi be-yisrael* [Gershom Scholem Festschrift] (Jerusalem: Israeli National Academy of Sciences, 1982), pp. 110–11 n. 99. See also Boaz Huss, *Sockets of Fine Gold: The Kabbalah of Rabbi Shim'on Ibn Lavi* (in Hebrew) (Jerusalem: Ben-Zvi Institute, 2000); id., "*Sefer ha-Zohar* as a Canonical, Sacred and Holy Text: Changing Perspectives on the Book of Splendor between the Thirteenth and Eighteenth Centuries," *Journal of Jewish Thought and Philosophy* 7 (1998): 257–307.

45. See chapter 4, "Breaking the Glass."

46. Isaiah Tishby and Fishel Lachower, trans. and eds., *The Wisdom of the Zohar*, 3 vols. (New York: Oxford University Press, 1989), 1: 137, 165.

47. Ibid., 2: 837.

48. The story putatively involves R. Isaac Luria. See Ya'ari, "History," p. 85.

49. See the seventeenth-century source cited in *EJ*, 8: 495.

50. Moshe Idel, "Kabbalah and Music," in *Judaism and Art* (in Hebrew), ed. David Cassuto (Ramat Gan: Kotlar Institute for Judaism and Contemporary Thought, Bar Ilan University, 1989), pp. 275–89. The quotation from the Jerusalem source (p. 285) makes the metaphor explicit: "like a groom going out to meet a bride, so the neshamah is happy with joy." On North Africa, see Frija Zuaretz et al., eds., *Sefer Yahadut Luv* [Libyan Jewry] (Tel Aviv: Va'ad Qehillot Luv Be-Yisrael, 1960), p. 398; Irene Awret, *Days of Honey: The Tunisian Boyhood of Rafael Uzan* (New York: Schocken Books, 1984), p. 62.

51. Gershom Scholem, *Major Trends in Jewish Mysticism* (New York: Schocken Books, 1941), p. 285; anon., *Hemdat Yamim* (Izmir, 1731/1732), pt. 3, "The Days of the 'Omer," ch. 2.

52. Yoram Bilu, "The Inner Limits of Communitas: A Covert Dimension of Pilgrimage Experience," *Ethos* 16 (1988): 302–25; Eade and Sallnow, *Contesting.*

53. Goldziher, "Veneration of Saints"; Ernest Gellner, *Saints of the Atlas* (London: Weidenfeld & Nicolson, 1969). Descriptions of celebrations at the tombs of marabouts, frequently called *musems*, are found in Vincent Crapanzano, *The Hamadsha* (Berkeley: University of California Press, 1973), pp. 114–18; Paul Rabinow, *Symbolic Domination* (Chicago: University of Chicago Press, 1975), pp. 89–95; and Dale Eickelman, *Moroccan Islam* (Austin: University of Texas Press, 1976), pp. 171–78.

54. Fieldwork both in Morocco and among Moroccan Jews in Israel has contributed to the understanding of the veneration of tzaddikim. See Issachar Ben-Ami, *Saint Veneration among the Jews in Morocco* (Detroit: Wayne State University Press, 1998); Bilu and Abramowitz, "In Search of the Saddiq"; Y. Bilu, "Dreams and the Wishes of the Saint," in *Judaism Viewed from Within and from Without: Anthropological Studies,* ed. H. E. Goldberg (Albany: State University of New York Press, 1987), pp. 285–314; and H. E. Goldberg, "The Mellahs of Southern Morocco: Report of a Survey," *Maghreb Review* 8, 3–4 (1983): 61–69.

55. Issachar Ben-Ami, *Veneration des Saints chez les Juifs du Maroc* (in Hebrew) (Jerusalem: Magnes Press, 1984), pp. 88–89; Ben-Ami, *Saint Veneration,* p. 96; Yosef Meshash, *Mayyim Ḥayyim* (Fez, 1934), pp. 169–79. Meshash's comments on the hillulot in Morocco complain about the transgressions of religious rules that sometimes result from the enthusiasm for visiting tzaddikim, such as traveling on the Sabbath and the licentious mixing of men and women. See also Oren Kosansky, "Tourism, Charity, and Profit: The Movement of Money in Moroccan Jewish Pilgrimage," *Cultural Anthropology* 17 (2002): 359–400.

56. M. Bloch and J. Parry, eds., *Death and the Regeneration of Life* (Cambridge: Cambridge University Press, 1982), p. 11.

57. This may take place in other religious traditions as well, as suggested by Victor and Edith Turner with regard to Jesus in Christian hagiolatry. See Turner and Turner, *Image and Pilgrimage,* p. 11.

58. Sylvie-Anne Goldberg, *Crossing the Jabbok: Illness and Death in Ashkenazi Judaism in Sixteenth- through Nineteenth-Century Prague,* trans. Carol Cosman (Berkeley: University of California Press, 1996 [orig. 1989]). See chapter 6 in this volume, "The Individual and the Organization of Death."

59. Haïm Zafrani, *Mille ans de vie juive au Maroc: Histoire et culture, religion et magie,* 2 vols. (Paris: Maisonneuve & Larose, 1983–86), 1: 101; Dobrinsky, *Treasury,* p. 76.

60. Ben-Ami, *Saint Veneration,* p. 324.

61. Zafrani, *Mille ans,* pp. 58–74; Goldberg, "The Mellahs." One book used for ritualized study was *Ḥoq le-Yisrael.* See chapter 3, "Adult Study and Rituals," and Huss, "*Sefer ha-Zohar* as a Canonical, Sacred and Holy Text," p. 297.

62. André Chouraqui, *Marche vers l'Occident: Les Juifs d'Afrique du Nord* (Paris: Presses universitaires de France, 1952), p. 281.

63. See chapter 3, "Bar Mitzvah."

64. See chapter 3, "The Torah as a Person." The scarcity of printed books in the rural communities in North Africa is evident in the Judeo-Arabic term for "printed book" common among the Jews of the Tripolitanian countryside in Libya. This term was *siddur,* whose more general meaning in Jewish culture is "prayer book." Prayer books were salient among the few printed volumes reaching this region. See Mordecaï Ha-Cohen, *The Book of Mordechaï,* trans. and ed. Harvey E. Goldberg (London: Darf, 1993), p. 112. A parallel situation (with different terminology) existed in southern Morocco.

65. Harvey E. Goldberg, "Torah and Children," in *Judaism Viewed from Within and from Without: Anthropological Studies,* ed. H. E. Goldberg (Albany: State University of New York Press, 1987), pp. 116–17.

66. Bracha Yaniv, *The Torah Case: Its History and Design* (Ramat Gan: Bar-Ilan University Press; Jerusalem: Ben-Zvi Institute, 1997).

67. See the case described in detail in A. L. Udovitch and L. Valensi, *The Last Arab Jews: The Communities of Jerba, Tunisia* (New York: Harwood Academic, 1984), pp. 56–57. A biblical prototype of this attitude may be found in the story of King David's bringing the divine ark back to Jerusalem and the blessing bestowed upon the house of 'Oved Edom ha-Giti while the ark resided there (2 Sam. 6:11–12).

68. Preferably along with the burial of a scholar: see *Shulhan Arukh, Yoreh De'ah* 282:10. Various forms that book burial takes are surveyed by Mark Cohen and Yedida Stillman, "The Cairo Genizah and Genizah Customs among Middle Eastern Jews" (in Hebrew), *Pe'amim* 24 (1985): 3–35.

69. See chapter 2, "Eve of Circumcision Celebrations." It might also have been used in instances of difficult childbirth (see chapter 2, "Recognizing Gender").

70. See chapter 3, "The Torah as a Person."

71. There were, however, other ways of "representing" the Torah by bringing home one of its appurtenances. Such practices were found in a variety of communities.

72. Goldziher, "Veneration of Saints," p. 259.

73. Ibid., p. 255.

74. Richard I. Cohen, " 'And Your Eyes Shall See Your Teachers': The Rabbi as Icon" (in Hebrew), *Zion* 58 (1993): 407–52.

75. I use the term "local religion" in preference to phrases with invidious connotations such as "folk religion" or "popular religion." The general problem is discussed, from the point of view of the religious lives of women, by Chava Weissler, *Voices of the Matriarchs: Listening to the Prayers of Early Modern Jewish Women* (Boston: Beacon Press, 1998), pp. 172–86.

76. I use "him" in reference to saints generally because female saints (*tzaddikot*) are rare. A few are discussed in Ben-Ami, *Saint Veneration*, ch. 18, pp. 305–21. See also the discussion of Rachel in "The Personal and the Political," later in this chapter.

77. Reiner, *Pilgrims*, p. 277.

78. Tishby and Lachower, *Wisdom of the Zohar*, 2: 862–63.

79. R. Cohen, " 'And Your Eyes . . . ,'" pp. 411–15. The prohibition against making "graven images" appears in the Ten Commandments (Exod. 20:4; Deut. 5:8).

80. TB *Berakhot* 31a.

81. Turner, *Ritual Process*; id., "The Center out There."

82. Here I follow the discussion of Moshe Greenberg, *Biblical Prose Prayer as a Window to the Popular Religion of Ancient Israel* (Berkeley: University of California Press, 1983), p. 22. *Lehitpallel* is related to the verb *pillel*, which carries the significations of "estimate, judge, [and] render a verdict." The linguis-

tic form *lehit-* indicates a reflexive action, so that *lehitpallel* might be translated: "to seek a judgment for oneself."

83. Ibid., p. 44. See also the discussion by S. D. Goitein of "the individual" in medieval Muslim society, *Mediterranean Society*, 5: 215. He contrasts the personal prayer of Muhammad, as it appears in the Quran, with earlier traditions of Jewish and Christian liturgical and hymnal prayer.

84. Victor Turner, "Pilgrimages as Social Processes," in *Dramas, Fields and Metaphors* (Ithaca, N.Y.: Cornell University Press, 1974), p. 175.

85. On the celebration, see Daphna Musnikov, "The Women of Elijah" (in Hebrew) (M.A. thesis, Department of Sociology and Anthropology, Hebrew University, Jerusalem, 1995). On the criticism, see H. S. Kehimkar, *The History of the Bene Israel in India* (Tel Aviv: Dayag, 1937), p. 65. The celebration is further discussed in chapter 7, "Family, Community, and Food." On Elijah in general, see chapter 2, "Rabbinic Circumcision."

86. Bilu and Abramowitz, "In Search"; Awret, *Days of Honey*, p. 75.

87. On R. Meir Baʿal ha-Ness, see *EJ*, 11: 1245–47, and "The Personal and the Political" later in this chapter.

88. Michael M. Laskier, *The Alliance Israélite Universelle and the Jewish Communities of Morocco, 1862–1962* (Albany: State University of New York Press, 1983); Aron Rodrigue, *French Jews, Turkish Jews: The Alliance Israélite and the Politics of Jewish Schooling in Turkey, 1860–1925* (Bloomington: Indiana University Press, 1990); id., *Images of Sephardi and Eastern Jewries in Transition: The Teachers of the Alliance Israélite Universelle, 1860–1939* (Seattle: University of Washington Press, 1993).

89. The words are from Prov. 3:2, and "they" are traditionally understood to be God's Torah and commandments. The verse is cited in the section of the Zohar describing Bar Yohai's death. See Tishby and Lachower, *Wisdom of the Zohar*, 1: 164.

90. R. Cohen, " 'And Your Eyes . . . ,' " pp. 443–44. Another instance of a reworked hillula is found in Ruth Fredman Cernea, "Flaming Prayers: *Hillula* in a New Home," in *Between Two Worlds: Ethnographic Essays on American Jewry*, ed. Jack Kugelmass (Ithaca, N.Y.: Cornell University Press, 1988), pp. 162–91.

91. Ben-Yaʿaqov, *Qevarim qedoshim*, p. 24. Rabbi Yosef Hayyim is also mentioned in chapter 3, "New Rituals of Education."

92. Weissler, *Voices*, p. 48.

93. Erik Cohen, "A Phenomenology of Tourist Experiences," *Sociology* 13 (1979): 179–201; Barbara Kirshenblatt-Gimblett, *Destination Culture: Tourism, Museums, and Heritage* (Berkeley: University of California Press, 1998).

94. Laurie Goodstein, "To Bind the Faith, Free Trips to Israel for Diaspora Youth," *New York Times*, 16 November 1998, p. A7. On these plans, see also *Haʾaretz-IHT*, Community Section, 7 January 2000, p. 23. On trips to Poland, see Kugelmass, "Rites of the Tribe."

95. Danielle Storper-Perez and Harvey E. Goldberg, "The Kotel: Toward an Ethnographic Portrait," *Religion* 24 (1994): 309–32.

96. Kenneth Brown and J. Mohr, "Journey through the Labyrinth," *Studies in Visual Communication* 8 (1982): 2–82.

97. Y. Bilu, "Dreams and the Wishes"; Ben-Ami, *Saint Veneration*, p. 179, n. 3; Harvey E. Goldberg, "Potential Polities: Jewish Saints in the Moroccan Countryside and in Israel," in *Faith and Polity: Essays on Religion and Politics*, ed. M. Bax, P. Kloos, and A. Koster (Amsterdam: Vrije Universiteit University Press, 1992), pp. 235–50; id., "Religious Responses among North African Jews in the Nineteenth and Twentieth Centuries," in *The Uses of Tradition: Jewish Continuity in the Modern Era*, ed. J. Wertheimer (New York: Jewish Theological Seminary with Harvard University Press, 1993), pp. 119–44.

98. Parallel to the Aramaic term for Torah, *oraita*.

99. Shoshana Ben-Dor, "The Sigd of the Beta-Israel: A Holiday of Covenant Renewal" (in Hebrew) (M.A. thesis, Department of Folklore, Hebrew University, Jerusalem, 1985).

100. Alex Weingrod, "Changing Israeli Landscapes: Buildings and the Uses of the Past," *Cultural Anthropology* 8 (1993): 370–87.

101. Vered Vinitzky-Seroussi, " 'Jerusalem Assassinated Rabin and Tel Aviv Commemorated Him': Memorials and the Discourse of National Identity in Israel," *City and Society*, annual review, 1998, pp. 183–203.

102. André Levy, "Ethnic Aspects of Israelis' Pilgrimage and Tourism to Morocco," *Pilgrimage, Jewish Folklore and Ethnology Review* 17, 1–2 (1995): 20–25; id., "To Morocco and Back: Tourism and Pilgrimage among Moroccan-born Israelis," in *Grasping Land: Space and Place in Israeli Discourse and Experience*, ed. E. Ben-Ari and Y. Bilu (Albany: State University of New York Press, 1997), pp. 25–46; Shlomo Deshen, "Near the Jerba Beach: Tunisian Jews, an Anthropologist, and Other Visitors," *Jewish Social Studies*, n.s., 3 (1997): 90–118.

103. Feldman, " 'Roots in Destruction' "; Oren B. Stier, "Lunch at Majdanek: The March of the Living as a Contemporary Pilgrimage of Memory," *Pilgrimage, Jewish Folklore and Ethnology Review* 17, 1–2 (1995): 57–66.

104. Darya Maoz, "My Heart Is in the East: The Journey of Israeli Young Adults to India" (in Hebrew) (M.A. thesis, Department of Sociology and Anthropology, Hebrew University, Jerusalem, 1999).

105. Anthony Giddens, *Modernity and Self-Identity: Self and Society in the Late Modern Age* (Stanford, Calif.: Stanford University Press, 1991).

106. Benedict Anderson, *Imagined Communities: Reflections on the Origin and Spread of Nationalism* (London: Verso, 1983).

107. Jonathan Boyarin, *"Storm from Paradise": The Politics of Jewish Memory* (Minneapolis: University of Minnesota Press, 1992), pp. 1–8.

108. Shifra Epstein, "Inventing a Pilgrimage: Ritual, Love, and Politics on the Road to Amuka," *Pilgrimage, Jewish Folklore and Ethnology Review* 17, 1–2 (1995): 25–32.

109. Reiner, *Pilgrims*, p. 237.

110. Ravit Naor, "Send Me a Groom (Charming and Smart)" (in Hebrew), *Ma'ariv, Signon*, 19 June 1996, pp. 8–11.

111. Laurence Loeb, *Outcaste: Jewish Life in Southern Iran* (London: Gordon & Breach, 1977), p. 230.

112. Kugelmass, "Rites of the Tribe"; Feldman, " 'Roots in Destruction.' " Probably in reaction to such criticisms, Polish youths were invited to participate in aspects of the "March of the Living" (see n. 103 above) in the spring of 2000.

113. Feldman, " 'Roots in Destruction.' "

114. Levy, "To Morocco and Back."

115. Oren B. Stier, personal communication.

116. Baila Shargel, "The Evolution of the Masada Myth," *Judaism* 28 (1979): 357–71; Edward Bruner and P. Gorfain, "Dialogic Narration and the Paradoxes of Masada," in *Text, Play and Story: The Construction and Reconstruction of Self and Society*, ed. E. Bruner (Washington, D.C.: American Ethnological Society, 1984), pp. 56–79; Nachman Ben-Yehudah, *The Masada Myth: Collective Mythmaking in Israel* (Madison: University of Wisconsin Press, 1995); Zerubavel, *Recovered*, chs. 5, 8, and 11.

117. Tamar Katriel, *Communal Webs: Communication and Culture in Contemporary Israel* (Albany: State University of New York Press, 1991), ch. 4; Ben-Yehudah, *Masada Myth*, p. 153.

118. Goldberg et al., *Israel Experience*, pp. 36–59.

119. Kugelmass, "Rites of the Tribe"; Levy, "To Morocco and Back."

120. Goldberg et al., *Israel Experience*, p. 308.

121. Ibid., p. 320.

122. Shalom Goldman, *The Wiles of Women / The Wiles of Men: Joseph and Potiphar's Wife in Ancient Near Eastern, Jewish, and Islamic Folklore* (Albany: State University of New York Press, 1995), pp. 131–43.

123. Naor, "Send Me a Groom." I have not been able to discover a historical source for this notion. One possibility is that there has been a popular merging of the name Ben Uzziel with that of Ben Azzai, a well-known mishnaic sage (who lived about a century later than Ben Uzziel), who never married (TB *Yebamot* 63b). The Talmud presents Ben Azzai as a focus of popular admiration who might appear in dreams (TB *Berakhot* 57b), a phenomenon closely linked to pilgrimage (Bilu and Abramovitch, "In Search"; Bilu, "Dreams and the Wishes"). Not much is known about Ben Uzziel, who is mentioned only a few times in rabbinic literature.

124. See chapter 2, "Rabbinic Circumcision."

125. See Claude Lévi-Strauss, *The Origin of Table Manners* (New York: Harper & Row, 1978), pp. 332–39.

126. Bilu, "Inner Limits."

127. Alex Weingrod, *The Saint of Beersheba* (Albany: State University of New York Press, 1990).

128. Shifra Epstein, "The New Month and Tu be-Av Pilgrimages as an Entryway to the Beliefs and Practices of Hasidim and Edot ha-Mizrah" (paper delivered at the Annual Meeting of the Association of Jewish Studies, Boston, December, 1990), pp. 18–19. A general perspective on rituals of this sort is found in Paul Fenton, "The Symbolism of Ritual Circumambulation in Judaism and Islam—A Comparative Study," *Journal of Jewish Thought and Philosophy* 6 (1997): 345–69.

129. Edith Turner, "Bar Yohai, Mystic: The Creative Persona and His Pilgrimage," in *Creativity/Anthropology*, ed. S. Lavie, K. Narayan, and R. Rosaldo (Ithaca, N.Y.: Cornell University Press, 1993), pp. 225–52, esp. 247–48.

130. Vince Beiser, "Casting a Spell," *Jerusalem Report*, 25 July 1996, pp. 32–34.

131. See chapter 3, "Adult Study and Rituals," for examples related to Torah study.

132. Susan Sered, "Women and Religious Change in Israel: Rebellion or Revolution?" *Sociology of Religion* 58 (1997): 1–24. On the recent decision, see *Haaretz*, Tuesday, 23 May 2000, p. B2. See also *Haaretz*, Friday, 14 July 2000, p. A9, and Friday, 1 June 2001, p. A9.

133. See article by Rami Chazut, *Yedioth Aharonoth*, Wednesday, 8 August 1997; Roger Friedland and Richard D. Hecht, "The Politics of Sacred Place: Jerusalem's Temple Mount / al-haram al-sharif," in *Sacred Places and Profane Spaces: Essays in the Geographics of Judaism, Christianity and Islam*, ed. Jamie Scott and Paul Simpson-Housley (Westwood, Conn.: Greenwood Press, 1991), pp. 35–49.

134. The search for a compromise was the initiative of the then minister of the treasury, Yaaqov Neeman, who was active in trying to find a modus vivendi for dealing with the controversy over conversions (see chapter 7, "Israel and Diaspora Links"). On the government agreement, see *Haaretz*, Tuesday, 23 May 2000, p. B2.

135. Friedland and Hecht, "Politics," pp. 21–62.

136. Wladyslaw T. Bartoszewski, *The Convent at Auschwitz* (New York: George Braziller, 1990).

137. See above in this chapter and Ben-Dor, *Sigd*. For an overall portrait of Ethiopian Jewry, see Steven Kaplan, *The Beta Israel (Falasha) in Ethiopia: From Earliest Times to the Twentieth Century* (New York: New York University Press, 1992); Hagar Salamon, *The Hyena People: Ethiopian Jews in Christian Ethiopia* (Berkeley: University of California Press, 1999).

138. On Gush Emunim, see Gideon Aran, "Jewish-Zionist Fundamentalism," in *Fundamentalisms Observed*, ed. M. Marty and S. Appleby (Chicago: University of Chicago Press, 1991), pp. 265–345. On the tomb of Joseph, see earlier in this chapter and Goldman, *Wiles*. In the fall of 2000, the Israeli authorities decided to relinquish their control of the site as a result of armed conflict with Palestinians that focused on Jewish presence there. Later, when Israeli forces frequently entered West Bank areas, small religious groups sought to establish themselves there.

139. Goldberg, *Judaism Viewed*, p. 229.

140. See Susan Starr Sered, "Rachel's Tomb: The Development of a Cult," *Jewish Studies Quarterly* 2 (1995): 103–48.

141. As pointed out by Turner and Turner, *Image*, pp. 63–64, female saints appear to provide potent images upon which sentiments of nationhood can be nourished.

142. W. Sollors, *Beyond Ethnicity* (New York: Oxford University Press, 1986), p. 71.

143. Susan Sered, "Rachel's Tomb and the Milk Grotto of the Virgin Mary: Two Women's Shrines in Bethlehem," *Journal of Feminist Studies in Religion* 4 (1986): 6–14.

144. See Susan Sered, "The Tale of Three Rachels: The Natural History of a Symbol," *Nashim: A Journal of Jewish Women's Studies and Gender Issues* 1 (1998): 5–41.

145. Goitein, *Mediterranean Society*, 5: 18; Kenneth Brown, "Religion, Commerce and the Mobility of Moroccan Jews" (in Hebrew), *Pe'amim* 38 (1989): 95–108.

146. Shlomo Deshen, "Political Ethnicity and Cultural Ethnicity in Israel during the 1960's," in *Urban Ethnicity*, ed. Abner Cohen (London: Tavistock Publications, 1974), pp. 285–313.

147. Miriam Greenberg, "Pilgrimage of a Non-Believer," *Pilgrimage, Jewish Folklore and Ethnology Review* 17, 1–2 (1995): 40–41; Marion S. Jacobson, "The Klezmer Club as Pilgrimage," ibid.: 42–46.

148. On Marranos, see chapter 7, "Seeds and Social Sites of the Modern Jewish World."

149. Jeffrey Shandler, "City of Jews, City of Gays: Amsterdam as an Impromptu Pilgrimage Site at the Tenth International Conference of Gay and Lesbian Jews," *Pilgrimage, Jewish Folkore and Ethnology Review* 17, 1–2 (1995): 47–52.

150. Nathanel Katzburg, "Halukkah," *EJ*, 7: 1207–16.

151. Gen. 23:19, 25:9–10, 49:29–31, 50:13, and chapter 6 in this volume, "Death in the Bible."

152. *EJ*, 15: 1132.

153. Danielle Storper-Perez and Harvey E. Goldberg, *Au pied du mur de Jerusalem: Approche anthropologique du mur du Temple* (Paris: Cerf, 1989).

154. Stuart A. Cohen, *The Scroll or the Sword?* (Amsterdam: Harwood Academic, 1997), p. 54.

CHAPTER 6. DEATH, MOURNING, AND REMEMBERING

1. See chapter 3, "Other Torah Education Ceremonies"; chapter 4, "Breaking the Glass"; chapter 5, "Popular Pilgrimages."

2. S. D. Goitein, *A Mediterranean Society: The Jewish Communities of the Arab World as Portrayed in the Documents of the Cairo Geniza* (Berkeley: University of California Press, 1967–93), vol. 5: *The Individual* (1988), pp. 160, 165.

3. Mishna *Yoma* 1:1.

4. See chapter 4, "Marriage, Women, and Menstruation."

5. The house, as a locus for the interpenetration of death and life, also appears in the memories of Algerian Jews now living in France. See the account by Joëlle Bahloul, *The Architecture of Memory: A Jewish-Muslim Household in Colonial Algeria, 1937–1962* (Cambridge: Cambridge University Press, 1996), p. 16. For a general approach to understanding aspects of life through

death, see Zygmunt Bauman, *Mortality and Immortality: And Other Life Strategies* (Stanford, Calif.: Stanford University Press, 1992).

6. Gen. 37:29, 34; 44:13; Lev. 10:6; 1 Sam. 15:27–28; 2 Sam. 1:11; and Job 1:20.

7. The reason the rule was stated in the case of an execution may have been the temptation for rulers to display the bodies of enemies who were executed (cf. Josh. 10:26). Immediate burial is also the norm in Islam.

8. Gen. 37:34; 2 Sam. 12:16–21, 14:2; Jer. 4:8.

9. Talmudic literature also refers to details in Ezek. 24:15–24 as a basis for customs of mourning.

10. Erich Brauer, *The Jews of Kurdistan,* completed and ed. Raphael Patai (Detroit: Wayne State University Press, 1993), p. 194.

11. Mishna *Mo'ed Qaṭan* 3:7; TB *Mo'ed Qaṭan* 25a; *Shulhan Arukh Yoreh De'ah* 340.

12. TB *Yebamot* 13b, links the verbal form *titgodedu* to a noun meaning "association"—*agudah.*

13. Mary Douglas, *Purity and Danger: An Analysis of Concepts of Pollution and Taboo* (New York: Praeger, 1966); id., *Natural Symbols: Explorations in Cosmology* (New York: Vintage Books, 1973).

14. The prohibition against tattooing appears in the same verse as a rule against scratching the skin as a gesture of mourning. On wholeness as a value in the Bible, see J. Pedersen, *Israel: Its Life and Culture,* vols. 1–2 (London: Oxford University Press, 1926), pp. 263–64, 358–59.

15. See chapter 4, "Marriage, Women, and Menstruation." The strict separation of death from life in biblical literature is reviewed by Neil Gillman, *The Death of Death: Resurrection and Immortality in Jewish Thought* (Woodstock, Vt.: Jewish Lights, 1997), ch. 3.

16. Gen. 42:38; Isa. 14:9; Ps. 88:4, 139:8; Job 11:8, 17:13.

17. See chapter 5, "The Personal and the Political."

18. The fact that the last verse in Genesis refers to Joseph's mummification (after his explicit request that his bones eventually be removed from Egypt [Gen. 50:24–26]) is perhaps a way of stating that the biblical narrative is "to be continued."

19. See chapter 5, "The Personal and the Political." Rachel, of course, was not the mother of all the children of Jacob (who was also called Israel), but only of two of them (Gen. 30:23–24; 35:16–18).

20. BT *Sanhedrin* 92b. Dan. 12:2–3 is also cited often as indicating a belief in personal resurrection.

21. There are many discussions of "body and soul" in Judaism with reference to the talmudic period. See Woolf Hirsch, *Rabbinic Psychology: Beliefs about the Soul in Rabbinic Literature of the Talmudic Period* (London: E. Goldston, 1947; reprint, New York: Arno Press, 1973). The following account is indebted to the sociological emphasis in Nissan Rubin, "The Sages' Conception of the Body and Soul," in *Essays in the Social Scientific Study of Judaism and Jewish Society,* ed. S. Fishbane and J. Lightstone (Montreal: Concordia University Press, 1990), pp. 47–103. Other recent formulations are found in Sylvie-Anne Goldberg, *Crossing the Jabbok: Illness and Death in Ashkenazi Judaism*

in Sixteenth- through Nineteenth-Century Prague, trans. Carol Cosman (Berkeley: University of California Press, 1996), ch. 1, and Gillman, *Death,* chs. 4–5.

22. Phrases indicating that God revives the dead (*meḥayeh metim,* or simply *meḥayeh*) appear five times in the second of the opening sections and its concluding benediction. See Joseph Hertz, *The Authorised Daily Prayer Book,* rev. ed. (New York: Bloch, 1948), pp. 130–35.

23. See TB *Berakhot* 60b; Hertz, *Authorised Daily Prayer Book,* p. 18. Dalia Sarah Marks, "Berakhot ha-pe'ulot ve-ha-berakhot ha-mavḥinot be-virkot ha-shaḥar" (M.A. thesis, Department of Hebrew Literature, Hebrew University, Jerusalem, 2000).

24. Hertz, *Authorised Daily Prayer Book,* p. 10.

25. Nissan Rubin, "Secondary Burial in the Mishnaic and Talmudic Periods: A Proposed Model of the Relationships of Social Structure to Burial Practices" (in Hebrew), in *Graves and Burial: Practices in Israel in the Ancient Period,* ed. Itamar Singer (Jerusalem: Yad Itzhak Ben-Zvi, 1994), pp. 248–69; id., *The End of Life: Rites of Burial and Mourning in the Talmud and Midrash* (in Hebrew) (Tel Aviv: Hakibbutz Hameuchad, 1997), pp. 145–53. Rubin's discussion elaborates a model suggested in Richard Huntington and Peter Metcalf, *Celebrations of Death: The Anthropology of Mortuary Ritual* (Cambridge: Cambridge University Press, 1979), p. 66, and also relates to work by Yehudi Cohen, "Macroethnology: Large-Scale Comparative Studies," in *Introduction to Cultural Anthropology: Essays in the Scope and Methods of the Science of Man,* ed. James A. Clifton (Boston: Houghton Mifflin, 1968), pp. 403–48.

26. Rubin, *End,* pp. 152–53.

27. The idea of soul is expressed in different words: see S.-A. Goldberg, *Crossing the Jabbok,* p. 87; Rubin, *End,* pp. 59–61. Gillman, *Death,* pp. 113, 284, n. 1, suggests translating the Hebrew phrase 'olam ha-ba as the "Age to Come," rather than the "World to Come," because the term 'olam can have a temporal connotation as well as a spatial reference.

28. Hertz, *Authorised Daily Prayer Book,* pp. 427–28.

29. The following paragraphs are based on Galit Hasan-Rokem, *Web of Life: Folklore and Midrash in Rabbinic Literature,* trans. Batya Stein (Stanford, Calif.: Stanford University Press, 2000).

30. Ibid., pp. 125–29.

31. For this story, see Midrash *Eikha Rabba* 42–49, proem 24, ed. S. Buber (Vilnius: Ram, 1899), pp. 25–28. See also the discussion in "The Personal and the Political" in chapter 5 above of Rachel's tomb.

32. See Goitein, *Mediterranean Society,* vol. 3: *The Family* (1978), pp. 2–6, 15; ibid., vol. 2: *The Community* (1971), p. 351. These customs were common to the Rabbanite and Karaite Jews of medieval Egypt. See Jacob Mann, *Text and Studies in Jewish History and Literature,* vol. 2: *Karaitica* (Philadelphia: Jewish Publication Society of America, 1935), pp. 256–57.

33. Goitein, *Mediterranean Society,* 3: 4, 7.

34. On different views in ancient sources about the effect of the words of the living on those who have died, see Rubin, *End,* pp. 154–55.

35. Ivan Marcus, "Mothers, Martyrs, and Moneymakers: Some Jewish Women in Medieval Europe," *Conservative Judaism* 38, 3 (1986): 34–45.

36. S.-A. Goldberg, *Crossing the Jabbok*, pp. 36–40.

37. David de Sola Pool, *The Kaddish* (New York: Bloch, 1929). See also *EJ*, 10: 660–62, and Leon Wieseltier, *Kaddish* (New York: Knopf, 1998).

38. TB *Shabbat* 119b; *Berakhot* 3a.

39. The source is a midrash, probably from the seventh or eighth century. See J. D. Eisenstein, ed., *Ozar Midrashim* (New York: Eisenstein, 1915), pp. 414–15. A translation is provided by Wieseltier, *Kaddish*, 36–38.

40. TB *Soṭah* 49a and Rashi ad. loc.

41. Pool, *Kaddish*, pp. 6–7.

42. On the siyyum, see chapter 3, "Adult Study and Rituals."

43. Hertz, *Authorised Daily Prayer Book*, pp. 1084–87; Wieseltier, *Kaddish*, pp. 30–33.

44. Moses Gaster, *The Exempla of the Rabbis* [*Sefer ha-maʼasiyot*] (London: Asia Publishing Co., 1924), pp. 92–93 (in Hebrew; summarized on p. 84 in English, item 134). A translation is found in Wieseltier, *Kaddish*, pp. 41–43, 126–27.

45. Israel M. Ta-Shema, "Some Notes on the Origins of the '*Kaddish Yathom*' [Orphan's Kaddish]" (in Hebrew), *Tarbiz* 53 (1984): 559–68; S.-A. Goldberg, *Crossing the Jabbok*, pp. 39–40; Rubin, *End*, pp. 154–55.

46. Pool, *Kaddish*, pp. 102–4 and the references he cites; n. 38 above.

47. On Sephardi perspectives, see A. Z. Idelsohn, *Jewish Liturgy and Its Development* (New York: Hebrew Union College, 1932), p. 87, and the discussion in Wieseltier, *Kaddish*, pp. 156–62.

48. Jack Riemer, ed., *Jewish Insights on Death and Mourning* (New York: Schocken Books, 1995), ch. 6. Wieseltier, *Kaddish*, depicts an intricate scholarly and personal journey tracing the history of the kaddish, which he undertook during his year of mourning. Kaddish, in Ashkenazi practice, is recited by a mourner for eleven months, rather than a full year, so as not to imply that the deceased was so wicked that he deserved twelve months in Gehenna. The specific rules regarding the twelfth month vary somewhat in different Sephardi traditions. See Herbert Dobrinsky, *A Treasury of Sephardic Laws and Customs* (Hoboken, N.J.: Ktav, 1988), ch. 5.

49. S.-A. Goldberg, *Crossing the Jabbok*, chs. 3–4.

50. See chapter 5, "*Hillulot* and the Zohar in Morocco."

51. There are brief references to organized groups that concerned themselves with some aspects of funerals and reburials in antiquity, but no solid evidence of anything resembling the later hevra kadisha. See TB *Moʼed Qaṭan* 27b; Tractate *Semaḥot* 12:5. In talmudic times, the family was responsible for arranging for burial, but there were communal religious norms that they had to follow.

52. S.-A. Goldberg, *Crossing the Jabbok*, p. 100.

53. Ibid., p. 90.

54. Dov Zlotnick, trans. and ed., *The Tractate "Mourning"* (New Haven, Conn.: Yale University Press, 1966). For summaries from the perspective of traditional halakha, see Maurice Lamm, *The Jewish Way in Death and Mourn-*

ing (New York: Jonathan David, 1969), and Isaac Klein, *A Guide to Jewish Religious Practice* (New York: Jewish Theological Seminary of America, 1979). A recent account that merges halakhic and historical information with an ethnographic perspective on contemporary America is found in Samuel C. Heilman, *When a Jew Dies: The Ethnography of a Bereaved Son* (Berkeley: University of California Press, 2001).

55. Zlotnick, *"Mourning,"* pp. 18–19.

56. See chapter 4, "Preserving, Reviving and Interpreting Customs."

57. *Shulhan Arukh, Yoreh De'ah* 339:1, which is based on the opening of Tractate Semahot.

58. See chapter 5 above, *"Hillulot* and the Zohar in Morocco."

59. S.-A. Goldberg, *Crossing the Jabbok*, pp. 91–92. Notions relating to the soul that appear in *Ma'avar Yabbok* and similar publications are discussed at length by Avriel Bar-Levav, "Sifrei holim u-metim be-sifrut ha-hanhagot" [Books for the Sick and the Dying in Jewish Conduct Literature], *Jerusalem Studies in Jewish Thought* 14 (1998): 341–91.

60. S.-A. Goldberg, *Crossing the Jabbok*, pp. 102–4.

61. See chapter 4, "Marriage, Women, and Menstruation."

62. Rubin, *End*, pp. 141–42.

63. See Mishna *Sheqalim* 1:1 and 2:5, TJ *Sheqalim* 2:5, TB *Mo'ed Qatan* 5a, and Maimonides, *Yad ha-Hazaqah, Shoftim* (Judges), *Avel* (Mourning) 4:4.

64. Ester Muchawsky-Schnapper, "The Use of Incense by Yemenite Jews," *Tema* 6 (1998): iii–xxx.

65. There is a great deal of variation within the liturgical traditions concerning prayers of supplication recited at this juncture of the morning service.

66. S.-A. Goldberg, *Crossing the Jabbok*, pp. 89–90.

67. Ibid., p. 106.

68. H. Pollack, *Jewish Folkways in Germanic Lands: Studies in Aspects of Daily Life* (Cambridge, Mass.: MIT Press, 1971), pp. 35–36; Avraham Hai Adadi, "Quntres maqom she-nahagu," in *Ha-shomer emet*, ed. F. Zuaretz and F. Tayyar (Tel Aviv: Va'ad Qehillot Luv Be-Yisrael, 1986), pp. 155 (orig. in *Vayiqra avraham* [Leghorn, 1865]).

69. See chapter 4, "Breaking the Glass."

70. This possibility was pointed out to me by Moshe Idel, mentioning a study by Eissler that I have not been able to identify.

71. S.-A. Goldberg, *Crossing the Jabbok*, pp. 142–45; Pollack, *Jewish Folkways*, p. 38 n.

72. See chapter 5, "Popular Pilgrimages," and the examples discussed below. See also chapter 7, "Mysticism, the Genders, and the Individual."

73. Gedalyah Nigal, *"Dybbuk" Tales in Jewish Literature* (in Hebrew) (Jerusalem: R. Mass, 1983). The term *dibbuk*, referring to what was seen as a generic phenomenon, developed in eastern Europe.

74. Yoram Bilu, "The Taming of Deviants and Beyond: An Analysis of Dybbuk Possession and Exorcism in Judaism," *Psychoanalytic Study of Society* 11 (1985): 1–32.

75. Michel Foucault, *The History of Sexuality,* vol. 1: *An Introduction* (New York: Vintage Books, 1980). This issue is further discussed in chapter 7, "Mysticism, the Genders, and the Individual."

76. Sometimes haqqafot took place in the room where a person died (see S.-A. Goldberg, *Crossing the Jabbok,* pp. 108, 116). For a general perspective on "walking around" rituals, see Paul Fenton, "The Symbolism of Circumambulation in Judaism and Islam—A Comparative Study," *Journal of Jewish Thought and Philosophy* 6 (1997): 345–69.

77. S.-A. Goldberg, *Crossing the Jabbok,* pp. 133–35.

78. One ethnographic example is found in Lloyd C. Briggs and Norina L. Guède, *No More For Ever: A Saharan Jewish Town,* Papers of the Peabody Museum of Archaeology and Ethnology, Harvard University, vol. 55, no. 1 (Cambridge, Mass.: Peabody Museum, 1964), p. 69.

79. Gershom Scholem, *On the Kabbalah and Its Symbolism* (New York: Schocken Books, 1965), pp. 153–56. See also Henry Abramovitch, "The Jerusalem Funeral as a Microcosm of the 'Mismeeting' between Religious and Secular Israelis," in *Tradition, Innovation, Continuity: Judaism and Jewishness in Contemporary Israel,* ed. B. Beit-Hallachmi and Z. Sobol (Albany: State University of New York Press, 1991), pp. 71–99, who adds a recent perspective to the custom.

80. See chapter 3, n. 80, for other references to influences developing in and emanating from Luria's circle and the Safed community. See also Zeev Gries, *Conduct Literature* (in Hebrew) (Jerusalem: Bialik Institute, 1989), pp. 80–99; Moshe Idel, " 'One from a Town, Two from a Clan'—The Diffusion of Lurianic Kabbala and Sabbateanism: A Re-Examination," *Jewish History* 7 (1993): 79–104.

81. TB *Mo'ed Qaṭan* 27a–b. Rabban Gamliel of Yavneh was a leader of the Jewish community at the turn of the second century C.E. He is viewed as responsible for a number of ordinances and practices with regard to burial. See Rubin, *End,* pp. 126–30, 135–37, 225–26.

82. Nissan Rubin, "Unofficial Memorial Rites in an Army Unit" (in Hebrew), *Megamot* 30 (1987): 139–50.

83. S.-A. Goldberg, *Crossing the Jabbok,* pp. 106, 131.

84. Wieseltier, *Kaddish,* pp. 177–91, 350, 456–57, notes a few exceptions to this generalization.

85. This usage appears, for example, in a lullaby composed by Yiddish author Sholem Aleichem. See A. Vinkovetzky, A. Kovner, and S. Leichter, *Anthology of Yiddish Folksongs* (Jerusalem: Magnes Press, 1983), pp. 109–11.

86. Susan W. Schneider, *Jewish and Female: Choices and Changes in Our Lives Today* (New York: Simon & Schuster, 1984), p. 146 (emphasis in the original); Avraham Burg, review of *Ha-datiyim he-ḥadashim,* by Yair Sheleg, *Ha'aretz,* Sefarim, 19 July 2000, pp. 1, 10. See also Marian Henriquez Neudel, "Saying Kaddish: The Making of a 'Regular,' " in *Jewish Insights on Death and Mourning,* ed. Jack Riemer (New York: Schocken Books, 1995), pp. 177–82.

87. Susan Sered, *Women as Ritual Experts: The Religious Lives of Elderly Jewish Women in Jerusalem* (New York: Oxford University Press, 1992). An

assessment of the notion of "domestic religion" as the sphere of women is found in Chava Weissler, *Voices of the Matriarchs: Listening to the Prayers of Early Modern Jewish Women* (Boston: Beacon Press, 1998), pp. 150–51, 170–71.

88. David de Sola Pool, ed. and trans., *Book of Prayer According to the Custom of the Spanish and Portuguese Jews* (New York: Union of Sephardic Congregations, 1941), pp. 206–7. See also the discussion above on Muslim lands, "The Middle Ages." In tracing the history of the kaddish, Wieseltier also notes the tension between mourning for a scholar and an ordinary individual. See his *Kaddish*, pp. 82–83, 88, 90–91, 158–59.

89. Meyer Fortes, "An Introductory Comment," in *Ancestors*, ed. W. H. Newell (The Hague: Mouton, 1976), p. 7.

90. Abraham Udovitch and Lucette Valensi, *The Last Arab Jews: The Communities of Jerba, Tunisia* (New York: Harwood Academic, 1984), pp. 64–66, 68.

91. Myer Samra, "Naming Patterns among Jews of Iraqi Origin in Sydney," *Jewish Journal of Sociology* 31 (1989): 25–37.

92. See chapter 3, "The Torah as a Person."

93. Harvey E. Goldberg, "Torah and Children: Symbolic Aspects of the Reproduction of Jews and Judaism," in *Judaism Viewed from Within and from Without: Anthropological Studies* (Albany: State University of New York Press, 1987), pp. 107–30.

94. See chapter 5, "*Hillulot* and the Zohar in Morocco."

95. *Shulhan Arukh, Yoreh De'ah* 282:10.

96. Joseph Tedgi, *Le livre et l'imprimerie hébraïque à Fes* (in Hebrew) (Jerusalem: Institut Ben-Zvi, 1994), p. 20.

97. Maya Melzer-Geva, "Constructing the Georgian Identity in the Israeli Social Context: An Inter-Cultural Learning Process" (Ph.D. diss., University of Haifa, 2001).

98. Riemer, *Jewish Insights*, p. 9.

99. S.-A. Goldberg, *Crossing the Jabbok*, p. 114.

100. Joseph Kafih, *Jewish Life in San'a* (in Hebrew) (Jerusalem: Ben-Zvi Institute, 1969), p. 251.

101. Aryeh Arthur Goren, "Sacred and Secular: The Place of Public Funerals in the Immigrant Life of American Jews," *Jewish History* 8 (1994): 269–305.

102. TB *Ketubbot* 111a.

103. Ibid. On the importance of being buried in the Land of Israel, see Rubin, *End*, pp. 133–36.

104. See chapter 5, "The Personal and the Political."

105. TB *Mo'ed Qatan* 28a.

106. Moshe Samet, "Halanat metim," *Asufot* 3 (1989): 413–65; S.-A. Goldberg, *Crossing the Jabbok*, pp. 195–99.

107. Ibid., pp. 415–16.

108. Briggs and Guède, *No More For Ever*, pp. 28–30. Goldberg, "Torah and Children," p. 127 n. 25.

109. TB *Berakhot* 58b.

110. Zvi Zohar, *Tradition and Change: Halakhic Responses of Middle Eastern Rabbis to Legal and Technological Change (1880–1920)* (in Hebrew) (Jerusalem: Ben-Zvi Institute, 1993), pp. 249–50.

111. Elliot Dorf, *"Choose Life": A Jewish Perspective on Medical Ethics*, University Papers, vol. 4, no. 1 (Los Angeles: University of Judaism, [February] 1985); Avraham Shteinberg, *Encyclopedia of Halakhah and Medicine* (in Hebrew), 5 vols. (Jerusalem: F. Schelzinger Institute, Shaárei Tzeddeq, 1988–96), 2: 219–29.

112. Shahar Ilan, "Minister of Health Promotes Halachic Ruling to Allow Religious and Traditional Community to Donate Organs," *Haáretz*, 9 August 1996.

113. A portrayal of this dilemma, in a family that moved from Egypt to Israel, is provided in an essay on "modern death" by Jacqueline Kahanoff, *Essais* (in Hebrew) (Tel Aviv: Hadar, 1978), pp. 225–71. A recent analysis of aspects these dilemmas is found in Sharon Kaufman, "In the Shadow of 'Death with Dignity': Medicine and Cultural Quandaries of the Vegetative State," *American Anthropologist* 102 (2000): 69–83.

114. Seymour Siegel, "Suicide in the Jewish View," *Conservative Judaism* 32, 2 (1978): 67–74. See "The Individual and the Organization of Death" above in this chapter on a gosses.

115. See Elliot Dorf, *"Choose Life"*; Fred Rosner, *Modern Medicine and Jewish Ethics* (New York: Ktav and Yeshiva University Press, 1986), ch. 17.

116. Klein, *Guide*, p. 273.

117. Leon R. Kass, "Death with Dignity vs. Euthanasia," in *Jewish Insights on Death and Mourning*, ed. Jack Riemer (New York: Schocken Books, 1995), pp. 244–56.

118. Yoel Kahn, "On Choosing the Hour of Our Death," in *Jewish Insights on Death and Mourning*, ed. Jack Riemer (New York: Schocken Books, 1995), pp. 237–44. A similar perception of the condition of sick elderly people is found in Kahanoff, *Essais*, p. 259.

119. Ḥesed is often translated as an act of "loving-kindness."

120. Raphael Patai, *On Jewish Folklore* (Detroit: Wayne State University Press, 1983), ch. 21; Susan Sered, "Religious Rituals and Secular Ritual: Interpenetrating Models of Childbirth in a Modern, Israeli Context," *Sociology of Religion* 54 (1993): 101–14.

121. Maimonides, *Yad ha-Ḥazaqah, Shofṭim* (Judges) *Avel* (Mourning) 1:6.

122. Jack Riemer, "How Can We Mourn the Stillborn," in id., *Jewish Insights*, pp. 260–79; Debra Orenstein, ed., *Lifecycles: Jewish Women on Life Passages and Personal Milestones* (Woodstock, Vt.: Jewish Lights Publishing, 1994), pp. 45–51.

123. Debra Reed Blank, "Three Responses to Miscarriage," in *Jewish Insights on Death and Mourning*, ed. Jack Riemer (New York: Schocken Books, 1995), pp. 271–74.

124. Barbara Myerhoff, *Number Our Days* (New York: Simon & Schuster, 1972); id., " 'Life, Not Death in Venice': Its Second Life," in Goldberg, *Judaism Viewed*, pp. 143–69.

125. Jacob Climo, "Transmitting Ethnic Identity through Oral Narratives," *Ethnic Groups* 8 (1990): 163–79. On ethical wills, see chapter 7, "Seeds and Social Sites of the Modern Jewish World," and Stanley J. Garfein, "A Rabbi's Ethical Will," in *Jewish Insights on Death and Mourning,* ed. Jack Riemer (New York: Schocken Books, 1995), p. 114.

126. Jack Kugelmass, *The Miracle of Intervale Avenue: The Story of a Jewish Congregation in the South Bronx* (New York: Columbia University Press, 1996); Lucette Valensi and Nathan Wachtel, *Jewish Memories* (Berkeley: University of California Press, 1991); Jonathan Boyarin, *Polish Jews in Paris: The Ethnography of Memory* (Bloomington: Indiana University Press, 1991).

127. See Jack Kugelmass and Jonathan Boyarin, *From a Ruined Garden: The Memorial Books of Polish Jewry* (1983; 2d expanded ed., Bloomington: Indiana University Press, 1998). The recorded memories of an immigrant from White Russia (Climo, "Transmitting") were later transcribed and analyzed by his grandson. Ruth Behar, "Death and Memory: From Santa María del Monte to Miami Beach," *Cultural Anthropology* 6 (1991): 346–84, unravels the threads linking her fieldwork in Spain to her Jewish identity carried forward by her paternal grandfather, who migrated from Turkey to Cuba. These links were highlighted by the death of her maternal grandfather, which occurred in the midst of her fieldwork in a rural community whose past was being threatened: "my preoccupation with the death of memory in Santa María provoked a resurgence of memory, for me, about my own Jewish heritage and the ways in which I had become alienated from it" (p. 375). Joëlle Bahloul, *Architecture,* provides an intricate portrait of the interweaving of personal, family, and communal memories of Algerian Jews in France who had shared a dwelling in a North African town. Esther Schely-Newman, *Our Lives Are but Stories: Narratives of Tunisian-Israeli Women* (Detroit: Wayne State University Press, 2002), reconstructs the life histories of women who moved from Tunisia to Israel, with her mother serving as one of the central narrators.

128. Kugelmass and Boyarin, *From a Ruined Garden;* Annie Benveniste, *Le Bosphore à la Roquette: La communauté judéo-espagnole à Paris, 1914–1940* (Paris: L'Harmattan, 1989); Saul Friedlander and Adam Seligman, "The Israeli Memory of the Shoah: On Symbols, Rituals and Ideological Polarization," in *Now/Here: Space, Time and Modernity,* ed. R. Friedland and D. Bowden (Berkeley: University of California Press, 1995), pp. 356–71.

129. For example, see David Weiss Halivni, *The Book and the Sword: A Life of Learning in the Shadow of Destruction* (New York: Farrar, Straus & Giroux, 1996), p. 32.

130. On "places of memory," see Pierre Nora, *Realms of Memory: Rethinking the French Past,* trans. Arthur Goldhammer, ed. Lawrence D. Kritzman (New York: Columbia University Press, 1996). On Yad Vashem, see James E. Young, *The Texture of Memory: Holocaust Memorials and Meaning* (New Haven, Conn.: Yale University Press, 1993); Friedlander and Seligman, "Israeli Memory."

131. Anne Frank, *The Diary of a Young Girl* (New York: Pocket Books, 1953).

132. Jackie Feldman, " 'Roots in Destruction': The Jewish Past as Portrayed in Israeli Youth Voyages to Poland," in *The Life of Judaism*, ed. Harvey E. Goldberg (Berkeley: University of California Press, 2001), pp. 149–72.

133. Jack Kugelmass, "The Rites of the Tribe: The Meaning of Poland for American Jewish Tourists," *Going Home, YIVO ANNUAL* 21 (1993): 395–453.

134. David Wolpe, "Why Stones Instead of Flowers?" in *Jewish Insights on Death and Mourning*, ed. Jack Riemer (New York: Schocken Books, 1995), pp. 128–30.

135. Yael Zerubavel, *Recovered Roots: Collective Memory and the Making of Israeli National Tradition* (Chicago: University of Chicago Press, 1995), chs. 3, 6, and 9.

136. This is almost certainly not David's burial place but a site "identified" in the sixteenth century. See Yoram Bilu, "The Sanctification of Place in Israel's Civil and Traditional Religion" (in Hebrew), *Jerusalem Studies in Jewish Folklore* 19–20 (1998): 65–84.

137. George Mosse, *Fallen Soldiers: Reshaping the Memory of the World Wars* (New York: Oxford University Press, 1990); Nachman Ben-Yehuda, *The Masada Myth: Collective Memory and Myth-making in Israel* (Madison: University of Wisconsin Press, 1995), pp. 285–87; Zerubavel, *Recovered Roots*.

138. Anita Shapira, "Historiography and Memory: Latrun, 1948," *Jewish Social Studies*, n.s., 3 (1996): 20–61.

139. Michael Laskier, *North African Jewry in the Twentieth Century: The Jews of Morocco, Tunisia, and Algeria* (New York: New York University Press, 1994), pp. 227–29; Alex Weingrod, "Dry Bones: Nationalism and Symbolism in Contemporary Israel," *Anthropology Today* 11, 6 (1995): 7–12.

140. Bilu, "Sanctification of Place."

141. Robick Rosenthal, *Ha-im ha-shekhol met?* (Jerusalem: Keter, 2001).

142. Abramovitch, "Jerusalem Funeral."

143. Frances Raday, "Religion, Multiculturalism and Equality: The Israeli Case," in *Israel Yearbook on Human Rights* (Tel Aviv, 1994), pp. 193–241, esp. 220.

144. Israel Supreme Court Decisions (1992), vol. 46, pt. 2, p. 464, civil appeal 294/91. See also Kahanoff, *Essais*, p. 266. Conflict over this issue appears in the first part of the nineteenth century as noted by Paula Hyman, *The Emancipation of the Jews of Alsace: Acculturation and Tradition in the Nineteenth Century* (New Haven, Conn.: Yale University Press, 1991), p. 128.

145. See chapter 7, "Israel and Diaspora Links."

146. *Haaretz*, June 4 1998, p. A-5; Shimon Shetreet, *Between Three Branches of Government: The Balance of Rights in Matters of Religion in Israel* (Jerusalem: Floersheimer Institute for Policy Studies, 2001), pp. 22–23.

147. Leon Wieseltier, *Kaddish*, pp. 48–49.

148. Riemer, *Jewish Insights*, p. 81.

149. Ibid., pp. 82–107.

150. Gillman, *Death*, ch. 9.

151. Examples of mid-century formulations are found in Milton Steinberg, *Basic Judaism* (New York: Harcourt, Brace, 1947), p. 160, and Walter Zenner,

"Memorialism—Some Jewish Examples," *American Anthropologist* 67 (1965): 481–83. On the phrasing in the Amidah, see n. 22 above.

152. See the beginning of chapter 5.

CHAPTER 7. BONDS OF COMMUNITY
AND INDIVIDUAL LIVES

1. See chapter 2, "Home, Synagogue, and the Role of Women in Circumcisions."

2. See chapter 3, "Adult Study and Rituals"; chapter 6, "The Middle Ages."

3. See chapter 3, "The Torah as a Person." An old Yiddish tale built around the drama of a hard-earned marriage has been interpreted as a foundation story of the Ashkenazi Jewish communities. It tells of a young man who, asked to prove his abilities to win the hand of a girl, was forced to face perils in the East until his scholarly abilities were recognized and he eventually returned to win his bride, just as she was about to be married to a competitor. This reading of the story is linked to Ashkenazi Jewry asserting its independence from the centers of learning further East. See Sara Zfatman, *The Jewish Tale in the Middle Ages: Between Ashkenaz and Sepharad* (in Hebrew) (Jerusalem: Magnes Press, 1993). See the discussion in the next section.

4. TB *Yebamot* 22a. See "Israel and Diaspora Links" below in this chapter.

5. Steven M. Cohen and Arnold M. Eisen, *The Jew Within: Self, Family and Community in the United States* (Bloomington: Indiana University Press, 2000).

6. Steven M. Cohen, *Religious Stability and Ethnic Decline: Emerging Patterns of Jewish Identity in the United States* (New York: Jewish Community Centers Research Center, 1998).

7. Sergio DellaPergola, "Arthur Ruppin Revisited: The Jews of Today, 1904–1994," in *National Variations in Jewish Identity: Implications for Jewish Education*, ed. Steven M. Cohen and Gabriel Horencyzk (Albany: State University of New York Press, 1999), pp. 53–84.

8. See chapter 5, "*Hillulot* and the Zohar in Morocco," "Bringing Close the Divine," and "The Personal and the Political." In chapter 6, see "The Individual and the Organization of Death," "Modern Death," and "Dealing with Death."

9. On the subtleties and inner tensions in the way the Bible portrays the relationship of the emerging Israelite nation, see Ilana Pardes, *The Biography of Ancient Israel* (Berkeley: University of California Press, 2000). See "Marriage and Community" in this chapter for an example of the way the Talmud utilized the theme of tribal structure in the Bible in relation to marriage patterns.

10. Another example of the strain for unification is the requirement that whenever an Israelite slaughters an animal, the act has a sacrificial element and must be carried out at the central sanctuary. This ideal rule appears in Leviticus in the context of the Tent of Meeting that was at the center of ritual life. It appears to be modified in Deut. 12:20–25, which takes into account the fact that Israelites will be settled far from the national center.

11. See chapter 3, "Receiving the Torah and Access to It." Jacob Milgrom, *Leviticus 1–16 (the Anchor Bible)* (Garden City, N.Y., 1991), pp. 1004–9, stresses how this process is found in the Bible, providing the basis for its development in later periods.

12. TB *Megillah* 29a. *Miqdash me'aṭ* is also taken there as referring to "houses of study" (*batei midrash*).

13. Lee I. Levine, ed., *The Synagogue in Late Antiquity* (Philadelphia: American Schools of Oriental Research, 1987), pp. 7–31.

14. Bernadette J. Brooten, *Women Leaders in the Ancient Synagogue: Inscriptional Evidence and Background Issues* (Chico, Calif.: Scholars Press, 1982).

15. Ezra Fleischer, "On the Beginnings of Obligatory Jewish Prayer" (in Hebrew), *Tarbiz* 59 (1990): 397–445.

16. See chapter 3, "Receiving the Torah and Access to It."

17. Shaye J. D. Cohen, "Pagan and Christian Evidence on the Ancient Synagogue," in L. I. Levine, ed., *The Synagogue in Late Antiquity* (Philadelphia: American Schools of Oriental Research, 1987), p. 175; id., *From the Maccabees to the Mishnah* (Philadelphia: Westminster Press, 1987), pp. 111–16. See now Lee I. Levine, *The Ancient Synagogue: The First Thousand Years* (New Haven, Conn.: Yale University Press, 1999).

18. Mark R. Cohen, *Under Crescent and Cross: The Jews in the Middle Ages* (Princeton, N.J.: Princeton University Press, 1994), provides an overview of the topic and the literature relating to it.

19. See chapter 1, n. 51.

20. Salo W. Baron, *Social and Religious History of the Jews*, 2d ed., rev. (New York: Columbia University Press; Philadelphia: Jewish Publication Society of America, 1952–83), 3: 99–110.

21. S. D. Goitein, *A Mediterranean Society: The Jewish Communities of the Arab World as Portrayed in the Documents of the Cairo Geniza* (Berkeley: University of California Press, 1967–93), vol. 2: *The Community* (1971), pp. 5–23, 195–205.

22. Menahem Ben-Sasson, *The Emergence of the Local Jewish Community in the Muslim World: Qayrawan, 800–1057* (in Hebrew) (Jerusalem: Magnes Press, 1997).

23. Gerson D. Cohen, trans. and ed., *The Book of Tradition (Sefer ha-Qabbalah)* by Abraham Ibn Daud (Philadelphia: Jewish Publication Society of America, 1967), pp. 63–90; Zfatman, *Jewish Tale*. See also Robert Bonfil, "Can Medieval Storytelling Help Understanding Midrash? The Story of Paltiel: A Preliminary Study on History and Midrash," in *The Midrashic Imagination: Jewish Exegesis, Thought, and History*, ed. Michael Fishbane (Albany: State University of New York Press, 1993), pp. 228–54.

24. Louis Finkelstein, *Jewish Self-Government in the Middle Ages* (New York: Feldheim, 1964).

25. Ibid., pp. 15–18; Simha Goldin, "The Synagogue in the Medieval Jewish Community as an Integral Institution," *Journal of Ritual Studies* 9 (1995): 15–39; Menahem Ben-Sasson, "Appeal to the Congregation in Islamic Countries in the Early Middle Ages" (in Hebrew), in *Knesset Ezra: Literature and*

Life in the Synagogue, ed. S. Elizur, M. D. Herr, G. Shaked, and A. Shinan (Jerusalem: Yad Ishak Ben-Zvi, 1994), pp. 327–50.

26. See chapter 3, "Receiving the Torah and Access to It."

27. Goldin, "Synagogue."

28. See chapter 3, "Receiving the Torah." Typically, the blessing is recited as part of the public repetition of the Amidah ("Eighteen Benedictions") prayer.

29. Frija Zuaretz, "Havai u-minhagim," in *Sefer Yahadut Luv,* ed. F. Zuaretz et al. (Tel Aviv: Vaʾad Qehillot Luv Be-Yisrael, 1960), p. 370.

30. Personal communications from Efrat Lapidot and Esther Schely-Newman. In Tripoli, little girls, including baby daughters, would gather under the prayer shawl on this occasion, but not women.

31. Chava Weissler, *Voices of the Matriarchs: Listening to the Prayers of Early Modern Jewish Women* (Boston: Beacon Press, 1998), ch. 6.

32. Susan S. Sered, *Women as Ritual Experts: The Religious Lives of Elderly Jewish Women in Jerusalem* (New York: Oxford University Press, 1992). In the Middle Ages, women might be seen as experts in aspects of rituals that were obligatory for men, such as properly preparing the fringes on the prayer shawl (tzitzit). See Avraham Grossman, *Pious and Rebellious: Jewish Women in Europe in the Middle Ages* (in Hebrew) (Jerusalem: Shazar Center, 2001), p. 338.

33. Jacob ben Asher, *Arbaʾah Turim, Even Ha-ʾezer,* introduction. In presenting this parallel, Ben Asher uses the Hebrew stem *mashol* (see chapter 4, "Marriage, Women, and Menstruation").

34. See chapter 5, "*Hillulot* and the Zohar in Morocco," and chapter 6, "The Individual and the Organization of Death."

35. Daniel Matt, trans. and ed., *Zohar: The Book of Enlightenment* (Ramsay, N.J.: Paulist Press, 1983), pp. 3–39.

36. Gershom Scholem, *Major Trends in Jewish Mysticism* (New York: Schocken Books, 1941), pp. 244–86; Boas Huss, "*Sefer ha-Zohar* as a Canonical, Sacred and Holy Text: Changing Perspectives on the Book of Splendor between the Thirteenth and Eighteenth Centuries," *Journal of Jewish Thought and Philosophy* 7 (1998): 257–307.

37. Scholem, *Major Trends,* pp. 227–30.

38. See chapter 4, "Marriage, Women, and Menstruation." See also Arlene Agus, "This Month Is for You: Observing Rosh Hodesh as a Woman's Holiday," in *The Jewish Woman: New Perspectives,* ed. E. Koltun (New York: Schocken Books, 1976), pp. 84–93. The relevant texts from the Midrash and the Zohar are presented and discussed in a paper that proposes a ritual for newborn girls. See Daniel Siegel, "Moon: White Silver of *Shekhinah*'s Return," in *Worlds of Prayer,* ed. S. H. Wiener and J. Omer-man (Northvale, N.J.: Jason Aronson, 1993), pp. 231–55. The following discussion was stimulated by that paper.

39. TB Ḥullin 60b.

40. Zohar, *Bereshit* 20b, in *The Zohar,* trans. H. Sperling, ed. M. Simon (London: Soncino, 1931), 1: 87.

41. See chapter 4, "Breaking the Glass."

42. Scholem, *Major Trends*, pp. 284–86.

43. TB *Shabbat* 119a.

44. See the discussion of a woman's poem in Judeo-Spanish in chapter 2, "Women and Torah." On various ritual uses of these verses, see Yael Levine, " 'Eshet ḥayil be-fulḥan yehudi" ("Eshet Ḥayil" in Jewish Rituals), *Beit Miqra* 31 (1986): 339–46.

45. In 1492, about 50,000 Jews left Spain for Muslim lands, and about 100,000 migrated to Portugal. Many of the latter left Portugal subsequently, either as Jews or as Marranos, Christians who practiced Judaism secretly (see below in this chapter). On Sephardim in the Balkans and the Ottoman Empire, see Esther Benbassa and Aron Rodrigue, *The Jews of the Balkans: The Judeo-Spanish Community, Fifteenth to Twentieth Centuries* (Oxford: Blackwell, 1995).

46. Robert Bonfil, *Jewish Life in Renaissance Italy*, trans. Anthony Oldcorn (Berkeley: University of California Press, 1991), p. 105.

47. Yosef Kaplan, "The Portuguese Jews in Amsterdam—From Apostasy to the Return to Judaism" (in Hebrew), in *The Sepharadi and Oriental Jewish Heritage*, ed. Issachar Ben-Ami (Jerusalem: Magnes Press, 1982), pp. 115–34; id., "The Travels of Portuguese Jews from Amsterdam to the 'Lands of Idolatry' (1644–1724)," in *Jews and Conversos: Studies in Society and the Inquisition*, ed. Y. Kaplan (Jerusalem: Academy of Sciences, 1985), pp. 197–224; id., "The Portuguese Community of Amsterdam in the Seventeenth Century between Tradition and Change" (in Hebrew), in *Society and Community: Proceedings of the Second International Conference for Research of the Sephardi and Oriental Jewish Heritage 1984*, ed. Abraham Haim (Jerusalem: Misgav Yerushalayim, 1991), pp. 141–71. Miriam Bodian, *Hebrews of the Portuguese Nation: Conversos and Community in Early Modern Amsterdam* (Bloomington: Indiana University Press, 1997).

48. Yirmiyahu Yovel, "Converso Dualities in the First Generation: The *Cancioneros*," *Jewish Social Studies*, n.s., 4 (1998): 1–28.

49. Robert Bonfil, "Change in the Cultural Patterns of a Jewish Society in Crisis: Italian Jewry at the Close of the Sixteenth Century," *Jewish History* 3 (1988): 11–30.

50. Michael K. Silber, "The Emergence of Ultra-Orthodoxy: The Invention of a Tradition," in *The Uses of Tradition: Jewish Continuity in the Modern Era*, ed. Jack Wertheimer (New York: Jewish Theological Seminary of America with Harvard University Press, 1992), pp. 23–84, esp. pp. 48–50.

51. Solomon Schechter, "Safed in the Sixteenth Century—A City of Legists and Mystics," in *Studies in Judaism*, vol. 2 (Philadelphia: Jewish Publication Society of America, 1908), pp. 182–285. Yosef Caro was also a mystic.

52. The following is taken from Menahem Friedman, "The Market Model and Religious Radicalism," in *Jewish Fundamentalism in Comparative Perspective: Religion, Ideology, and the Crisis of Modernity*, ed. Laurence Silberstein (New York: New York University Press, 1993), pp. 192–215. Friedman cites a paper by Y. Ahituv, "Repentance and Religious Extremism—An Examination of These Phenomena from the Point of View of the Individual and the Community" (in Hebrew), *'Amudim*, Heshvan, 1988, pp. 43–49.

53. Strict observance of the laws of tithes and heave-offerings (with regard to the produce of Jews) was among the ritual issues stressed by Pharisees in Second Temple times to set themselves apart from the less punctilious "people of the land" (ʿamei ha-ʾareṣ). See the discussion in chapter 5, "Pilgrimage in the Bible and Second Temple Times."

54. Moses Maimonides, "Letter to the Jews of Lunel" (in Hebrew), in *The Letters and Essays of Moses Maimonides*, vol. 2, ed. Itzhak Shilat (Jerusalem: Shilat Publishing, 5755 [1995]), pp. 555–59.

55. H. S. Kehimkar, *The History of the Bene Israel in India* (Tel Aviv: Dayag, 1937), p. 41.

56. Schifra Strizower, *Exotic Jewish Communities* (London: Yoseloff, 1962), p. 63.

57. Zvi Friedhaber, "The Dance in Jewish Mediterranean Communities since the Expulsion from Spain until the Beginning of the Nineteenth Century" (Ph.D. diss., Hebrew University, Jerusalem, 1986). Examples of traditional Jews flouting rules against dancing are still recorded for the nineteenth century. See Paula Hyman, *The Emancipation of the Jews of Alsace: Acculturation and Tradition in the Nineteenth Century* (New Haven, Conn.: Yale University Press, 1991), p. 77.

58. Friedhaber, *Dance*, pp. 29–30.

59. Leah Bornstein-Makovetsky, "Life and Society in the Community of Arta in the Sixteenth Century" (in Hebrew), *Peʿamim* 45 (1990): 126–55.

60. Further study of relations between Sephardi women and men in this period is desirable. See Renée Levine Melammed, "Sephardi Women in the Medieval and Early Modern Periods," in *Jewish Women in Historical Perspective*, ed. J. R. Baskin (Detroit: Wayne State University Press, 1991), pp. 115–34; Bornstein-Makovetsky, "Life and Society in the Community of Arta," pp. 143–45.

61. Friedhaber, *Dance*, pp. 96–98.

62. Leah Bornstein, "The Ashkenazim in the Ottoman Empire in the Sixteenth and Seventeenth Centuries" (in Hebrew), in *East and Maghreb: A Volume of Researches*, ed. H. Z. Hirschberg with the assistance of E. Bashan (Ramat Gan: Bar-Ilan University, 1974), pp. 81–104; Michael Littman, "Relations between Different Jewish Communities in Egypt in the Sixteenth and Seventeenth Centuries" (in Hebrew), *Peʿamim* 16 (1983): 29–55, see p. 42.

63. See Hayyim Vital, *Shaʿar ha-Gilgulim*, the account printed at the end and signed by his son Samuel (Tel Aviv: Eshel, 1963), pp. 186–87, and Gedalyah Nigal, *"Dybbuk" Tales in Jewish Literature* (in Hebrew) (Jerusalem: R. Mass, 1983), pp. 85–88. The story is actually more complex than indicated. After a Gentile judge neutralizes the Gentile spirit, a second errant Jewish soul still remains in the woman and is exorcised by Vital.

64. See Judah Goldin's foreword to Israel Abraham, *Hebrew Ethical Wills* (Philadelphia: Jewish Publication Society, 1976), and Natalie Z. Davis, "Fame and Secrecy: Leone Modena's *Life* as an Early Modern Autobiography," in Mark R. Cohen, trans. and ed., *The Autobiography of a Seventeenth-Century Rabbi: Leon Modena's Life of Judah* (Princeton, N.J.: Princeton University

Press, 1988), pp. 50–72. A twentieth-century rabbi has tried to encourage the adoption of this practice. See Stanley Garfain, "A Rabbi's Ethical Will," in *Jewish Insights on Death and Mourning,* ed. Jack Riemer (New York: Schocken Books, 1995), pp. 113–18. Elisheva Baumgarten, "As Families Remember: Holocaust Memoirs and Their Transmission," in *Jews and Gender: The Challenge to Hierarchy,* ed. Jonathan Frankel, *Studies in Contemporary Jewry* 26 (2001): 265–86, has documented and analyzed the will among Holocaust survivors to transmit personal experiences in writing to the following generations of their families.

65. David B. Ruderman, *Kabbalah, Magic, and Science: The Cultural Universe of a Sixteenth-Century Jewish Physician* (Cambridge, Mass.: Harvard University Press, 1988).

66. See chapter 4, "Breaking the Glass."

67. Cohen, trans. and ed., *Autobiography of a Seventeenth-Century Rabbi.*

68. Glueckl of Hameln, *Memoirs of Glueckl of Hameln,* trans. M. Lowenthal (New York: Schocken Books, 1960); Natalie Z. Davis, *Women on the Margins: Three Seventeenth-Century Lives* (Cambridge, Mass.: Harvard University Press, 1995).

69. Vivian Mann and Richard Cohen, eds., *From Court Jews to the Rothschilds: Art, Patronage, Power, 1600–1800* (Munich: Prestel-Verlag; New York: Jewish Museum, 1996).

70. Shlomo Deshen, *The Mellah Society: Jewish Community Life in Sherifian Morocco* (Chicago: University of Chicago Press, 1989), pp. 22–23.

71. See chapter 2, "Some Modern Challenges."

72. Alexander Altmann, *Moses Mendelssohn: A Biographical Study* (Philadelphia: Jewish Publication Society, 1973), pp. 455–57.

73. The impact of Enlightenment thought and emancipation on the practice of circumcision is discussed in chapter 2, "Some Modern Challenges."

74. Hyman, *Emancipation;* Harvey E. Goldberg, ed., *Sephardi and Middle Eastern Jewries: History and Culture in the Modern Era* (Bloomington: Indiana University Press; New York: Jewish Theological Seminary of America, 1996), pp. 2–18.

75. See Jack Wertheimer, ed., *The Uses of Tradition: Jewish Continuity in the Modern Era* (New York: Jewish Theological Seminary of America, 1992).

76. Jacob Katz, "Traditional Jewish Society and Modern Society," in *Jews among Muslims: Communities in the Precolonial Middle East,* ed. S. Deshen and W. P. Zenner (New York: New York University Press; Houndmills, Hants, U.K.: Macmillan, 1996), pp. 25–34.

77. Joëlle Bahloul, *Le culte de la table dressée: Rites et traditions de la table juive algerienne* (Paris: A. M. Métailié, 1983); id., *Parenté et ethnicité: La famille juive nord-africaine en France* (Paris: Mission du patrimoine ethnologique de la France, 1984), pp. 135–64; id., "What You Remember and Whose Son You Are: North African Jewish Families and Their Past," in *Essays in the Social Scientific Study of Judaism and Jewish Society,* ed. S. Fishbane and J. Lightstone (Montreal: Concordia University Press, 1990), pp. 217–29; id., "The Sephardi Family and the Challenge of Assimilation: Family Ritual and Ethnic Reproduction," in *Sephardi and Middle Eastern Jewries,* ed. H. E. Gold-

berg (Bloomington: Indiana University Press; New York: Jewish Theological Seminary of America, 1996), pp. 312–24.

78. Recently, historians have begun to pay more attention to these topics. See Marion A. Kaplan, *The Making of the Jewish Middle Class: Women, Family and Identity in Imperial Germany* (New York: Oxford University Press, 1991).

79. Barbara Kirshenblatt-Gimblett, "Coming of Age in the Thirties: Max Weinreich, Edward Sapir, and Jewish Social Science," *YIVO Annual* 23 (1996): 1–103, p. 23.

80. Philip Roth, *Portnoy's Complaint* (New York: Bantam Books, 1969).

81. The following is largely based on Daphna Musnikov, "The Women of Elijah" (in Hebrew) (M.A. thesis, Department of Sociology and Anthropology, Hebrew University, Jerusalem, 1995). See also Orpa Slapak, ed., *The Jews of India: A Story of Three Communities* (Jerusalem: Israel Museum, 1995), pp. 144–46.

82. Kehimkar, *History*, pp. 26, 28.

83. See, e.g., Kehimkar, *History*, pp. 20, 65, 119, 180.

84. See ibid., pp. 20, 25.

85. Ibid., p. 65. See also chapter 6 in this volume, "Bringing Close the Divine." *Tu bi-Shvat*, in midwinter, is the "new year for [laws concerning] trees," according to Hillel's school in the Mishna (*Rosh Ha-shanah* 1:1), and was elaborated as a holiday with kabbalistic meanings in the seventeenth century. Celebrating the holiday entails eating fruits of the Land of Israel.

86. See Lev. 11:45 and Deut. 14:21. For a general discussion of the importance of food in ancient Jewish culture, see Gillian Feeley-Harnik, *The Lord's Table: The Meaning of Food in Early Judaism and Christianity* (Washington, D.C.: Smithsonian Institution Press, 1994).

87. See chapter 5, "Pilgrimage in the Bible and Second Temple Times."

88. Menahem Friedman, "Life Tradition and Book Tradition in the Development of Ultraorthodox Judaism," in *Judaism Viewed from Within and from Without*, ed. H. E. Goldberg (Albany: State University of New York Press, 1987), pp. 235–55.

89. Menachem Friedman, "The Lost Kiddush Cup: Changes in Ashkenazic Haredi Culture—A Tradition in Crisis," in *The Uses of Tradition*, ed. Jack Wertheimer (New York: Jewish Theological Seminary of America with Harvard University Press, 1992), pp. 175–86.

90. Haym Soloveitchik, "Rupture and Reconstruction: The Transformation of Contemporary Orthodoxy," *Tradition* 28 (1994): 64–130.

91. See *EJ*, s.v. "Dietary Laws," "Food," "Kasher," "Meat," and "Shehitah" (slaughtering). See also Stuart Schoffman, "Lettuce Was Lettuce," *Jerusalem Report*, 2 April 1998, p. 50.

92. There was a small movement of religious kibbutzim that sought to combine the new ideals with Orthodoxy. See Aryei Fishman, *Judaism and Modernization on the Religious Kibbutz* (Cambridge: Cambridge University Press, 1992).

93. Aviva Opaz, ed., *Sefer ha-qvutza: The Sharon Group, 1922–1936* (in Hebrew) (Jerusalem: Yad Yizhak Ben-Zvi, 1996).

94. Yonina Talmon, *Family and Community in the Kibbutz* (Cambridge, Mass.: Harvard University Press, 1972); Melford Spiro, *Kibbutz: Venture in Utopia* (Cambridge, Mass.: Harvard University Press, 1956).

95. Opaz, *Sefer*, pp. 32–33.

96. Melford Spiro with the assistance of A. G. Spiro, *Children of the Kibbutz* (Cambridge, Mass.: Harvard University Press, 1958).

97. Zvi Friedhaber, "Evidence of the 'Hora' Danced by Pioneers of the Second and Third Aliya" (in Hebrew), *Jerusalem Studies in Jewish Folklore* 16 (1994): 113–25.

98. Opaz, *Sefer*, p. 106. The term "purify our hearts" is taken from the *musaf* (additional) Sabbath service.

99. Talmon, *Family*, p. 12.

100. See Mattat Adar-Bunis, "Kinship and an Urban Community in Israel: The Case of Maale Adumim" (Ph.D. diss., Hebrew University, Jerusalem, 1991).

101. Opaz, *Sefer*, p. 120.

102. Tsili Doleve-Gandelman, "The Symbolic Inscription of Zionist Ideology in the Space of Eretz Israel: Why the Native Israeli Is Called *Tsabar*," in *Judaism Viewed from Within and from Without*, ed. H. E. Goldberg (Albany: State University of New York Press, 1987), pp. 257–84.

103. Spiro, *Children*, p. 189 n. 265.

104. Lea Shamgar-Handelman and Don Handelman, "Celebrations of Bureaucracy: Birthday Parties in Israeli Kindergartens," *Ethnology* 30 (1991): 293–312; Shalva Weil, "The Language and Ritual of Socialization: Birthday Parties in a Kindergarten Context," *Man* 21 (1986): 329–41.

105. Tamar Katriel, *Communal Webs: Communication and Culture in Contemporary Israel* (Albany: State University of New York Press, 1991). For recent trends in kibbutzim, and the tension between communal and more private interests as expressed in life-cycle events, see Yoram Carmeli and Rina Roth, "The Cake and the Plate: Family and Community in a Kibbutz's Bar-Mitzvah Ceremony," *International Journal of Comparative Family and Marriage* 1 (1994): 49–63.

106. See chapter 3, "Adult Education and Rituals."

107. Soloveitchik, "Rupture and Reconstruction," p. 79, notes the importance of this period with reference to Orthodoxy.

108. Janet Dolgin, *Jewish Identity and the JDL* (Princeton, N.J.: Princeton University Press, 1977).

109. Yossi Klein Halevi, *Memoirs of a Jewish Extremist: An American Story* (Boston: Little, Brown, 1995), pp. 78–79.

110. Ehud Sprinzak, *Israel's Radical Right* (New York: Oxford University Press, 1991), ch. 7.

111. Jacob Neusner, ed., *Contemporary Judaic Fellowship in Theory and in Practice* (New York: Ktav, 1972); Joseph Reimer, "The Havurah as a Context for Adult Jewish Education," in *The Uses of Tradition*, ed. Jack Wertheimer (New

York: Jewish Theological Seminary of America with Harvard University Press, 1992), pp. 393–410.

112. Riv-Ellen Prell, *Prayer and Community: The Havurah in American Judaism* (Detroit: Wayne State University Press, 1989).

113. Chava Weissler, "Making Davening Meaningful: Worship in the Havurah Movement," *YIVO Annual* 19 (1990): 255–67.

114. See chapter 3, "Confirmation and Bat Mitzvah."

115. See the discussion on knowledge and authority in chapter 3, "Adult Study and Rituals."

116. Harvey E. Goldberg, "Becoming History: Perspectives on the Seminary Faculty at Mid-Century," in *Tradition Renewed: A History of the Jewish Theological Seminary of America*, vol. 1, ed. Jack Wertheimer (New York: Jewish Theological Seminary of America, 1997), pp. 353–437.

117. Paul Ritterband and Harold S. Wechsler, *Jewish Learning in American Universities: The First Century* (Bloomington: Indiana University Press, 1994), ch. 9.

118. Jacob Neusner, "Fellowship through Law: The Ancient Havurah," in *Contemporary Judaic Fellowship in Theory and in Practice* (New York: Ktav, 1972). It should be noted however, that much is unclear about the historical content of "the havura." See Cohen, *From the Maccabees*, pp. 118–19.

119. Reimer, "Havurah," p. 405.

120. Riv-Ellen Prell, "Sacred Categories and Social Relations: The Visibility and Invisibility of Gender in an American Jewish Community," in *Judaism Viewed from Within and from Without*, ed. H. E. Goldberg (Albany: State University of New York Press, 1987), pp. 171–93.

121. Frida K. Furman, *Beyond Yiddishkeit: The Struggle for Jewish Identity in a Reform Synagogue* (Albany: State University of New York Press, 1987); Reikoh Itoh and Leonard Plotnicov, "The Saturday Morning Informal Service: Community and Identity in a Reform Synagogue," *Ethnology* 38 (1999): 1–19. See also Peter Margolis, "The Role of the Reconstructionist Movement in Creating Havurot in America" (M.A. thesis, Institute of Contemporary Jewry, Hebrew University, Jerusalem, 1993).

122. Daniel Landes, "The Role of the Synagogue in Jewish Identity," in *Jewish Identity in America*, ed. D. M. Gordis and Y. Ben-Horin (Los Angeles: University of Judaism, 1991), pp. 173–80.

123. See chapter 4, "Marriage, Women, and Menstruation." See also Arlene Agus, "This Month"; Penina Adelman, *Miriam's Well* (Fresh Meadows, N.Y.: Biblio Press, 1986); Susan W. Schneider, *Jewish and Female: Choices and Changes in Our Lives Today* (New York: Simon & Schuster, 1984), pp. 94–97; Judith Plaskow, *Standing Again at Sinai: Judaism from a Feminist Perspective* (San Francisco: Harper & Row, 1990), pp. 51, 57–58, 67; David M. Rosen and Victoria P. Rosen, "New Myths and Meanings in Jewish New Moon Rituals," *Ethnology* 39 (2000): 263–77.

124. Moshe Shokeid, *A Gay Synagogue in New York* (New York: Columbia University Press, 1995).

125. Fran Markowitz, "Rituals as Keys to Soviet Immigrants' Jewish Identity," in *Between Two Worlds: Ethnographic Essays on American Jewry,* ed. Jack Kugelmass (Ithaca, N.Y.: Cornell University Press, 1988), pp. 128–47.

126. See Sergio DellaPergola, "New Data on Demography and Identification among Jews in the U.S.: Trends, Inconsistencies and Disagreements," *Contemporary Jewry* 12 (1996): 67–97, for a discussion of how demographic trends, including intermarriage, point to the need for anthropological studies of new articulations of identity.

127. See the different perspectives in Charles S. Liebman and Elihu Katz, eds., *The Jewishness of Israelis: Responses to the Guttman Report* (Albany: State University of New York Press, 1997).

128. Menachem Friedman, *Society and Religion: The Non-Zionist Orthodoxy in Eretz-Israel, 1918–1936* (in Hebrew) (Jerusalem: Yad Izhak Ben-Zvi, 1977). For an example, see the story of an Israeli circumcision in chapter 2, "Recent Developments."

129. Sylvie-Anne Goldberg, *Crossing the Jabbok: Illness and Death in Ashkenazi Judaism in Sixteenth- through Nineteenth-Century Prague,* trans. Carol Cosman (Berkeley: University of California Press, 1996 [orig. 1989]).

130. On the special ritual roles of the kohanim, see the beginning of chapter 3. The rule forbidding marriage to a divorced women is found in Lev. 21:7.

131. Aviva Lory, "To Cyprus with Love and with Protest" (in Hebrew), *Ha'aretz,* Weekend Supplement, 3 April 1998, pp. 18–19, 20, 22, 24.

132. Yokhi Brandes and Ruhama Weiss-Goldman, *Lirqod 'al kamah ḥatunot: The Complete Guide for Registering Marriages and Arranging Alternative Wedding Ceremonies* (in Hebrew) (Jerusalem: Ḥidush, 1996). There are also short, readable, booklets presenting a "standard religious" (Orthodox) perspective on the wedding. See Dov Herman, *Ḥatunah: A Guide to the Perplexed for the Groom and Bride* (in Hebrew) (Tel Aviv: Prolog, 1994). Another initiative, by some Orthodox rabbis, makes available halakhic marriage ceremonies in a fashion that can be appreciated by non-Orthodox couples.

133. *Ha'aretz,* editorial, 11 May 1998. See chapter 4, "Tensions in Marriages: Divorce and Polygyny."

134. The growing realization of this trend is reflected in the holiday supplement of the Israeli daily *Yedioth Aharonoth,* issued on the eve of the seventh day of Passover, 16 April 1998. Articles in the supplement are based on coordinated surveys carried out by the Israeli newspaper and the *Los Angeles Times* and examine the lives of Jews in both countries.

135. See chapter 4, "Tensions in Marriages"; other examples concern education (chapter 2, "Adult Study and Rituals") and worship at the Western Wall (chapter 5, "Pilgrimages, the Personal and the Political"). See also Harvey E. Goldberg, "A Tradition of Invention: Family and Educational Institutions among Contemporary Traditionalizing Jews," in *National Variations in Jewish Identity: Implications for Jewish Education,* ed. S. M. Cohen and G. Horenczyk (Albany: State University of New York Press, 1999), pp. 85–106.

136. The Conservative Movement in Israel is known as the Masorti (Traditional) Movement, and Reform Judaism has adopted the name Mitqademet (Progressive).

137. See the discussion of the demands of the Israeli rabbinate regarding Jews from Ethiopia, in chapter 2, "Some Modern Challenges." On the recent developments in Reform Judaism, see *Haʾaretz,* 28 June 2001, pp. A1, A10.

138. *Haʾaretz,* 1 June 2001, p. A9.

139. See website www.israelemb.org/articals/2002/February/2002022502.html.

140. Moshe Samet, " 'Who Is a Jew?' (1958–1977)," *Jerusalem Quarterly* 36 (1985): 88–108; id., " 'Who Is a Jew?' (1978–85)," ibid. 37 (1986): 109–39. Samet (vol. 36, p. 103) reports the view, expressed in the late 1970s, that the controversy really revolves around "Who is a rabbi?" because it essentially reflects a struggle over the recognition of religious authority.

141. Exod. 12:48; Deut. 21:10–14.

142. A collection of talmudic-like books, known as the Minor Tractates (Masekhtot Qeṭanot), includes a tractate called *Gerim,* but these tractates are not based on mishnaic compositions. See *EJ,* 12: 49–51.

143. TB *Yebamot* 46a.

144. Ibid. 47a–b.

145. Avi Sagi and Zvi Zohar, *Conversion to Judaism and the Meaning of Jewish Identity* (in Hebrew) (Jerusalem: Bialik Institute and Shalom Hartman Institute, 1994), pp. 122–33.

146. See chapter 4, "The Marriage Ceremony," and Moshe Samet, "On Conversion to Judaism," in *Gevuroth Haromah: Jewish Studies Offered at the Eightieth Birthday of Rabbi Moses Cyrus Weiler* (in Hebrew), ed. Z. Falk (Jerusalem: Mesharim, 1987), pp. 293–308; id., "Conversion in the First Centuries, C.E.," in *Jews and Judaism in the Second Temple, Mishna and Talmud Period: Studies in Honor of Shmuel Safrai* (in Hebrew), ed. I. Gafni, A. Oppenheimer, and M. Stern (Jerusalem: Yad Yitzhak Ben-Zvi, 1993), pp. 316–44.

147. Arnold van Gennep, *The Rites of Passage,* trans. M. B. Vizedom and G. L. Caffee (London: Routledge & Kegan Paul, 1960 [orig. 1909]); Avi Sagi and Zvi Zohar, "The Halakhic Ritual of Giyyur and Its Symbolic Meaning," *Journal of Ritual Studies* 9 (1995): 1–13. The latter authors remark that there is nothing in classic rabbinic conversion that corresponds to the liminal phase identified by van Gennep. Shaye J. D. Cohen, *The Beginnings of Jewishness: Boundaries, Varieties, Uncertainties* (Berkeley: University of California Press, 1999), pp. 236–37, explicitly criticizes the understanding of conversion as a rite of passage. On the status of *haver,* see Shaye J. Cohen, *From the Maccabees to the Mishnah* (Philadelphia: Westminster Press, 1987), pp. 118–19, as well as the brief discussions in chapter 5, "Pilgrimage in the Bible and Second Temple Times," and above in this chapter, "Orthodoxy and Separation."

148. Sagi and Zohar, *Conversion.*

149. Harvey E. Goldberg, "Torah and Children: Symbolic Aspects of the Reproduction of Jews and Judaism," in *Judaism Viewed from Within and from Without,* ed. H. E. Goldberg (Albany: State University of New York Press, 1987), ch. 3; Soloveitchik, "Rupture and Reconstruction," pp. 89–90.

150. Moshe Greenberg, "A Problematic Heritage: The Attitude toward the Gentile in Jewish Tradition—An Israel Perspective," *Conservative Judaism* 48

(Winter 1996): 23–35. See also the discussion of racial ideas in chapter 1, "Roots of an Anthropological Approach to Jewish Culture."

151. Samet, "Who Is a Jew?" (1986), states that this argument was stressed by the lobby of the Habad movement, from the early 1970s. See chapter 4, above, "Tensions in Marriages."

152. The central prayer of the liturgy, also known as "the Eighteen Benedictions."

153. Moses Maimonides, "Letter to Ovadiah the Proselyte" (in Hebrew), in *The Letters and Essays of Moses Maimonides*, vol. 1, ed. I. Shilat (Jerusalem: Shilat Publishing, 5755 [1995]), pp. 195–205.

154. Mordecai Roshwald, "Marginal Jewish Sects in Israel," *International Journal of Middle East Studies* 4 (1973): 219–37, 328–54; Zvi Zohar, "Between Alienation and Brotherhood: Karaite-Rabbinite Intermarriage according to Egyptian Jewish Scholars in the Twentieth Century" (in Hebrew), *Pe'amim* 32 (1987): 21–39.

155. Yossi Beilin, *The Death of the American Uncle* (in Hebrew) (Tel Aviv: Yedioth Aharonoth–Chemed, 1999), pp. 147–58.

156. *Ha'aretz*, 4 June 2001, pp. A1, 8.

157. Moshe Z. Sokol, ed., *Rabbinic Authority and Personal Autonomy* (Northvale, N.J.: Jason Aronson, 1992).

158. Avi Sagi and Zeev Safrai, eds., *Between Authority and Autonomy in Jewish Tradition* (in Hebrew) (Tel Aviv: Hakibbutz Hameuchad, 1997). The opening article in the Sokol collection (cited in the preceding note) is reprinted in the Sagi and Safrai volume. Since the assassination in 1995, the state religious school system in Israel has been trying to deal with the topic of "Judaism and Democracy" in its curriculum. On the impact of Rabin's assassination on attitudes to religious autonomy within the national religious community in Israel, see also Ya'aqov (Jackie) Levi, "Elohim sheli, raşiti she-teda'," *Yedioth Aharonoth, 7 Yamim*, 16 June 2000, pp. 34–38.

159. See, e.g., Chaim I. Waxman, "The Haredization of American Orthodox Jewry," *Jerusalem Letter / Viewpoints* (Jerusalem Center for Public Affairs), no. 376 (15 February 1998), who even considers the possibility of "separation from Haredi orthodoxy." On France, see Shmuel Trigano, *Un exil sans retour? Lettres à un juif égaré* (Paris: Stock, 1996).

160. Jay M. Harris, *How Do We Know This? Midrash and the Fragmentation of Modern Jewry* (Albany: State University of New York Press, 1995); Ezra Kopelowitz, "Three Sub-Cultures of Conservative Judaism and the Issue of Ordaining Women," *Nashim* 1 (1998): 136–53.

161. David Roskies, "S. Ansky and the Paradigm of Return," in *The Uses of Tradition*, ed. Jack Wertheimer (New York: Jewish Theological Seminary of America with Harvard University Press, 1992), pp. 243–60; Kirshenblatt-Gimblett, "Coming of Age."

162. Blu Greenberg, *On Women and Judaism: A View from Tradition* (Philadelphia: Jewish Publication Society of America, 1981), p. 23.

163. Susan M. Kahn, *Reproducing Jews: A Cultural Account of Assisted Conception in Israel* (Durham, N.C.: Duke University Press, 2000).

164. Bonfil, "Change in the Cultural Pattern"; Harvey E. Goldberg, "Coming of Age in Jewish Studies, or Anthropology is Counted in the Minyan," *Jewish Social Studies*, n.s., 4 (1998): 29–64.

165. Mishna *Ta'anit* 4:8.

166. TB *Ta'anit* 30b–31a.

167. Another explanation of the festival appearing there refers to the political split between Judah and the northern Israelite kingdom. The split, according to the Talmud, prevented pilgrims from reaching Jerusalem to the south, and Tu be-Av marked the renewal of pilgrimage travel. If pilgrimages were opportunities for match-making (chapter 5, "Contemporary Travel and Identity"), the resumption of the flow of pilgrims would also imply the widening of the marriage pool. Earlier, the Mishna (*Ta'anit* 4:5) links the date of Tu be-Av with Jews in the Second Temple period who were unclear as to their original tribal origin.

168. In recent years, more than one-fourth of the Jewish marriages in Israel have been between individuals from European and Middle Eastern backgrounds. Differences based on religious ideology are currently a more salient barrier to marriages between social groups than is ethnicity.

169. See Michael Satlow, *Jewish Marriage in Antiquity* (Princeton, N.J.: Princeton University Press, 2001), pp. 259–71 (Conclusion), for thoughts on marriage among Jews today after detailed consideration of earlier historical patterns.

Glossary

Italicized words also appear as separate entries; see also the List of Abbreviations.

Aguna:	A woman who is no longer effectively in a relationship with a marriage partner but is formally married according to rabbinical law and is unable to secure a *get* to release her.
'Aliya:	Immigration to the Land of Israel.
'Am ha-àreṣ:	A person of a lower religious status who is perceived as not following certain strictures; one ignorant of religious law.
Aron kodesh:	The cabinet in a synagogue in which the *Torah* scrolls are housed (the term is common in the tradition of *Ashkenaz*).
Ashkenaz:	A place/people in the Bible (Genesis 10), which medieval Jews applied to the Rhineland when communities developed there. The *Yiddish* language and Ashkenazi laws and customs were later carried eastward, so that eastern European Jews also belong to the Ashkenazi tradition. People who lived in the area or who originated from it are known as Ashkenazim.
Bar (fem. Bat) Mitzvah:	Religious majority. Reached at the age of thirteen by boys and twelve by girls.
Beit Din:	Rabbinical court.
Bekhor:	Firstborn male (see *pidyon ha-ben*).
Brit Milah:	The covenant of circumcision; the ritual marking it.
Davening:	Praying. From the *Yiddish* word *daven,* with an English suffix.

Dibbuk: The soul of a person who has died and has possessed
                                 a living human.

Elijah: The prophet described in the Books of Kings, who
                                 plays many roles in Jewish lore by "reappearing" in
                                 contemporary circumstances.

Erusin: The betrothal phase of a wedding ceremony, also
                                 known as *kiddushin*.

Gematria: A symbolic system in which each Hebrew letter is
                                 assigned a number, thereby allowing interpretations
                                 by the discovery of numerical equivalences between
                                 words.

Geniza: A place where worn sacred texts, or any document
                                 containing God's name in Hebrew, are stored until
                                 ultimate burial in a cemetery.

Geonim: Heads of the religious academies (*yeshivot*) in Iraq
                                 from the seventh to the eleventh centuries, whose
                                 centrality was recognized throughout the Jewish
                                 world.

Get: A rabbinical bill of divorce.

Gosses: A person who is close to death.

Habad: A movement originating within *Hasidism* that
                                 now emphasizes influencing Jews to become more
                                 observant.

Haftara: A portion from a prophetic book of the Bible read
                                 publicly in the synagogue on Sabbaths, festivals, and
                                 fast days, following the reading from the *Torah*
                                 scroll.

Haggadah: The text used during the Passover *seder* containing
                                 the rituals and the narration celebrating the exodus
                                 from Egypt.

Halakha: The rabbinical traditions from the time of the *Tal-
                                 mud* and onward that deal with ritual, ethical, civil,
                                 and criminal law.

Haredim   Ultra-Orthodox Jews characterized by their critique
  (adj. haredi):   of modern society and a tendency to observe rabbini-
                                 cal law in its strictest fashion. They also reject *Zion-
                                 ism* and the claim that the State of Israel represents
                                 the fulfillment of Jewish aspirations for national and
                                 religious redemption.

Hasid (pl. hasidim;   A pious person. Hasidism began in the eighteenth
  Hasidism, a   century in regions of southeastern Poland and
  religious movement):   Ukraine. It stressed worshiping God through per-
                                 sonal piety and ecstasy. Hasidic communities formed

around charismatic rabbinic leaders, often called *tzaddikim,* who were known by the name of their towns. Often portrayed as being in tension with the learned leadership cultivated in *yeshivot,* Hasidism and its rabbinic opponents joined forces in the nineteenth century within the streams of Orthodoxy and *haredi* Judaism.

Haskalah: The Jewish enlightenment movement beginning in central Europe in the late eighteenth century and spreading eastward during the nineteenth.

Havdalah: A ceremony at nightfall on Saturday nights that marks the distinction between the Sabbath and weekdays.

Haver (pl. haverim): Fellow; member of a *havura.*

Havura: A group of people coming together for purposes of prayer or study based on shared religious viewpoints and sociality.

Heikhal: The cabinet in a synagogue in which the *Torah* scrolls are housed (the term is common in the tradition of *Sepharad*).

Hevra Kadisha: Burial society.

Hillula (pl. hillulot): A feast day and celebration marking the anniversary of the death of a venerated rabbi or *tzaddik,* and often involving a pilgrimage to his tomb (see *Lag ba-'Omer*).

Ḥumash: The Pentateuch or Five Books of Moses.

Ḥuppah: Wedding canopy.

Judeo-Arabic: Arabic dialects spoken by Jews in Arabic-speaking regions; the Arabic language written in Hebrew characters.

Judeo-Spanish: Dialects of Spanish that developed among Jews in the Iberian Peninsula through the fifteenth century and were maintained by some Sephardi groups living elsewhere thereafter: Judeo-Spanish, sometimes known also as Ladino, or Judezmo, was originally written in Hebrew characters but more recently has been written in Latin characters.

Judezmo: See *Judeo-Spanish.*

Kabbala: Traditions of mysticism that developed in Spain and Provence in the twelfth century. Sometimes, the term "kabbala" is used to refer to Jewish mysticism in all periods.

Kaddish:	A prayer sanctifying God, associated with mourning and remembering the dead.
Karaites:	A group following a stream within Judaism that coalesced in the ninth century and opposed the majority rabbinite tradition. Small communities of Karaites continued to exist in modern times both in Egypt and in eastern Europe, and today may be found in Israel and some Diaspora settings.
Kashrut:	Ritual dietary rules based on biblical injunctions and their rabbinic elaborations. See also *kosher.*
Ketubba (pl. ketubbot):	Rabbinic marriage contract.
Kibbutz (pl. kibbutzim):	Collective settlement in Israel.
Kiddushin:	The betrothal phase of a wedding ceremony, also known as *erusin.*
Kohen (pl. kohanim):	A member of the priestly class, putatively descended from the biblical Aaron, the brother of Moses. Kohanim have certain ritual privileges and duties.
Kosher:	The term, meaning "fitting," or "permitted according to law," is used most commonly with regard to food. See also *kashrut.*
Kotel:	The Western Wall, or "Wailing Wall," in Jerusalem.
Lag ba-'Omer:	The major *hillula* in Jewish tradition, taking place in the spring and marking the death of *Rabbi Shim'on Bar Yohai,* the putative author of the *Zohar,* whose traditional tomb is in Meron in the Galilee.
Maimonides:	Rabbi Moses the son of Maimon (d. 1204). Originating from *Sepharad,* he eventually moved to Cairo, and his writings were and are highly regarded in the realms of philosophy and *halakha.*
Mamzer:	A person born as a result of a forbidden marriage according to biblical rules, who may not marry other Jews, except within restricted categories, such as other mamzerim (pl.).
Matzah:	Unleavened bread for *Passover* because of the rule forbidding the eating of bread or any form of leaven during that festival.
Mezuza (pl. mezuzot):	A ritual case containing short sections of the *Torah,* written on parchment, that is attached to the doorpost in Jewish homes (see *tefillin*).
Midrash:	Rabbinical literature that elaborates upon the text of the Bible, often including legendary materials that

go far beyond the plain meaning of the biblical text. Midrashic material is found in the *Talmud* and in separate compositions from that period and from later centuries.

Minyan:
A quorum of ten Jews, which is the minimum number required to conduct public prayers.

Mishna:
The earliest codification of rabbinical law, which took its final form about 200 C.E.

Miqveh:
A ritual bath. Its most essential contemporary use is for the purification of women in the state of *niddah* so that sexual intercourse may be resumed.

Mishe-berakh:
A prayer, beginning with the phrase "May He who blessed," typically recited by a representative of a congregation, that invokes a blessing for an individual upon special occasions both of fortune and of illness.

Mishpaḥa:
In the Bible, the term refers to a clan based on male descent; in modern Hebrew, the word for family.

Mitzvah (pl. mitzvot):
A commandment; a deed of religious merit.

Mohel (pl. mohalim):
A circumciser trained to carry out a *brit milah.*

Moshav:
A cooperative settlement in Israel.

Nazirite:
A person, described in Numbers 6:1–21, who temporarily takes certain vows such as not to drink wine or to cut his or her hair.

Nesuin:
The phase of a wedding ceremony that completes the marriage, as opposed to the first phase of *erusin* or *kiddushin.*

Niddah:
The state of a woman during her menstrual period, and the series of rules regulating behavior during that time and purification subsequent to it.

Passover:
The seven-day festival (eight days in the Diaspora) beginning on the fifteenth of the month of Nisan (in the spring) that commemorates the exodus of the Israelites from Egypt.

Periah:
A phase of circumcision, after the cutting of the foreskin, in which the prepuce is removed.

Pidyon Ha-ben (also pidyon):
Redemption of the firstborn; a thirty-day-old firstborn male of a woman is "redeemed" from a *kohen* by the symbolic payment of five coins ("shekalim").

Piyyutim:
Liturgical poetry written for occasions defined by the ritual calendar and life-cycle events.

Rosh Hodesh:	The initial day or days of a new month, which is (are) defined as a minor festival.
Rabbi Shimʾon Bar Yohai:	A second-century sage. The mystical *Zohar* book is traditionally attributed to him. The putative date of his death, the eighteenth of the month of Iyyar, or *Lag ba-ʾOmer* (thirty-three days after *Passover*), has become a minor festival.
Rosh Hashanah:	New Year holiday at the beginning of the month of Tishri (in the fall).
Sandek:	The man who holds a baby boy during a *brit milah*.
Seder:	The domestic celebration on the first night of *Passover* in Israel and on the first two nights in the Diaspora. It consists of reading and discussing the story of the exodus from Egypt, performing related rituals, and singing psalms and hymns, all of which bracket a festive meal.
Sefer Torah:	The scroll of parchment, wound around two wooden poles, upon which the text of the Five Books of Moses are hand-written.
Sepharad:	A biblical place-name (Obadiah 1), applied to the Iberian Peninsula in medieval times. After expulsions from Spain and Portugal at the end of the fifteenth century, Spanish Jews (Sephardim) spread to Mediterranean lands, to northwestern Europe, and to the New World. Later, Jews who had been forced to convert to Catholicism, but maintained their Judaism secretly (Marranos), rejoined the ranks of Diaspora Spanish communities. Today, Sephardi may refer to Jews who speak a *Judeo-Spanish* language, or to those descended from the émigrés from the Iberian Peninsula. More broadly, the term refers to Jews who came under the influence of these émigrés and who accepted Sephardi law, liturgy, and customs.
Shabbat:	Sabbath.
Shavuʾot:	The Feast of Weeks. One of the pilgrimage festivals, prescribed by the Bible to take place fifty days after the first day of *Passover*. Tradition designates it as the day on which the *Torah* was given on Mt. Sinai.
She-heheyanu:	A blessing recited by an individual upon reaching milestones in the cycle of festivals and personal life that praises God "for having kept us alive" for the occasion.

Shivah:	The seven days following upon a burial, during which immediate relatives of the deceased sit at home and are visited by those who console them.
Shofar:	A ram's horn. Used in antiquity during the anointing of kings or the proclamation of the jubilee year, sounding the shofar is now an integral part of the *Rosh Hashanah* service and concludes the prayers of *Yom Kippur*.
Shloshim:	Literally "thirty": The period of thirty days of mourning for a relative after burial that are less intense than the first week of mourning (*shivah*).
Shma' Yisrael:	The first words of Deuteronomy 6:4, which came to constitute the central declaration of faith in Jewish life and was incorporated into daily prayer (see appendix 3).
Shtetl (*Yiddish: small town*):	A town, usually with a market, in the countryside in eastern Europe.
Shulhan Arukh:	A sixteenth-century compilation of rabbinical law by Rabbi Yosef Caro that rapidly became the standard reference work with regard to *halakha* and everyday guidance for observant Jews.
Siyyum:	A celebration marking the completion of study of a *tractate* of the *Talmud*, but which can also mark other occasions of concluding study as well.
Sukkot:	The pilgrimage festival of Tabernacles (booths), on the fifteenth of Tishri, in the fall, which continues for seven days (eight days in the Diaspora).
Tallit:	A shawl, with four ritual fringes, used during prayer, mainly during the morning service (see *tzitzit*).
Talmud:	The term is most commonly used comprehensively to include both the *Mishna* and the rabbinic corpus called the Gemara, which developed over the subsequent centuries in both a Palestinian version and a Babylonian version. The term can also refer to the later work alone.
Targum:	A translation of the Bible into Aramaic in ancient times. Several targumim exist.
Ṭeʾamim:	Notations appearing in printed versions of biblical books indicating how the text is to be chanted when read aloud in the synagogue.
Tefillin:	Phylacteries. Set of two black cubes and attached straps, all made of leather, which house specified passages of the *Ḥumash* and are worn on the arm

and forehead as part of morning worship each weekday (see appendix 3).

Temple: The structure(s) at the center of sacrificial worship in
Jerusalem in ancient times, carrying the implied
meaning of Jewish sovereignty. There were two Temples, the first corresponding to the biblical period before the destruction of Jerusalem in the early sixth
century, B.C.E., and the second, restored at the end of
the biblical period (late sixth century B.C.E.) and
eventually destroyed under Roman rule in 70 C.E.

Tishàh be-Av: A fast day, the ninth of the Hebrew summer month
of Av, which commemorates the destruction of the
First Temple by the Babylonians and the Second
Temple by the Romans.

Torah: The term has many referents, including (1) the
physical Torah scroll, which must be hand-written
on parchment and is prepared by a scribe; (2) the
contents of the Torah in the form of a book, the *Ḥumash*, which may be glossed "the five books [of
Moses]," corresponding to the Pentateuch; and (3)
the whole tradition of Jewish sacred literature, including the *Ḥumash* and other sections of the Hebrew Bible (the Prophets and the Holy Writings),
along with the works of rabbinical culture like the
Talmud and the subsequent discussions and codifications of talmudic literature produced from ancient
times to the present.

Tractate: A book in the *Mishna* or of the *Talmud* that elaborates upon the *Mishna*.

Ṭumàh: Ritual impurity, defined by rules in the Bible and
elaborated in rabbinical writings.

Tzaddik Literally: righteous person. Among North African
(pl. tzaddikim): Jews, a sainted rabbi believed to have the power of
curing and miracle-working both while alive and
after death. Graves of *tzaddikim* often became pilgrimage sites (see *hillula*). In *Hasidic* tradition, a
tzaddik is the charismatic center of the community.

Tzitzit: A set of four ritual fringes on the corner of a garment, or of a *tallit*, which are worn to fulfill a biblical commandment (see appendix 3).

Ultra-Orthodoxy. See *Haredim*.

Yahrtzeit: In *Yiddish*, the anniversary of a close relative's
death.

Yeshiva
(pl. yeshivot):
An academy of higher *Torah* study. Although known primarily for the study of *Talmud,* some yeshivot emphasize other styles and branches of learning as well. Most commonly, men study in yeshiva settings.

Yiddish:
The Jewish language (called Judeo-German by linguists) that took form about the tenth century and characterized *Ashkenazi* Jewry.

Yizkor:
A memorial prayer in the tradition of *Ashkenaz* recited on the occasion of the three pilgrimage festivals, *Passover, Shavu'ot,* and *Sukkot,* and on *Yom Kippur.*

Yom Kippur:
The Day of Atonement, on the tenth of the month of Tishri (in the fall).

Zekher la-ḥurban:
A phrase usually explaining an act as recalling the destroyed *Temple.*

Zionism:
A movement, originating in nineteenth-century Europe, that stresses the national existence of the Jews. It claims that, as a nation, Jews have the right to return to their own land to freely realize their collective life.

Zohar:
The central text of Jewish mysticism, or *kabbala.* Much of the Zohar was composed in late thirteenth-century Spain, but it was attributed to the second-century sage *Rabbi Shim'on Bar Yohai,* and this was accepted by much of the traditional Jewish world.

Index

Italic type indicates illustrations.

Compositor:	Impressions Book and Journal Services, Inc.
Text:	10/13 Aldus
Display:	Aldus
Printer and binder:	Thomson-Shore, Inc.